PAIN

PAIN

Thomas D. Ackerman

RESOURCE *Publications* • Eugene, Oregon

PAIN

Copyright © 2024 Thomas D. Ackerman. All rights reserved. Except for brief quotations in critical publications or reviews, no part of this book may be reproduced in any manner without prior written permission from the publisher. Write: Permissions, Wipf and Stock Publishers, 199 W. 8th Ave., Suite 3, Eugene, OR 97401.

Resource Publications
An Imprint of Wipf and Stock Publishers
199 W. 8th Ave., Suite 3
Eugene, OR 97401

www.wipfandstock.com

PAPERBACK ISBN: 979-8-3852-0703-9
HARDCOVER ISBN: 979-8-3852-0704-6
EBOOK ISBN: 979-8-3852-0705-3

05/29/24

Contents

Author's Note	vii
Acknowledgments	ix
Introduction	xi

PART 1

1	Depression in the Bible	3
2	The Sea	17
3	Pain	34
4	God Answers You	76

PART 2

5	Be cleansed of your filth	171
6	Walk Uprightly	217
7	The Future is a Miracle	279

The New Mount	335
Bibliography	343

Author's Note

THIS BOOK USES THE King James Bible for all of its Bible quotes except for two, while making occasional reference to word choices in other Bible versions. Most of the italics you see in quotations, from the Bible or from literature, are added by me for emphasis, except in one or two quoted articles, where they were added by the author for the same reason. Other italics in the Bible verses were already there to show implied words added by the translators. I use various names or titles for God throughout the book. These include Yahweh, as the sacred name, along with God, the Almighty, and several others.

Acknowledgments

I AM VERY GRATEFUL to the help of Pastor Jack Shannon, of Saint Athanasius Church in Fort Collins, who offered to read a draft of my book, and who has given me much helpful and detailed commentary on it. That was a valuable gift of much time and effort on his part. I also want to thank Jerry Newcombe, who without hesitation, sent me a copy of his book with D. James Kennedy, *What if Jesus Had Never Been Born?*, to use for research, which provided me what I needed for my book, and which I will enjoy reading apart from research as well. I was also provided helpful knowledge and insights about the "holy fool" in Eastern Orthodoxy by Father Andrew at St. Nicholas Church in Weirton, West Virginia.

Introduction

I HAVE WRITTEN THIS book over the past three years to explain why pain exists, and what each of us can do about it. If you don't want to read so many pages just to find out why pain exists, you can skip ahead to the last page of the final narrative section called The New Mount, and read the final four words. There's your answer. I hope you are willing to hear the longer answer, however, and the details of how God heals us from what is a truly deadly state.

I was inspired to write this book initially to discuss the experience of depression, and examine it from the Bible. I wanted to offer what the Bible along with the Christian life offer regarding pain, which is a way of peace for the soul, and spiritual medicine for our sufferings. Having personally experienced severe depression, and left it far in the past, I can describe it in some depth, describe its development, and show in what path we can find freedom. Yet in doing this, I wanted to address the reason and purpose of suffering and evil to begin with, as well as how God heals the human soul and puts suffering away forever; in short, explain the Christian faith — the fallen human condition, and the gospel of Jesus Christ. That means while I want to offer understanding of depression, and offer hope for those who experience it, there is no way to separate this from the faith of God's children, its present and its glorious future. The book is at least in part a catechism which has been personalized through my journey with depression.

There are many people tied up and disturbed by suffering, who find they have no answer to its very purpose. Others claim the existence of suffering as a reason they continually deny God, or as a reason they abandoned their faith in God and in Jesus Christ. For those who are confounded by suffering, Christianity has a great "problem of evil" which it must answer, or which it cannot answer. Yet the opposite is really true: Christianity has the answer to our pain, not only the explanation for its existence, but the remedy to pain in actuality. It communicates the meaning and value of this human experience. It does so very clearly. It also brings us beyond that experience, to a whole new creation, a state of incorruptibility, and a union with God forever. It is actually the unbeliever who has a problem of pain, and a problem with existence itself. He has meaningless pain, purposeless evil, and a final insignificant end in the blackness of death. Now that's a problem.

The Bible, if we trust it, provides us the reason for the existence of suffering, as well as what God does with it. It promises us an end to all suffering that will occur for the regenerate and restored world that comes to Christ. I have never found a problem of pain in the Christian faith or the Holy Bible, and I have known Christ now nineteen years. The Bible addresses suffering, loss, and evil in detail many times. It even has an entire book dedicated to the case of a righteous man suffering. If we trust in the Bible, we will be strong in our faith, and we will know what the answers are. They aren't always the answers man wants to hear. However, they are answers that demand we respect God's headship, that we trust in his decisions as sovereign Lord, and that require our own humility and sacrifice as we participate in the glorious goal. They turn upside down some of our assumptions, requiring we come to Christ as little children, and accept what the world calls foolishness, rather than accept the wisdom the world promises us. They don't allow that we rely on our own solutions and strength. Yet they are answers that should satisfy a humble and repentant heart.

I want to stick to what Scripture says as much as possible. I will make mention of some of the philosophical models that have been offered, but as far as faith teaching is concerned, I want to root it clearly in the word of God. Often philosophical answers are mere guess work, or they probe secondary questions, where the main answer does not lie, and which even can distract from what the Bible teaches. Great harm has been done in the Christian faith by relying on philosophy and academics. So mostly I will give them passing mention. The Bible has the answers for us, answers which feed the soul, and which require our own participation in the remedy for pain. To share that remedy for pain with others. It is both an explanation, and a playbook for battle. It offers the theory of nutrition, as well as the food which nourishes us. God is the healer of our souls, and uses you as the healer and minister to do his work. God makes you get involved, once you understand the answer, and by getting involved, you know the answer more fully and deeply than you ever did. The Christian should know about pain more than anyone else.

PART 1

1

Depression in the Bible

I OFTEN HEAR CLAIMS about the many biblical persons who experienced depression. I think they are well meaning claims, and those who make them seek to offer a solution by pointing to these men, and what we can learn from them. They seek to offer encouragement. Yet when I hear them, I find claims of depression in the Bible greatly exaggerated. I find they mostly are experiences of sadness, grief, suffering, and anxiety, none of which truly encapsulates clinical depression, or represents a severe case of it. They are normal human reactions to bad events. Granted, people have a hammered flat version of the word depression that seems to include nearly any downer emotion, but I do not use that definition, and I find it meaninglessly broad. While there are a few arguable cases, in most passages I find the experience of mental distress is better described by other words, and that's why we have those other words in the first place, to describe different experiences. I see no clear cases of severe clinical depression in Scripture.

Let's first look at some of the proposed depressed men, and briefly evaluate their suffering. Then let's look at what depression is as a mental illness and spiritual affliction. Perhaps the most common claim of depression in the Bible is that of David, who describes a good amount of personal suffering in the Psalms.

For example, Ps 13 is sometimes cited as an expression of depression. Since it's short, I'll cite the whole psalm, minus the heading:

> How long wilt thou forget me, O LORD? for ever? how long wilt thou hide thy face from me?

> How long shall I take counsel in my soul, having sorrow in my heart daily? how long shall mine enemy be exalted over me?
>
> Consider and hear me, O LORD my God: lighten mine eyes, lest I sleep the sleep of death;
>
> Lest mine enemy say, I have prevailed against him; and those that trouble me rejoice when I am moved.
>
> But I have trusted in thy mercy; my heart shall rejoice in thy salvation.
>
> I will sing unto the LORD, because he hath dealt bountifully with me.

David describes God hiding his face from him, apparently for an ongoing period of time. He is certainly experiencing anxiety because he is attacked by his enemies over and over. Sorrow is on his heart daily. Yet despite all this, David says he trusts in Yahweh, and his heart will rejoice. He knows Yahweh will help him in the future. Like many psalms, it begins with suffering or fear, and ends with trust in God. This is one of the great lessons in reading the Psalms in general, the peace they promise in the Almighty in the midst of affliction.

I am not prepared to say this psalm describes depression. If a person is attacked over and over, and betrayed, as David was by family members and trusted associates, it is a normal human reaction to be sad. It is normal to be dismayed that God is not showing you favor, or offering the solution just yet. Being dismayed and unhappy is not a mental illness. It is not the spiritual malaise that depression really is, a malaise that transcends sadness, or anger, and truly saps all hope and joy out of a human being. In fact, the very attitude of trust in God and hope that David reveals at the end show that he is not mentally ill, but is simply going through ordinary human suffering. Tears are not a mental illness. This man knows he will be singing joyously in the future, and has a Rock that gives him peace in the times of suffering. The man is distraught, and not depressed.

Let's go through a few other expressions of sadness in the Psalms and put them together:

> My God, my God, why hast thou forsaken me? why art thou so far from helping me, and from the words of my roaring?
>
> O my God, I cry in the daytime, but thou hearest not; and in the night season, and am not silent.
>
> But thou art holy, O thou that inhabitest the praises of Israel.

Our fathers trusted in thee: they trusted, and thou didst deliver them.

They cried unto thee, and were delivered: they trusted in thee, and were not confounded.

But I am a worm, and no man; a reproach of men, and despised of the people.

All they that see me laugh me to scorn: they shoot out the lip, they shake the head, saying,

He trusted on the LORD that he would deliver him: let him deliver him, seeing he delighted in him.

But thou art he that took me out of the womb: thou didst make me hope when I was upon my mother's breasts.

I was cast upon thee from the womb: thou art my God from my mother's belly.

Be not far from me; for trouble is near; for there is none to help. (Ps 22:1b–11)

My tears have been my meat day and night, while they continually say unto me, Where is thy God?

When I remember these things, I pour out my soul in me: for I had gone with the multitude, I went with them to the house of God, with the voice of joy and praise, with a multitude that kept holyday.

Why art thou cast down, O my soul? and why art thou disquieted in me? hope thou in God: for I shall yet praise him for the help of his countenance.

O my God, my soul is cast down within me: therefore will I remember thee from the land of Jordan, and of the Hermonites, from the hill Mizar.

Deep calleth unto deep at the noise of thy waterspouts: all thy waves and thy billows are gone over me. (Ps 42:3–7)

Judge me, O God, and plead my cause against an ungodly nation: O deliver me from the deceitful and unjust man.

For thou art the God of my strength: why dost thou cast me off? why go I mourning because of the oppression of the enemy?

O send out thy light and thy truth: let them lead me; let them bring me unto thy holy hill, and to thy tabernacles. (Ps 43:1–3)

Have mercy upon me, O LORD; for I am weak: O LORD, heal me; for my bones are vexed.

My soul is also sore vexed: but thou, O LORD, how long?

> Return, O LORD, deliver my soul: oh save me for thy mercies' sake.
>
> For in death there is no remembrance of thee: in the grave who shall give thee thanks?
>
> I am weary with my groaning; all the night make I my bed to swim; I water my couch with my tears.
>
> Mine eye is consumed because of grief; it waxeth old because of all mine enemies.
>
> Depart from me, all ye workers of iniquity; for the LORD hath heard the voice of my weeping.
>
> The LORD hath heard my supplication; the LORD will receive my prayer. (Ps 6:2–9)
>
> DALETH. My soul cleaveth unto the dust: quicken thou me according to thy word.
>
> I have declared my ways, and thou heardest me: teach me thy statutes.
>
> Make me to understand the way of thy precepts: so shall I talk of thy wondrous works.
>
> My soul melteth for heaviness: strengthen thou me according unto thy word.
>
> Remove from me the way of lying: and grant me thy law graciously.
>
> I have chosen the way of truth: thy judgments have I laid before me.
>
> I have stuck unto thy testimonies: O LORD, put me not to shame.
>
> I will run the way of thy commandments, when thou shalt enlarge my heart. (Ps 119:25–32)

This is only a small selection from many examples of suffering in the Psalms. I don't believe any describe depression, although it is subjective. What I see continually is that there is usually something which is immediately causing the sadness or fear, often persecution and attacks by others. The sadness does not appear to be something which is ongoing for years, or that arises in the heart apart from any persecution. Moreover, the psalmist still has hope, and finds great peace by placing trust in God. He knows that Yahweh will hear his prayer. Being persecuted, feeling terrible, and then turning to God to find peace, do not in my mind represent depression in any serious sense of the word. They are passing negative emotions anyone would feel if attacked or betrayed. One of the psalms, Ps 22, is a great messianic psalm, and pictures the sufferings of Christ, down to describing his gaunt body and his wounds. The entire latter half of the psalm goes on to describe the glorious redemption that would come through his suffering, and the many who would be saved by it. Was Christ suffering depression on the cross, or just suffering from abuse and physical pain? I see no depression on the cross at all. In fact, not all suffering is depression. Not everyone who cries out for help is depressed. Not everyone who weeps is depressed.

The righteous man Job, whom we will speak about much more later, is a more serious contender for depression in the Bible. Yet even in this case of incredible loss and pain, I am not confident that Job was clinically depressed, but rather see him as an individual suffering because of the immediate tragedies in his life. In his very own words, he is "mourning" (30:28). That's how Job defines it. Is a parent who just lost a child and is crying out in incredible grief suffering clinical depression? Or are they just in pain? Grieving at loss is a normal human reaction, and as the book shows, Job gets over the depth of the suffering by changing his attitude, and growing in his faith, after a period which Job 29:2 suggests is less than a year. Many people grieve for months over the loss of a loved one.

Job, who lost his home and his children to tragedy, and then was afflicted with a painful illness, describes some of his suffering his way:

> I loathe it [my life]; I would not live alway: let me alone; for my days are vanity. (Job 7:16)
>
> Oh that I might have my request; and that God would grant me the thing that I long for!
>
> Even that it would please God to destroy me; that he would let loose his hand, and cut me off! (Job 6:8–9)
>
> He hath made me also a byword of the people; and aforetime I was as a tabret.
>
> Mine eye also is dim by reason of sorrow, and all my members are as a shadow. (Job 17:6–7)
>
> Though I were perfect, yet would I not know my soul: I would despise my life.
>
> This is one thing, therefore I said it, He destroyeth the perfect and the wicked.
>
> If the scourge slay suddenly, he will laugh at the trial of the innocent.

> The earth is given into the hand of the wicked: he covereth the faces of the judges thereof; if not, where, and who is he? (Job 9:21–24)
>
> My days are swifter than a weaver's shuttle, and are spent without hope.
>
> O remember that my life is wind: mine eye shall no more see good. (Job 7:6–7)

Job communicates feelings that are common in depression. He hates his life. He wishes it were over. He feels abandoned by God. He feels sorrow. He lacks hope. While these are common to experiences of depression, if they result from immediate loss and are short-term reactions, I do not see them as mental illness either. It is normal to grieve deeply for the loss of loved ones, especially children. It is normal to want extreme suffering to be over, even if death is what ends it. It is normal to come to hate life when you have a painful illness that afflicts you every day. So while Job is clearly in great pain, he may simply be reacting to immediate loss and pain in a normal way. A normal healthy human soul really goes through grieving and weeps. The fact Job is still seeking answers to his situation, trying to understand, albeit errantly, why God has done this to him, is a sign Job is still strong in the spirit in many ways. Even in the midst of doubts he cries out, "For I know that my redeemer liveth, and that he shall stand on the latter day upon the earth" (19:25). The fact he interacts with his friends, responding in detail and rebuking them, and is willing to turn to God in his distress, shows the life and energy he still possesses. Job wants answers to his suffering in light of his being righteous and God being righteous. If he had truly given up hope I don't see that he'd be discussing it with his friends in the first place, or mulling over the problem looking for solutions. He would be deadened to the world as many of the depressed are. He would not care about anything. I do see the pain in Job that is associated with depression, but not necessarily the deadness of soul.

Many people point to the author of Ecclesiastes, the revered King Solomon, as suffering from depression. Indeed, the majority of the book paints life as meaningless, and with little hope, sentiments that often come from a depressed soul. Could it describe depression in Solomon's present or past? Some of the more powerful expressions of the purposeless of life say this:

The thing that hath been, it is that which shall be; and that which is done is that which shall be done: and there is no new thing under the sun.

Is there any thing whereof it may be said, See, this is new? it hath been already of old time, which was before us.

There is no remembrance of former things; neither shall there be any remembrance of things that are to come with those that shall come after. (Eccl 1:9–11)

I said in mine heart, Go to now, I will prove thee with mirth, therefore enjoy pleasure: and, behold, this also is vanity.

I said of laughter, It is mad: and of mirth, What doeth it? (Eccl 2:1–2)

And I turned myself to behold wisdom, and madness, and folly: for what can the man do that cometh after the king? even that which hath been already done.

Then I saw that wisdom excelleth folly, as far as light excelleth darkness.

The wise man's eyes are in his head; but the fool walketh in darkness: and I myself perceived also that one event happeneth to them all.

Then said I in my heart, As it happeneth to the fool, so it happeneth even to me; and why was I then more wise? Then I said in my heart, that this also is vanity. (Eccl 2:12–15)

Therefore I went about to cause my heart to despair of all the labour which I took under the sun.

For there is a man whose labour is in wisdom, and in knowledge, and in equity; yet to a man that hath not laboured therein shall he leave it for his portion. This also is vanity and a great evil.

For what hath man of all his labour, and of the vexation of his heart, wherein he hath laboured under the sun?

For all his days are sorrows, and his travail grief; yea, his heart taketh not rest in the night. This is also vanity. (Eccl 2:20–23)

So I returned, and considered all the oppressions that are done under the sun: and behold the tears of such as were oppressed, and they had no comforter; and on the side of their oppressors there was power; but they had no comforter.

Wherefore I praised the dead which are already dead more than the living which are yet alive.

> Yea, better is he than both they, which hath not yet been, who hath not seen the evil work that is done under the sun. (Eccl 4:1–3)
>
> I considered all the living which walk under the sun, with the second child that shall stand up in his stead.
>
> There is no end of all the people, even of all that have been before them: they also that come after shall not rejoice in him. Surely this also is vanity and vexation of spirit. (Eccl 4:15–16)
>
> I said in mine heart concerning the estate of the sons of men, that God might manifest them, and that they might see that they themselves are beasts.
>
> For that which befalleth the sons of men befalleth beasts; even one thing befalleth them: as the one dieth, so dieth the other; yea, they have all one breath; so that a man hath no preeminence above a beast: for all is vanity.
>
> All go unto one place; all are of the dust, and all turn to dust again.
>
> Who knoweth the spirit of man that goeth upward, and the spirit of the beast that goeth downward to the earth?
>
> Wherefore I perceive that there is nothing better, than that a man should rejoice in his own works; for that is his portion: for who shall bring him to see what shall be after him?
>
> (Eccl 3:18–22)

This book includes many statements you'd assume shouldn't be in the Bible. There are some real whoppers, such as "a man hath no better thing under the sun, than to eat, and to drink, and to be merry" (Eccl 8:15). Over and over the writer points to the meaninglessness in life; in our hard work, in our having children, in our pursuit of knowledge, in attempts at being righteous. It shows all of this comes to nothing, and fades away. Whether one is righteous or wicked, rich or poor, it is all the same. It goes to waste in the end. Since all our pursuits are vanity, suggests the writer, it is best to simply pursue pleasure in life. The author also expresses that death would be more pleasant, or superior to life, with its worthlessness and evil. He envies the dead.

Despite all of this dark sentiment, I do not assume these morose sections mean the writer of Ecclesiastes was depressed, although it is possible. The biggest reason is because, once we read to the end of the book, we see the author has trust in God, and knows what our life should be all about—trusting and obeying God. Life is not empty to the author. Life has purpose. We can see he is only describing what life is like *apart* from knowing God, and the true uselessness of man's efforts when done for himself. Everything we try and base our life on besides God is indeed vain, and passes away like dust. It is only God who is good and eternal. That is where we find meaning in life, and we must come to him before we face death:

> And further, by these, my son, be admonished: of making many books there is no end; and much study is a weariness of the flesh.
>
> Let us hear the conclusion of the whole matter: Fear God, and keep his commandments: for this is the whole duty of man.
>
> For God shall bring every work into judgment, with every secret thing, whether it be good, or whether it be evil. (Eccl 12:12–14)

Perhaps Solomon is describing depression he experienced *before* he grew in faith, or what his former outlook was like. He may be describing a sense of emptiness in life, a view common to the depressed mind, though not unique to it. Solomon indeed spent much of life pursuing pleasures of all kinds, including great wealth, and many women. These things can gut the soul. Surely Solomon learned firsthand the uselessness of these things he surrounded himself with. We should also remember it is possible to intellectually recognize the vanity of man's actions, while not being spiritually depressed at all. We can easily recount man's emptiness and failures apart from God, while at the same time having satisfaction in our souls because we know the true God. Ecclesiastes can easily be seen as a thesis on man's efforts in the material world apart from God, and showing the imperative of faith in light of that. Any man without depression can communicate those truths. It does not take clinical depression to see the utter vanity in all our efforts. Thus, I am not convinced the author of Ecclesiastes was depressed.

I believe it *is* more likely, as far as a mental and spiritual ongoing affliction, that King Saul experienced depression. Saul appeared to have an affliction that arrived without cause in his life, other than a terrible spirit which came upon him. It brought him great distress when he was experiencing it, but could go away quickly as well. David's music was sometimes the healing balm for his sadness. Saul's affliction also came with what seem like irrational decisions, such as trying to kill David, who had never once threatened him, and who even spared Saul's life when he could easily have killed him (1 Sam 24:1–7). His affliction was ongoing for years. While we don't see many detailed descriptions of Saul's distress or madness, we can get a layout of the situation from various texts:

> But the Spirit of the LORD departed from Saul, and an evil spirit from the LORD troubled him.
>
> And Saul's servants said unto him, Behold now, an evil spirit from God troubleth thee.
>
> Let our lord now command thy servants, which are before thee, to seek out a man, who is a cunning player on an harp: and it shall come to pass, when the evil spirit from God is upon thee, that he shall play with his hand, and thou shalt be well.
>
> And Saul said unto his servants, Provide me now a man that can play well, and bring him to me. (1 Sam 16:14–17)
>
> And it came to pass, when the evil spirit from God was upon Saul, that David took an harp, and played with his hand: so Saul was refreshed, and was well, and the evil spirit departed from him. (1 Sam 16:23)
>
> And the women answered one another as they played, and said, Saul hath slain his thousands, and David his ten thousands.
>
> And Saul was very wroth, and the saying displeased him; and he said, They have ascribed unto David ten thousands, and to me they have ascribed but thousands: and what can he have more but the kingdom?
>
> And Saul eyed David from that day and forward.
>
> And it came to pass on the morrow, that the evil spirit from God came upon Saul, and he prophesied in the midst of the house: and David played with his hand, as at other times: and there was a javelin in Saul's hand.
>
> And Saul cast the javelin; for he said, I will smite David even to the wall with it. And David avoided out of his presence twice.
>
> And Saul was afraid of David, because the LORD was with him, and was departed from Saul.
>
> Therefore Saul removed him from him, and made him his captain over a thousand; and he went out and came in before the people. (1 Sam 18:7–13)

We do not see detailed descriptions of Saul's mental state in First Samuel or elsewhere. We do see that Saul was fearful, jealous, and sad. He had murderous anger inside of him. His mental state and spiritual affliction also precede his jealousy of David, so we can't see it as a mere reaction to David's popularity. Saul is cast down, apparently without reason, when this spirit from the Lord comes upon him. The spiritual affliction, I imagine, is also connected to his prior sins which perhaps he had never sincerely repented, such as his unlawful sacrifice, or failure to destroy the Amalekite king (1 Sam 13, 15). God sent this spirit to torment him as a matter of justice. On reflection, this is consistent with the fact that terrible depression and hopelessness are often wrapped up in the sufferer's own sins, which help bind him to the darkness. In its lack of immediate cause and ability to dominate his soul, I see a stronger case for depression here than elsewhere in all Scripture, despite our lack of detail on the subject. It is also clearly ongoing, producing suffering for years. Saul's soul was oozing with impurities that dominated him, and the Lord had a hand in it, providing a supernatural torment with no easy solution. David's music provided relief that was temporary, and Saul returned to his unstable and murderous ways.

Surprisingly, many people point to one brief experience of Elijah as an example of depression. Elijah suffered persecution by Ahab and Jezebel, and had to flee into the wilderness because of it. He felt dismayed and without help. In the wilderness God answered Elijah, cared for him, and provided a direction for him in the future. Scripture provides only a brief description of his feelings, and I think it's a stretch to call it serious depression:

> Then Jezebel sent a messenger unto Elijah, saying, So let the gods do to me, and more also, if I make not thy life as the life of one of them by to morrow about this time.
>
> And when he saw that, he arose, and went for his life, and came to Beersheba, which belongeth to Judah, and left his servant there.
>
> But he himself went a day's journey into the wilderness, and came and sat down under a juniper tree: and he requested for himself that he might die; and said, *It is enough; now, O LORD, take away my life; for I am not better than my fathers.*
>
> And as he lay and slept under a juniper tree, behold, then an angel touched him, and said unto him, Arise and eat.
>
> And he looked, and, behold, there was a cake baken on the coals, and a cruse of water at his head. And he did eat and drink, and laid him down again.
>
> And the angel of the LORD came again the second time, and touched him, and said, Arise and eat; because the journey is too great for thee.
>
> And he arose, and did eat and drink, and went in the strength of that meat forty days and forty nights unto Horeb the mount of God.

And he came thither unto a cave, and lodged there; and, behold, the word of the LORD came to him, and he said unto him, What doest thou here, Elijah?

And he said, I have been very jealous for the LORD God of hosts: for the children of Israel have forsaken thy covenant, thrown down thine altars, and slain thy prophets with the sword; and I, even *I only, am left; and they seek my life, to take it away.*

And he said, Go forth, and stand upon the mount before the LORD. And, behold, the LORD passed by, and a great and strong wind rent the mountains, and brake in pieces the rocks before the LORD; but the LORD was not in the wind: and after the wind an earthquake; but the LORD was not in the earthquake:

And after the earthquake a fire; but the LORD was not in the fire: and after the fire a still small voice.

And it was so, when Elijah heard it, that he wrapped his face in his mantle, and went out, and stood in the entering in of the cave. And, behold, there came a voice unto him, and said, What doest thou here, Elijah?

And he said, I have been very jealous for the LORD God of hosts: because the children of Israel have forsaken thy covenant, thrown down thine altars, and slain thy prophets with the sword; and I, even I only, am left; and they seek my life, to take it away.

And the LORD said unto him, Go, return on thy way to the wilderness of Damascus: and when thou comest, anoint Hazael to be king over Syria:

And Jehu the son of Nimshi shalt thou anoint to be king over Israel: and Elisha the son of Shaphat of Abelmeholah shalt thou anoint to be prophet in thy room.

And it shall come to pass, that him that escapeth the sword of Hazael shall Jehu slay: and him that escapeth from the sword of Jehu shall Elisha slay.

Yet I have left me seven thousand in Israel, all the knees which have not bowed unto Baal, and every mouth which hath not kissed him. (1 Kgs 19:2–18)

This is a very beautiful passage. It is also one the speaks to the New Covenant powerfully, as Paul cites those final words of Yahweh, "I have reserved to myself seven thousand men, who have not bowed the knee to the image of Baal" (Rom 11:4b), in proving that Israel has continued through the remnant who believe in Christ, despite the unbelief of the rest (vv. 2–5). The passage offers great encouragement for those who feel dismayed in serving the Lord, or who are alone in their spiritual struggle. They strengthen those who are persecuted. They are words of comfort and hope.

I don't believe that Elijah's few words as he hides in the wilderness make for a case of depression. "It is enough; now, O LORD, take away my life" (1 Kgs 19:4), he says, when faced with his overwhelming circumstances. However, when we consider there are men seeking to murder him, and that he is in the wilderness where he may die by the elements themselves, crying out that it would be better to go ahead and die right now is not very strong evidence of depression. People say things like that for a variety of reasons, including immediate fear. People in great physical pain sometimes commit suicide only to end the pain, not because they are depressed. Elijah is reacting naturally to having his life threatened and having no obvious solution before him. The idea he has a mental illness because he utters that he might as well die right now is ridiculous. People feel dismayed, helpless, and not much like living when they are being chased by men who want to kill them, and have no obvious help. Elijah is simply in pain and wanting help, which he soon receives. He knows enough in his distress to turn to Yahweh in prayer, and Yahweh answers his servant.

Looking at these examples of potential depression I've reviewed, they show a wide variety of negative emotions, as well as a lack of desire to live, or a longing for death. They show sadness, anxiety, fear, and loathing. Yet often, they are normal reactions to the events around us. They are what we would expect from a normal human being in response to incredible loss or pain. They are how countless people naturally react in states of grief, and when they see no solution to their problem. I do not view them as clear cases of depression, because of their rooting in recent events, and often because the person still has trust in God and finds peace in him. If we call dismay, pain, and helplessness "depression," then the word is nearly useless in defining a unique mental or spiritual state. Depression is not sadness. It is not pain. It is not grief. I find that most purported examples of depression in the Bible describe something else, unless we rely on a very liberal definition of the word. Job is a real possibility, although his suffering has only been going on for months and he's still got a spark in him. Saul I find a more possible example because of the inscrutability of his affliction, its spiritual character, and its lengthy ongoing nature. At the minimum, we can say there are indeed many cases of great sadness and suffering in Scripture. We don't have to call it depression to recognize it as suffering.

I find only one clear and explicit description of depression in the Bible. It is from a passage that is not even attempting to describe depression, or portray someone's immediate mental state. Yet it provides the perfect picture of depression anyway. You could not choose better words. While giving a warning against sin, the Lord Jesus describes a state that is dark and truly fearful, but one step better than hell. The Lord Jesus tells us this:

> It is impossible but that offences will come: but woe unto him, through whom they come!
>
> *It were better for him that a millstone were hanged about his neck, and he cast into the sea*, than that he should offend one of these little ones. (Luke 17:1b–2)
>
> And whosoever shall offend one of these little ones that believe in me, it is better for him that *a millstone were hanged about his neck, and he were cast into the sea*. (Mark 9:42)
>
> But whoso shall offend one of these little ones which believe in me, it were better for him that *a millstone were hanged about his neck, and that he were drowned in the depth of the sea*. (Matt 18:6)

2

The Sea

THE SEA AND ITS many waters have a deep impression on the soul. The sea's influence on us is powerful, and complex, and at time frightening. Being near the sea brings an immediate sense of rest and stillness to our soul. The great distance of the waters, and the sound of it waves falling and receding, seem to cleanse our soul without even touching us. It is washing over us within. Forms of great beauty rise up, as well as scenes of violence and chaos in its waters. Waves tower above as approaching sea beasts. Its reach across the horizon and its incredible depth seem to touch on the infinite, and the eternity of God, as on the horizon is only more water and sky. We see no end. This is even more so as the seas go on and on, touching on each other, and circling the rock on which we live. Its currents are for thousands of miles, and you could follow its courses endlessly. The sea also touches on how temporal all things are, being a force that gradually, beyond the sight of our eyes, wears down rock, taking it so slowly despite its strength to softness, collapse, and finally into scattered pebbles and sand. Its waves repeat, and as the author of Ecclesiastes might point out, just go on and on without change, saying the same thing to our mute ears. It ticks off the time endlessly.

It is the depth of the sea, and its darkness, that can truly frighten us. The very thought of hundreds, or thousands of feet of water beneath out feet can cause immediate alarm in an individual. Just thinking about having those great depth below us, with nothing under our feet, can cause fear, cause the heart to pound. Our legs kicking in the waters, with an abyss of darkness beneath us causes the hairs to stand on end. We don't want to think about what's down there. It brings up a nightmare of what could be living and swimming below us, brushing up against our feet, or slowly lurching up from the darkness. The idea of sinking down into that darkness, being unable to come up, is almost more frightening than death. Without the power to swim, or with some great grasp pulling us down, the light would gradually disappear into a darkness thicker than night. Darkness would surround us. Lack of form. Penetrating coldness. The disappearance of all directions. As we go down and down it is an abyss and truly a picture of hell. The waters that bring cleansing and refreshment to the soul, walking along the beach and hearing them call out, also promise a nightmare, a tight death grasp no man could escape from. Falling further and deeper from the light.

The Bible echoes nature in its presentation of the seas, and then takes us further in our understanding, as it does in many other subjects. Speaking of the waters of the ocean, or merely of the element of water itself, it reveals the attractive cleaning and life-giving power of water in God's creation—a power that represents the communion of the Holy Spirit and God's grace and love. His Spirit overflows, like wells of life-giving water in the desert, blessing all people around. It also reveals its destructive nature, through the flood over all the earth, which quenched all life but those on the ark, water which brings trouble, chaos, and death. It is a truly unstoppable force. Both Jonah and Paul nearly met death on the waters of the open sea.

Water is saving in a way connected to how it is destructive. The same flood waters that drowned the whole earth, also lifted the ark of Noah and his family up above them and carried them safely. The same waters of baptism that bring us down to death, so that our old man perishes, are also the ones which bring new life, as we rise in Jesus Christ, receiving the life of the spiritual man—the old man went under, the new man arose. Water is also a grand creative force. It is acted on by God. Water is present in the beginning of creation (Gen 2, 6–7), and used by God's force to bring shape to creation (2 Pet 3:5). God in the Old Testament, as well as through Christ in the New, reveals his power by showing mastery over water, parting the sea, parting the river, walking on water, stilling a storm, and bringing one up. Despite the power in water, and the great awe we experience at the sea, God exhibits his mastery by moving it and holding it at his desire. He is Lord over this awesome and mysterious force. Perhaps this is why, as the soul responds to the ocean, we feel it truly touches on God and speaks to his eternity. It pictures him, and is the basic primordial material of the cosmos.

It is the sea and its depth that provide for me the only clear picture of depression in the Scriptures. Christ's words and his warnings promise that this fate is terrible, but still better than the punishment for leading a child of God into sin: "It were better for him that a millstone were hanged about his neck, and that he were drowned in the depth of the sea" (Matt 18:6b).

Those are carefully chosen words, and rightly should instill terror on hearing them. It is that falling and that blackness endlessly that accurately describes depression; that being pulled under as if by a great weight. Even thinking about a fate like that, imagining it vividly, is terrifying. Deep water is among some men's greatest fears. To be falling, and to be heavily weighted to as to sink without end, unto the depth of the sea, is a fate with no way out. You cannot tell up from down. The weight is more powerful than you are. The crushing forces destroy the body. You cannot see the other dangers that may lurk even an inch from your face. There is silence and darkness, with no distinction, and it goes on in every direction.

Depression, if we really want to speak of it as a mental disorder, and as the spiritual curse that it is, is enormously more than sadness. Depression usually comes in stages, and does not just jump to its worse form, which is what truly is represented by the words I have chosen. It starts with various assaults on the soul, and falling into habits of being far down, and unable to come up. Habits also of self-loathing, and anger. The mind becomes apathetic to ordinary goals and previous dreams, and seems without a thought to detach itself. It just starts to shut down. While there may be a few initiating causes from which it appears to stem, depression as an experience becomes removed from any cause, and seems like misery with no cause. An illness that you just caught in the air. A spiritual cancer regardless of your life circumstances. When the curse has reached its greatest depth, the soul is numb, and there is absolute emptiness. There is not sadness, but an incredible silence, and lack of feeling. An entire soul experience of deadness, purposelessness, torturing silence.

PERSONAL EXPERIENCE

I experienced depression for over ten years, in growing stages until I reached the most extreme. I hope that my experience can help you in some way, and I want to describe it before I speak more broadly about pain and about the Almighty. I hope you can recognize it in yourself, or in others, and are there to offer hope and comfort to those who are lost to it. There is no easy solution to this affliction, but human contact and help is invaluable, as is love.

The first stage of depression I experienced was the random, on-and-off again pits I could fall into. It was a long period of highs and lows. Almost at random, or by small insignificant triggers, I could immediately become silent, apathetic, and unhappy. Usually this came along with a good deal of self-hatred, hatred for my incapacity to act normally, or the many past experiences that troubled my heart. As it continued, the weight of self-hatred increased, as you see yourself missing more and more experiences due to being spiritually down, and unable to feel warmth and joy. When I was not afflicted by these comings and goings of tortured spirits, I could feel normally, laugh, have fun, enjoy life. The only thing that continued beyond these times of depression was a detachment I felt in my mind, which I see being at the root of the depression, but I will speak of that cause later on, since I view it as separate from the blackness called depression.

I had many years of ups and downs. It became a normal and expected part of my life. Over time, the downs became worse, as misery from missing life due to depression increased, and as depression left me more isolated and lonelier. As hope disappeared of ever having a normal life, it seemed only that this was my terrible experience that I was locked into, and the future could be no different. The constant thought was—I will not be a part of this world, because I am not normal, and I cannot feel the joy that others do. I do not walk or talk or think like them. I tried at times to figure out causes for when this affliction would come upon me. That is simply because its onset often was without apparent cause, just a button being pushed. At times it could be triggered by something as small as a word, or a topic of conversation, or a thought. The ground could just collapse beneath me. I could wake up with the darkness in the morning, and find it depart a few days later. I tried to guess if the affliction would only come on certain days of the week. I tried counting the stages of the moon, to see if the moon affected my inner state. In the long run of course, neither did. Over time, I associated my mental state, whether high or low, with the coming and going of spirits. When I felt exuberant, and enthusiastic towards life, I had been filled with spirits of life, and when I was tortured and dark inside, the evil spirits had come.

Looking back, I see an element of King Saul's experience, in the radical change of emotional and spiritual state. My soul was an empty vessel, cracked, and open to spirits to come and dwell.

Generally, pain would come apart from what I was doing, or whom I was with, and even if my current attitude was more positive than usual, it would find a way in. Eventually what seemed like discernable forms of sadness, anger, self-hatred, and apathy simply forged themselves together into one affliction: pain. Like the nails, bolts, and sharp metal shreds the suicide bomber packaged into his belt, they unite and make the inner life a place of destruction. They became one debility as well, making normal happiness, hope, and human connection unimaginable. My mind attacked itself, becoming my enemy. The human contact, friendships, feelings, and warmth others feel were a part of the world that I watched occur before me from a distant unfeeling land. They were merely on a screen in front of me. Yet they were not meant for me at all. They did not cross over into my world of darkness and death. Pain became what I expected, and what I lived with. Normal life goals seemed laughable. Happiness was a dream, that only appeared in the soul by force of imagination. I spent many years spending much of the time wishing for death so that it would end; thousands of days and nights. That terrible state I describe is what I thought to be serious depression, until one day I finally arrived at serious depression. Then it seemed like the overture.

The second stage of depression is the one I can speak most clearly of as being like the fearful warnings of Christ; like having a heavy millstone hung around your neck and thrown into the depth of the sea. It is indeed a spiritual experience, as dark and satanic as it is, and pervading the soul. It transcends any sadness, grief, or anger. I entered this stage after many years of ups and downs, and many attempts at normal connection with the world, and normal friendships. I went down in my mood one day, fully expecting to come up again. The days passed, and I did not return out of the depth. Then weeks passed, and I knew this was something totally different. I knew I was in trouble, and finally sought mental help, as well as help from friends. Stage two is the utter collapse of feelings. What had been assaulted over and over finally is defeated. The tower collapses. The soul settles into a mire of complete lack of feeling. Desires go away. One can feel an incredible weight hanging off one's chest, almost pulling one to the ground. When this state struck, I immediately stopped doing some of the activities I was involved in, and still found myself with little energy to do the rest. I could command myself to get my responsibilities done, but I kept them to a bare minimum. I could pick up my guitar and attempt to lift myself out of this state with music, which if I was very focused on the music I could for a short time, and then immediately after I ceased, the heavy weight returned, pressing on my chest, pulling me down. Like others who suffer deep depression, you think that one of the solutions is to force yourself to go out to do things, and that will lift your spirits. Perhaps if you're just a little unhappy that will work. I found no success at all in this. I would walk somewhere miserable. Sit there miserable. And then walk home still miserable. There was no desire even to reach my destination, and I could stop in the middle of the street, and simply stare at my feet, wondering what I am doing. There is no point in reaching my destination, I sense, and no point in returning home. There is no point in turning left or right. There is a great silence in depression. Those thoughts and stimulations that usually come to you and engage your mind, become quieted. The soul is empty, like a burnt-out husk. You listen to that silence, hoping to hear something, and you do not. It just goes on and on endlessly. Each moment you feel you fall further and sink more deeply into the sea. Its depth surrounds you. Its darkness is deadening. Any human being would wish for death to end it.

There are physical elements to this terrifying curse. The soul and the body of man touch on each other, so this should be expected. On the mild end, I could experience mild nausea, a warmth, and of course a lack of energy in all my limbs. Other times I felt hotter or colder than usual. Perhaps the most shocking, proving the dominance of this curse over the human soul, is when I found one day I could no longer taste my food. I chewed it up like cardboard. It was an undistinguished mush in my mouth. I tried making my favorite meals, but they lacked all flavor and enjoyment. I took a bite out of a chocolate bar, and it too was cardboard, flavorless. For a period I ate very little, having no desire to eat, and getting no pleasure from it. I would force myself to swallow down a few bites just to have something in my stomach. Otherwise, it was empty, and with time I could smell my stomach in my mouth, as it had nothing to digest, and wafted upward looking for kill.

You should know how much of a new land, a new territory this darkness is. It surrounds you and it fills you. You have truly crossed over. I think of the patient who has suffered a terrible accident who finds themselves now in a little room, in a bed, hooked up to a respirator and other machines, completely apart from their normal life. I think of the hiker who takes a wrong turn, and ends up in the thick jungle, with night coming, and few supplies. The loneliness and lack of connection in depression is overwhelming, as if there is nothing real you can touch, nor any mark that sets your direction, up or down. You simply exist. Keep breathing. Your heart beats. Yet there is silence and nothingness all around. For some reason you are alive, yet you feel as if dead. Imagine an astronaut, who has set off from his ship on a spacewalk, and the tether holding him in is cut. He is abandoned by his ship, set only to drift and float aimlessly, not even at his own command. Just staring at the big black universe, to the sound of breathing; that void which goes on to unfathomable depth.

Today, when I reflect on those dark experiences, I immediately think of the verse in Revelation, which heralds the final kingdom of God: "He that is unjust, let him be unjust still: and he which is filthy, let him be filthy still: and he that is righteous, let him be righteous still: and he that is holy, let him be holy still" (22:11). All that we are in this life on earth is now brought to eternity. Those who are wicked now remain wicked for eternal days. Those who are righteous remain righteous for eternal days. My ocean of darkness seems an example of hitting that final state, but as the unjust and the wicked. The filth of the soul now stretches out to eternity, and anywhere you look there is no light, no joy, no hope. In heaven there is no need for light, as the light of Christ illuminates all. In hell you receive no light at all. You get to be with yourself forever, in your own godlessness. Depression is what life without God and goodness looks like, and it appears an image of the eternal abyss.

HELP FOR DEPRESSION

It is not hard to recognize someone like myself when I was under the power of this affliction. I show it. There is apathy, deadness, sadness, pain, often in my voice. My face shows my anguished mental state. Other sufferers are not like that. You may have friends who can keep a fine performance at many tasks while they suffer terribly within. Others can smile nearly the whole time. They are miserable and want to die, but you'd never know it, unless you were very intuitive and sought to know them better. Anyone who saw me most of the time would recognize me as a troubled person and an outcast; being unhappy, and in some minds dangerous; being distant and unknown. Daily life for many people can be characterized by work, by leisure, by boredom, by an aching body, by tiredness, by excitement. For the depressed it is characterized by pain. The unbelievable emptiness and meaninglessness is a suffering of unspeakable kind. That is your life. You have pain, and you live it day after day after day, and you have no signal it will ever end. It has gone on for so long it seems all that you know, and you wonder what normal people feel like. You wonder why, and have no answer. You only know you continue to live, and your life is pain.

I tried, like countless psychiatric patients, varying medications for depression. Psychiatrists will hand out prescription drugs very easily, and it really doesn't take much to get some, including for a variety of conditions beyond depression. By the time I went, I would have begged for it, but they will give it to you quickly anyway. Those who wish to be medicated should know this—there is no such thing as a happy pill. I have never been prescribed a drug for depression that changed my mood from deadened, miserable, and empty, to lighthearted and full of mirth. The pills I have tried either did nothing in my mind or body at all (Prozac for example), or zonked me out in a pleasant way, being kind of a tranquilizer (such as Zoloft and chemically related drugs). Their effects seem little more than a placebo.[1] None of them make you happy. In fact, I went through some of the worst, nightmarish depression while taking the latter kind of drugs. However, they do have an indirect effect that might be helpful in living with depression: the drugs make you care so little that you care less that you are depressed. You are too tranquilized to care. In that way, they may take off the spiraling effect depression can have, where you don't merely feel miserable, but you feel miserable about the very fact you are miserable, and how long you have been miserable. By drugging you up then, it might numb you to the certain edge depression can have, and help you function. That's only my opinion, but it comes from plenty of experience with the drugs.

The best thing you can give someone who suffers horribly is company, if they desire it, and support. Be able to offer them hope for the future, and listen to them. While I found that forcing myself to go out and do things was a failed strategy, just the opposite strangely did some good. I had a friend who would come over when I was at my worst, and we'd turn off the lights and listen to *The Godfather* soundtrack. Sounds kind of intentionally dark and spooky, but in a way by embracing the darkness, there was less terror in it. There was some soothing to it. When

---

1. Kelley, "Antidepressants."

I could not eat, my friend took me over to her house and forced me to eat chicken noodle soup, so I could get something in my stomach, and get used to food again. That was not a cure, but it was therapy, and treatment as good or better than any paid professional. Long before they had psychiatrists, not everyone was committing suicide over depression. Their faith, strength, and relationships all helped them live in peace, or rise out of it. Similarly, today we would have little need for professional mental help if we lived the right way and had support. Right attitudes and right behavior are better than any anti-depressant in the world.

When someone has depression, you should also be able to recommend a healthy path for that person to go on, even though in the midst of depression it can seem too dark to see one. Realize that the life choices people make helps to lead them into the darkness. I don't believe many people fall into depression merely because a chemical in the body suddenly increases or decreases too much. Depression is much more than a mood. It is a spiritual state. Wicked choices increase the distance to which the soul enters this deadness, and there are real choices that can help lead the soul out of it. Attitudes such as pride, unforgiveness, anger, hatred; if left lingering on the soul, continuous over time, will begin to bring anyone down, no matter what his personality. Shallow living; that includes immorality, drunkenness, and a life purely based on self; provides high risk of a collapse, since it has so little grounding beneath it. Unbelief, and outward rejection of the Creator bring misery and deep emptiness to any soul. For a thinking, feeling being to embrace the idea they are just a piece of meat that evolved by accident over billions of years is shattering to the soul. It is shattering to mental health. To actually believe you have zero intrinsic value, and that there is no eternal moral law, leaves anyone in confusion, and vulnerable to mental illness, up to and including severe depression. The idea that there is nothing fundamentally wrong with murdering a child, as materialistic secularism demands, is devastating to our inner life and our ability to love the life God has blessed us with. Further, social isolation, and unstable, unhealthy relationships in general rot out the core of our being. We are built for stable, loving, productive bonds, and to have a meaningful role among family and community. The lack of such bonds can increase our fear, isolation, and sadness, and remove a sense of purpose in existence. The use of drugs further brings bondage, and locks many into evil behavior either to get their drug or because of its effects on their mind. It truly unleashes instability and confusion. Many of these pitfalls come down to our choices in belief, attitude, and behavior. A healthy and loving life is much lower risk for depression. One with family, stability, morality, and goals for the future are the groundwork for inner satisfaction. Trust in God and a life in Jesus Christ thwart the adversary, and take down many attacks against us. They provide us a safe shelter, a purpose, a hope for the good.

One thing to remember is not to be bamboozled by the labels psychology gives to our mental phenomena. At times those labels are useful, and at times they are grossly inadequate. In responding to mental suffering, recognize there are often multiple reasons, or one specific reason you may be suffering, beyond what psychology calls depression. If you can see that cause—and it's not always possible—recognize and respond to that cause. It may be different for different people. Mental anguish can come from ongoing grief, self-loathing (which is often anger turned inward), fear, isolation, hopelessness, loss, lack of activity, diet, or other factors. Definitions that are very broad become almost useless, and this is true of the label depression. Deal with the cause of the anguish, not some phantasm of a mental illness, which often does not really exist in the first place.

Even the worst kind of depression, which I describe in this book, and which does bear more of a resemblance to an actual mental illness, does not need to be put wholly in the box in which psychology puts it. It needs to be recognized that such a dark and overpowering state also has origins. It must be understood the spiritual nature of the abyss which the spirit falls into, and spiritual avenues to freedom must be explored. There is depression which is a cursing, or which is demonic. Just as Saul was tormented by an angel from God, there may be instances today of depression caused by the same spiritual visitation. There is depression rooted in a lack of prayer, or trust in God. Nothing in the created world can be easily put in a box by science, much less by the field of psychology, which is such a soft science, and which often is totally unnecessary.

Psychology, while not wrong about everything it teaches, is only going to the reflect godless thought it was founded on, as well as the values of the secular world. In this it can be very dangerous. The tendency that psychology has to create a psychological label for broad and possibly unrelated phenomena, as I have discussed here, is followed by pushing a cure, most often through medication. This is true of depression in which the use of medication is epidemic, and is often the first thing given to the patient as a solution. It is true of other umbrella labels, like ADHD, which similarly likely describes a variety of phenomena caused by a variety of things, and which usually does not need to be medicated. It can be dealt with successfully through other means. Millions of children in the U.S. have been medicated with stimulants because they fit this broad label, one which its inventor, shortly before his death, said was over diagnosed and called a fictitious disease.[2]

Even in the current push towards transsexualism in the culture, which is aberrant in its very attempt to bend gender, we see the broad label of a gender disorder slapped on all kinds of experiences. Many of these people are simply uncomfortable with some of the pressures that come with their sex, and if treated like a normal person, which they are, would likely get over their insecurities. It is actually very normal to be uncomfortable with the sex God made you. Others have been bullied or abused, and come to think that means they would be better off being the opposite sex. They look to that as the only necessary escape. Still others are craving attention and a sense of importance. The label of gender dysphoria gets placed on young people who actually have totally different mental problems, but have become convinced that pretending to be the opposite sex will relieve them of their pain. Then psychology swoops in and makes a killing by giving these confused people drugs, or even operations, under the guise of helping them. Even if it were not wrong to pretend to be the opposite sex, this kind of mass herding of patients, and mass medicating, is just ignorant and does not even try to address a man's real problems. It labels normal human problems as mental illnesses. Leave it to a team of PhDs to make fools out of everyone.

What finally brought me past the unbelievable experience of mental illness was one thing: spending time in an open, and loving environment, to share friendship with people daily. It was not professional therapy, or drugs, though it's possible those things bring some temporary relief. Being surrounded by acceptance, learning to communicate myself, and experiencing brotherly love brought my soul back to life in a matter of months. It placed the living fire within me. It gave me something to do with that fire, people to love, and made the deadened world I had known reveal its splendor. Medications had never done that. Love did that. People who were like family, who did not leave me, were not angry with

---

2. Blech, "Melancholy Without Shame." Eisenberg also states during the interview that psychiatrists often rush too quickly to medication, and points out that psychological factors and home life need to be looked at for a cause. He greatly laments the overmedication of the condition. It should be noted that he calls ADHD fictitious as a genetic disease, and is not denying that anyone has serious problems with attention.

me, and showed understanding for my pain and for the odd character that I was. My debilities did not stop them from showing me warmth and connection. Everything flowed from love.

The society that relies on psychiatric drugs is confused and impotent in the face of pain. It has been made blind and stupid by its reliance on highly educated medical professionals. You really have to ask yourself, if you see someone sinking in the sea, if you want to numb them to their pain, or rescue them. Do you want them to be full of chemicals, or of love? Do you want them to drown more comfortably, or come out of the depths and live? If you see someone whom you think is miserable, they probably are. Talk to them. Show that you care. Show them acceptance and draw on whatever light they have within. There is still a desire to live and to love in their souls, despite obvious inner misery and hopelessness. The deadened soul does come to life. For some people all it took was one phone call when they were about to kill themselves. For others it was a group of friends who made them feel normal. We are each other's safety nets, and while depression can truly dominate and torture the soul, it is not forever and it can vanish like a bad dream, fade away as a morning mist. You won't even remember what it was like anymore.

ORIGINS

Nearly any sufferer of terrible pain wants to know its root cause. It seems less fearsome if you know its cause. He may find it wrapped up in life events, his thought life, spiritual forces, or simply genetics. While I can speak in detail about going through depression, for me it stemmed from what I consider a wholly separate affliction, which was present from the beginning of my life. As early as two years old, and I have no memories before that, I can recall a sense of separateness in my being from other people. I vividly remember lapsing into states of detachment periodically throughout my early childhood. It could be likened to a wall coming down, or a thin transparent veil. Separateness, numbness of feelings, and lack of joy characterize this cutting off.

This was an experience which grew in frequency over time. It became triggered by more and more events. I specifically remember a friend's birthday party when I was little, and as I sat there at a table watching other children run around and play, laughing, and having fun. I felt no ability to join in, and no laughter at all. One of the parents at the party asked me if I wanted to play, and though I did, I refused. I simply lacked the ability to. Whatever happiness was there I was unable to feel. Whatever cord between the outside world and the inner which exists had been cut. These experiences began to happen for longer periods, and soon became a normal part of my life. Like depression, which also grew over time, it appeared to be random, or triggered my unexplainable or small factors.

Coupled with detachment came an overwhelming number of thoughts; thoughts so plentiful and complex and rich it would be hard to communicate many of them. I could see vivid scenes, as if watching a play in my mind, and at times be very emotionally connected to them. I could laugh or weep at the images in my head. These thoughts and imaginations dominated my mind to the degree I could not focus on the outside world, or would miss some of what occurred before me. An overflow of thoughts could perhaps be a benefit in writing or similar creative work, but it functions as a debility in much else, preventing communication, and making my listening and understanding very difficult. The life experience becomes heavily rooted in the mind, and less in the outside world. If the detachment were like an egg, then perhaps my plentiful imaginings would be like the chick which grows within this egg, finding its natural place in a little world apart from this one, but very near. I knew this was not normal, but did not know what strange disease it was a part of. It was, like much of my experience, a curse.

I spend many of my school years in that state. My final six years of school were completely dominated by this affliction. I cannot remember ever looking forward to walking in the door of school, but only knew it as a place of detachment, a place to simply shut down. I would have gone anywhere to escape it, to escape my school and home life, and to escape my future. For what future can you have? From this one curse came another—that of depression —and it's not hard to see how depression organically grew from being cut off from the world. A sense of separateness leaves you with few friends, and no sense of closeness with others to begin with. It leaves you unable to interact. You watch the world happen as a foreigner, or a visitor from outer space. The world is not yours, but something which happens around you. Yet at the same time, you know others are experiencing friendship, fun, emotional bonding, and those things in life you desire. Any human being it seems, being so cut off, would fall into inner misery, and eventually clinical depression. Being cut off alone is a state of torture, and inspires pain throughout the soul. One wants to be rescued, but one finds no help.

LIFE IN PAIN

The results of growing up with despair, and having little attachment to the goals of this world are predictable to anyone. There was nothing I desired of the world, except the passing fleeting fantasy. I had no hope in any life path or career. The possibility of family appeared like a misery, and not a relationship of any satisfaction or value. Why would I want to pass on my pain to children anyway? I could imagine doing any job including an attractive one, but those fantasies disappear when you realize most bosses don't really want someone who stares vacantly, and doesn't say anything. The nerves and anxiety I had simply being around people and interacting with them were usually visible, and quite awkward, and made me prefer solitude much of the time. I had been kicked out of this world, and at a point I wholly rejected it. I saw it as little but wicked; a bleak, dull, grey landscape before me. There is no future.

I embraced this emptiness. I predictably made a personal religion of it. I searched for meaning in other confused men, such as existential writers, beat writers, or people I knew who equally impressed me. Disturbed French playwright and actor Antonin Artaud seemed like my image and likeness, even in his looks. Like others who were drowning in unhappiness, I found temporary relief and meaning in music which proclaims the lost. Even a few minutes, or an hour of music could be a medicating drip, to provide soothing until the pain returned, the inevitable feeling of spiritual acid eating the soul. Songs about anger, misery, and suicide naturally attract those who feel that way. One therapist I saw told me it was common for mental patients to be very attached to Pink Floyd's *The Wall*, because of its theme of alienation and self-destruction. I would similarly listen to that band's last album, the *Final Cut*, as well as bands like Metallica and the Misfits. The Violent Femmes had a rousing song depicting drug use or suicide called "Kiss Off," and an equally rousing one suggesting murder and suicide, "Add It Up." That is not all I listened to, but these things provide momentary relief, and a connection to someone else who feels the same as you do.

When you are openly abnormal, and unhappy, you tend to attract two kinds of people. The first are others who are disturbed and unhappy themselves, and the second are regular people who want to be your friend because they want to help you. They may not be that crazy about you, but they see you are lost and want to provide you friendship. This provides temporary relief as well, but ultimately no cure. It gives you at the minimum someone kind or interesting to talk to. One Mexican friend of mine described me as *medio loco* ("half crazy"), and another as *un perdedor de la sociedad* ("loser of society"), and such descriptions are typical by people who knew me even a brief time. You garner some amount of sympathy, and at times disgust. Once a person is wrapped up in wrong thoughts and abysmal attitudes, they tend to continue with that pattern, and reject newer better ones. Misery becomes a way of life. My unstable life, and constant relocations also added to how little possible friendships could help, making relationships easily broken. I became quite committed to the idea this world was evil, and that I desired to be different from it. Easing back into the norm, even if it were possible, would be an option my soul repelled. I felt a foreigner here, and born for another world.

Once one gives in to temptation to sin, that sin becomes much more the trap and the prison cell than it had ever been. Walk a few steps forward, and the door slams and locks behind you. Many of the poor influences that I chose for myself, which often relieved my pain, were themselves further warping and damaging to the soul. In fact, my mirror image Artaud, shortly before he died, and while frequently a mental patient, wrote a radio play called, *To Have Done With the Judgment of god*. It included a section called, "The Abolition of the Cross." Living a life in rebellion against God, and suffering from his sin, he sought to lead others away to the same hell he would know. Other musicians I listened to played a self-aware pied piper role, which they essentially bragged about. They were proud to instill rebellion. In the liner notes of one popular band, they told parents—we love your children more than you do.

It is certain during this time that a few people must have shared the gospel with me, but very few. If I ran into people who mentioned Jesus, it was usually in a feel-good kind of way, or as a matter of proclaiming the end of the world at the subway station. I don't recall many gospel presentations at all. Surely if I had heard it, I would have rejected it immediately like the rest. Such talk of God to fallen man is like human talk to a dog, being meaningless blabber, except in the case of the dog, there is a stronger bond of love there. I once had a girlfriend take me to the meeting of a Christian college group, which came off to me basically as group therapy. Nothing religious was meaningful to me, but it was pleasant, and I would have gone again. Nevertheless, the same girl was committing fornication with me, and we sometimes brought other people to bed with us. While probably not uncommon among college Christians, it wouldn't have been the best of witnesses.

Perhaps the only person I can think of who made me listen with an open mind was my close musician friend in Spain. He was a vagabond like myself, drank heavily, and did drugs. He and another close friend taught me how to work on the streets, and showed me the bohemian side of the city. My friend ended up getting talked to by Jehovah's Witnesses, and for a short time proclaimed that he believed in Jesus. He gave me a tract about the end of the world, and asked me if I believed these things. It was touching, because he was such a close friend, more than a brother. It made me think much more than if anyone else had asked me or handed me a tract. I told him I believed the world would end one day, surely, but nothing he said led me to faith in Christ. There was just something truthful about loving each other, as Christ commands. I doubt my friend had much of a biblical knowledge at that time, and soon after he returned to his lifestyle, and no longer professed belief. Today, from brief communication on social media, I see he lacks faith in Christ, and lives in the secular world, still playing music. When I have tried to speak with him about the Lord, he politely brushes me off. His soul does not want to see a glimmer of it.

I have spent much time on and off throughout my life trying to figure out what my condition was. Did it have a name? What are the causes? Is there a cure so I don't have to feel like this anymore? All of the possibilities I read about, until recently, did not match my reality. There was no physical or mental condition that summarized what I experienced. Any pattern I tried to find to discover when my mind would be cut off and become distant proved to be unhelpful. There was no cure. On a rare occasion I saw another young man who appeared the same as me, and immediately recognized the curse in him; in his eyes, facial expression, and awkward reactions. I knew I must have a brother somewhere. The separateness had grown over the years from starting under unique circumstances, to happening frequently, and then to taking over my life. In practical terms, it has not only been painful, but also been a debility, and heavily limited what I can do in work or relationships. In part it is the mystery, and dominating power it has, which makes it so terrifying, and leaves no escape from the darkness. Your soul seems simply to belong to another. Beyond human understanding it is the worst of monsters.

THE SEA

The questions Why, How, When, are near to your lips when you suffer continually. You want to know the reasons for your affliction, and how to get out of it. When will this terrible state of existence end? You want to know the curse's name, as if that would give you power over it. You want to know what is bringing it on. Was it something you did? Was it something you inherited? You look for small glimmers of reasons to hope. As the curse endures endlessly and there seems little escape, you want little from life, and only want to die. You're simply a broken person.

3

Pain

For if God spared not the angels that sinned, but cast them down to hell, and delivered them into chains of darkness, to be reserved unto judgment;

(2 Pet 2:4)

And the angels which kept not their first estate, but left their own habitation, he hath reserved in everlasting chains under darkness unto the judgment of the great day. (Jude 1:6)

Hell and destruction are before the LORD: how much more then the hearts of the children of men? (Prov 15:11)

For anyone suffering depression, it's no exaggeration to call depression an image of hell. The emptiness and darkness that seems to consume you points to what man understands to be the deep prison and pit apart from God. The burning torment of fires, or the endless void of the abyss. Depression is an experience of much of what hell is, albeit in a limited sense on the earth. A lack of God's grace. A lack of hope. A lack of true, and meaningful living. A lack of spiritual understanding. A lack of a foundation for anything in our life. A lack of love. A lack of joy. A lack of light in the soul. Were man to taste hell for some reason or another in this life, and by the purposes of God, it seems depression would be the taste, for this short time we are on this earth. It seems a prison of torment, even though you know the entire time that prison is in your heart, and you are still unable to escape. But why, the sufferer of pain calls out? Why? What can I do to end it? Why would a God pour fire upon me on this earth? Is this a purely brutal, cruel, meaningless beating?

Just as the sufferer of pain or illness wants to know the source and solution of his misery, every human being wonders about his own condition. The more or less happy souls wonder too. He knows he is corrupt. He can see moral wickedness in himself and be ashamed of it, and even as he tries to cover up his own wrongdoing, he knows it is dark and filthy. He experiences pain, and knows one day he will grow decrepit and die, facing the blackness beyond. He likely has suffered because of his own evils, as we all have suffered from the evils of those around us. Even the mostly contented soul knows everything he holds onto dearly will be washed away. Everything he treasures will be destroyed. What kind of life is this, and how can I know relief? I want purity and goodness and rest. Why can we not find it in this life?

The Holy Scriptures provide answers to these universal questions. They are not the answers everyone prefers to hear, and some reject them. However, the Scriptures reveal truth any man can rest on, along with the reason for our suffering, and the solution to it in the long run. We can trust in God's answers and build our life around them. Sadly, many people continue to use the reality of pain and of evil to attack the faith which will actually save us from it. Similarly, many Christians who do not trust in the truth of the Scriptures are confused about their pain too, and doubtful about their God. They're not sure they believe what the Scriptures teach them, although they should, and more to the point must as a Christian believe them. If we trust in the Almighty, we must also trust in the truth he teaches.

That lack of acceptance of God's answer for us is in fact a big part of the reason for pain to begin with. Not only did mankind start his existence by sinning, as Adam did shortly after creation, but we continually bring more confusion, anxiety, sadness, and suicide by thinking we have no bearings to live our lives, and by not realizing the love which truly has been given us. We continually bring more evil to this earth by dismissing the Bible's moral and spiritual instructions. By making the human heart the well of life and source of commandments, instead of God, we permit and encourage what is a dirty bomb on all humanity, including violence down through the generations, drug addiction, broken families, immorality, and the spirit of rebellion that got us all in trouble in the first place. We have a truthful guidebook to our lives, but we disregard it, only to create more pain and evil we can complain about, and claim we want to solve. The answer is very close at hand,[1] but it seems most men do not want it. They instead want their pain.

I am a product of that foolishness as much as anyone else is. I also became an active cause of suffering as I grew up, joining in the rejection of God and his word, replacing it instead with the desires of man's heart, and whatever sinful desire I had. I made the decision to replace God with man. That lack of awareness of truth leads any life to become untethered, whether in the great obvious ways of sinful lifestyles, or the quieter dissatisfaction of a neat, clean, yet self-serving and empty life. For most of my life, someone could have given me the answer and the cure to my terrible pain, and I would have blindly rejected it. Very few people ever shared the gospel with me over the years, but anyone who ever spoke about God with me, I dismissed and ignored. Man rejects the real solution because of his unbelief, and because he knows if he comes to trust in God, he will have to step down. That is very unattractive. He will lose his puffed-up sense of autonomy, and will have to give up some pleasurable sins. He will have to admit he is weak. Others accept the truths on the surface, because they offer some ethical grounding, or emotional relief, but remain filthy on the inside, never trusting in God and his Son, and remaining in a fleshy mindset that will lead any man to death. We do not wish to look at the root of the problem, or at the solution. It is not comfortable.

The real root of our universal pain is in the fall of mankind into sin. It is not an individual moral evil which you or I do, nor a single flaw in the body that allows it to become ill, suffer pain, and die. Rather, it is in an event which unplugged humanity from the source of true life who is God our Creator. In detaching man from intimate connection to the Lord of Creation, the fall brought deadness and darkness to the soul. Our forefather Adam sinned, and every child who would come from Adam subsequently fell into sin with him. His family would inevitably suffer from death and from the spiritual leaning toward sin that would destroy them. Apart from the saving mercy of God, and from faith, the end of every life would be physical death, and spiritual torment for the soul after death, under the judgment of God. That is why you and I can suffer so: The sin of Adam and all of his race.

Some will claim boldly—I don't believe in sin, because I don't believe in your god (lower case g). Yet when this same person reads about

---

1. See Deut 30:14. It is "very near you, in your mouth and in your heart" (NKJV).

children at a school being molested, they will immediately believe in sin, and want that sin to be cured. They will cry out with righteous indignation that it be cured. When they learn that a store has been ripping off its customers, including them, they will believe in sin again, and seek justice to be done. They will want the relevant authorities to protect us from this sin, and for the wrong to be made right. When a friend is raped, a person beaten cruelly, a judge bribed to sway justice, they will find sin fully incompatible with their belief system, and wonder why this world is so corrupt and what we can do about it. They will be actively seeking a cure. Even those who with words reject the truth of God, accept it in many other ways. They love the moral law, they just don't want to obey all of it, or be accountable to the Almighty. They want to complain about evil in others, but they want to be left alone, unbothered by God, to practice evil themselves.

It is also the perennial response of the unbeliever, or simply of the confused, to say this: But why am I suffering for what Adam did? Why am I disposed to do evil because of his evil? The complaint is followed by the predictable accusation: This is unfair. I should not suffer because of what someone else did. The accusation of being unfair is often hurled at God in both this arena, and of sin in general, but it is always a false accusation. Before I get into specifically why it's false accusation, I want to explain how we are all under that curse that came from Adam's sin, as well as how it affects us. Remember, before we go on, God is eternal and God is all powerful and God is loving. Therefore, as we discuss this darkness which pervades and domineers us, there is not only a reason for that darkness to be there, but a cure that will end it. There is a solution in principle and in practice. Whimsy has nothing to do with it. Whatever sin you are imprisoned by, or physical or mental suffering you undergo, you can be freed forever. It may not be in the way you want. It may not be in the way you imagine. The treatment isn't always easy. But there is a cure for the human situation.

Sin, suffering, and death, find their way into humanity in three main ways. The first is through our conception; being in sin from birth and by nature separated from God. We inherit a sin nature along with a corruptible body, one which not only predisposes us toward sin but places us from birth into a rebel kingdom. The second is through the oppression of sin in the world, which pressures men, groups, and entire nations to commit evil. Corrupt systems, intergenerational sin, a flood of falsehoods, make any individual overwhelmed by corruption the same way a tsunami would make a coastal village overwhelmed by water. It's power and weight and destruction are unavoidable. The third is through our own wicked choices; our willful decision to show solidarity with Adam and the devil, voting every time we sin for Adam as our head, and for hell as our preferred destination. Our personal wicked choices, you might say, are the sacrament of Confirmation into a fallen people—our birth brought us into this rebellion, our Confirmation gave our more knowing consent. In each of these three ways we are given over to it. In each of them we exist apart from God's kingdom, and in an open ongoing rebellion. We are Adam's people, through the ages, continuing what he started. That is why we suffer and sin. Let's look at each one of these reasons in turn.

FIRST—CONCEPTION INTO SIN

The death, pain, and sinful character that came with Adam's fall, is inherited by each individual descendant. We can understand this in terms of receiving our nature from Adam, because he is our father, as well as in terms of being in his family and so naturally under his headship. While Scripture does not contain the specific phrase "sin nature," it does teach that we are in a sinful state from birth, and that our heart itself is wicked. It does teach the universality of sin in all mankind.

In his great psalm of confession, David writes, "Behold, I was shapen in iniquity; and in sin did my mother conceive me" (Ps 51:5). Reinforcing to us that he speaks of our innermost being, David goes on to contrast it with what God desires of us, "Behold, thou desirest truth in the inward parts: and in the hidden part thou shalt make me to know wisdom" (v. 6). In speaking of evildoers in an imprecatory psalm, David writes, "do ye judge uprightly, O ye sons of men? Yea, in heart ye work wickedness; ye weigh the violence of your hands in the earth. *The wicked are estranged from the womb*: they go astray as soon as they be born, speaking lies" (Ps 58:1b–3).

The book of Job, which has much to teach us about the meaning of suffering, asks this about the state of mankind: "What is man, that he should be clean? and he which is born of a woman, that he should be righteous? Behold, he putteth no trust in his saints; yea, the heavens are not clean in his sight. *How much more abominable and filthy is man*, which drinketh iniquity like water?" (Job 15:14–16). Later it likewise asks, "How then can man be justified with God? or *how can he be clean that is born of a woman?* Behold even to the moon, and it shineth not; yea, the stars are not pure in his sight. How much less man, that is a worm? and the son of man, which is a worm?" (25:4-6).

Holy Scripture just as powerfully speaks of man's condition when describing the state of humanity before the flood. It reveals, "And GOD saw that the wickedness of man was great in the earth, and that *every imagination of the thoughts of his heart was only evil continually*. And it repented the LORD that he had made man on the earth, and it grieved him at his heart" (Gen 6:5-6). Lest you think this merely describes the worst of behavior at that time in history, we can still see that wickedness is universal and is present in our youth after the flood has wiped out all but Noah's family. In receiving Noah's sacrifice, it teaches, "And the LORD smelled a sweet savour; and the LORD said in his heart, I will not again curse the ground any more for man's sake; for *the imagination of man's heart is evil from his youth*; neither will I again smite any more every thing living, as I have done" (Gen 8:21).

Sin is in the fabric of human nature. That fabric is with us from our conception, even before we learn willfully and with knowledge to act on it. It is there from childhood and into adulthood. In describing our new state as Christians, and contrasting it with our state before coming to Christ, Eph 2 teaches:

> And you hath *he quickened, who were dead in trespasses and sins*;
>
> Wherein in time past ye walked according to the course of this world, according to the prince of the power of the air, the spirit that now worketh in the children of disobedience:
>
> Among whom also we all had our conversation in times past in the lusts of our flesh, fulfilling the desires of the flesh and of the mind; and *were by nature the children of wrath*, even as others. (vv. 1-3)

Here we see the deadness before being born again in Christ described in light of our newness and life, which Paul will go on to describe. It is a state of deadness, in which we seek to fulfill the desires of our flesh and our mind, meaning selfish ones and sinful ones. He specifically teaches that we are children of wrath "by nature," as opposed to by sinful choices that we made here and there. The sinfulness is a part of our being. When we see "children of wrath," we shouldn't only think evildoer, but also see it connotes being under condemnation, under God's wrath. We are, in our nature, guilty. We are sons of guilt. It is not merely our deeds, but our being itself which is flawed. Just as it is that every person has a body that can suffer pain, grow old, and die, finally to rot in the grave, we each have an inner character which is corrupt, separate from fellowship with God, and will make our mind and willpower instruments of serving the self and serving sin. Our sinfulness, like our mortality, is in our bones. Should we be surprised this is a world of pain and death?

It's interesting to note that the term Paul uses here for "nature" (Greek: *physis*) is the common word indicating nature, or birth. While it may occasional be used in reference to a learned habit, it's normal use and common definition is for innate properties within us. In fact, this is the exact same word Paul uses multiple times for people who are Jews or Gentiles "by nature." Some Bible versions translate the phrase in Gal 2:15 as "Jews by birth,"[2] because that would be by far the most common way to be a Jew. Likewise, *physis* describes the "natural branches" (Jews) who were broken off from the olive tree in Rom 11, and describes the olive tree which is wild "by nature" (vv. 21, 24). *Physis* is also the same word used in Rom 1 to say that same-sex behavior goes "against nature" (v. 26), being against the natures we are born with, and designed by God with. It describes that inborn natural design, which homosexual behavior rebels against. In fact, it would not be odd to read the description of our pre-Christ state in Eph 2 as "and were *by birth* the children of wrath, even as others." That would be consistent with how the word is used elsewhere. When James refers to different kinds of animals, he writes, "For every *kind* of beasts, and of birds, and of serpents, and of things in the sea, is tamed, and hath been tamed of mankind" (Jas 3:7). That word "kind" uses the same word Paul uses for our sinful state before conversion, and here it also refers to something in the nature of a creature, which they have from birth. Each different kind of animal is born that way. So are we when we're born in sin.

Our fundamental sinfulness fits naturally with the kind of salvation we can receive in Christ, which Paul goes on to expound. It is a salvation in which we are given something by God's mercy, and not by any work we did, and this gift gives us new life, which is eternal. We are born into peace with God, just as we had been born into wrath:

> But God, who is rich in mercy, for his great love wherewith he loved us,

---

2. These include the ESV, NIV, NET, and CSB.

> *Even when we were dead in sins*, hath quickened us together with Christ, (by grace ye are saved;)
>
> And hath raised us up together, and made us sit together in heavenly places in Christ Jesus:
>
> That in the ages to come he might shew the exceeding riches of his grace in his kindness toward us through Christ Jesus.
>
> For *by grace are ye saved* through faith; and that not of yourselves: it is the gift of God:
>
> Not of works, lest any man should boast.
>
> For we are his workmanship, created in Christ Jesus unto good works, which God hath before ordained that we should walk in them. (Eph 2:4–10)

While it is the previous passage that provides the specific words which teach we are sinners in our very nature, this teaching confirms its truth as well. That fallen nature is why we are to be made a new creation in Christ, and not merely be taught good ethical teachings and given motivation to be good. We are given life (quickened) when we are dead by God's mercy, and not by anything we have done. God lifts us up by his power in Christ to heavenly places. This is our salvation. As I point out to many who deny we have a morally corrupt nature, the new birth only confirms our natural deadness in sin. The nature of the gospel as being by grace of God through faith only confirms it. In a world where you had a basic goodness before God, you'd have a very different kind of salvation, and remedy for your pains. It could be accomplished through teaching men to do good works, and subsequently doing them. But that's not what God gives us as a glorious gift, although he certainly teaches us too. It is a supernatural rebirth, one that is likened multiple times to being raised from the grave. Thus, it is clear we possess a dead and sinful nature that needs rebirth. A more or less good person who just needs to right his wrongs doesn't need rebirth at all. Christ died for our sins, because we are dead in sin.

Most of us may not recognize our childhood sins as truly sinful, because of our young age, but being aware of them and witness to them reminds us that this universal uncleanness is deep in our nature. We can all remember an early time we chose to strike a friend or a family member, rather than respond normally. We can recall an early fit we threw just because we did not get what we wanted. We don't need to be fully informed at the time for these things to reflect the fallenness of the human souls, because pure souls don't do things like that. Pure souls don't walk over to their brother and sister and push them off a chair to be mean. Pure souls don't lie to get what they want. Pure souls don't smash things up because they are angry. I can recall getting into a fight in my grade school, allowing myself to be goaded into it, and then later doing my best to make excuses for it, as if it weren't really my fault and I had no say in the matter. I crossed a line I knew was wrong to cross, and then I pretended like it wasn't so bad. I instinctually knew the wicked art of blaming somebody else. Just as Adam and Eve immediately tried to excuse or defend their sin in the garden, it is an instinct in fallen man to try and excuse his own sin. I can remember sneaking out of class early in grade school, only for the excitement of doing something forbidden. I could feel a thrill in it, as others feel a thrill in their own evil. My lack of full development at the time did not make that a virtuous act, nor did my lack of development excuse it. I knew it was wrong, but covered it in my own mind with excuses as man does: it's not so bad, it doesn't harm anyone, everyone does something wrong . . .

While it may not relate to my own wicked choices, I can see my early development of mental problems as a sign of our deadness in sin. Sin and pain, despite the moral difference, are deeply linked, and came together in the fall, both resulting from an act of disobedience by our forefather. The fact that I can recollect feeling separate and unable to communicate from as early as two-years old, and have other similar memories in the single digits of age, only tells me in a way that harmonizes with the Bible, that I was born dead spiritually. As Paul comments in Rom 5, even apart from the commandments of Scripture, mankind still experienced death, showing they all fell in Adam collectively (v. 14). So the wicked deeds of a child are no more evidence than the suffering of a child that we are conceived in sin, and there is a stain on all mankind. The experience of mental suffering when young also confirms to me that life is not all about our personal choices. We did not choose to be in a body that suffers, or have a mind that can experience pain. We did not choose an inherited personality. We did not choose some of our inherent strengths and weaknesses, both physical and mental. Those who are born in very poor or war-torn areas did not choose that dangerous location, just as those from wealthy or virtuous families did not choose that upbringing either. That should give us a perspective on the sin which we inherit too, so we cannot offhand reject the idea. We know already we inherit pain and other disadvantages. It should not be shocking that we inherit sin too.

The topic of children suffering in any way is predictably a difficult one for Christians, but God provides us the only truth there is, despite how bitter the truth can taste. There is nothing so especially hard about this reality that makes it radically different from adult suffering. The Christian can speak about it, and know why it exists. The current Catholic pope as of this writing was asked about why children suffer. Even though this man holds the position of highest cleric in a church of over a billion people, he replied by saying, "I have no answer for that."[3] This man has studied for many years and professed his faith for many years and he has "no answer." I would suggest, even if you feel sympathy for this man, that he quickly resign his post as chief cleric in his church. He does not know his own faith. In contrast to this professed ignorance, the Almighty provides all Christians an answer to why we suffer, including why children suffer: It is the sin of Adam, the sins of Adam's race, and behind that the will of God. That is why children suffer.

Federal Headship

We can also understand our inherited sinfulness and suffering through our being a part of the family of mankind; the family of the sinner Adam. Since he is our head, when he became separate from God, we also became separate. While being morally stained from conception looks at it almost through a law of inheritance, being under Adam's headship and a part of his body, looks at it from the perspective of a nation. If Adam is estranged through his sin, then all who are under Adam are estranged also. You might think of it as being part of a country, and recognize how all citizens of a country suffer for the ills of its leadership, and suffer together when tragedy or invasion befalls the entire people. There were representatives of the nation who made poor choices, and all those whom they represent come under the consequences. Being redeemed in Christ follows a similar principle. We are redeemed through being under Christ's kingship, and being a part of his people. We come into the new and pure human nature, and participate in it. Since God views his Son as righteous and beloved, we are righteous and beloved when we come into his family. That's not the way the westerner in the contemporary world likes to view reality, but it is the reality God teaches us, and it is intrinsic to biblical

---

3. Clench, "Pope Francis Has 'No Explanation.'"

revelation many places. The individual is often held accountable for the deeds of their leader, or of their group.

We see a few examples of this unity of the head and the whole group in Scripture. We see that when Ham sins, by pointing out the nakedness of his father Noah, it is the sons which would come from Ham who fell under the curse on him (Gen 9:25). The entire people of Canaan were cursed to be slaves because of their father. In contrast, we can see that God's promises to Abraham, who was a righteous man, greatly blessed all of his children, who became the nation of Israel. In fact, Yahweh specifically says that he placed his love on Israel because of his oath to the patriarchs and *not* their own goodness (Deut 7:7–8). That was the oath to Abraham, which passed down to Isaac and Jacob, and assured Israel was God's people. They inherited the blessing because of the patriarch, and not their own good deeds.

The main passage about headship as it pertains to fallenness in Adam is Romans 5. While it is a complex passage, that makes various related subpoints, I will cite the most relevant verses to our guilt: "Wherefore, as by one man sin entered into the world, and death by sin; and so death passed upon all men, for that all had sinned" (Rom 5:12). "Therefore as by the offence of one *judgment came upon all men* to condemnation; even so by the righteousness of one *the free gift came upon all men* unto justification of life. For as by one man's disobedience many were made sinners, so by the obedience of one shall many be made righteous" (vv. 18–19).

We can see that "one man," who is Adam, brought sin and death into the world, and that death spread to "all men," along with sin. Sin like death is something universal to us then. It is rooted in Adam's sin. The final phrase, "for that all had sinned," can be taken to mean that the universality of sin can be witnessed since all people sin. We may also take the same phrase to mean that all mankind sinned in Adam, as a part of him at the time. Thus, all suffer the consequences. That latter interpretation goes against much of our thinking, but it does make sense in light of the fact we are all descended from Adam, and we are all under his headship until we are reborn. If he sins and brings wrath on himself, he brings sin and wrath on all his people also. We may be extremely individualists today, but God's revelation is not extremely individualistic, and most societies through nearly all human history weren't either. We're a part of Adam, either literally or figuratively, and when our head falls, we all fall.

We see more of the results in the final two verses I've cited. We see that "all men" receive judgment and condemnation because Adam fell, and "many" were made sinners by one act. Condemnation is merely something we received, not something we acquired through bad actions. This goes far beyond having a leaning toward sin within our nature, describing also an overall condemnation that lies over Adam's race. Sin is more than a disease of the soul. We are judged and condemned as Adam's people, with him as our head.

The glorious redemption in Christ works by similar, though not identical, principles. Through Christ's perfect life and his sacrifice, "all men" received a free gift of justification (being made right with God). We have eternal life because of "one man." Because of Christ's obedience to God, in contrast to Adam's disobedience, "many" are made righteous. This is clearly not a matter of Adam merely motivating some people to sin, or Christ encouraging them to be good enough to be saved. It comes down to who our leader is. It comes down to who our father is. If it is Adam (as it is naturally for the human race), we die because of our unrighteous father, all of us. We are under condemnation because he is under condemnation. If our father is Christ (as it can be for us through faith), we are at peace with God and God looks at us as righteous people, though we still have sin to overcome and filth to wash off. One man represents *all* his family. One man saves the entire group. Therefore, we are impure and needing redemption even as babies, for we are born into Adam's race. Sin is not merely a moral sickness, but our state of alienation in Adam. We must lose that sonship in his fallen family, and come into a new one. We cannot pretend to be clean and pure, even in youth.

As it relates to the universality of death, and our physical corruption, the same reality is described in brief in 1 Cor 15. In speaking of the resurrection from the dead, Paul teaches, "But now is Christ risen from the dead, and become the firstfruits of them that slept [died]. For since by man came death, by man came also the resurrection of the dead. For as in Adam all die, even so in Christ shall all be made alive" (vv. 20–22). Headship sets the order for the situation here. Death entered for everyone through Adam. The resurrection and eternal life come to all God's people through Christ. It is impossible to fully separate the subject of our corrupt bodies from the sin in our souls, for we can see that those raised in Christ physically are the same ones morally and spiritually washed clean. Those in unbelief and sin may be raised from the grave, but they will be cast into hell and suffer forever. In this passage we speak of God's people, so the physical healing and the spiritual cleansing go together.

The condemnation is enacted in Adam. The life comes to pass in Christ. We are either saved or cursed depending on who our father is.

Sin in Children

The average human being doesn't enjoy the thought that children are sinful, or ungodly in their natures. We like to think of them as cute and innocent creatures. We don't put babies on trial for anything. However, anyone who has spent time around children, or been a parent, can tell you that wicked attitudes and wicked actions manifest themselves very early in life. You don't have to wait long after birth. As a parent, I believe I have witnessed wickedness in children within one year of age, but even if you're not able to notice it so early, you certainly will see it by two years. Then you will see the vast array of human sin over the coming time they grow to adulthood. Even a well raised and virtuous child will sin from the youngest of age.

If children are born morally pure, this would be absurd. We would expect to see good attitudes and right actions until some age of consent, when a person suddenly becomes a sinner, sinning with full mental knowledge and informed consent. Yet every child shows his wickedness, and shows it early and repeatedly. Even in the period before a child does much abstract thinking, or even can talk, we see rage, greed, and deception. Very few parents teach their children to lie, yet they almost instinctively deceive, and when they are a little older, tell conscious lies. Even parents who are gentle and wise will find their children do not react with gentleness or wisdom, but become jealous of their siblings, fight over small things with them, and become enraged. This is universal. Even at the youngest of ages, because of all the evidence of sin in children, I am convinced there is the baby who cries when he is hungry, and there is the baby who cries because of his selfish desire and egoism. Those traits live inside small children long before they can express them intelligently. Any parent will need to correct and discipline their child many times, and will see the wrong attitudes and behaviors countless times before they even enter adolescence. Pure creatures do not act that way. Corrupt ones do.

It is foolishness to believe babies are born free from sin. Not only does the Bible tell us in plain language that they are born in sin, but the observable evidence supports this. Human nature is tainted from conception, and no one needs a Bible to see that stain. Some like to claim that man is born with merely a "death nature," and that a sin nature grows out of this over time and experience, but is not essentially a part of us from the start. This explanation is wrong. If we were only born with a death nature, why do we see sin very shortly after a child is born? That alone is powerful evidence to the contrary. Moreover, this also assumes that the sin nature is not present until its full manifestations are reached—some kind of fully informed consent, or mature kind of sinfulness. But this is bad logic. If we applied the same logic to the claim we have a "death nature," we could say we do not have one until later in life, because it is later in life when we start to die, our body shows signs of aging, and we grow weaker and die. Since we don't see this in our youth, then we would have to assume we only acquire a death nature later in life. Right? Of course not. We do not need to see the full manifestations of something to know that thing exists in the first place. The same is true of the image of God in us. If we consider the image of God reflected in willful virtue, use of reason, or fellowship with God, then we'd assume that children are not made in the image of God, because they have not manifested that nature in a fully informed way, or in its mature expression. According to that logic children must acquire the image of God later in life.

We should all see how faulty this logic is. Clearly, we are born with a sin nature, and we don't need to wait for the full expression of it to occur before we acknowledge its existence. One does not need to sin beyond an age of consent to be corrupted morally in one's nature. That corruption shows its signs long before informed consent. As others have asked long before this writing, if a man is planting from a bag of seeds, and he plants one seed, and another, counting thousands in a row, and each seed grows up to be a lemon tree, what will we conclude about that bag of seeds? We naturally will conclude that it is a bag of lemon seeds. We know the nature of the seed by knowing it will grow up into a lemon tree. So now we don't really need to wait until it grows into a tree, wondering if the universality of lemons has been one great coincidence. We just know what kind of seed we're planting and have no problem telling people they are lemon seeds, and we're going to get lemons from them. That's the logic anyone would follow with seeds, and it is fair logic to use with human beings too. We're all made of the same basic material and have the same basic nature. We can know confidently from observation alone: We are flawed both physically and morally. We can debate the exact name to give it, but suffice to say we are a fallen race. That's not pessimism, but is the human situation any of us must face. If you don't face the problem clearly, you won't see the solution clearly either.

It is important to know how intertwined are the experiences of sin and death. They are both consequences of the fall and seem nearly impossible to separate. The act that led mankind to depart from God and be cursed was an act of disobedience (Gen 3:6). The warning God gave for this particular act was death (Gen 2:16–17), but we also know it was not ordinary or immediate death. Adam and Eve kept living physically for a very long time. It was spiritual alienation from God along with suffering and mortality. Part of the curse itself included suffering, for Adam in his labor and for woman in her childbearing, and also in her rebellion against her husband (Gen 3:16–19). We are taught that sin leads to death (Rom 6:23, Jas 1:15), some sins more than others (1 John 5:17). We are taught that sin and death go together in our state, and freedom from both comes as part of our salvation. First Corinthians 15 teaches: "The sting of death is sin; and the strength of sin is the law" (v. 56). Romans 8 promises that Christ sets us free "from the law of sin and death" (v. 2). They are both in us together, and it is irrelevant to our situation to know which one came immediately prior. They are just two manifestations of being cut off from God.

Moreover, we all experience those consequences and those impurities in a united way most of the time, suffering pain because of our sin and the sin of others, or likewise finding our life suffering entices us to commit sin. It is a cycle both ways. The average man or woman, even those who profess not to believe in God, can sense that corruption, knowing the darkness of evil deeds, and desiring peace and goodness in their place; knowing the pain of disability, illness, and the loss of loved ones, and wanting a world of health, comfort, bliss in its place. One does not need to be a Bible believer to know we are corrupted together in all of these ways, and long for the cure. We have bodies which will grow old and die, and a mind full of sins which are rightly judged. None of our power, or our efforts to do what is ethical change this. Sin and death work together in us. They have been rooted next to each other since man sinned.

Does God make sinful souls?

There is a related question in understanding man's soul and man's fallenness which, while not consequential to the point of this book, nor to any major doctrine, is very interesting and opens up many other windows to view our human state. People often ask—well if God does not make anything wicked, then how did he "make" our soul, which is sinful? Likewise, people ask—if God is perfectly good, how could he make a soul that has wickedness in it, or suffering for that matter? Doesn't that go against how God made creation good, and how he is good in character? Now if we can accept that Yahweh makes men with bodies that will die and with disabilities, we ought to also accept he can make souls morally corrupted, regardless of how he does it. However, we gain insight by looking at the possible methods God may use.

On a mechanical level, there is no certain answer, and it doesn't ultimately affect any of the major answers the Bible gives us. However, there are two main ways that Christians can understand this. The first, which has been the mainstream view through Christian history, is that Yahweh makes our souls spiritually good, yet when he places them in our bodies, they receive that sinfulness along with physical corruptions from the flesh. Modern Christians usually believe the soul enters the body at conception, so at this point, the good soul receives the impurity from Adam's sin through being in the body. Earlier Christians speculated the soul might enter the body slightly later, still very soon after conception, but the point was still the same: entering the flesh brings the moral impurity. The alternate and minority view, one which I formerly wrote off entirely and now believe to be true, is that our souls pass down to us through our ancestry, being received from Adam, and from all of our fathers. We receive our soul through our fathers, and we receive the scar on our soul that way too, since it comes from our sinful fathers. We inherit it.

Many immediately object to this latter explanation, saying it conflicts with the Bible's teaching that Yahweh fashions our soul himself, but there is really no conflict with any biblical teaching. God can fashion our souls down to the last detail through the agencies of our parentage, and any other method he desires to use. Thus, God is in complete control the entire time. The scar of sin is already there, but he fashions how all the pieces fit together. Others might object because of the teaching that God made man upright (Eccl 7:29), a teaching which if interpreted broadly enough would contradict original sin entirely. However, this phrase refers to the creation of Adam before the fall, and naturally is in harmony with the notion of other souls being inherently corrupt since then, and with the notion we inherit our soul from Adam. It only means that mankind was upright at the start.

Not only that, but the idea we receive our souls from parentage makes good sense of biblical Scriptures that would be otherwise without clear explanation, and agrees with what we know from science. As many readers of Scripture often miss, the Bible states only one other time besides the creation of Adam in Gen 1 that a human being was made in the "image" and "likeness" (v. 26) of someone else. Yet of whom is that image and likeness? It says that Adam, "begat a son in his own likeness, after his image; and called his name Seth" (Gen 5:3b). It does not say that Seth was begotten in God's image, but in Adam's image, who himself had been made in the image of God. So unless you want to imagine that image and likeness here is purely physical, then it includes his soul, and Seth received his soul from his father. That would be the consistent way to understand it, especially in light of the only previous use of the phrase. He received his soul from his father, and with it spiritual corruption.

Our parentage can be seen as the source of our soul also in the doctrine that the child can act through his father, a point made by Paul when building the doctrine of Jesus' higher priesthood. To show that Jesus did not need to be legally a part of the Levitical priesthood to be our high priest, Paul shows that the priesthood of Melchizedek is higher than that of the current Levites. How does he teach this? He says that the children paid tithes to Melchizedek through their forefather Abraham, when Abraham paid tithes. Thus, when the father was acting, they were acting, and since tithes are paid to one greater, the current Levites proved Melchizedek was greater by paying tithes to him through Abraham. Sounds fanciful to some ears, but the Bible teaches it, and it is a key part in building the necessary doctrine that Jesus is part of a higher priesthood. Are mere fanciful expressions part of building a doctrine, or is truth part of building it?

Paul concludes thusly:

> And as I may so say, Levi also, who receiveth tithes, *payed tithes in Abraham.*
>
> For he was *yet in the loins of his father,* when Melchisedec met him.
>
> If therefore perfection were by the Levitical priesthood, (for under it the people received the law,) what further need was there that another priest should rise after the order of Melchisedec, and not be called after the order of Aaron? (Heb 7:9–11)

The principle that we are participating in the actions of our father, being in his loins, also shows some of the logic of how we fall as an entire group. In effect, we sinned as an entire group, since we were in Adam at the time he sinned and went away from God. We participated in that, since we were a part of him. This means that when Paul says that "all have sinned" in Rom 5, we can legitimately read it to mean that all sinned *in Adam* through participation: "Wherefore, as by one man sin entered into the world, and death by sin; and so death passed upon all men, for that all have sinned" (v. 12). Surely if the first century AD priests can pay tithes in the second millennium BC Abraham, we today can sin in our forefather Adam. Moreover, if the Levites paying tithes in Abraham made them a lower priesthood, our sin in Adam makes us a fallen people. We are a group then, and not merely individuals, and have a life that carries through the generations.

The passing down of the soul, and of the blot of sin, also seems to agree with what we know from science. For if the other theory is to believed, and our perfect soul is merely placed in the sinful body by Yahweh, genetics would be meaningless. Yet much of the knowledge genetics provides us with relates to things we call the soul. Genetics affects our personality, mind, and feelings, not just our body. Researchers find genetic links not just to physical illnesses, but to various evil predilections, and to intellectual gifts. These are aspects of our being we associate with the soul, not with the body. These facts lend support to the theory that our souls pass down to us from our parents, since our genetics is passed to us too. Nothing is at all accidental, with every detail of its passing down managed by God.

It is possible we could combine these two ways of viewing how we receive our soul and our fallenness. That would bring it all together. Perhaps we could recognize the spirit simply as that spark of spiritual life, and relegate the giving of that to God's supernatural spark. Then we recognize the soul as the other elements of our inner being I have mentioned, and see that as handed down, rather than mere bodies being handed down. The spiritual awareness and ability to fellowship with God can legitimately be seen as distinct from some of our other functions, so perhaps this might work. There are many who already distinguish between spirit and soul, although biblically they are at times viewed the same, and at times different.

How we view the creation of the soul is not the most consequential doctrine. By itself it does not prove or refute the consequences of sin I've discussed. I believe a true Christian can understand the matter either of the two ways I mention. However, whichever one adheres to, the headship of Adam plays a role in the alienation and sinfulness of all his children. Whether it is understood more as his representation of his children, or more literally as his children acting through him, the fall is a singular act that affects the entire group. The smallest of children are not immune.

SECOND—OPPRESSION OF SIN IN THE WORLD

Pain and sin also enter our lives through the overwhelming tide of sin in the world. The universality of evil is revealed by Scripture and through human observation. It wells up from within our souls due to our sin nature, and it pushes at us from beyond ourselves from people, laws, and institutions that are all corrupted by evil. Falsehood penetrates our belief system and we receive falsehood from others; errors and lies that the world has come to believe. It is not sin out there in the world that condemns us, but it is sin out there in the world that has helped make obedience to God a missed goal by every man born except Jesus of Nazareth. A small child will be exposed to the sins of his family. That means a multitude, whether simple selfishness, laziness, greed, or anger; or immediately dangerous and criminal acts, such as drug use, violence, and murder. The small child also is taught falsehood, and taught it at an age when they easily receive it as truth, and cannot think critically about it. They may be taught that God is not real, or that God does not judge sin. They may be taught, as is common in the West today, that immorality is good, and the law of God is evil. They will be taught to hate some people, and love others. One may ask how they ever stand a chance. Some parents in the worst situations encourage their children to be violent, or teach them to use vulgarities, blasphemy, and take the name of the Lord in vain. In the news the other week, in a singular demonstration of leading astray the children, a criminal gave his 4-year-old child his gun, and told him to shoot the police. The child held the gun, pointed it, and shot at them.[4] Thankfully no one was hit. The child was disarmed and remained unharmed himself, but each of us will be just as inevitably overrun by sin on the earth, like that small child, entering into wicked schemes we do not even suspect, we will get spiritually mugged.

4. Kaonga, "Child Shoots at Cop."

Sin and falsehood are there in institutions as well. The average scientific study, which some in the secular world treat like the highest authority, is vulnerable to falsehood through error or willful fraud. Doctors are pressured to give medicine where no medicine may be necessary. They are also censored in the West from speaking out against sodomy, or warning people away from same-sex behavior, even though scientifically it is against our design and it is harmful to human life. The belief system of the age, and political pressure would cause a doctor—who ought to be telling the truth—to lose his job if he actually did tell the truth. Churches as well are vulnerable to sin and falsehood. They follow the trends of the era, sacrifice biblical doctrine for what is popular, and contain ministers who are not sincerely men of faith, and will give the secular world's answer to questions, rather than God's answer. When Paul teaches, "the love of money is the root of all evil" (1 Tim 6:10a), this teaching describes the church as well. A desire to receive a salary, or grow rich as a pastor, has led to all manner of false teachings in the church, and an openly decadent lifestyle by many ministers. Popularity becomes the deciding factor on whether a doctrine is true, not whether it is expressed in the Bible, since more people in a church will bring more donations, and many ministers refuse to downsize for the sake of God's truth. The children of God are led astray more often by churches, than are led rightly in the way of Jesus. People learn from ministers that sin is acceptable, and a worldly life is acceptable. Souls go to hell because of false teachings. Businesses likewise play a role in making evil all pervasive in human society. Whether it is their own love of money, or fear of public pressure, they drop ethics when it is convenient. Perhaps the most well known of business sins is to steal money or cheat people out of money, but businesses assault the world with sin in other ways too. It is normal now in the West for businesses, even those run by Christians, to have worldly entertainment and play secular music for their customers. It was larger businesses which played a major role in normalizing immorality in my own country; whether celebrating fornication, immodesty, or homosexual behavior, large businesses helped force this all into western culture, until that immorality and lewdness was all pervasive in society. They continue to spread it across the globe. One cannot go anywhere and avoid it. Movies and music make a secular belief system look universal as well, while mocking God and his law. Nearly everyone in society has come to view those entertainments as normal, and participate in at least some of them, placing their minds under control of the devil. People sit under secular media for countless years, and that media shapes their values, hopes, self-image, and behaviors. Children soak in vulgar, godless, sexualized content through their eyes and ears from the youngest age. Parents, teachers, and governments permit this.

One cannot step outside, or even look at the news on the internet, without being assaulted through the eyes and ears with sin. Even in a more christianized society, the burden of sin is everywhere, but in a society that openly mocks God, sin is encouraged as a religious dogma, and protected like a human right. Sin takes over entire communities, and is passed on to the children. Fornication leads to children who are not taken care of, who usually lack a father (or occasionally a mother), who are more likely to learn violence, to commit suicide, to commit crimes, and become immoral when they grow up. Criminals take over neighborhoods, turn the local women into whores, and recruit the young children into their gang. Beyond the age of five it is nearly certain children will enter a life of crime in such neighborhoods, making violence an intergenerational culture. Education and the light of God are kept out. Darkness becomes the norm in the populace. Ego, money, fornication, and drugs destroy the bulk of the people. Sin is saturated into the soul this way, penetrating the fiber of its being.

On the less obvious level, entire communities are taken over by the worship of self, despite being outwardly ethical in many ways. They live a life built around pleasing one's desires, giving a mere nod to God's existence, and living a life according to the worldly sacraments of higher education, heavy debt, fornication, abortion, careerism, homeownership, vacations, and retirement. A mount of luxury becomes a necessity. They glorify this pleasurable life, chanting: "As it was in the beginning, is now, and ever shall be, world without end. Amen."[5] It is a template for hundreds of millions of lives, and lacks God. It locks people into the service of self, and disregards the way of the spirit. Any child growing up in such a community will see that narrow path as their future, and nearly always follow the pressure to live it out. They won't see the other options. Along with that will come taking on the same attitudes, expectations, longings of the world, while learning to admire what the world admires and loathe what it loathes. It leaves room at best for a nominal Christian belief, and a careful picking and choosing of truths one finds likeable. It is at heart the service of mammon, and not of Yahweh.

5. EWTN, "The Glory Be (Gloria Patri)." This is an ancient and common Catholic prayer.

I am reminded of entire nations where corruption is normal. There's no way out of it. I got to hear some details of this system when I was teaching overseas. I had an adult student in South America who told me that as a part of her job, she had to find out what bribe to pay various people. She knew it was wrong, but felt she had to do what her boss told her anyway, because he was the boss. She wished she could stop, but saw no opportunity to stop. The pressure of making money and keeping her job, kept her doing what she knew was evil. Bribes are also common in Asian countries in order to get a client to work with you, to get a school to allow entrance to your child, or to pay off officials of all kinds. Entire institutions function this way. A friend of mine in Asia couldn't figure out why a university wasn't letting her rent offices on their campus. Her friend then told her she was very naive for a Chinese person, and she needed to come to them with an envelope of cash, which she did to immediate success. Many businesses get away with far lower standards and endanger the public through this system. I met a young man, also in South America, one night sitting down with him right by the beach having drinks, and he told me how he does business. He sells fake products of all kinds, including fakes of life-saving equipment like fire hoses, pays the necessary people to have the stamps put on them that will authenticate them as real, and nothing in the current laws could stop him. He does so without any legal problems and is successful selling them. No one has any idea how to stop it. The officials whose job it is to inspect things are themselves paid off, and unwilling to do the oversight they must. This young man, who is not originally from that continent, told me he loves doing business, and makes plenty of money that way. Pointing at the hippies at the other table he said, "I'm just like those guys over there, except I'm a businessman." Corrupt systems and corrupt institutions keep him in business.

Similarly, when churches see the trends of the times swinging one way, they quickly become the illicit businessmen of the religious world. The desire to be popular and to keep their salaries, will pressure them to change doctrine. Countless churches have embraced false doctrines this way and mislead their people. Once the pressure is on, they embrace first the feminizing and gender bending current in our culture, then they either downgrade immorality as not very serious, or change their doctrines entirely and permit the currently popular sins of sodomy and transsexualism. You can watch it happen over and over in real time. Churches today have actually apologized for teaching what God's truth says about sodomy in the past. One popular female "teacher" had a short passage against sodomy removed from one of her very old books, in a cowardly attempt to avoid criticism. The pressure of the times does this and weak people comply with that pressure. Not only that, but the ministers and others who work for those churches typically go along with the moral collapse, even when they know it is wrong. They are willing to utter lie after lie, or close their eyes to wrongdoing, convincing themselves that at least at the end of the day someone got to hear about Jesus. Ministers who stand up against the gender bending, or the changed doctrine regarding morality, are either silenced or quickly shown the door. They will not be able to work in any major ministry. The entire group becomes filthy, and all its members committed to filthiness. The majority go along with the conspiracy. The evil takes over the entire body.

The state of mankind then, in principle, is not far from being like a criminal organization or a gang. One member won't refuse to commit a crime, since that would put him at odds with the other members. He would be threatened. He would end up dead. He will go along with criminal schemes he knows are wrong in part to protect himself. Moreover, the moment he thinks to inform to authorities on another member of the gang, he implicates himself too, since he is involved in the very same activity. In mankind, as in a criminal gang, everyone has his hands dirty. Everyone depends on others who have their hands dirty for their bread and butter. We're all part of the scheme. No one is prepared to bring the whole house down, and lose everything themselves. Forces far beyond our own choice, or even the choice of other individual members are at work. Institutions, like organic bodies, carry and pass along sin, as a body might carry and pass along a disease. The oppression is too much for the individual to bear.

One is reminded of the assessment made in Rom 2:

> Therefore thou art inexcusable, O man, whosoever thou art that judgest: *for wherein thou judgest another, thou condemnest thyself*; for thou that judgest doest the same things.
>
> But we are sure that the judgment of God is according to truth against them which commit such things.
>
> And thinkest thou this, O man, that judgest them which do such things, and doest the same, that thou shalt escape the judgment of God? (vv. 1–3)
>
> Thou therefore which teachest another, teachest thou not thyself? thou that preachest a man should not steal, dost thou steal?

PAIN

> Thou that sayest a man should not commit adultery, dost thou commit adultery? thou that abhorrest idols, dost thou commit sacrilege?
> Thou that makest thy boast of the law, through breaking the law dishonourest thou God?
> For *the name of God is blasphemed among the Gentiles through you*, as it is written. (vv. 21–24)

Remember, much of this oppression in the world around us, that makes it appear inevitable to do evil over and over, is our own sin coming back at us. The liar ends up deceived by others, and his lie touches many more people than he originally intended it. The fornicator is used cruelly by another fornicator. The sins of the parents return to them by the sins of the children, and also go out into the world through many generations. The cheater is cheated. The violent man runs into someone stronger than him, and becomes a victim. The bureaucrat who compromises one time engenders many more and more serious compromises. While we are assaulted by evil all the time, and subsequently imprisoned by it, we must remember, humbly, we have our own hand in the affairs. We are dirty too. We have given our assent to it many times through our actions, and often do the same wrongs which we condemn in others. It is a small-scale act of justice to suffer oppression of sin in this world. Its power and all-pervasiveness is a small picture of hell, just as the darkness of depression is. There is no avoiding evil in the bottomless pit.

THIRD—SINFUL CHOICES

While we may not consciously choose to experience impurity at birth, we confirm our agreement with it the first time we choose to sin with full knowledge of its wrong. Then we say we agree with it every time we sin. We cast thousands and thousands of votes throughout our lives for Adam over Christ. We declare Satan to be our rightful master with our full voice and dedication. We parade him down the street with tickertape. You might say we're yellow dog satanists. Every single human being who has ever lived, except for Jesus of Nazareth, votes this way.

It was the fall in the garden that made us part of a rebel race, but each human being goes through a fall in miniature in his own life. He experiences the same temptation, and he gives in. He knows it is evil, he shoves aside that knowledge, he makes excuses that try to justify it, he gets the idea that maybe Yahweh was wrong, and then he does it. Man goes from the less consciously impure state of a child, to one who knowingly experiences that blackness in their soul, and even tries to wield that blackness as a weapon: one who is ready for war against the Most High. He is prepared with his pride, with his clever justifications for sin, with his lusts and desires uplifted as if they were gods, and he goes out to war with his Adamic weapons, confident he's a champ, and he will lose every time. He puts on the breastplate of self, the helmet of false assurance, the sword of man's empty philosophies, and the shield of doubt and skepticism, and is a front-line warrior for a devil he usually doesn't believe exists. He's riding out prepared to lose for a lost cause.

It becomes very difficult to complain that we are guilty for an ancestor's sin, when we all choose to sin ourselves. Every single one of us. Not only that, but when faced with our sin, we commonly just make excuses for it, and proceed to do it again. It may be the urge to take what is others, and steal it for ourselves. It could be the anger and rage at a human brother who has bested us, or who simply has more than we have. It may be the arrogance of looking down on the other man as the stupid, the unfashionable, the uneducated, and unrefined one. It may be violence, lust, greed, or gluttony of possessions that reveals our inner nature as sinner through our personal choice. Even inner invisible attitudes are sin. The many meditations of the heart that are unkind, selfish, or lustful—the fantasy world in which we reign as carnal king anytime we wish. Apostle John taught that to hate your brother in your heart is akin to murder, a teaching which echoes the law in Leviticus (1 John 3:15). Jesus taught that whoever is angry with his brother without a cause is in danger of judgment, and whoever calls him a "fool," will face the fires of hell (Matt 5:22). These are all hidden sins of the heart before they manifest as outward ones. There is no man's life which is not awash with such choices to do evil, internal or external, aligning him with Satan. This simply manifests to the world their nature from birth.

Worship of the Devil

It is common in our time for westerners to deny the existence of the devil. They will even mock the idea that there could be a personal spiritual entity who inspires sin, and mock the devil as a caricature with a pointed tail and horns on his head. Who's afraid of that? Who takes that seriously? Even those who ascribe to modern-day satanism usually deny a personal devil. Ask them, and they will tell you the devil is only an idea to them—an idea of human freedom and empowerment, and rebellion against the religious beliefs which they hate. He's not a real being in their mind. At least that's what they'd have us believe.

Yet for all this denial, the modernist openly shows his worship of the devil. He shows it by following the devil's will, and being overcome by his temptations. He shows it by covering up the devil's work, or excusing it. The devil's master plan is not simply to inspire people to do something very evil such as murdering children, but rather to turn mankind away from Yahweh, away from trusting Yahweh, thus attacking God's precious creation. The devil in the garden did not take a knife and murder the two residents, but he brought about countless deaths and suffering simply by one lie—that God didn't really say what he said, that man can be like a god himself. Yet this is quite robustly what the modernist who denies the devil believes—that we can't really trust in God's word, and for all practical purposes, we are the rulers of all things. We can simply follow our heart and be the king of our domain, as long as we don't "hurt anyone," according to various man-made views of hurt. We dictate what good and evil are. A perfectly nice and non-violent person can hold to such a worldview, and be worshipping the devil. If you are making yourself the god of your life, you are a servant of the devil.

I can look at my own attitudes and choices in my prior life, and see the same conscientious decision. The worship of the devil absolutely rules unbelief. I may also have mocked the idea that the devil was a real personal being, yet I loved to draw satanic symbols, occult symbols, and even light candles before them. The experience inspired me towards something I could not see, which excited me. The symbols held beauty and mystery. I took hold of my belonging to the devil through my choices, affirming my membership in the lost family of our father Adam. I may not have believed the devil was "real" so to speak, but I affirmed he was real in every other possible way. I was asked once as a young man whom I wanted to be like in my life, presumably what well known personality I wished to imitate. With little thought I said I'd like to be like Ernest Hemingway. Why? Because Hemingway got to travel the world and sleep with a lot of women. That was my stated goal as well, so I found him inspiring. It's hardly original, but it shows a choice to align with the devil, a choice which fulfills his goals of harming God's precious creation. Every single child that is born into deadness, confirms as I did his own deadness through choice. Every single one. Ironically, I was given by God the freedom to live out that wish, and through much of my life indeed travelled the world and slept with many women. What a coincidence. Also like the person I identified myself with, I suffered horrible depression, and experienced the incredible emptiness of the life I led. The only difference other than the fame of my personal leader, was the fact that Hemingway finally took a shotgun and blew his head off, while I am still alive to talk of my lost state. I took a step into the territory of my leader, and I enjoyed the temporal pleasures of his reign, as well as his just agonizing suffering. As my hero suffered, I suffered. It is only by God's grace I did not experience the rewards of my choice, which would have been death.

There are those who would still scoff at the idea we worship Satan, but the evidence is before them all the time. Even the denial that the devil is a personal spirit serves Satan, since those who are not wary of him are much more vulnerable to be used by him. They become his easiest tools to attack God's creation. They are his unknowing agents, whom many will believe have good intentions. They repeat to the public, "Did God really say . . . ?"

I can recall when I was living overseas, I was out one night as usual with several male and female friends. We planned to go down to the beach and commit immorality together. As we walked down the narrow streets, we came upon a small plaza we frequently passed through. It was empty, and beautifully still. In the middle a small fountain stood and reflected the gentle moonlight. We strode to the fountain and gazed into the moonlit water. My friend looked at me and said: "*Tomás, pon la cabeza encima del agua*" (Thomas, put your head over the water). At first I was confused, and didn't know what he wanted me to do or why. He repeated, gesturing to me with his hand: "*pon la cabeza sobre el agua.*" I started lowering my head, not sure how close I must go. My friend raised his hand and lowered my head slowly to just above the water. I rested it there, as he put his hands together, scooped up some water from the fountain, and poured it on my head. I felt the warm water trickle gently down the sides of my head and caress my neck. I raised myself back up, realizing what he'd done, and saw he had a great smile on his face. I felt refreshed despite my surprise, and moved by his brotherhood. My friend had just baptized me. He had given me the new birth into the night. Then we all preceded to walk to the beach together and fulfill our sinful desires. A man who does anything like that knows he worships something greater, but it is not God.

The Ultimate Universal

While Scripture speaks of our corrupt nature, as I have pointed out, it also speaks of the universality of our sinful choices. It speaks of the universality of our corrupt heart. This teaching is present from Genesis, but the New Testament puts a focus and a highlight on it, because it is this universality of sins which demonstrates we are condemned. As Paul teaches in a well-known and significant passage in Rom 3:

> As it is written, There is none righteous, no, not one:
>
> There is none that understandeth, there is none that seeketh after God.
>
> They are all gone out of the way, they are together become unprofitable; there is none that doeth good, no, not one.
>
> Their throat is an open sepulchre; with their tongues they have used deceit; the poison of asps is under their lips:
>
> Whose mouth is full of cursing and bitterness:
>
> Their feet are swift to shed blood:
>
> Destruction and misery are in their ways:
>
> And the way of peace have they not known:
>
> There is no fear of God before their eyes. (vv. 10–18)

Paul is clear through this citation of various passages from the Psalms, Isaiah, and Ecclesiastes that sinfulness is in everyone. No one does good. All men do evil. None seek after God. Some will claim that these passages he cites are only speaking about certain very wicked eras or very wicked people, but if that were true, then Paul would be misinterpreting the Bible. That is not possible. Paul uses these passages in fact to show one thing—how all of us are under sin, and logically how we also all need a Savior (vv. 19–26). It is the very universality of sin that reveals the necessity of salvation. We can't pretend to be the good guys. We're all bad.

Similar passages throughout the Bible show that all men sin and all are sinners. This is in principle what Paul is building from, even if he does not cite each one:

> And enter not into judgment with thy servant: for *in thy sight shall no man living be justified*. (Ps 143:2)
>
> If they sin against thee, (for *there is no man which sinneth not*,) and thou be angry with them, and deliver them over before their enemies, and they carry them away captives unto a land far off or near (2 Chr 6:36)
>
> The good man is perished out of the earth: and *there is none upright among men*: they all lie in wait for blood; they hunt every man his brother with a net. (Mic 7:2)
>
> *All we like sheep have gone astray*; we have turned every one to his own way; and the LORD hath laid on him the iniquity of us all. (Isa 53:6)
>
> The heart is deceitful above all things, and *desperately wicked*: who can know it? (Jer 17:9)

The New Testament further speaks of man's inability to avoid sin in his life. It speaks of our wicked behavior before being born new, and also speaks to the assembly of saints about their own sin. In speaking of our need for confession and forgiveness, even once we are Christian, Apostle John teaches:

> *If we say that we have no sin, we deceive ourselves*, and the truth is not in us.
>
> If we confess our sins, he is faithful and just to forgive us our sins, and to cleanse us from all unrighteousness.
>
> If we say that we have not sinned, we make him a liar, and his word is not in us. (1 John 1:8–10)

Confession is a part of the Christian life, for even though he is a new creation, he still suffers temptation, and needs to put behind him the habits of the flesh. He is not flawless, but must be made holy, through turning from sin and receiving forgiveness. This is true of every Christian.

Similar to Eph 2, which we looked at regarding our fallen nature, Titus 3 speaks broadly about our life before coming to know Christ. It includes disobedience and a variety of sinful acts and sinful passions:

> For we ourselves also were sometimes foolish, *disobedient*, deceived, serving divers lusts and pleasures; living in malice and envy, hateful and hating one another. (v.3)

Paul points to the same pre-Christ reality in Colossians, writing:

> And you, that were sometime alienated and enemies in your mind by wicked works, yet now hath he reconciled (1:21)

In the famous monologue in John 3, Jesus teaches why mankind does not come to the light of God, which in the long run will show why most men did not receive him. It is their wicked deeds, which they love, and desire to keep:

> And this is the condemnation, that light is come into the world, and men loved darkness rather than light, *because their deeds were evil.*
>
> For every one that doeth evil hateth the light, neither cometh to the light, lest his deeds should be reproved. (19-20)

Just as we see with our corrupt nature, one need not possess a Bible or have read a word of it to know that all men sin. All men are guilty. Our lives universally do not live up to the standards of the Creator. People who wish to justify mankind before God like to point to some kind person they know, or their dear sweet grandmother, but human observation alone shows us those very same people, sweet as they are, also commit sin and are guilty. They are rightly judged for their evil.

Some years ago, in a truly odd and disturbing series of events, dead rabbits started turning up along the side of the road and in other open places. Disgustingly, the rabbits had also been sexually violated by a man. Surely, we like to imagine a person who would do such deeds as totally dark, twisted, inhuman individual. However, when the culprit was unmasked, it was an honored member of the community, one who gave generously to the poor. All who knew him were shocked. The criminal was openly a loving humanitarian, and was privately into raping and killing bunny rabbits. This reality presents a little picture of the human situation. There is no "good" person out there who will live up to the law of God. The Bible tells us all are guilty. None are good. None seeks after God. It is situations like this, which you will find occur over and over perpetually, which illustrate the truth of the Bible, and confirm it for any who doubt. There can be no more blaming Adam for our deeds, or claiming that being condemned for his sin is unjust. Every last one of us confirms our alliance with his sin by embracing sin ourselves.

One may ask, if we are not sinlessly perfect after coming to Christ, then what is the difference between the previous life, which we lived in the flesh and the new Christian life. The answer is twofold. Firstly, the difference is that we have restored fellowship with God, and are made clean through Christ. God can look on us as his child, rather than as a rebel sinner in Adam. Our state has changed, from one of alienation, to one of communion with God. Secondly, we are sanctified, and sin is made much less in our life. We recognize it. We learn to hate it. We are given the power and guidance to confess and repent of our sin. The Holy Spirit acts in us to free us from sin and its grip, even if we do not reach flawless perfection in this life. We will know it in the next life, but for now live with a restored union with God, and the cleansing of the Holy Spirit.

ACCUSING GOD

Even when I was living with severe depression, and was not a Christian, I couldn't say I was angry or disillusioned about the Almighty. How could I be angry with a God I did not even believe in. I might have thrown out a pain argument occasionally for the sake of denying God, but in actuality I thought about the connection very little, because I was an unbeliever. I simply lived with ongoing, meaningless pain. It seemed like the torture of an innocent animal, with me being the animal. It was also apparent to me that not only was there suffering in the world, but evil too, and that man's evil clearly brought about the vast bulk of the suffering. It was a world of darkness anyway, so pain seemed to fit in. Meaninglessness, suffering, and evil all seemed to go together. Who can you blame anyway if there's no Creator? Suffering is what it is. It's in the nature of being itself. As a young man and adult who looked kind of disturbed in his countenance, and who wore a lot of black, you might have guessed that was my worldview. I may not have been able to clearly look at my own sin, and sinfulness, but I did look at mankind's evil, and suffering seemed to make sense in light of it. I didn't blame God. God didn't exist anyway. Rather it was the world which was a place of evil and death, and I as a part of this world, just wanted an exit from pain.

I look at pain very differently today, in light of much of what I share in this book. I am grateful to Yahweh for each moment of life I have, and know that moment was given to me as a gift, and that moment is for his glory. I also recognize the fact that for nearly all of us, severe pain is a small fraction of our lives, and we should recognize that despite pain, we have been given the resources we need to live as we should. We can act as brothers, work for human welfare, provide for our own needs, take care of our children, live in virtue, and rejoice in the blessings Yahweh gives us. It shows a great exaggeration of pain, and an irrational fear of pain, to think we are robbed of all this because of one small fraction of our lives. I also know the value in suffering. God uses our pain to build us, to refine us, and to judge us for our sins. We can reject none of this from God, as it is his place and his place alone to do that. Our misfortune, furthermore, can build up his kingdom, as he may use our loss in ways we do not see to create new saints, miracles, and bring justice to this earth. My loss is always going to be much greater gain. If I could crash into a ditch, rather than a man on a much greater mission than I, so that he is able to fulfill his mission, I should be grateful: to God, for the ditch, for the wreck, and for the man. My wreck has a place in God's purpose. I know it is right to accept lowliness, and I have never been promised grandeur anyway.

Angry men, and disillusioned men, are looking at the view the wrong way when they look at pain in this world, and at evil. They're simply not seeing the whole picture. This includes many Christians who try failingly to get God to think and act as they would think and act about these subjects. They believe pain somehow impugns God, or denies him. They become dampened in their faith, or lose it entirely. World prominent critic of the Bible, Bart Ehrman says that it was the "problem" of suffering and evil that caused him to lose his faith,[6] although from my standpoint I would say if he lost his faith, he never had a sincere, saving faith in Jesus to begin with. He now spends considerable effort convincing others to doubt the credibility of the Scriptures. Doubt is his career. A recently "deconverted" Christian apologist says he lost his faith in Jesus when God did not comfort him through his recent ugly divorce.[7] He had prayed for comfort, and he had not received it, so he left Christ to profess a much looser theism. Suffering disproved the God of the Bible in his mind. One British man I knew, and ex-military man, said he just could not believe God would allow him to do the evil he had done in his own life. If God was real, God would have stopped him. Atheists and agnostics of varying intellectual stripes claim these negative matters must prove Yahweh does not exist, or is not of good enough character to worship. It is one long litany of complaint. Their complaint bundle sounds like a book written by Job's wife, and they seem to think arrogantly that they have God in a corner. This is purely a battle of man's self-righteousness against God's righteousness.

6. Ehrman, "Leaving the Faith."
7. Staff Writer, "Christian Apologist Tyler Vela."

Yet these bitter deniers do not have God in a corner, nor is God's character anything less than perfectly righteous. Attacks, doubts, and confusion about the God of the Bible all come from several wrong views of the matter, as well as from enormous human pride. Trying to find failing with Yahweh because of pain or evil misses a number of essential truths. It demands blindness to our actual situation. Here are a few of those truths you need to see:

Number One

Accusing God over suffering assumes we somehow deserve a moment of life as well as a life of comfort. This continues to be unproven, yet it lies beneath every ounce of dissatisfaction, anger, accusation, and unbelief. The lack of evidence for this central assumption shows how hollow are any claims based on it. It shows how false the accusations are. If we deserved a long life, it would indeed be an injustice if we did not receive one. However, we do not deserve a long life, and we did nothing at all to earn one. In fact, we did not even earn one instant of life. If we exist for even an instant, it is a gift of God which he gave to us freely by his power. If we exist for three seconds, it is a gift from God, and no injustice has been done when those three seconds are over. If we exist for five minutes, each minute is a gift from God, and we have been neither wronged nor oppressed when our five minutes of life are over. If we die at forty of a heart attack, no injustice has been done that we did not die instead at ninety. If we die at twenty in a car wreck, we have been neither mistreated nor denied our just rewards. If we die at one hundred in the comfort of our bed, with our family all around us, we have not been wronged either. It is simply our time to die. Death is not robbery of us, because we did not earn our life to begin with. It is simply the ending of our gift, an ending God has every right to bring about, and plan in every facet for his purposes, including the time of its death. Our life was not ours to begin with. It is right to love our life in the right way, in the sense that we are grateful for the many blessings Yahweh provides us, and feel inner satisfaction at life's pleasures, certainly, but it is wrong to love that life in the wrong way, by coveting it, and hanging on to it, and making it about our personal pleasure and fulfillment. It's a life whose only purpose is to glorify Yahweh. We did not deserve a moment of it. No injustice then has been done, even when a young person dies.

Similarly, we have not been promised comfort. Why should we think Yahweh has done us any wrong if we experience pain, even severe pain? Most of our lives most of the time include either comfort or bliss. Few times involve severe pain. We eat, we work, we relax, we play, we experience the many varied pleasures of this earth, which even in its fallen form are delightful. How thankless we are to think we can curse Yahweh when pain comes. What part of that comfort did we deserve? What part did we earn? If we did not earn or deserve our comfort we have not been wronged if we lack comfort, and for most of us, we only lack it a small minority of the time. We should reverse our attitude if we are bitter at experiencing pain. We should instead be thankful for the truly countless joys we have, and then know that Yahweh's meaning and purpose must be within that pain, because he is God and he is good. No charge then can be made against God for pain, when we cannot prove it was undeserved.

As I would say to anyone who really does not understand suffering: Before you seek an answer, try thanking God personally for the blessings you receive every day. Thank him for the food, the life, the friendship, the protection, the pleasure, the earth, the heavens, the beauty, the breath in your lungs, and do that every day sincerely for a year. Then after that year, start to consider how you view pain. You will see it in a much better context, and with more clarity, if you look at it that way, first showing gratefulness to the one who gives you gifts each day. It is truly unfair, selfish, and irrational not to thank God for everything you have, and one who is so selfish to begin with, likely will be blind to the meaning of pain too. He's already made the universe about himself.

Number Two

It places man above God to even consider he must be in error over pain, as Job at least began to consider before God corrected him. Truth and goodness flow from the Creator, and not from the human heart. Decisions are governed by God's will and character, and not by our opinions and preferences. We don't get to decide what's good. We no more established the foundations of the moral law, than we established the foundations of the universe at its beginning. Yahweh did both of these things. It is his right, as he is above us in position, power, and knowledge. He doesn't just judge better than we do, but he actually creates the measuring stick by which we judge, and has given it to us to help us.

Once we recognize we are below God, we can see how futile man's arguments against his Creator are. For example, we could not even judge pain or evil as wrong if it were not for a God of life and goodness. It is God's perfection that lets us know there is something off, something fallen about suffering. If it were left to the materialist, and evolutionary view, pain merely exists, and has no fundamental value[8]. It happens, you don't like it, but you can't show it to be wrong. The same is true of evil. Without God's perfect moral standards and perfect essence in the first place, we could not say that evil is wrong. We could not claim that wrong has been done to us if we are robbed, cheated, slandered, or abused in any manner. It relies upon Yahweh, and upon his law, to claim that these acts are sinful. Without Yahweh, acts of murder, cruelty, torture, rape, are simply neutral acts, which we have no business condemning. You can find any number of articles and debates with atheists in which they plainly admit this point: there is nothing fundamentally wrong with genocide, or with molesting small children. At least they are being honest here.

Therefore, if by God's life we know there is wrong in suffering, and if by his perfection we know there is wrong in sinning, we are comically prideful, and quite hypocritical, to blame God for our suffering and our sin. We only know goodness and life because of him. To blame God for sin is ultimately self-refuting, because the moment we choose to blame God, we deny the very standards by which we know these things to be wrong. So if we deny that very standard, we need to stop complaining anyway, and just accept it. No real standards exist.

Number Three

To blame God ignores God's sovereignty. If there is anything clear from Scripture, it is that Yahweh is ruler over all. Man is a creation, and is the one to be ruled. That means man cannot dictate how Yahweh governs creation. You simply are not in the position to do so. Not only that, but the Scripture explicitly teaches, and also demonstrates, that God is

---

8. The atheist may disagree here, and claim that he can examine the world, and find a useful purpose for pain. He may claim suffering and death will "better" the species over time. However, here he has the same problem as he has with asserting a moral law apart from God; he is unable to say what "better" is, apart from his own personal opinion, and the trends of the current culture. This is also a failed attempt at natural revelation, without a God to reveal anything. Evolution wouldn't care if all life ended tomorrow, and the cosmos ceased to exist. Evolution is not a person, and it does not care.

sovereign over evil which occurs: that includes both natural disaster and moral evil. He may not do evil himself, but he is sovereign over those acts, even appointing them to occur. This is revealed truth. Evil may not be good, but what God uses evil to bring about *is* good. His plan and goal are perfect. The Scripture clearly teaches that Yahweh brought about the brutal and unjust murder of his own Son, and even that the act pleased him. If we can accept that God was sovereign over the crucifixion, morally the most evil act to ever occur, we can have no objection that God is sovereign over the death of a child. If we have no problem with God appointing the crucifixion to occur, we should have no problem with God appointing the death of a child to occur. Jesus Christ is perfect, and is by nature God. A child is not perfect, nor is a child God. If a single soul dies it is by God's plan, and is for God's perfect purpose on this earth.

One thing you must realize in this regard: Yahweh gave his law to us. He gives us a moral law that we can know in our conscience, and which we can know with more clarity and certainty through the prophets, whose words have become Scripture. All mankind, whether pagan, atheist, or Christian, has received the moral law from God and must obey it. It is wicked to rob, to cheat, to blaspheme, to gossip, to lie, to do violence, to commit adultery, sodomy, and murder. We harm God's creation when we break his law, and we also offend God, who will judge us for that. In contrast, we did not give a law to God which he must follow. We are in no position to do so because we are the creation and not the Creator. We have no absolute moral law with which we can command Yahweh to behave as we wish him to behave. We have no ability to bind God to ethics or any other behavior. God commands us, not the other way around.

It is equally absurd to suggest that Yahweh must obey the law which he sent into his creation, as it is to suggest a computer programmer must do all the different tasks he programmed the computer to do. His program may reflect his personality and his will, but the programmer certainly is not going to be doing everything in his script, as he is not a little bit of light inside a machine. He is a man. He is fully beyond the machine and has authority over it. Similarly, God's law teaches us greatly about his character and will, but it is not intended for him nor given to him. He's not the computer, but the programmer.

There is no moral law that demands Yahweh cannot end a human life. There is no moral law that demands Yahweh cannot end the life of a child either. It simply does not exist, and the same people who malign the perfect Creator with accusations of wrongdoing, always find it impossible to prove that God is doing wrong. Yahweh has not broken any law if he ends the life of a child, because God is beyond those laws, and completely free. All he does is good, and all he does flows from that good nature, but by no means does that mean he would never cause a life to end or a person to experience pain. It simply means it is all for the good because it is from God. I realize that is hard for many to accept, but if we respect Yahweh as ruler, and have a simple trust in him, we do accept it. There may remain some mystery as to God's reasons, but we embrace that mystery as we embrace God. No man has made any law that God must follow, but rather the other way around—the moral law was made for us, and we are obliged to follow the moral law, which blesses us greatly when we do. We are blessed with peace, contentment of the soul, material resources, harmonious relationships, and often pleasure when we follow his laws. We are rightly judged when we break them.

Number Four

Accusations against the Almighty also leave out man's sin. You are willfully refusing to look at the evidence if you close your eyes to the fact we are sinners, and will blind yourself to the problem as well as the solution. Man's sin comes into play in two ways. Firstly, it is clearly man's sin which brings about the vast majority of suffering on the earth, and all of its moral evil. Man made those choices. Therefore, if there is anyone we need to take a good hard look at, it is man. We need to grieve over his actions. We need to recognize his actions are worthy of judgment. It's not Yahweh we should be judging, but man. Every act of human cruelty is committed through man's will. Moreover, man's sin also allows us to see earthly suffering as a judgment, and a clearly deserved one. All of us deserve God's wrath due to sin, and rightly face the fire of hell, so if a tiny portion of that judgment falls during our time on this earth, no injustice has been done to us. We are all sinners. It's a fraction of what we deserve. That's not to say that every act of suffering is a divine judgment, as we know that some are not, but we need to realize that much of it is judgment, and we brought it on ourselves from the evil we do. Scripture teaches us clearly and repeatedly that various invasions that came upon Israel were judgment for her deeds. That includes the killing, looting, starvation, and rape that was a part of those enemy attacks.

While I brought up before that we are wrong to assume we deserve life or deserve pleasure, we are also wrong to ignore that we deserve judgment, and pretend Yahweh is unfair if we must undergo judgment, even if it is temporal. If Yahweh were perfectly fair, we would every one of us be condemned. Every one of us is guilty. Yet even though we are sinners God holds back judgment nearly all of the time, and often for many years. He continually brings teachings that will heal our pains, and sends preachers who will proclaim to everyone the way to end pain forever and know eternal peace. He further gives us the ability to develop technology and medicines which bring comfort and convenience to our sinful lives. Therefore, we should not wonder why anyone receives judgment. We should marvel at God's mercy, at the ongoing chances he gives us to be restored, and to know peace. It should be a source of deep gratitude.

The Good Guys

We can look at it another way. Before we imagine that we are one of the good guys, and don't deserve condemnation, we need to look sin square in the eye. We need to recognize how serious even the average man's sins are. The idea there is a world in which only the mass murderers end in hell, but everyone else is pretty decent, is laughable and self-serving. It ignores the bulk of humanity's evil, including our own. I do not claim to be a better person than the killer, except by the goodness of Christ. I do not find any virtue in the fact I do not commit the most condemned crimes, such as rape, murder, or pedophilia, since I do not desire to do them in the first place. However, the sins I have done are wicked in themselves.

It is an assault on human life to lie, cheat, commit fornication, inebriate the mind with drink or drugs. These are sins which millions of people think nothing of doing daily. Yet all of these acts do more slowly what murder does quickly. All these things bring the pain and loss which comes with murder, through their betrayal, inherent instability, and infusion of filth and danger to human life. If you could imagine for the moment the number of people who committed suicide merely because of betrayal in intimate relationships, you'd know you could fill up a city with corpses. If you considered the amount of risk to human life done by shoddy products, unsafe building practices, and financial dishonesty, you'd see the same connection. If you remembered the percent of young violent criminals on the street who came from a broken home, you'd see that sexual immorality means death. If you reviewed history to see the wicked leaders who came to power due to the lie, you'd see the atomic destruction of this sin, which if we remember, brought death to all mankind in the garden. We like to pretend we are better people than the child killer. Yet human beings, through their sin, agree with every stab wound that comes down to kill the child.

I am always struck when I read about today's school shooters how much I have in common with them. I relate to their background. I feel the same for certain of the diabolical serial killers now popular in mass media. The only difference I see between myself and them is the grace of God. I am not a better person. There is One in heaven who protected me from becoming like them. It seems most of the time I look at their stories, it is one of alienation, unhappiness, often a fatherless or broken home. Many are on psychiatric medication. They would often be described as odd, cold, or distant. They are obsessed with darkness, and fascinated with death. I say to myself—that person is just like me. They are my brethren. I am only grateful to God that his grace protected me from becoming them. I did not muster any goodness up inside myself to warrant such protection. My anger and loathing were inward. I did not choose it to be that way, rather than outward, but it's merely my life experience. I feel some sympathy for other human life, merely by my instincts. I did not put those instincts there by my will, to make sure they accomplished their goal.

One can look at the childhood of such killers, and feel great sadness for them, even if they made their choice to do evil deeds later on. In many cases if they had been treated differently, they would not have taken steps into murder. Wisdom, kindness, and right relationships would have made them more stable inside, and less full of rage. The love of godly parents and community would have steered them away from cruelty or the denial of God. Serial killer Edmund Kemper was from a broken home, raised by his alcoholic mother who blamed him for all her problems, and forced him to live in the basement.[9] Robert Hansen, who also murdered women, grew up an unattractive child, and was mocked and shunned by his peers in school.[10] He was an outcast for many years. American icon Charles Manson was abandoned by his real father at birth, to be raised by his alcoholic and criminal mother, and by whatever men were passing

---

9. Bonn, "The Twisted Tale."
10. Team Seven, "The Butcher Baker."

through her life. For years he only got to see her through the glass panes of the prison, and being raised by his uncle, who considered him a sissy, was once forced to go to school wearing a dress.[11] Can you not honestly weep for those men? Are you not your brother's keeper? We need to ask ourselves if those killers could even exist without the allegedly smaller sins of the family and community which raised them, and were content to mistreat them. It is only God's grace that prevents any of us from possessing the rage these men have, or from possessing the coldness to human suffering it must take to commit murder. Whether by his hand in our lives, or by our innate spiritual makeup from the start, Yahweh can guard us from such evil.

When you and I do have the chance to sin, we confirm that we agree with those condemned killers about death. We put our personal goals and pleasure above what is good for the life of humanity. We break the law of God, and the laws of men. If we cannot refrain from committing what we view as smaller sins, how can we expect them to refrain from committing what we view as bigger ones? If every time a man gave in to the temptation to fornicate, a child molester gave in to the temptation to molest a child, how many children would be molested? Ask yourself that about your own favorite sin. It humbles the pretentious self. You are not a better person, and neither am I. Sin is all an assault on life, and an offense against a holy God. Every last one of us chooses to cloak ourselves in darkness like the killer.

Not a Guy in the Sky

One of the main causes for the multiple errors I've mentioned, is that we tend to look at the question by imagining that the Almighty is essentially a very powerful person, and then imagine what a very powerful person would or should do. This tendency will always lead us to wrong answers. Yahweh is not a very powerful person. If you imagine things this way, expect to be left with confusion and frustration, as you've just treated God as a part of the created order. That does not provide answers. The Bible has the answers, and we need to understand that Yahweh is not a man. Yahweh is beyond our world; his thoughts are beyond our thoughts. God is the source of goodness and truth itself, and is sovereign Ruler over all things. He is completely free, and unbound by the limitations of creation,

---

11. Sederstrom, "'Wasn't What I Would Call a Bad Person.'"

and by the laws we have on earth, including the laws of society. Yahweh gave us this creation, and he can decide how it works. He decides what is right and wrong. He gave us our life and if he chooses to end it, we have not been wronged. These things are true of God but not of man. If God chooses to end the life of your neighbor in order to judge him, or in order to bring about the goodness of his plan, Yahweh—as sovereign ruler and source of all life—can do that. If you end the life of your neighbor for those reasons, in contrast, you are a murderer. You sin and you are rightfully judged by society as well as by God. You cannot impose man's way of life upon the Creator. God is not a man.[12]

Brings about Perfection

Yahweh is also perfect, and being perfect can always act to bring about the good. Even in appointing evil or suffering to occur, God purposes this for good, and God does no wrong. Man's doubts, despair, and even accusations against Yahweh are often made from a standpoint of the now, and are made with eyes only on his suffering, or the loss of his goals. It is ultimately superficial. It allows our feelings to wrongly sway our view of reality. We can be surprised to see some of what righteous Job says, as he is feeling abandoned by God, or oppressed by God, and wanting to plead his case in heaven. We as the reader know better, but he is overwhelmed by his situation, and his eyes are fixed on his pain. If man is doubting God because of pain, he has the long-term good out of his vision. He needs to turn his eyes to God to see a clearer, broader, and more distant view. The final destination will be glorious. We know this when we have patience, continue to trust in God, and to pray.

Joseph's abuse by his brothers, and selling into slavery was a temporary fall for him, but those very circumstances brought him through God's plan to become the right-hand man of the ruler of Egypt, and to have authority over those who persecuted him (Gen 37, 39–41). This rulership is what the young Joseph had seen in his dream to begin with. He knew that end would come, and his apparent distance from that goal did not stop that end from occurring. The same is true of the whole nation of

---

12. It should be remembered that God became a man for our sake. However, this immanence does not deny his transcendence. Moreover, when living in human nature, God showed us how to live: he followed the law of God, obeyed the Father, trusted in the Father, and worshipped the Father. He lived out our creaturely life in full submission to the Creator.

Israel, which knew slavery for generations, but was brought by miracles, and a hard journey into the land, fulfilling the promises of God (Josh 21:43–45). They knew they had a circumstance and a future greater than what they saw. Joseph had even told them to take his bones when they left Egypt (Gen 49:29–30), assuring that this land was not their final one, but the land of promise was. Momentary suffering will never take us away from the good which God has planned for us. In the larger scale, that includes the good of his perfect kingdom, with an end to sin and death.

As Apostle Paul wrote about the horrific sufferings of the early church: "For our light affliction, which is but for a moment, worketh for us a far more exceeding *and* eternal weight of glory" (2 Cor 4:17). The "light affliction" he wrote of included imprisonment, torture, and death. These are things that would cause some to start doubting God and lose hope, yet these sufferings were momentary compared to the eternity that awaited. They were "light" compared to the heavy weight of glory. In the long run, I don't think you and I will be complaining about a mere moment of suffering here on earth, when we are living in beautiful communion with God and each other, in a world with no suffering and death. We will look back on that suffering as a distant, memory in another world, and see clearly its purpose in God's perfection of the world. It will be washed away in the bliss of love infused forever in our soul.

Do you honestly think that Jacob or Joseph will be complaining about their hardship in heaven, or could it be they will be grateful to have been able to do a few things God, and for his people? Will Apostle Paul or Stephen be embittered over the sacrifices they made, or glory in the results which came about for the ones they love? Will David be despairing the betrayal of friends and wounding by enemies, or will he know God greatly honored him on this earth by using him as his instrument? It is only in the moment when we fail to see the meaning, and when suffering seems overwhelming, that we cannot see the good. Despair itself is very shortsighted. If we love Yahweh, and we come into his family, we will see how much suffering was worth, both for our own growth as a saint, and for the good of the whole world. We will rejoice that we were able to suffer.

4

God Answers You

THINGS TOO WONDERFUL FOR ME

The Bible in the Old Testament answers the question of suffering in a very clear way. It is called the book of Job. Really, it is an answer that can be summed up in a few words, even though the book of Job is quite long, and is full of wordy meditations. It does not give us the fullest answer, although it hints at it multiple times. The fullest answer is found in the New Testament, being realized in Jesus Christ. Job does give us the answer though with crystal clarity. If people reject this answer—and I found it unsatisfying when I was an unbeliever too—it is because they simply do not like it. It is an answer that requires man's humility and understanding, and often humility and understanding are the last things on a man's heart when he is upset about pain, or desires to charge Yahweh with evil. Yet the answer from Job stands, and it is simply one of God's rulership and freedom.

Job deals with pain from the standpoint of a righteous man. This is a man that no one could charge with sin, and which the book seems to affirm was not being judged by Yahweh for his sin, although later by doubting God's goodness he had something for which to repent. Yet personal sin is not the source of his suffering from the start. That means the book addresses the aspect of suffering that most upsets people—when bad things happen to "good people." The book also deals with suffering of the more severe form—a man who loses his children to tragedy, loses his home and wealth, and is then struck with a terrible painful illness, which disfigures him. He suffers daily.

While these are some of the same sufferings that would lead a man to shake his fist at God, Job immediately responds the way a saint would, and the way any Christian would. He understands that all that happens comes from God, and we must continue to honor and praise him even in loss. When his wife suggests he "curse God, and die" (Job 2:9b), Job immediately rebukes her. When he learns of his children's death, he only says, "the LORD gave, and the LORD hath taken away; blessed be the name of the LORD" (1:21b). These are the words of a good man when faced with terrible loss and suffering. God takes away and he still blesses God's name.

Job's wife, although presented very briefly, and in a negative light, makes me think of the way many Christians think about pain, as well as how unbelievers consider it. They may be tentatively prepared to accept that Yahweh brings pain to punish serious sin, but they are horrified by the idea that Yahweh brings pain upon the "innocent" simply by his own free will, and for purposes we cannot see. They must envision pain as a mere response by God to man's bad behavior, or else it is God who is being bad. "I would never worship a God like that," is the catch phrase of the Christian nearly as much as the atheist, suggesting that unless Yahweh interacts with evil just the way we think he ought to, he's not worth our honor, despite being God. The Christian makes that atheist's mistake quite frequently. He thinks he, being a mere man, is the one to decide how the universe functions, how sin should affect us, whom should be held responsible, who should suffer, and that God must respond to man's dictates about the universe instead of the other way around. Then when faced with a case of evil or suffering that does not fit his expectations, he says so to speak—let us curse God and die. This is not a God I would worship. Man turns things on their heads, and becomes as Job's wife, and we must remind him similarly, "You speak as one of the foolish women speaks" (Job 2:10 NKJV). For it is God who decides how things work, and the Christian who thinks God is not free to cause suffering needs to learn the simple lesson of Job again, and humble himself as Job did.

While Job responds to his terrible situation the right way to begin with, he soon lapses into questioning Yahweh's judgment, and thinking his tragic situation is unjustified. While his several friends try repeatedly to convince him that his suffering must be due to hidden sin, Job is certain he is righteous, and begins to express doubt in God's goodness and

God's judgment. He wants to be able to enter courts in heaven and plead his case. Statements of great faith are punctuated by long outpourings of despair. "He teareth me in his wrath, who hateth me: he gnasheth upon me with his teeth; mine enemy sharpeneth his eyes upon me" (16:9), he cries out, presenting the God he has walked with many years as his enemy. Job never becomes as rebellious as his wife did, but he becomes foolish enough that he earns the correction of his friend Elihu, and finally a rebuke, and clear answer from Yahweh. That answer is as relevant today, to every single human being, as it was to Job, who even in his doubt was humbler than many believers today. Job would not fully see that answer until the end.

Since I am not writing a book about Job, I only will summarize the Lord's answer to this righteous man. It is not the pat on the back that we would prefer to hear. Nor is it an answer that explains all the reasons for which Job is suffering. It is the answer of God's sovereignty. God's right to rule and his freedom. Yahweh teaches Job that God is the Creator of all things, and Job is a mere creature. Seeing this truth, it is not Job's place to question God or suggest he decides wrongly. Yahweh teaches this mostly in a series of questions, which reveal their different positions as Creator and creature:

> Then the LORD answered Job out of the whirlwind, and said,
>
> Who is this that darkeneth counsel by words without knowledge?
>
> Gird up now thy loins like a man; for I will demand of thee, and answer thou me.
>
> Where wast thou when I laid the foundations of the earth? declare, if thou hast understanding.
>
> Who hath laid the measures thereof, if thou knowest? or who hath stretched the line upon it?
>
> Whereupon are the foundations thereof fastened? or who laid the corner stone thereof;
>
> When the morning stars sang together, and all the sons of God shouted for joy?
>
> Or who shut up the sea with doors, when it brake forth, as if it had issued out of the womb?
>
> When I made the cloud the garment thereof, and thick darkness a swaddlingband for it,
>
> And brake up for it my decreed place, and set bars and doors,

> And said, Hitherto shalt thou come, but no further: and here shall thy proud waves be stayed?
>
> Hast thou commanded the morning since thy days; and caused the dayspring to know his place;
>
> That it might take hold of the ends of the earth, that the wicked might be shaken out of it? (Job 38:1-13)

This doesn't sound too sympathetic or comforting, but Job needs the truth more than sympathy right now. Yahweh's answer is an extended way of saying—I am God and you are not. Yahweh first reminds Job that he is Creator of all things, the heavens and earth, the seas, the lands, the animals. None of these things did Job do, but he is simply one of countless creatures in God's creation. The simple comparison makes it laughable to even think to rebuke God. Anyone reading should also notice a lack of an appeal to Job's libertarian freedom, and a full appeal to God's authority.

> Wilt thou also disannul my judgment? wilt thou condemn me, that thou mayest be righteous?
>
> Hast thou an arm like God? or canst thou thunder with a voice like him?
>
> Deck thyself now with majesty and excellency; and array thyself with glory and beauty.
>
> Cast abroad the rage of thy wrath: and behold every one that is proud, and abase him.
>
> Look on every one that is proud, and bring him low; and tread down the wicked in their place.
>
> Hide them in the dust together; and bind their faces in secret.
>
> Then will I also confess unto thee that thine own right hand can save thee. (Job 40:8-14)

Yahweh continues to remind Job that his complaints put himself above God and God's purpose. He also reminds Job that moral judgment comes from God. As Yahweh is the source of physical creation, he is the source of rightness, law, judgment, and justification. Man does not have either the strength or the moral perfection to correct the proud and the sinful. In fact, even in the limited way we need to correct one another, we are not the source of goodness itself, but try only apply what God has given in the way God says to do it. Only Yahweh can truly judge the wicked, or justify a man. Considering God is the source of the moral plane of existence, it is preposterous to think we can tell God his judgment was wrong, or he dealt with a man in the wrong fashion. We have not the ability to judge as he does, as we ourselves are imperfect.

> Canst thou draw out leviathan with an hook? or his tongue with a cord which thou lettest down?
>
> Canst thou put an hook into his nose? or bore his jaw through with a thorn?
>
> Will he make many supplications unto thee? will he speak soft words unto thee?
>
> Will he make a covenant with thee? wilt thou take him for a servant for ever?
>
> Wilt thou play with him as with a bird? or wilt thou bind him for thy maidens?
>
> Shall the companions make a banquet of him? shall they part him among the merchants? (Job 41:1-6)

God sounds mocking when he further presents Job's powerlessness as a man compared to God's mighty power. It was God who made the great beast Leviathan, and it is man who is unable to tame or defeat this beast. He's not going to play with Leviathan like a pet animal, and even his weapons are useless against him. Job is faced with his weakness compared to God's might. If he cannot even defeat a mighty beast made by Yahweh, how can he judge Yahweh, or think to rebuke him? Men are trampled by beasts made by God every day. They are eaten as they swim in the sea.

There are many proud rebel men who would answer back to being put in their place. They might say that man, over time, has learned to tame much of God's creation, yet even such a proud answer is left with the same problem. Those same people are limited and defeated by other parts of God's creation, and are defeated continually. Moreover, even those problems and challenges which they have overcome, were only overcome by abilities given by Yahweh in the first place, through resources he placed on the earth. We also see that man only overcomes problems within the creation, a domain which is infinitely small compared to Yahweh himself who made it; yet with one problem overcome, finds another defeat following it. Whether it is the many dead from the recent Coronavirus, with the entire global economy shut down and men locked inside out of fear, or the mass destruction of tornadoes and hurricanes wiping out entire neighborhoods, man's centuries of advances leave him crushed by a mere creation of the Creator. The comparison made to Job over three thousand years ago remains apt to a rebellious mind today—we are feeble, and are easily crushed by the creation itself.

What this means, and what Job as a righteous man realizes, is that we cannot judge God for bringing pain into our lives. Yahweh is completely free to do as he wills. That does not mean he is being whimsical or cruel, as we know Yahweh is a God of truth and of goodness. It only means it is his place and not our place to decide what occurs. He is completely righteous in bringing suffering upon a man, even one who has no obvious sin in his life.

It's not the feel-good response most men would like, but Job realizes his own pride in doubting God. Even before Yahweh is finished rebuking him, Job says:

> Behold, I am vile; what shall I answer thee? I will lay mine hand upon my mouth.
> Once have I spoken; but I will not answer: yea, twice; but I will proceed no further. (Job 40:4–5)

He realizes the very foolishness of his words, and doesn't wish to speak another one. He is willing to just listen, and knows he has no answer to Yahweh's queries. This is the quietness of heart than any man should have in listening in prayer. God is God. He is awesome and ever-powerful, and beyond us. Job is a man, and was becoming very proud. If only all of us could stop ourselves when we become so proud, and listen to the voice of God. He speaks out of the storm here, and out of the silence elsewhere.

When Yahweh finishes with his lengthy rebuke, Job shows he has learned the truth, and will repent of his doubt. He respects God's sovereignty over all things:

> I know that thou canst do every thing, and that no thought can be withholden from thee.
> Who is he that hideth counsel without knowledge? therefore have I uttered that I understood not; things too wonderful for me, which I knew not. (Job 42:2–3)

Job clearly accepts that there are things beyond his understanding, and things beyond his position as a mere creature in God's creation. Yahweh knows more than him and Yahweh has the right to act in his creation as he sees fit. Job recognizes God's rulership and freedom. God can "do every thing" and "no thought can be withheld" from him. Despite our lack of knowledge of God's purpose much of the time, God has the unlimited power, and true right to rule over us. We must trust in those purposes ourselves even if we do not see them. All that Yahweh desires he will accomplish.

Clearly, this realization leads Job to deepen his faith in Yahweh and his understanding of Yahweh. He concludes this episode saying:

> I have heard of thee by the hearing of the ear: but now mine eye seeth thee.
>
> Wherefore I abhor myself, and repent in dust and ashes. (Job 42:5–6)

Job realizes that his faith, while real, has been shallow by comparison to what he has just learned, through his suffering and the Lord's answer to it. He only had heard of God, but now he *sees* God. To see God is a very powerful way to express understanding, since God is spirit, and is invisible to us. Job has come to an awesome understanding of his Creator which he had lacked. He now has a deepened intimacy with God. Many years of worship and ethical living did not provide that for Job. Only suffering and the rebuke of God did. These are the great riches that can be found through trials. In his repentance from doubt, Job finally was restored, having many more children, and becoming wealthy again. His daughters were very beautiful and were married and themselves provided him many grandchildren. Even though not everyone does, Job lived to see the day his suffering ended, and he lived in God's abundant blessings.

While Job's response is the right response, and Yahweh's answer is still the answer today, they truly are the last things many people want to hear when confronted with their own Jobian situations. You can relate the right message to them, but they still want to repeat Job's error, or perhaps even worse errors. Some wish to respond as Job's wife. They wish to curse God. Yahweh's answer is not one which promises us understanding of why each particular act of suffering occurs. We are not promised any such thing. It is not an answer that tells us our pain will always be cured, or that we will have better in the future in this life. It is an answer that rests fully on God's right to rule the universe. That strikes at man's pride when we really want to hear another answer, and dictate what the answer is ourselves. If we responded as Job did, we would repent in dust and ashes as well. We would realize our incredible smallness in this world, and God's incredible power, goodness, and freedom. God can do no wrong. Whatever unseen reason there is for our current suffering, God is in command and our situation is bound to his purposes. God must ultimately purpose that event for the glorious good. It is his right to decide. It's not our right to decide. That truth would deepen our knowledge and love of God, and the awe with which we see him. Who are we to tell God what to do?

It's important to see that Yahweh has clearly been in command from the start of the events the book describes. Satan may be the one specifically to make the attacks on Job's family, and then on Job, but it is Yahweh who needs to give Satan permission, and he even sets limits on what Satan can do, restraining him from taking Job's life. We can even see an initiation of sorts into the entire event when Yahweh asks Satan, "Hast though considered my servant Job" (Job 1:8), perhaps the ultimate rhetorical question of all time. God is in charge despite Satan's direct involvement, something we need to keep in mind in considering other facets of God's rule over acts of evil. God never ceases to be in command, even when he merely gives permission. Yet God is good, and commands these events perfectly and justly. From the perspective of a believer, God's right to rule should be no problem for us. It becomes a problem when we are wrapped up in ourselves, presume we are gods, and refuse to see God's purpose in this existence. It is small-minded and proud to blame God for pain.

The ending of Job also cannot be ignored. While Yahweh's children are not promised a restoration for every loss on this earth, we are promised a final restoration and many rewards. Job's return at the end of the book to having children and to wealth pictures Yahweh's glorious purpose in suffering—the blessing of his children, the bliss they will have in his kingdom. God's will is always good, even when what is on our plate is terrible to endure. In suffering with faithfulness, and in willingness to repent, Job shows he is truly God's child, and experiences the fullness of God's love again. This is what the Christian can expect as well, while not always earthly wealth or immediate deliverance from problems, a secure home in eternity where there is no pain or death. The Christian's restoration is far greater than Job's. We need to know this when seeing pain in perspective with God's good purpose, and in perspective with eternity. Pain is only there for a relative instant, and God is using it to bring his salvation to many. Who would refuse to go through that brief pain if we really knew how glorious his end is? Wouldn't we all volunteer? Not only did Job's suffering end in his restoration, but it also resulted in a book that has brought wisdom to billions, and that hints at the Savior of mankind various times. When read with a humble heart, this book has brough peace to the souls of countless men, a blessing far greater than what Job receives at the end of his trials. What a small and short thing his tortures were. You can ask him when you meet him if he would ever take back all that trial and suffering he went through, despite all the good it brought about. Job is a child of God in heaven. He would tell you no.

Why Not Put an End to Pain?

It is common to wonder why God does not simply end our pain. We wonder since God is all powerful, what purpose is served in continuing to send suffering upon us, and continue to allow this corrupt world of sin and death to go on. Why not produce his desired results in another way. I am reminded in my own life that the bulk of my suffering I've experienced did end. My depression lifted, as almost supernaturally as it had come. It faded away as a mist in the sunlight, as the sun rises, and I cannot even remember it anymore. How did I react? Did I praise God as Nebuchadnezzar did? Did I make my life all about living for righteousness? Did I commit myself to helping others? No, like most people, the end result of having my pain go away was to live more efficiently and effectively for myself. It was to glorify me better. It was to continue in immorality, but only continue more comfortably and confidently than before. That was my attitude when my suffering was lifted, an act I can only attribute to the hand of God. I responded with greater worship of the self.

This is true of many others besides myself. When comfort comes, it is an opportunity to get rich, to do pricier drugs, to shower on ourselves more pleasure and a greater variety of pleasure. One can easily see the link in European culture between the great leaps in accomplishments that began to occur around the Renaissance, and the subsequent growing unbelief in the Bible, along with the sensuality, decadence, and humanist philosophy of the age. One only needs to look at the fleshiness of the artwork at the time to see where their minds were at. Growing wealth, comfort, and education led many to unbelief. This is frequently the case when burdens are lifted. Poor populations start to take on middle class living, and soon their children, as the fruit of their hard work, push coke up their noses, start attending nice clubs, can pay for more abortions, and dump insane amounts of money into luxurious cars, clothing, and any manner of excess. They can afford hotels for their whores, and rent nice apartments for their concubines. This is what an end to suffering leads to, when man is in the flesh. It is a more comfortable version of hell.

Consider that God knows he will accomplish much more through suffering. The human heart can turn to depend upon him greatly. It can see the reality of its own sin, and truly long for righteousness, not only a purity of the body from illness, but the purity of the soul from destructive lusts. Through suffering, even those who do not suffer can take part in this cleansing of the soul. The inner being is not an easy thing to cleanse. It can be hard as a rock, bitter, uncaring, and take many blows of the chisel to break off the deadening shell. Often it's pain which does this uniquely. Family must sacrifice themselves to care for the ill brother, or to pay for the needed medical help. They must take their time and money, attention and energies to help their disabled friend or neighbor. They must put aside their love of the flesh to do backbreaking work for free. They minister to those in prison, who have led a life of evil and are quite dangerous. They job train prostitutes who have lived a life of lewdness, so they can become pure and lead a life of virtue. Men at every turn, simply because of pain and evil, must help one another. They must give up what they have. They must accept loss.

An old friend of mine, who was considering the truth of Jesus, worked at a medical establishment and research facility. He regularly saw patients from overseas, who bore marks of horrible treatment on their bodies, things some of us really cannot imagine. Hellish images you will not forget. He was deeply troubled by seeing how men treated other men, and did not know why God allowed it. I tried to remind him that his own job is a part of the reason why—so he can serve them, be humble, use his mind and God-given gifts to heal. It forces servanthood on us all. There is great blessing in being presented with a suffering man, just as there is greater blessing in the cross of the murdered Jesus. God was not presenting my friend with the problem. He was presenting him with part of the solution. Pain is often better for the spirit and mind than comfort is. It is better for all of society.

A Fool for Christ's Sake

Often, when people are given comfort, strength, earthly education, what they do with it is the opposite of what my friend was doing now, when he helped heal this man. People simply become high on themselves. They deny God. They blaspheme him. They use that peace and apparent blessing pursuing a life devoted to self, most often seeking out immorality because it is pleasurable, and caring little whom they hurt. If God simply gave people all these things, free mostly of pain, it would often create a monster. The man living between the warm beach and the snow-capped mountains with a glass of wine in his hand, and fine food before him, smirks arrogantly at the thought of needing his Maker, and gives not a thought to the law of God. His law is himself. I have all of this kingdom every day, he thinks, what do I need God for? Comfort then, prosperity, becomes a source of damnation. A source of cruelty. An inspiration to sin, and to sin so arrogantly that you believe you need no one to deliver your soul.

God's economy works differently, and I urged my friend to see this. He seemed to listen and honestly understand. You see, God takes the insignificant one, and lifts him up. He takes the suffering, and uses him as healer. The dead, as a source of life. He mocks the comfortable sinner, and mocks the earthly power of all the governments in history, turning their presumptions upside down. The Almighty ordered this world that way, by his wisdom, so that it would be the blind who see, the fools who know the path of salvation, the imprisoned who are free, the dead who live. So only the humble, and lowly, and servants will come to him. That's how God handles this world, and it gives us light on why a man with the scars of torture on his body, which no one even desires to see, should come before us one day, that we should do what is the will of God.

Scripture reveals this way of working plainly, and even points to how it deceives people. It fools those who think they are wise. It is not what men think. To start with the shortest of references, the Spirit reveals the strange nature of his salvation, and the strange nature of his people in Paul's words to the Corinthians, describing the ministry. In doing so Paul makes an obscure remark, that ministers are deceiving, even though they are true:

> Giving no offence in any thing, that the ministry be not blamed:
>
> But in all things approving ourselves as the ministers of God, in much patience, in afflictions, in necessities, in distresses,
>
> In stripes, in imprisonments, in tumults, in labours, in watchings, in fastings;
>
> By pureness, by knowledge, by longsuffering, by kindness, by the Holy Ghost, by love unfeigned,

> By the word of truth, by the power of God, by the armour of righteousness on the right hand and on the left,
>
> By honour and dishonour, by evil report and good report: *as deceivers, and yet true;*
>
> As unknown, and yet well known; as dying, and, behold, we live; as chastened, and not killed;
>
> As sorrowful, yet alway rejoicing; as poor, yet making many rich; as having nothing, and yet possessing all things. (2 Cor 6:3–10)

I only want to make one small point here, but I cite most of the passage so you can see the panorama of service to God that Paul gives us. This is the nature of the redeemed people, the church, and its labor which is never in vain. It is a mission that includes much work and suffering, yet we also see it is in ways built on strange contrasts, and even opposites. In verse 8 the apostle says servants of Christ are "deceivers, and yet true." This is immediately very strange to any reader, since how can one both deceive and also be true. It's furthermore strange, and almost wrong-sounding, as we know that Yahweh cannot lie, but God's people are said to deceive. Where is this deception? How is it rightful?

The Spirit does not reveal the answer in these verses. How I understand it, in context with other similar passages is this: the gospel message and the suffering of God's people deceive those who live in the flesh. Those who desire the flesh will only see foolishness in believing on a dead Jewish religious teacher. They will moreover be deceived by the suffering state of this people, who are meek and humble, and everywhere being arrested, flogged, executed by the Jews and Romans. They are deceived by the truth, you might say. They see a weak people, when really God's people have incredible and eternal power. They see a failure, when the Spirit that lives in these mere men overcomes even death. He can lift the dead from the grave. Therefore, we are always being deceivers, and in a righteous sense. Similar opposites in these verses resound with the same tone, showing ministers have honor and dishonor, receive both good and evil reports. One reality comes from eyes enlightened by the Spirit, the other by those which are enslaved to the flesh. Paul also points out how the lowly state of God's people brings forth its opposite—sorrowful, yet always rejoicing, poor, yet making many rich. This is how God works, and he works this way for his glory. Man's way is contentment, self-gratification, and self-importance. God's way is to lift up the lowly and bring down the proud. It truly makes fools of many.

A similar set of contrasts, and similar observations are present in Paul's teaching in 2 Cor 4:1–15. It is a powerful description of how Christ accomplishes his goal through simple, lowly men. While I won't cite the entire passage, these few central verses show how God uses his truth:

> But having renounced the hidden things of dishonesty, not walking in craftiness, nor handling the word of God deceitfully; but by manifestation of the truth commending ourselves to every man's conscience in the sight of God.
>
> But if our gospel be hid, it is hid to them that are lost:
>
> In whom the god of this world hath blinded the minds of them which believe not, lest the light of the glorious gospel of Christ, who is the image of God, should shine unto them. (vv. 2–4)

Here the apostle explicitly teaches that they handle God's word truthfully, which is the light and the glory of Christ. They preach the truth. Yet that message of salvation is hidden to those who are blinded. They cannot see it for what it is. They will not believe. When the Christian sees one thing, they see another. For the followers of Christ are not preaching what the world would desire to hear or to understand—ideas that fit our understanding or promise to meet our goals—but rather preaching what is important to God, and a salvation which comes to humble, repentant men. He explains in the following two verses:

> For we preach not ourselves, but Christ Jesus the Lord; and ourselves your servants for Jesus' sake.
>
> For God, who commanded the light to shine out of darkness, hath shined in our hearts, to give the light of the knowledge of the glory of God in the face of Jesus Christ. (vv. 5–6)

It is not the message of personal happiness, wealth, sensuality, or even religious works that might elevate us, but is the unadorned message of the man Jesus Christ nailed to the cross. We are only his slaves. The message, despised as unsophisticated by some, is the light of God and from God. Therefore, the man of the spirit will receive it, and the rest will be deceived by it, despite its perfect truth.

Paul is explicit about the fact this odd nature of the message is by God's design in the first chapter of First Corinthians. God has ordered the world this way, and it is for our good:

> For the preaching of the cross is to them that perish foolishness; but unto us which are saved it is the power of God.

> For it is written, I will destroy the wisdom of the wise, and will bring to nothing the understanding of the prudent.
>
> Where is the wise? where is the scribe? where is the disputer of this world? hath not God made foolish the wisdom of this world?
>
> For after that *in the wisdom of God the world by wisdom knew not God*, it pleased God by the foolishness of preaching to save them that believe.
>
> For the Jews require a sign, and the Greeks seek after wisdom:
>
> But we preach Christ crucified, unto the Jews a stumblingblock, and unto the Greeks foolishness;
>
> But unto them which are called, both Jews and Greeks, Christ the power of God, and the wisdom of God.
>
> Because the foolishness of God is wiser than men; and the weakness of God is stronger than men. (vv. 18–25)

This is a most incredible revelation. God could have designed this world so that anyone could receive the message. He did not. In his wisdom, the world through wisdom would *not* know God (v. 21a). The way God designed it was for his pleasure, because it glorified him for men to be saved by another method than their own wisdom and strength. The way that God has chosen for our redemption reveals his power, and reveals the weakness of prideful men. He makes a mockery of human pride, and the powers of the devil. Even God's foolishness is greater than all the knowledge at our finest universities. Considering Adam, we can see this design even present in the garden. Adam and his mate would have received blessing and knowledge straight from God, and eaten of the pleasures of the tree of life. In humility, they would have received all things like children. Yet they chose to find knowledge for themselves, and to be like God, replacing him in a way. They came stealing instead of receiving. That arrogance led to Adam's loss of paradise, and mankind's disconnect from the divine. Right living has always been about learning from God's wisdom and relying on God's strength.

God could have chosen to reveal to us all the mysteries of this cosmos, the secrets of every star, a thousand physical laws we have not discovered yet, and then used that kind of knowledge to deliver us from death. He could have shown us the most moving works of art, breathtaking symphonies, or grand architectural constructions so that we would learn to build them. But no. He taught us to learn another way, which would be received by those who are simple. He revealed the death of the living God-man. He gave us his blood pouring out from grotesque wounds to make us clean. He said to believe that a man rose up from the grave. It is the opposite of what man's sophistication would desire, or even our ethical sense would discern to make us better people. He said—put your trust on a man hated and murdered. Those who believe will be saved, and have eternal riches. This simple wisdom of God, not even touching upon the countless facts that must be known to run the entire cosmos, is far greater than anything we have learned or will ever learn in human history. God brought low our mind, our works, our sense of righteousness with only a tiny fraction of what he knows. This man died for you. Believe and you will be saved.

This is how Yahweh cleanses the world of pain and death. It is how he delivers us from sin, and from its claws that sink into us, holding us in place, and enslaving us. It is how he removes our righteous sentence of death. God does not end it our way, because our way is only pride, and our way is the source of the problem. He ends it his way, and puts the wicked to shame:

> But God hath chosen the foolish things of the world to confound the wise; and God hath chosen the weak things of the world to confound the things which are mighty;
>
> And base things of the world, and things which are despised, hath God chosen, yea, and things which are not, to bring to nought things that are:
>
> That no flesh should glory in his presence.
>
> But of him are ye in Christ Jesus, who of God is made unto us wisdom, and righteousness, and sanctification, and redemption:
>
> That, according as it is written, He that glorieth, let him glory in the Lord. (vv. 27–31)

There is glory in being foolish and simple. In caring about a few simple truths of God, and little about the passing attractions of this world. God reveals to them the secrets of the spirit, which he has hidden from the rest. By lifting up the poor and the simple, he ultimately shows his own power and goodness, riches which would not be on display by simply letting the powerful stomp on people, or the educated telling people what to think, and then assume they will have eternal life doing it. In the end lifting up the foolish honors God. It also demands our dependency on him, and not on ourselves, a dependency which finally brings uplifting and honor to the humble. A simple Christian with a Bible has more wisdom than the scholar. A Christian in a wooden hut more riches than a movie star.

> Let no man deceive himself. If any man among you seemeth to be wise in this world, let him become a fool, that he may be wise.
>
> For the wisdom of this world is foolishness with God. For it is written, He taketh the wise in their own craftiness.
>
> And again, The Lord knoweth the thoughts of the wise, that they are vain. (1 Cor 3:18–20)

If you can imagine making yourself a fool, it doesn't have to mean being stupid. A fool for Christ, however, would not be wise about this world. He would be intentionally not attached to it, and not enchanted by its attractions. He would have faith, and work, and service to proclaim, but little to speak of the latest movies, popular singers, or diet fads. He couldn't chant with the latest songs. His thought for others is how he may love them, not how he may use them. It would not be a life that stood out to others, or seemed fashionable, or outwardly exciting. He would not sparkle the eyes of many people with a life of hard work and prayer. Those who seek popularity and honor from men would not desire to be like him, and would find he's not one of their own. He has made himself a fool, and doing so retained wisdom from God. It may seem at times to be turning away from much usefulness and pleasure in the world, but really it is turning away from a trap of death. It takes the simple man away from the snares of the world's vain attractions, from its truly godless philosophies, and from many useless paths which would waste his energy much needed for serving God. He wholeheartedly rejects what the world calls wisdom.

The simplicity, and foolishness of the gospel to the world is something I can clearly remember encountering as I learned to share my faith as a new believer. I was someone used to viewing life philosophically or romantically, and to forging answers that fit my way of thinking and my personal philosophy. It took some exercise of willpower to teach myself to share such a simple truth as the gospel, which at times felt like childishness. I had to will myself to be a little child inside and to speak simply, even when its simplicity embarrassed me. Whenever my predilection was to let my mind explain things, I had to stick to what Scripture says instead. I just had to say what it said. Long before I spent much time with the passages we review here, the reality they express was evident in my life. It dropped down on me right after I came to faith. I had to throw out the wisdom of the world, with which I was saturated, and trust in God's word, even when it didn't sound very sophisticated. It was the truth of God and all I had to do was represent it to the hearer. So I taught myself to say such foolishness as—we are lost in sin, and Jesus Christ is the only way to peace with God. To say—this man died for your sins and rose from the grave, and if you trust in him, you will have eternal life. It sounds childish to say this ancient Jewish teacher is God in the flesh, but that is what I learned to say.

That is the power of God, my friends. The simplicity of that, and the apparent impossibility of that are a part of its power. They are also a part of the reason so many are blinded to it, including the devil, who must have thought he had the Son of God in a real bind. How could a murdered man nailed to a piece of wood really be truly God? How could a bloody and beaten man defeat his enemies? This is the last thing that sophisticated man would have devised, so perhaps that is why it is the foolishness that God chose. Every Christian learning to live as a Christian will face this challenge too. The wise man will have to shut his mouth. He will have to give up trying to offer smart and educated solutions to our fallen nature. He will learn to speak as a child speaks. He will learn that his own logic goes out the window, and he has to trust in God to reveal how salvation works. It is humbling, and it takes some courage to speak such simple words the first time, especially if you come from a life of worldliness, and no small amount of intellectual pride, as I did.

The Orthodox Church itself has an interesting doctrine on becoming a fool for Christ's sake. It is based on this passage and several similar ones. I don't know if I accept it entirely, but in their understanding, they believe some people, perhaps even slightly off in the head, are used by God through doing the most absurd acts. In doing so they speak to the church spiritually and also assure they will be scorned and despised, rather than given credit for their good deeds.[1] Several of their revered figures, and even those titled saints, managed to reveal truth through what most of us would call absurd, if not vulgar behavior. For example, Blessed John of Moscow wore heavy chains and a large metal cap. In freezing weather, he would go about nearly naked.[2] Simeon the Holy Fool

---

1. Cook, "Holy Fools." While being a holy fool is generally a religious discipline with a purpose, various articles and Orthodox Christians I have spoken to suggest a handful in history may have been legitimately mentally ill.

2. OCA, "Blessed John of Moscow the Fool-For-Christ."

once dragged a dead dog into the city, and extinguished all the lights in the church.[3] Now I don't see that the context of Paul's words in First Corinthians relate to truly absurd behavior such as this. It's clear they speak of rejecting worldly wisdom for the simple truth of the cross. However, there is a point to be made that God can use men who are apparently half mad to reveal what never would have been revealed by the more serious and balanced people. Their absurdity breaks through the silence of normal communication. It breaks through to the soul in a way that routine prayer and even beautiful liturgy never could. The people who teach this doctrine are generally serious and sound men themselves, but they are open that true foolishness, if coming from a child of God, has something to teach us. Even the absurd have more say in the church than those who only have human smarts.

A GOD OF LOVE APPOINTS EVIL

The book of Job teaches us several things boldly and clearly. It teaches that God is Lord over all, including our suffering. It teaches us that we cannot judge God. It teaches us that he is good, even when we are suffering without apparent cause. Our suffering is for a reason, even when we do not see it. Job knew his doubts and accusations against Yahweh were something to repent, and he was blessed when he repented. Let God work his purposes and continue to trust him.

Many people have trouble in their hearts and mind with that first point—God is Lord over suffering. It causes them to think it is impossible for a God of love to bring about such suffering, since clearly love does not wish to do harm to another. Likewise, when it relates to moral evil, they find it impossible that a God of love could not only appoint such evil to occur, but that he would necessarily impede man's free will. God must merely sit back and allow it to happen, and then later work something good with the end result.

I think it is best to go to Scripture and see what it teaches, rather than rely on our preconceptions or preferences in how God ought to work. I think we find with Scripture that several things are clear, even if they are counter-intuitive to many of us. Firstly, God indeed appoints acts of evil to occur, without committing sin himself. Number two, God holds those men who commit evil responsible and he judges them, even if he decreed

---

3. Forcén and Forcén, "Symeon the Holy Fool," 94.

that act to occur. They made a choice and they will be judged for it. God also freely chooses his own children whom he will bring into paradise forever, without violating their choices, which they make for good or evil. One cannot go much further than that in describing God's lordship over man's actions and over evil without getting into really hypothetical areas. We can speak in theory about how God's sovereignty and man's liberty interact, but not much of it should be treated as doctrine, since it is purely speculative. According to Scripture Yahweh can appoint acts of evil to occur, and Yahweh also judges man for his evil decisions. Both are true. How they fit together is not for us to understand completely.

Let's look first about passages on God's rulership of the universe and his power over all things. Then we will go over a number of passages which show his lordship over evil, both moral and natural evil. We will see clearly that Yahweh is Lord over all according to Scripture. Man cannot thwart God's aims by making bad decisions. God rules all while being pure love, pure light, and containing no darkness in him. He is eternal, good, and all powerful.

> Behold, the heaven and the heaven of heavens is the LORD'S thy God, the earth also, with all that therein is. (Deut 10:14)
>
> The LORD hath prepared his throne in the heavens; and his kingdom ruleth over all. (Ps 103:19)
>
> Yours, O LORD, *is* the greatness,
>
> The power and the glory,
>
> The victory and the majesty;
>
> For all *that is* in heaven and in earth *is Yours*;
>
> Yours *is* the kingdom, O LORD,
>
> And You are exalted as head over all.
>
> Thine, O LORD, is the greatness, and the power, and the glory, and the victory, and the majesty: for all that is in the heaven and in the earth is thine; thine is the kingdom, O LORD, and thou art exalted as head above all.
>
> Both riches and honour come of thee, and thou reignest over all; and in thine hand is power and might; and in thine hand it is to make great, and to give strength unto all. (1 Chr 29:11-12)
>
> He will keep the feet of his saints, and the wicked shall be silent in darkness; for by strength shall no man prevail.
>
> The adversaries of the LORD shall be broken to pieces; out of heaven shall he thunder upon them: the LORD shall judge the

ends of the earth; and he shall give strength unto his king, and exalt the horn of his anointed. (1 Sam 2:9-10)

These several passages—and there are many more like them—show that Yahweh is creator of all, and rightfully owns all. Everything in creation is his possession. The passages extol his power and show he is due all honor. The blessings and honor we receive as men only derive from Yahweh, who is our head. Our own honor would mean nothing without him. It shows his just protection of his saints, and also that he justly judges the wicked. Yahweh will break them into pieces, a picture of their utter destruction. The kings of the earth must draw their strength from him or they have no strength at all. No man can win by his own strength, since our strength is nothing compared to God. Yahweh is ruler and also the source of those more limited powers we as men have. Clearly any man who rose up against the Lord would be destroyed, even if Yahweh gives him a few moments to glory in himself. The rebel will be cast into darkness. That is the awesome might and rightful authority God has.

Now I'd like to look at a number of other passages that show God's freedom and power are limitless. That includes over our life history, and over human debility:

> And Moses said unto the LORD, O my Lord, I am not eloquent, neither heretofore, nor since thou hast spoken unto thy servant: but I am slow of speech, and of a slow tongue.
>
> And the LORD said unto him, *Who hath made man's mouth? or who maketh the dumb, or deaf, or the seeing, or the blind?* have not I the LORD?
>
> Now therefore go, and I will be with thy mouth, and teach thee what thou shalt say. (Exod 4:10-12)
>
> Ah Lord GOD! behold, thou hast made the heaven and the earth by thy great power and stretched out arm, and *there is nothing too hard for thee:* (Jer 32:17)
>
> For I know that the LORD is great, and that our Lord is above all gods.
>
> *Whatsoever the LORD pleased, that did he* in heaven, and in earth, in the seas, and all deep places. (Ps 135:5-6)
>
> Not unto us, O LORD, not unto us, but unto thy name give glory, for thy mercy, and for thy truth's sake.
>
> Wherefore should the heathen say, Where is now their God?

> *But our God is in the heavens: he hath done whatsoever he hath pleased.*
>
> Their idols are silver and gold, the work of men's hands.
>
> They have mouths, but they speak not: eyes have they, but they see not:
>
> They have ears, but they hear not: noses have they, but they smell not:
>
> They have hands, but they handle not: feet have they, but they walk not: neither speak they through their throat.
>
> They that make them are like unto them; so is every one that trusteth in them.
>
> O Israel, trust thou in the LORD: he is their help and their shield. (Ps 115:1–9)
>
> My substance was not hid from thee, when I was made in secret, and curiously wrought in the lowest parts of the earth.
>
> Thine eyes did see my substance, yet being unperfect; and *in thy book all my members were written, which in continuance were fashioned, when as yet there was none of them.* (Ps 139:15–16)
>
> For we are his workmanship, created in Christ Jesus unto good works, *which God hath before ordained that we should walk in them.* (Eph 2:10)
>
> And hath made of one blood all nations of men for to dwell on all the face of the earth, and *hath determined the times before appointed, and the bounds of their habitation;*
>
> That they should seek the Lord, if haply they might feel after him, and find him, though he be not far from every one of us: (Acts 17:26–27)

A few things are essential to see here. First, is that God's freedom is unlimited. Yahweh does whatever he pleases. That is in contrast to our own freedom, which is limited by God's law, by our human limitations, and by the decrees of God over our lives. God is perfectly free. There is no greater God or power than he that might stop him. These passages among others shatter in an instant the notion that Yahweh is merely looking at man's actions, shaking his head in disbelief, and then trying to figure out a way to make the best of the end results of our bad behavior. That's not the God revealed in the Bible. Yahweh is completely free and his power can do anything.

Another essential point is that Yahweh is Lord over things we consider flaws in creation. Even though we know that suffering and illness came along with the fall of man, Yahweh says that he makes the mute, the deaf, and the blind. So regardless of the effects of the fall, God is still Lord over creation, and has decided on whether we will have a disability or not, many of which come to us in the womb. As one man has speech according to God's will, another man is mute according to God's will. As one man is born seeing, another is born blind. Yahweh made each one of them, and has a purpose in it. We regard those ailments of the body in the category of natural evil, but Yahweh does no wrong when he appoints us to be born in that state. His omniscience and his omnipotence are behind whatever state you are in. If you are suffering then, simply ask God why. There is a reason for it.

We also see in these passages on God's power that he is Lord over our life history and over human history. Before we were born the days of our life were prepared for us. Our life's journey was given shape and a purpose by the Creator. Before the saints were born again, their good deeds were planned out by God, along with how they will serve his perfect kingdom. The dwelling places of entire nations and people groups have been determined. God shaped human history just as he shaped the geography of the earth itself. He gave boundaries to the seas with the continents, and he gave boundaries to tribes, kingdoms, and empires of the earth. He even chose their times, and when they would arise in human history, each of them fitting into his plan for us and for human redemption. Our choices did not prevent him from having that authority or power. Being Lord over all he established our days, our deeds, our national boundaries. There is no mention at all of human choice getting in his way.

Now let's look at a number of passages that reveal God's sovereignty over human behavior, the human heart, and reveal the unstoppable nature of his decrees. I know I said let's "look at" them, but I could better say, let's "dwell in awe" on them. Let us marvel:

> Daniel answered and said, Blessed be the name of God for ever and ever: for wisdom and might are his:
>
> And he changeth the times and the seasons: *he removeth kings, and setteth up kings*: he giveth wisdom unto the wise, and knowledge to them that know understanding:

He revealeth the deep and secret things: he knoweth what is in the darkness, and the light dwelleth with him. (Dan 2:20–22)

Let his heart be changed from man's, and let a beast's heart be given unto him; and let seven times pass over him.

This matter is by the decree of the watchers, and the demand by the word of the holy ones: to the intent that the living may know that *the most High ruleth in the kingdom of men*, and giveth it to whomsoever he will, and setteth up over it the basest of men. (Dan 4:16–17)

And at the end of the days I Nebuchadnezzar lifted up mine eyes unto heaven, and mine understanding returned unto me, and I blessed the most High, and I praised and honoured him that liveth for ever, whose dominion is an everlasting dominion, and his kingdom is from generation to generation:

And all the inhabitants of the earth are reputed as nothing: and *he doeth according to his will in the army of heaven, and among the inhabitants of the earth: and none can stay his hand, or say unto him, What doest thou?*

At the same time my reason returned unto me; and for the glory of my kingdom, mine honour and brightness returned unto me; and my counsellors and my lords sought unto me; and I was established in my kingdom, and excellent majesty was added unto me.

Now I Nebuchadnezzar praise and extol and honour the King of heaven, all whose works are truth, and his ways judgment: and those that walk in pride he is able to abase. (Dan 4:34–37)

All of these passages are from the book of Daniel, who prophesied in Babylon and Persia during the captivity. Two relate to how the Babylonian king was afflicted with madness, and thought he was a beast. He went to live like a beast in the fields until God ended his madness and he was restored to the throne. He rightfully honored the Most High when his affliction was ended. The final portion relates the king's prayer about God after he had been cured. We see from these scriptures that Yahweh is God over political kingdoms. He chooses leaders and places them over whom he desires. There is nothing there to say that Yahweh may only place a benevolent king over a kingdom, but it teaches simply that Yahweh rules nations. That will naturally include when there is a wicked king.

We also see that Yahweh can change the heart of a man, here to the point the man thinks he is a beast, and lives in the wild like a beast. That very idea threatens many of our notions of ourselves and our autonomy, but clearly it is God here who is in charge of the heart and not us. God is free to change our heart, and in this case he does so in an apparent judgment, and to bring the king to glorify God in the future. Even our heart is not a barrier to God doing his will, nor is our alleged freewill. If God wills us to go mad, we will go mad, and if he wills to come back to sanity, we come back to sanity. Finally, the prayer of the grateful Nebuchadnezzar is even more amazing, stating with clarity that Yahweh does according to his will (not according to ours), and that not one of his creations can stop him from doing what he wills, in heaven or on earth. None can judge him either. We do not see a picture in these passages of Yahweh passively changing his will depending on man's actions. Rather, we see God ordaining things to come to pass. He changes men's hearts. He makes a king mad, and he heals that king. Yahweh does what he wills as Lord of creation because he is the Lord of creation. It is of the nature of God that he is absolutely sovereign, and nothing you do can restrain his will.

Remember, Nebuchadnezzar, that great pagan king, who is like a vapor in the hand of God, does not respond to God's chastisement by saying, "I would never worship a God like that!" He doesn't say, "What kind of a God would turn a man into a cow and have him eating grass in the field. *Not* a God of love, I'll say!" Nor does the king say, "God has no right to change my heart, because my thoughts are my own and I am fully independent, being a king with free will! I am no robot." No, not by any means. Rather, the pagan, who is far wiser than many Christians today and than many atheists, immediately glorifies Yahweh, and praises God's majesty, might, and goodness. He wants the name of this God to be known throughout his kingdom. This is the true God. Yahweh has shown the king who is in command, and the king has been humbled and learned his lesson. His desire is to praise Yahweh, not scorn him for causing his madness, nor deny that God has the right to do that. He is humble. He is wise. He praises God.

> The king's heart is in the hand of the LORD, as the rivers of water: *he turneth it whithersoever he will.*
>
> Every way of a man is right in his own eyes: but the LORD pondereth the hearts.
>
> (Prov 21:1–2)
>
> There are many devices in a man's heart; nevertheless the counsel of the LORD, *that shall stand.* (Prov 19:21)

> The lot is cast into the lap; but the whole disposing thereof is of the LORD. (Prov 16:33)
>
> O LORD, I know that the way of man is not in himself: it is not in man that walketh to direct his steps.
>
> O LORD, correct me, but with judgment; not in thine anger, lest thou bring me to nothing. (Jer 10:23–24)

Here are four passages from Scripture on God's control over our actions. Indeed, most startlingly, God even can turn our hearts, one way or another. Even Thomas Aquinas, in dealing with Yahweh turning the hearts of kings, does not deny that God turns their hearts, but simply says that God doesn't accomplish this by doing violence to their will.[4] Taken at face value, the word of God teaches that Yahweh decides the direction the heart of the king will go. We need to let the words speak for themselves, despite the threat they pose to our notions of autonomy. The other passages reveal God's order and plan for our lives, laying our path, placing his plan above our own. It is his decision which chooses our direction and our steps. We may make decisions on a certain level, but the final sovereign choice is God's. As I've heard some preachers say—we do have a will, but when our will conflicts with God's will, God's will wins. Who but a God who matches the description of Scripture could do this? Who but a God who makes all things, who owns all things, who fashions our hearts, who can make us seeing or blind, who decides the times and the borders of nations, who brings down empires, who dwells in the heavens and does just what he pleases? *This* is the God who can decide our steps, and he has rightful rulership over all.

Perhaps the most stunning passages revealing Yahweh's power are from Isaiah. We'll start with a few that show the immutability of God's will, and go on later to look at a few which show his rulership over evil. Just as Isaiah reveals that Yahweh is one and there is no other, the prophet also reveals that that God is thwarted by no man, and is not passively responding to the decisions of man. He makes his plan and it will come to pass. His will surpasses man's will.

> The LORD of hosts hath sworn, saying, *Surely as I have thought, so shall it come to pass; and as I have purposed, so shall it stand*:
>
> That I will break the Assyrian in my land, and upon my mountains tread him under foot: then shall his yoke depart from off them, and his burden depart from off their shoulders.

---

4. Aquinas, *Summa Theologica*, 1a2ae, Q6, Art. 4, in Pegis, *Introduction*, 486–87.

> This is the purpose that is purposed upon the whole earth: and this is the hand that is stretched out upon all the nations.
>
> *For the LORD of hosts hath purposed, and who shall disannul it? and his hand is stretched out, and who shall turn it back?* (Isa 14:24–27)

These words from Isaiah themselves summarize the nature of Yahweh's rule and his power. When he plans to do something, that event will come to pass. There is no man and no nation that will stop it from coming to pass. God's will trumps man's will. Yahweh describes his purpose in bringing down the Assyrian empire, which he had also used to punish Israel, through his very same unbreakable will. Now that unbreakable will is going to bring down the same nation he used as his instrument, and nothing can stop that from coming to pass. Who will annul it? Who will turn it back? Those are questions that could be made as statements: No one will annul it. No one will turn it back. That is the nature of God's rule of creation.

> Have ye not known? have ye not heard? hath it not been told you from the beginning? have ye not understood from the foundations of the earth?
>
> It is he that sitteth upon the circle of the earth, *and the inhabitants thereof are as grasshoppers*; that stretcheth out the heavens as a curtain, and spreadeth them out as a tent to dwell in:
>
> *That bringeth the princes to nothing; he maketh the judges of the earth as vanity.*
>
> Yea, they shall not be planted; yea, they shall not be sown: yea, their stock shall not take root in the earth: and *he shall also blow upon them, and they shall wither*, and the whirlwind shall take them away as stubble.
>
> To whom then will ye liken me, or shall I be equal? saith the Holy One.
>
> Lift up your eyes on high, and behold who hath created these things, *that bringeth out their host by number: he calleth them all by names* by the greatness of his might, for that he is strong in power; *not one faileth*.
>
> Why sayest thou, O Jacob, and speakest, O Israel, My way is hid from the LORD, and my judgment is passed over from my God?
>
> Hast thou not known? hast thou not heard, that the everlasting God, the LORD, the Creator of the ends of the earth, *fainteth not, neither is weary*? there is no searching of his understanding.

> He giveth power to the faint; and to them that have no might he increaseth strength.
>
> Even the youths shall faint and be weary, and the young men shall utterly fall:
>
> But they that wait upon the LORD shall renew their strength; they shall mount up with wings as eagles; they shall run, and not be weary; and they shall walk, and not faint. (Isa 40:21–31)

Here Isaiah again reveals God's might, and his greatness above his creation. We cannot even begin to grasp the knowledge that he has. That is greatness which his people Israel can know will bring justice for their sin, and that also is unstoppable in delivering them from their suffering when they repent, and in establishing his messianic kingdom. That is a God you can trust in *all* of those things, because he is the God we have known through Scripture from the beginning; the God who made the heavens and the earth, and sits above all creation. Not only does the prophet show Yahweh's ownership and power over creation, but he again shows that the most powerful men on earth are "nothing" and are "vanity" before the power and authority of Yahweh. He could make them die in an instant when he desires. How strange that some think God incapable of doing anything when man does not act according to plan. Yahweh himself is the one to make the plan, and his plan cannot be thwarted by our choices.

This passage also shows the intricate detail of Yahweh's rule of creation. He numbers the countless creatures in his creation, and not one is missing. No amount of error or sin on the creation's part changes this. Yahweh ordains the number of his creatures and that is the number he arrives at. This truth also hints at what is revealed elsewhere—God's choosing of his people, his elect. In a similar passage, we see that God has chosen his special people from the beginning, and they are his, and he will lose not a single one (John 6:37). If he has called out a billion, that is how many will be with Yahweh in his kingdom. If he has called out ten times that, so too that is the number who will come to him in faith and dwell with him forever. God chooses his people and their exact number will never change.

> Remember the former things of old: for I am God, and there is none else; I am God, and there is none like me,

> *Declaring the end from the beginning,* and from ancient times the things that are not yet done, saying, *My counsel shall stand, and I will do all my pleasure:*
>
> Calling a ravenous bird from the east, the man that executeth my counsel from a far country: *yea, I have spoken it, I will also bring it to pass; I have purposed it, I will also do it.*
>
> Hearken unto me, ye stouthearted, that are far from righteousness:
>
> I bring near my righteousness; it shall not be far off, and my salvation shall not tarry: and I will place salvation in Zion for Israel my glory. (Isa 46:9–13)

This portion, like others, reveals that God's decision and plan are not changeable by man. His plan will come to pass. It even calls the people "stouthearted" (v. 12), meaning here obstinate or stubborn-hearted. This reveals that our own poor choices or poor character will not change his plan, or prevent it from occurring. It is the belief of some that God may purpose an act, but he needs our permission or cooperation to also do it. Yet these words of the Lord say God purposes it and he *will* bring it to pass. It's not a maybe. The passage also points like several other scriptures to God's foretelling of events in the future. He can speak the future before it happens. He is not merely looking into the future and responding to what he sees there, but actually deciding the future from the start. It is very interesting, and truly wonderful, that a book that extols the oneness of Yahweh at the same time extols his incredible power over all things. It seems just as there is no real competition from other gods, so there is no competition from any man on earth. The fact that Yahweh is one goes hand in hand with the fact that Yahweh is all powerful, and thwarted by no one. This is the God who has been revealed from Genesis, and who is revealed through Revelation: Creator, Ruler, Judge, Deliverer. You can trust in him because there is no other.

> Ye are my witnesses, saith the LORD, and my servant whom I have chosen: that ye may know and believe me, and understand that I am he: before me there was no God formed, neither shall there be after me.
>
> I, even I, am the LORD; and beside me there is no saviour.
>
> I have declared, and have saved, and I have shewed, when there was no strange god among you: therefore ye are my witnesses, saith the LORD, that I am God.

> Yea, before the day was I am he; and *there is none that can deliver out of my hand: I will work, and who shall let it?* (Isa 43:10–13)

This passage is similar to some of the previous. I just want to note, I don't know how Isaiah does any less to refute the doctrine of man's free will than he does to refute the doctrine of Mormonism, which is polytheistic. Just as I would cite for the Mormon, that God says "before me there was no God formed, neither shall there be after me" (v. 10), I would also cite for the libertarian, "*there is* none that can deliver out of my hand; I will work, and who shall let it [reverse it]?" (v. 13). They are both equally clear and strong in their meaning. There is only one God. No one can reverse his decision. God is one. God's will trumps yours. If anything, there are more verses from this prophet about God's sovereignty than there are about God's oneness, to the point it truly takes importing foreign ideas to avoid what is obviously being taught.

> Thus saith the LORD the King of Israel, and his redeemer the LORD of hosts; I am the first, and I am the last; and beside me there is no God.
>
> And *who, as I, shall call, and shall declare it*, and set it in order for me, *since I appointed the ancient people? and the things that are coming, and shall come, let them shew unto them.*
>
> Fear ye not, neither be afraid: *have not I told thee from that time, and have declared it?* ye are even my witnesses. Is there a God beside me? yea, there is no God; I know not any. (Isa 44:6–8)

Isaiah 44 offers a challenge to the false gods. That challenge is—who can proclaim the future like I can? Show that you are really a god by making the future happen as you proclaim it. The challenge reminds me of Elijah's challenge to the pagan prophets, to bring fire down from heaven. As they dance around and call out to their gods, the prophet mocks them, and suggests maybe their gods are too busy elsewhere to answer (1 Ki 18:22–27). They are out on a journey, just as human beings might be. Then he prays to the true God over all, and fire comes down from heaven, right upon the altar, and all of the people fall on their faces and worship Yahweh (vv. 36–39). Similarly, I see a mocking tone in this passage from Isaiah. How absurd it is for false prophets to claim their gods can do what Yahweh does. How worthy of ridicule. How vain it is to think a man or a spirit could speak the future into existence. He follows with a reminder of their blindness, saying, "They that make a graven image are all of them vanity; and their delectable things shall not profit; and they are their own witnesses; *they see not, nor know; that they may be ashamed*" (v. 9). It is Yahweh who has authority to declare what will come to pass, and he does, so we can trust in it. Just as no false god can turn his hand, no man can turn his hand either. His decrees will come to pass regardless of our decisions. God is in command.

There is nothing in these verses about Yahweh basing his declaration of the future on man's foreknown decisions. There is nothing to show Yahweh merely responding to man's poor choices and then trying to fix things up afterward. Rather the Almighty autonomously and authoritatively declares the future before it comes to pass. Anything different would need to be added in from outside. Yahweh is not responding to man when he proclaims future events. He is acting on his will and has all authority to do so, being God.

> For my thoughts are not your thoughts, neither are your ways my ways, saith the LORD.
>
> *For as the heavens are higher than the earth, so are my ways higher than your ways, and my thoughts than your thoughts.*
>
> For as the rain cometh down, and the snow from heaven, and returneth not thither, but watereth the earth, and maketh it bring forth and bud, that it may give seed to the sower, and bread to the eater:
>
> So shall my word be that goeth forth out of my mouth: *it shall not return unto me void, but it shall accomplish that which I please, and it shall prosper in the thing whereto I sent it*. (Isa 55:8–11)

The opening lines of this section perhaps more than the lines about God's sovereignty address some of the problems that men have accepting that Yahweh rules over suffering and sin. How so? It teaches how far beyond us are God's thoughts and ways. If we try to imagine a human being ruling over suffering and sin, while still being good, it's very difficult to impossible. But we need to approach this, as I've pointed out already, by recognizing God as God, as the source of all things, even as the source of the value measurements by which we call something evil, and containing what is to us mystery. We do not understand all the ways of Yahweh because he is God. It is presumptuous to think we can just use our logic, however grand, to figure out his thoughts and intentions. We only need to worship, trust, and obey him. By nature of Yahweh being God, of being higher, of being all knowing, of living in eternity, we are not going to understand all he does, including how he rules over sin while being perfectly righteous. We must accept that as his creatures.

This portion also reiterates and gives us a new angle on God's power. It shows that Yahweh will accomplish his will, as do the other passages, and also that his word will do what he sent his word out to do. In the local context, that is the historical restoration of his people Israel. In its broader messianic meaning, it includes the gathering of his saints in Christ and the calling together of his elect. No amount of poor human decisions will stop the Almighty from bringing his people from death to life, or from establishing his eternal kingdom. This is just as no disobedience from national Israel, and there was abundant disobedience, was able to stop him from bringing them into the land of promise, restoring the kingdom after the captivity, and bringing forth Messiah from their womb. Yahweh's decision supersedes all human bad decisions. His word will return with all his children together, and no human rebellion can stop that. His word will accomplish its aim, and hit the mark.

> Let all the earth fear the LORD: let all the inhabitants of the world stand in awe of him.
>
> For he spake, and it was done; he commanded, and it stood fast.
>
> The LORD bringeth the counsel of the heathen to nought: *he maketh the devices of the people of none effect.*
>
> The counsel of the LORD standeth for ever, the thoughts of his heart to all generations.
>
> ... The LORD looketh from heaven; he beholdeth all the sons of men.
>
> From the place of his habitation he looketh upon all the inhabitants of the earth.
>
> *He fashioneth their hearts alike*; he considereth all their works. (Ps 33:8–11, 13–15)

Psalm 33 extols God's might in creation, and goes on to give us great revelation about God's will. It specifically places God's will in contrast with man's will, and like other passages shows which comes out on top. Yahweh's word overrules any plans or decisions entire nations make. Yahweh is not passively sitting in heaven shaking his head at human behavior, but can with his power change the course of nations. His counsel and plans are forever. Human behavior does not change his plans. Not only that, but this psalm, like several other passages, shows that Yahweh crafts the very hearts of men. That is the Hebrew word *yāṣar*, which can mean to form, to fashion, or to frame. It is also used as a noun many times to mean a maker or potter. This is the same word used when Yahweh formed man out of the dust of the earth (Gen 2:7a), and when Aaron fashioned the golden calf with tools (Exod 32:4a). Yahweh fashions our hearts as a builder would a building, making all of them. Just as we are told Yahweh creates the seeing and the blind (Exod 4:11), we can also be sure that Yahweh creates hearts that are more disposed to love, and those which are more disposed to violence. He creates hearts with more natural self-control, and those more coursing with lust. He crafts all human hearts individually. We are the passive clay and the Lord is the Potter. He provides us the shape of our inner being, and he gives it the exact shape which he desires.

That revelation does not eradicate the fact that we indeed make choices, but it puts into perspective the fact that Yahweh is not merely reacting to our choices, but is in control of the very source of those choices. He is not merely predicting how we will react to a given situation, but is crafting the very source of our reaction. You and I are not as free as we like to imagine. Nor does this revelation eradicate that man was responsible for the fall, but rather shows God fully in control of the consequences of that act, the curse on man and creation, and how it affects every one of us. Therefore, just as there are those born blind, there are likely those born with a tendency to violence and cruelty, and none of that ever occurs apart from the will of God. Just as there are those with genetic diseases from conception, there are likely those with adulterous hearts from conception, who are more sensual and more easily led astray than others. Surely if Yahweh can make Nebuchadnezzar like a wild beast later in life, he can make us that way from birth. According to Scripture God crafts our heart, God can turn our heart as he desires, and God appoints our days. He is ruler over all.

> And said, O LORD God of our fathers, art not thou God in heaven? and rulest not thou over all the kingdoms of the heathen? and in thine hand is there not power and might, *so that none is able to withstand thee?* (2 Chr 20:6)
>
> And command them to say unto their masters, Thus saith the LORD of hosts, the God of Israel; Thus shall ye say unto your masters;
>
> I have made the earth, the man and the beast that are upon the ground, by my great power and by my outstretched arm, *and have given it unto whom it seemed meet unto me.*

> And now have I given all these lands into the hand of Nebuchadnezzar the king of Babylon, my servant; and the beasts of the field have I given him also to serve him.
>
> And all nations shall serve him, and his son, and his son's son, until the very time of his land come: and then many nations and great kings shall serve themselves of him. (Jer 27:4–7)
>
> Are not two sparrows sold for a farthing? and *one of them shall not fall on the ground without your Father*.
>
> But the very hairs of your head are all numbered.
>
> Fear ye not therefore, ye are of more value than many sparrows. (Matt 10:29–31)

These first two passages speak of God's unstoppable power, specifically over kingdoms of the earth. Yahweh chooses kings. He chooses kingdoms. He puts many others under their authority. Because Yahweh is the ultimate authority, he dishes out authority on earth to whom it pleases. In many Old Testament passages like these it refers to nations and empires. More broadly, it speaks of all authority systems, be it parents, husbands, or masters. God has infinite unbreakable power, so he bestows limited earthly power to those under him. As people under authority, we must recognize that God wills us to obey them. To obey that authority can be likened to obeying God. Those kings may seem great to us on earth, but none can withstand the one who gave them power in the first place. On a smaller note, I find it interesting that Yahweh here says that even the "beasts" would serve Nebuchadnezzar (Jer 27:6), when he would also make Nebuchadnezzar like a beast himself, and then later restore him as a king who praised Yahweh. The king knows he is little more than a small creature in the hand of Yahweh, and now he rules over all those small creatures.

The fact that Yahweh does as he sees fit does not sit well with many people. They believe that would be purely arbitrary, and do not like a world in which God rules over all according to what he desires. Nor would many accept the simple statement than no one is able to withstand Yahweh, because they think people are stubbornly withstanding him all the time, and frustrating his plans. Any God who makes his will come about, and who cannot be stopped, is an affront to the way they view the universe, and in their minds is labeled a cruel dictator. They don't like being so humbled, and put in the passenger seat. Yet to rule as he desires, and to bring about his plan unstoppably is exactly what the Bible teaches

Yahweh is able to do, and actually does. He does so as a God of love, out of love, and for the good of all creation.

One of the more interesting passages relating to God's rule over the universe is this last one from Matthew, alongside a similar passage from Luke. In giving encouragement to the disciples, and letting them know God will take care of them in their journey, Jesus compares them to two sparrows. Those sparrows are very small, and don't have much value to us, but God is concerned with them very much. In fact, he is concerned with them to the point not even the sparrow could die apart from his will. If this is the case, the logic concludes, God is even *more* concerned with your life. Nothing in it will happen apart from his will. He will provide for all your needs. There is no need to fear loss or persecution. God is in control.

This teaching alone shows God's comprehensive mastery over all that occurs in the cosmos. The physical world, and more so the human world, is known and overseen by our Creator. This passage and others also make it impossible to portray God's control as rather laissez-faire much of the time, with God only jumping in to help us in our lives here and there. Rather, God is in control of the details. God is in control of sparrows (which we generally don't even see affecting our lives). God is in control of death. Not only that, but if you consider that God decides when a little bird will die, he also must be in control of the countless facts, and the countless forces, over time, that led to a single bird's death. Whether it was age, or the temperature, or illness, or a predator, God was in control of that cause of death too, and all the forces which affected that cause of death, and in doing so was in control of that little bird which fell to the ground. Its life from start to finish, for the death to occur at the moment God wills, must be guided by God.

Once you see this, look even more intently at God's mastery over man's life, and his choosing of the day that we die. How could God merely jump in to choose a day of death, but not be in control of all the rest? If you consider the trillions of physical occurrences and human interactions that had to occur a certain way for a man's life to follow God's chosen path, and for his death to arrive according to God's will, the mastery of the Almighty over *all* things is clearly present. Nothing occurs ever apart from the will of God. The same point can be seen powerfully if we look at the fulfillment of prophecy. Yahweh spoke prophecies which were fulfilled hundreds of years later. For that historical fulfillment to occur, events over hundreds of years needed to be managed in perfect sync, otherwise history would have worked out differently. Just as scientists today speak of how the flapping of a butterfly's wings can interact with the atmosphere so as to create a great storm somewhere else, all those tiny events in history can interact with the world in such a way as to change major historical events many years later. God does not simply watch things occur as they happen. No, he is Master over all, and no one is able to withstand him.

God's Will in Sin and Death

> Go to now, ye that say, To day or to morrow we will go into such a city, and continue there a year, and buy and sell, and get gain:
>
> Whereas ye know not what shall be on the morrow. For what is your life? It is even a vapour, that appeareth for a little time, and then vanisheth away.
>
> For that ye ought to say, *If the Lord will, we shall live, and do this, or that.* (Jas 4:13–15)

In teaching us about prayer, James teaches us the right attitude, and even some of the right words to have on our lips. He reminds us we should not even assume the future exists for us, as we can disappear at any time, being so fragile, comparing us to a vapor, as the Psalms do (62, 39). He shows us to appreciate that God is in charge of each day of our life, and we only have one more day if God grants it. Implicit in that is that we have no more days if God does not grant it. Our life is in his hands. Each day is only from the Lord's grace and mercy. The same apostle who teaches that God is unwavering, unending light (Jas 1:17) also teaches that God can end our life at any time, still being benevolent. This truth can be hard to wrap our heads around if our thoughts are on our own feelings, and our own goals, and our sense of importance. We don't want what we have taken away. Yet when we look at God's grandeur, and the greatness of his plan for us, we realize there is no way we could resist his choice that our life must end. Our life was never deserved in the first place. It was only here for his glory. Now it is for the glory of the Lord and the goodness of his purpose that our life end. We go to serve him elsewhere. Only a blind man could accuse God of anything for the ending of our lives.

> The LORD hath made all things for himself: yea, *even the wicked for the day of evil.*

> Every one that is proud in heart is an abomination to the LORD: though hand join in hand, he shall not be unpunished. (Prov 16:4–5)
>
> Who is he that saith, and it cometh to pass, when the Lord commandeth it not?
>
> Out of the mouth of the most High *proceedeth not evil and good*?
>
> Wherefore doth a living man complain, a man for the punishment of his sins?
>
> Let us search and try our ways, and turn again to the LORD.
>
> Let us lift up our heart with our hands unto God in the heavens. (Lam 3:37–41)
>
> That they may know from the rising of the sun, and from the west, that there is none beside me. I am the LORD, and there is none else.
>
> I form the light, and create darkness: *I make peace, and create evil*: I the LORD do all these things. (Isa 45:6–7)

I'm going to group these three incredible passages together. One thing we see in each is Yahweh's command over evil. God creates even wicked men, and he does so for the day of destruction, which is the day they will be judged. He does not force them to sin, but he creates them body and soul, and will also judge each one of them. Take notice of the fact Yahweh makes the wicked man, just as he makes anything else "for himself." He makes the wicked to suit his purposes, and to glorify himself. Romans 9 affirms that God makes vessels of wrath, which have been prepared for destruction, and that as the clay of such vessels, men are in no position to charge God with unfairness (vv. 20–24). You may ask how a wicked man could glorify God, but this is clear in that the wicked both chastise and refine the righteous, and furthermore reveal God's righteousness and justice through their own final destruction. Yahweh is shown to be righteous when evil is judged. Some people take it basically to be a rule that God isn't allowed to make wicked people, even since the fall, but the God of all creation has not heard of this rule, and it appears nowhere in the Bible. It is man's preference that God does not make wicked people, because we imagine we would suffer less without them, but the choice really isn't up to us. Yahweh glorifies himself, reveals his character, and refines his saints through these godless men. God has the right and authority to create them.

The next passage from Lam 3 starts with a similar statement to some we've looked at; God is sovereign over our words and our accomplishments, our very plans in life. We are only able to make anything come to pass by the power of God. No one is able to speak apart from the will of God. In this short book mourning over Jerusalem's destruction, one which recognizes Israel's sin that brought the judgment of God, Yahweh is extolled as just, and also as merciful. Israel brought this destruction upon itself, but God will restore plentifully when the people repent. It also recognizes Yahweh as bringing about this evil, just as he brings about good. For from God's mouth proceed "evil and good" (v. 38). While various other Bible translations today give these words as something like "woe and well-being" (NKJV), if read according to the common meaning of the Hebrew words, Jeremiah is saying "evil and good proceed." *Raʿ* is the common Hebrew word for evil or wickedness. *Ṭôḇ* is the common Hebrew word for good. They are commonly set as opposites. In fact, the word *rāšāʿ* is used throughout the Hebrew Scriptures for a wicked man (Gen 18:23, Exod 23:7, Deut 25:1), and that word is rooted in the word used here, which is *raʿ*, or evil.

There are some translators that don't like writing it that way. They think it sounds too much like evil is coming from God who is good, so they use words like "woe" or "calamity" instead of evil, sometimes leaving good with its literal translation. However, read literally the verse says "evil" and "good." We ought to be able to see this moral component when we realize the mass destruction of Jerusalem, the destruction of the temple, and all sorts of other horrors were not merely a case of natural disaster. They included much moral evil. The invading nation worshipped false gods, it was proud, it slaughtered the citizens in the streets, raped women, and murdered children. So this is not comparable to natural disaster. We may call it "woe" if we want, but it's a kind of woe that includes a great deal of sin. I do not suggest that the passage teaches that God creates sin ex nihilo as a thing, but that God brings these terrible events to pass, and they include sin. He made it happen. That doesn't absolve the Babylonians for the wrong moral choices they made, but it clearly shows that God brought about this event. They proceed from God, as the verse teaches.

Then the prophet, in nearly the reverse of how many men would respond, and the reverse of how many Christians respond, says that his people have no right to complain. Who are we to complain against Yahweh when we are punished for our sins? God is perfect and God is just. He is fair when he brings a wicked pagan nation down upon us. We need not complain, but only repent. That is what the prophet teaches in this book to a suffering Israel. We ought to learn the same things today. If the righteous could learn a lesson of repentance from the scourge of the Babylonians, we can learn the *same* lesson in later times; from the attacks of 9/11, from school shootings, or from the scourges of AIDS and COVID. The modern cruelties done by groups like ISIS or Hamas are no greater than the ones done by ancient near-eastern empires, whom we know from Scripture were a scourge in the hand of Yahweh. We have just as much of a need for prophets today who will remind us of the reason for our pain and call us to repent. Many have a hard time seeing such destruction as just or fair in any way. They object to the pain. They cannot imagine it is fair to loose on a helpless population brutal soldiers to cut people to pieces, and violate the women. Yet the prophet knows this suffering is fair. We only try to imagine it is unfair when we completely minimize sin, and close our eyes to what it is. We have to pretend our own sin is very small, and of little consequence. In that light, being punished with utter destruction, and being the victim of moral evil, seems a preposterous consequence to our tiny little sin. However, sin is not tiny and little. Sin blots out the name of the Savior so others may not see it. Sin turns people from God, to seek after death and to suffer death. Sin denies the source of life, who is God, and uplifts death, man, and the devil. Sin causes pain, trauma, mistrust, illness, and death; and does so often in the lives of children. From our heart comes mass destruction and it deserves to be repaid!

Like anyone else I can read with horror a news story about a young lady, working alone in a convenience store at night, who becomes victim to a criminal, who treacherously enters the store, violates her, and kills her for his pleasure. I can sense the darkness in that act, and the fear. Yet I also know that every single day, the same pleasant and peaceful woman might choose to go down to an abortion clinic downtown, having found her child an inconvenience in life, and pay a doctor to put that child to death. That is typical in the life of the civilized. The doctor then takes cold hard "medical" instruments and rips her child to pieces for money. Then she goes about her life of pleasing herself, fornicates with another man, and in time murders another child in utero. How is it possible to view the one who has a small child killed as innocent, but find the robber, rapist, and murderer, lurking outside the gas station at night as somehow guilty? That bad man is guilty but we're all not? Nonsense. We are all guilty, and sin is no little mistake. It rips mankind out of the life and peace of

God, and brings him to utter destruction. That is what we do when we sin. That's why it is so wicked. It is truly thoughtless to claim that God is unjust. Our suffering is just indeed.

In Isa 45, the prophet again teaches in one breath about Yahweh being the *only* God and also about his incredible sovereignty. Here, as in Jeremiah's Lamentations, the prophet says that God creates "evil" (v. 7), although other translations write this as "calamity." That is the same word for evil as we see in the tree of the knowledge of good and evil (Gen 2:9), when God sees the intent of man's heart is evil continually before the flood (Gen 6:5), when the godly wife does her husband good and not evil (Prov 31:12), and when Amos teaches Israel to do good and not evil so they may live (Amos 5:14). Just as Yahweh creates all other things, Yahweh creates evil. That is a plain teaching of Scripture. Now there is not in this context any question about God creating evil as a "thing" ex nihilo, nor any question about evil being the lack of a thing, and not needing creation, as a mere absence of the good. I don't see that philosophical question there at all. Rather, it is simply proclaiming that Yahweh brings evil to pass. He brings the destroyer down on us.

Nevertheless, many people prefer the translation "calamity" to "evil." They will point out that this word parallels "peace," and the previous phrase pairs two opposites (light and darkness), so evil would not be a perfect opposite to peace. Calamity or woe would be better. However, this is poor reasoning and comes to a wrong conclusion. To begin with, calamity is not a perfect parallel to peace either, but merely falls within a range of strongly contrasting words. Moreover, a review of parallelism in the Bible will easily show that not every similar pairing is exactly the same, and not every contrasting pairing is exactly opposite. To demand an exact pairing is faulty logic. Proverbs 10:21, for example, contains pairs of what are not true opposites, nor are several other contrasts in the same chapter opposites.[5] They're simply contrasts, as are peace and evil. Therefore, I see no reason not to read verse 7 of Isa 45 normally as "create evil," as the King James Bible renders it. That's simply the meaning of the Hebrew word.

---

5. Another example (and there are many) is Prov 12:4: "A virtuous woman is a crown to her husband: but she that maketh ashamed is as rottenness in his bones." There are two pairs of contrasts in this one verse, and neither one is a true opposite. If you think there is a rule that a pair of exact opposites needs to be followed by another pair of exact opposites, go and read through passages of Hebrew poetry in Scripture and you'll see quickly there is no such rule.

Moreover, if we are going to understand the word *ra'* in context, the broader context of how God deals with Israel as well as with the pagan nations has to be understood. When those nations sin, God deals with them by bringing destruction, and that destruction, as I point out above regarding Lamentations, frequently involves moral evil. There's no avoiding that. This context locks us into an understanding of the word *ra'* much more than a glimpse at the previous line's opposites do. Therefore, if you want to read the word to mean "calamity," you fairly ought to understand it is not an earthquake or illness we're primarily talking about here. It is calamity that includes moral evil, and often being the victim of it. When Israel suffered that way, and when pagan nations suffered that way, their suffering was just.

In fact, just two verses later Yahweh is giving warnings against striving against God. He also goes on to speak of the subjugation of pagan nations who previously had persecuted Israel, but in the future restoration of Israel, will be in chains. It is also in the context of Cyrus the Persian emperor, who would subjugate many nations. Therefore, the calamity that God brings about cannot possibly be limited to natural evil.

Let's look at the following section:

> Woe unto him that striveth with his Maker! Let the potsherd strive with the potsherds of the earth. *Shall the clay say to him that fashioneth it, What makest thou? or thy work, He hath no hands?*
>
> *Woe unto him that saith unto his father, What begettest thou? or to the woman, What hast thou brought forth?*
>
> Thus saith the LORD, the Holy One of Israel, and his Maker, Ask me of things to come concerning my sons, and concerning the work of my hands command ye me.
>
> I have made the earth, and created man upon it: I, even my hands, have stretched out the heavens, and all their host have I commanded. (Isa 45:9–12)

It is interesting that this is the same passage that Paul alludes to in Rom 9, when he says, "Nay but, O man, who art thou that repliest against God? Shall the thing formed say to him that formed it, Why hast thou made me thus? Hath not the potter power over the clay, of the same lump to make one vessel unto honour, and another unto dishonour?" (vv. 20–21). There is no purpose in striving against God or accusing him of injustice. It's vain to even try. The opening of Isaiah's passage declares woe on him who fights with God in this way (Isa 45:9). We are a lump of clay. He is the potter. He can do with us as he wishes. It is further as absurd to tell the potter what he can make as it is to tell our parents whether to produce us or not. Our conception was their decision, and we did not even exist when they decided to produce us. We are passive in both these examples and our maker is the one who creates us. Yahweh likewise is free in his creation. He is free to show mercy on some of us, and he is free to judge others. He is free to make some of us his children, and not make others. We only need to repent of our own sin, and trust in the Savior God has sent for us. We can't be telling God how to govern mankind. Yahweh declares himself sovereign countless times throughout Scripture, as he does here.

Amos says essentially the same thing as other passages we've looked at. In assuring the necessity of the prophets, and the truth of their message, Yahweh says through the prophet:

> Shall a trumpet be blown in the city, and the people not be afraid? shall there be evil in a city, *and the LORD hath not done it?* (3:6)

The message is that we need to know the Lord is behind these things, and it is through the prophets that we learn in what way Yahweh is acting. The same word *ra'* (evil) is used as in other statements that God causes evil, and it fits within the context of God's judgment we see at the start of the section in verse 2: "You only have I known of all the families of the earth: therefore I will punish you for all your iniquities." As noted before, it is not a judgment by natural disaster, but primarily by evil men invading to do evil things.

Let's look at another passage about God's active control over evil men:

> Wherefore it shall come to pass, that when the Lord hath performed his whole work upon mount Zion and on Jerusalem, I will punish the fruit of the stout heart of the king of Assyria, and the glory of his high looks.
>
> For he saith, By the strength of my hand I have done it, and by my wisdom; for I am prudent: and I have removed the bounds of the people, and have robbed their treasures, and I have put down the inhabitants like a valiant man:
>
> And my hand hath found as a nest the riches of the people: and as one gathereth eggs that are left, have I gathered all the earth;

and there was none that moved the wing, or opened the mouth, or peeped.

Shall the axe boast itself *against him that heweth therewith?* or shall the saw magnify itself *against him that shaketh it?* as if the rod should shake itself *against them that lift it up,* or as if the staff should lift up itself, *as if it were no wood.*

Therefore shall the Lord, the Lord of hosts, send among his fat ones leanness; and under his glory he shall kindle a burning like the burning of a fire.

And the light of Israel shall be for a fire, and his Holy One for a flame: and it shall burn and devour his thorns and his briers in one day; (Isa 10:12–17)

Yahweh is humbling the Assyrian king who thinks he conquers by his own power and not by God's. Very much is revealed in the process. If there is any doubt that God actively moves evil rulers, this is one of several passages that soundly put that doubt to rest. Here Yahweh speaks of how he does judgment on sinful Israel, and it is through the "axe" of a pagan Assyrian king (v. 15). The passage does not present Yahweh doing justice merely by permitting the pagan king to attack Israel, but Yahweh is clearly in the active role. He is the one who lifts the axe and chops with it. He is the one who picks up the saw and saws with it. As he says previously, the nation is "the rod of mine anger," and the staff that they wield is "mine indignation" (v. 5). Clearly the pagan king would have no power to conquer without God. Yahweh is lifting up this pagan nation and this pagan king like a weapon, and bringing it down upon Israel by his own power. Yet we see in the same chapter that the pagan king is sinful. He is boastful, and uplifts himself. He is cruel, and he is arrogant. He will ultimately be destroyed by Yahweh when he no longer is useful as an instrument of judgment: "Wherefore it shall come to pass, that when the Lord hath performed his whole work upon mount Zion and on Jerusalem, I will punish the fruit of the stout heart of the king of Assyria, and the glory of his high looks" (v. 12).

Yahweh wields a sinful ruler to punish a sinful people. Then Yahweh judges that sinful ruler for his sin. There is no space here to imagine God merely responds to our actions and tries to make the most of our mistakes. No, the Almighty can wield entire nations, and decide their course, bring them to invade another, provide everything they need to do his will, and fill them with the power to act. This is completely within the authority of the God of creation. While human philosophies believe there is a contradiction here, the Bible shows no such contradiction, but merely reveals it as truth. Our response is not to accuse Yahweh of unfairness, or the claim he has no business judging a king whom he has used to do his will. Our response must only be to recognize our sin, repent, and seek to be restored. Yahweh wields the evil man to judge us, then he rightly judges the evil man.

We should remember that the Assyrians were among the cruelest of nations in this ancient world. They were known for slaughter and sadistic torture of their enemies. What the Turks were in modern history, as an empire known for getting thrills by slaughtering people, the Assyrians were before them. Israel's punishment was not merely being ruled by a foreign ruler, but the wicked actions of that foreign ruler and his soldiers. God handles that evil like a weapon, for his perfect purposes, and then he judges the evil men who do it, who deserve the punishment they have coming. That is the God of all creation. He is not a man, and is not charged with murder. He is the source of all life and truth, and can bring us to nothing in an instant. If you are horrified by the violence of it, if you are distressed by its darkness and hellish nature, you have nothing to charge God with. But be moved by that horror at human sin to get down on your knees, ask God forgiveness, and repent. He has atoned for the sins of all man at the cross, in the blood of the Lamb, and it is his blood that will bring us perfect peace and an end of all sin to come. You will live in a land with no evil if you come to Christ.

King Solomon in writing Ecclesiastes points out much the same truth as we see in the prophets and elsewhere. This shows his words are not merely motivated by a dreadful outlook or by depression, but are eternal truths from Scripture. While not using the word for evil, Solomon writes:

> Consider the work of God: for who can make that straight, *which he hath made crooked?* (Eccl 7:13)

The Hebrew word for to make crooked, ʿāvaṭ, is generally used for things which are made crooked, bent, or perverted from the good. It is used elsewhere in Scripture to mean "deal perversely" with a person. The psalmist writes in Ps 119, "for they *dealt perversely with me* without cause" (v. 78), using the same word. Amos 8:5 accuses Israel of "*falsifying* the balances," also using the same word.

Similarly, the individual Hebrew word for crooked, while not used here, is pəṭaltōl. It is frequently used to describe wrongs, such as in Deuteronomy 32:5, which tells the nation they are "a perverse and *crooked* generation." Other Hebrew words generally translated as crooked or perverse also seem appropriate to this passage from Ecclesiastes. The Hebrew ʿăqalqāl is used in Ps 125:5 to say, "As for such as turn aside unto their *crooked ways*," referring to workers of iniquity. To be crooked or to make things crooked is certainly not a good thing.

We cannot assume then that only human beings make things crooked, or pervert things. The Scripture may teach on one hand that God never perverts justice (Job 8:3), but here it teaches plainly that God makes something crooked. That is to make something perverted from the good. We can rectify these two truths by understanding that God makes it crooked through human beings, who are themselves making evil choices. He appoints it to occur through those men, just as he appointed the crucifixion to occur through men. The Almighty does so for his own purposes, which are not the same as those of evil human beings whose goals are their own.

We get a broader picture of the purpose in this if we read the following verse Solomon gives us in chapter 7:

> In the day of prosperity be joyful, but in the day of adversity consider: God also hath set the one over against the other, *to the end that man should find nothing after him*. (v. 14)

We should first notice that God "set" the day of adversity, meaning he made or produced it. This is the same Hebrew word (ʿāśâ) used in Gen 1 to say that God "made" certain things during creation week. Yahweh appointed that day to happen, as through his foreordaining power, assuring that it would happen. He did not do the evil as by his own hands, yet he is Lord over the good and the evil in our lives. We should also notice, as we do elsewhere, that the Hebrew for prosperity and adversity is ṭôḇ and raʿ respectively. That is good and evil. God appoints the day of good and the day of evil both. That day of evil isn't just the time we had a hard day at work, or when our car broke down. It's the day our children left the faith, or the day they became selfish hedonists. It's the day we were struck with cancer, or were viciously abused by other men. God appointed that day to occur.

When Solomon writes one day is "over against" the other, that word for "over against" (ʿummâ) is a word which is relational. It can be used for things that are very close together. Its usages include close by, side by side with, alongside of, and corresponding to. To be fair, ʿummâ is also translated elsewhere as opposite to. It is the same word used to describe items in the tabernacle in Exodus: "*Over against* the border shall the rings be for places of the staves to bear the table" (25:27). First Chronicles 26 describes the gatekeepers in the temple "having wards [duties] *one against* the other" (v. 12). There is a great intimacy in relationship revealed here. It seems this brings to light the relationship between the days of good and of evil which God gives us, and the way they act together in our life, one supporting the other. If we think of evil as the temporary scaffolding erected to build the cathedral, we can see that scaffolding is indeed very near and up against the cathedral it is used to build. They are in a unique and very close relationship, even though indeed the evil will be destroyed.

Why has the Holy One made parts of our life journey crooked? I believe the final line of this verse offers a significant piece of the puzzle. It is so that we will be ignorant of what will come in the future once we are gone. If everything worked according to our plan, or if we were fully capable of solving our own problems, we would know much more of the future. As it is, we do not know what will happen to our legacy, to our children, to our money and possessions, to our life's work. It may pass down rightly, or it may be perverted or destroyed. Who knows? Everything we worked for may be lost.

As I show you in great detail elsewhere, a significant biblical reason for this is so that we do not become prideful and self-reliant. If we knew what would come after, we would be far more likely to glory in ourselves and our own accomplishments. Yet as it is, with these crooked things which God has made, we must know all our accomplishments are quite small, and God can wipe them away in an instant, as you wipe away the condensation from your car's windshield in the morning. They are like the breath of the wind. They are vanity. We must know we depend only on the Holy One. Righteousness depends only on him. The kingdom depends only on him. The future of our children depends only on him. We're not the ones in control. That is one reason God makes these crooked things, and appoints these days of adversity. So that we may not know everything, or think that we do.

We can have a similar awe at God's working in the trials of the patriarch Joseph:

> Now therefore be not grieved, nor angry with yourselves, that ye sold me hither: for *God did send me before you to preserve life*.

For these two years hath the famine been in the land: and yet there are five years, in the which there shall neither be earing nor harvest.

And *God sent me before you* to preserve you a posterity in the earth, and to save your lives by a great deliverance.

So now *it was not you that sent me hither, but God*: and he hath made me a father to Pharaoh, and lord of all his house, and a ruler throughout all the land of Egypt. (Gen 45:5–8)

So shall ye say unto Joseph, Forgive, I pray thee now, the trespass of thy brethren, and their sin; *for they did unto thee evil*: and now, we pray thee, forgive the trespass of the servants of the God of thy father. And Joseph wept when they spake unto him.

And his brethren also went and fell down before his face; and they said, Behold, we be thy servants.

And Joseph said unto them, Fear not: for am I in the place of God?

But as for you, *ye thought evil against me; but God meant it unto good*, to bring to pass, as it is this day, *to save much people alive*. (Gen 50:17–20)

I find the passages about Joseph among the most powerful and moving in the Bible. Joseph is perhaps the clearest type of Christ in the Old Testament, expressing in his life what Christ would do in detail and in many ways. Joseph's final forgiveness of his brothers sheds light also on God's headship over evil events, along with God's glorious purpose for those events. The Bible reveals both in teaching and in demonstration what Yahweh accomplishes through the evil men do. This realization touches magnificently on the cross, and touches on any trial or suffering we may endure in this life as Christians.

When Joseph's brothers think he is going to punish them for the wrong they have done him—for accosting him and selling him into slavery—Joseph forgives them instead. This same forgiveness is repeated later, after their father Jacob dies, and the brothers worry that now Joseph will deliver his wrath on them. Joseph assures them of his forgiveness a second time, with nearly the same words. In doing so, he then sheds light on God's purpose in what has happened. What the brothers did for evil, Yahweh did for good—the saving of many people from the famine, which would surely have killed them. The brothers still did the evil act. Their purpose in the act was wicked, inspired by jealousy, and seeking to cause harm. God's purpose in the act was good, saving life from the famine.

The brothers did it. God did it. Both are true according to the word of God, yet God's purposing of it assured the saving of life through it.

Notice, the passage does not say that what the brothers did for evil, God merely allowed to take place and later used for good. Rather, the passage teaches that God intended the act, and he did it for the good. The word *hasab*, translated both as "thought" and "meant" in verse 20, has a meaning of plan or devise, showing that God's part in the act is as active as the brothers'. Joseph even goes so far as to say, "It was *not you* who sent me hither, but God" (45:8). He is the ultimate cause. The brothers of Joseph are guilty, and need either punishment or forgiveness for their act. God is not guilty, and needs neither. The acts the brothers did are still sinful, as jealousy is a sin, and violence is a sin, and even before the law of Moses, kidnapping an innocent person and selling him as a slave was wrong. In the law of Moses it would be punished by execution (Exod 21:16). Sin did not stop being sin just because Yahweh was behind this act. However, God's part in the act was pure, and the brothers' part in the act was impure. That difference comes down to the nature of God and his authority, as well as to the fact that as creatures we need to obey his law.

This makes little sense if Yahweh were a man. However, once we recognize Yahweh for whom he is, we understand it is natural to him to be able to wield man's evil in righteousness. We do not harbor grudges to those who hurt us, as they suspected Joseph might have, but are in wonder at God's glorious purpose in the act, at God's mercy in forgiveness, and at all the lives saved through God's sovereignty over the sin that occurred. That's a whole lot better than purposeless sin that much of the world believes in. It's even better than purposeless sin which God later uses to fix things. There is an actual purpose in the cruelty that befell us. It is not a random meaningless act, but is a scalpel in the hand of a surgeon. It deepens our wonder in God and our love for him to know this. We do not try and judge Yahweh. We marvel at him.

> And the LORD said unto Moses, When thou goest to return into Egypt, see that thou do all those wonders before Pharaoh, which I have put in thine hand: but *I will harden his heart*, that he shall not let the people go. (Exod 4:21)
>
> And *I will harden Pharaoh's heart*, and multiply my signs and my wonders in the land of Egypt. (Exod 7:3)
>
> And *I will harden Pharaoh's heart*, that he shall follow after them; and I will be honoured upon Pharaoh, and upon all his

> host; that the Egyptians may know that I am the LORD. And they did so. (Exod 14:4)
>
> And *the LORD hardened the heart of Pharaoh* king of Egypt, and he pursued after the children of Israel: and the children of Israel went out with an high hand. (Exod 14:8)
>
> For the scripture saith unto Pharaoh, Even *for this same purpose have I raised thee up, that I might shew my power in thee, and that my name might be declared throughout all the earth.*
>
> Therefore hath he mercy on whom he will have mercy, and *whom he will he hardeneth.*
>
> (Rom 9:17–18)

The hardening of Pharaoh is perhaps the most well known hardening in the Bible. It results in Pharaoh refusing to allow the people of Israel to leave and go worship in the desert, and even overcomes his previous permission of it. It causes him to turn from a good choice to a bad choice. That hardening assures that Pharaoh would choose the wicked and foolish route of prohibiting Israel to leave Egypt. Ultimately, it ensures he would chase after Israel when he finally allowed them to go, bringing about their mighty salvation in the Red Sea, and the destruction of Pharaoh's army. Yahweh saves Israel and makes them a nation through this hardening. He humbles a wicked, idolatrous, pagan nation as well. The exodus and the giving of the law at Sinai are arguably the most important events in salvation history until the incarnation and the cross. These are incredible revelations and acts of God's power. Yahweh provided for them through hardening a man's heart to do wrong. He did it through affecting his decisions. Yahweh was lord of Pharaoh's heart as he is Lord over all.

Many will point out that the long passages detailing Pharaoh's decisions include that Pharoah hardened his own heart (Exod 8:32, 9:34). It is natural to ask then, does this mean man and God were acting kind of 50–50 here? Was Yahweh not in control, but merely sharing the decision with the Pharaoh? While I believe there are a multitude of passages in Holy Scripture that would lead us to a resounding "no," the passage itself shows that Yahweh is in full command. Yahweh's hardening comes before the entire events occur, and it is also reiterated after the events occur. It contains several summary statements of the entire time period: "I will harden Pharaoh's heart" (4:21, 7:3). As a summary statement, each makes it clear any hardening or choices by Pharaoh are underneath God's decision to harden him, a fact made even clearer since Yahweh also hardened him and the Egyptians in their final decision to chase after Israel into the wilderness (14:4, 8, 17). Pharaoh made real sinful choices, but it was God's will from the beginning that came to pass. He even tells Moses the end goal that comes with the hardening, saying, "And I will harden Pharaoh's heart, and *multiply my signs and my wonders* in the land of Egypt. But Pharaoh shall not hearken unto you, *that I may lay my hand upon Egypt*, and bring forth mine armies, and my people the children of Israel, out of the land of Egypt *by great judgments*" (Exod 7:4). Yahweh's will is to judge Pharaoh and Egypt, and to glorify his name through wonders. The hardened heart of Pharaoh is simply one of his means.

We also know that Yahweh was not sharing the hardening 50–50 with Pharaoh by Apostle Paul's interpretation and application of the text in Rom 9. Paul multiple times in this chapter shows that God's will is not changed by our decisions. He teaches that God raised up Pharaoh for the very purpose of glorifying his own name when Pharaoh was destroyed. He chooses to have mercy on whom he wills, and harden whom he wills (Rom 9:17–18). Clearly, Paul is teaching that the hardening is God's decision. It is by God's will just as mercy is by his will. God can make a human vessel for the purpose of destruction if he desires (vv. 21–22). In fact, Egyptian history and the previous decades of Pharaoh's life were there only to glorify God in the exodus and at the Red Sea. Yahweh was in charge long before he hardened the leader of the kingdom. Therefore, Pharaoh's decisions were secondary, and simply fall in line with what Yahweh had willed. We know that it is God's hardening at the start, then, which simply assures Pharaoh's hardening as mentioned later. We also need to keep in mind this divine action over the heart if we begin to imagine that God is merely reacting to man's personal decisions, and trying to make the best of the mess after man has acted. We know the Almighty is sovereign over the heart, and can change the heart of kings one way or another. This really rules out God's sitting back while we make decisions that may block his will. Even our heart is in his hands. He can harden, and mercy as he wills.

The exodus may portray the most well-known example of God hardening man's heart, but there are various other clear examples in Scripture:

> But Sihon king of Heshbon would not let us pass by him: *for the LORD thy God hardened his spirit, and made his heart obstinate, that he might deliver him into thy hand, as appeareth this day.*

> And the LORD said unto me, Behold, I have begun to give Sihon and his land before thee: begin to possess, that thou mayest inherit his land. (Deut 2:30–31)

The subject of Yahweh accomplishing his purposes by hardening the heart of a man appears several times in Scripture. God's hardening apart from a specific mention of his purpose also appears several times. Here in Deut 2, Yahweh states his purpose in hardening the heart of the King of Heshbon—Yahweh intended to deliver the king and his land into the hands of Israel, and to destroy his people. Hardening the king assured the king would not allow them to pass through, and brought about the military conflict. The king was still responsible for his decision, but it was God's hand that assured that decision through his act upon the king's heart. He provided for his people Israel this way, brought forward a step in salvation history, and also judged a wicked and depraved pagan nation. Yahweh acted to assure that King Sihon refused to allow them through. The king himself acted to refuse entrance, and was guilty for his choice. You might say, in line with Joseph's words, what Sihon did for evil, God did for good. The long historical march to the cross into the land moved forward.

> Nay, my sons; for it is no good report that I hear: ye make the LORD'S people to transgress.
>
> If one man sin against another, the judge shall judge him: but if a man sin against the LORD, who shall intreat for him? *Notwithstanding they hearkened not unto the voice of their father, because the LORD would slay them.* (1 Sam 2:24–25)

This situation comes about early in the work of the young prophet Samuel. Eli the priest has let his children commit immorality and profane the sacrifices, and has done little to restrain them. When he finally gives them verbal correction, it seems the response is decided by God. Yahweh is Lord over the decision of Eli's sons when they refuse to hear the correction of their father. Plainly, they did not accept it because Yahweh had different plans for them: their own destruction. Because of their sins they would die, and the house of Eli would never produce a priest again. It was not finally the will of the sons that decided their refusal, but the will of Yahweh.

> And Absalom and all the men of Israel said, The counsel of Hushai the Archite is better than the counsel of Ahithophel. For the Lord had appointed to defeat the good counsel of

Ahithophel, to the intent that the Lord might bring evil upon Absalom. (2 Sam 17:14)

In another obvious case which subordinates human choice to God's will, Yahweh causes Absalom to listen to the counsel of David's friend Hushai, rather than the counsel of the Ahithophel, who was esteemed like a prophet (2 Sam 16:23). Absalom is seeking to kill David after David has fled into the wilderness. Ahithophel's counsel offered him a chance to catch David quickly, and Absalom could even stay at home, leaving Ahithophel to lead the battle. Hushai, who is looking for a way to save David, gives advice which takes more time to gather forces, allowing David the time to find an ideal place of battle and prepare his own men. His advice also requires Absalom lead the battle, putting his life in danger. It is Hushai's advice which Absalom chooses, and this leads to his defeat, and to his death. It is also in answer to David's earlier prayer, in which he had asked, "O LORD, I pray thee, turn the counsel of Ahithophel into foolishness" (2 Sam 15:31b). Why did Absalom choose to take the advice of a man who was a friend of David, and possibly still loyal to him? This passage gives us the answer: because it was the Lord's will. The Lord willed Absalom to ignore the counsel of Ahithophel, which from his perspective was good counsel, and listen to the counsel which would lead to his own destruction. That is because the Lord willed to bring down Absalom. Therefore, he blinded him to what would have been wise advice for him. Whatever Absalom's power of choice was, it was God who made the choice first, and God's choice came to pass. Absalom chose just as God had intended.

> And the ten horns which thou sawest upon the beast, these shall hate the whore, and shall make her desolate and naked, and shall eat her flesh, and burn her with fire.
>
> For *God hath put in their hearts to fulfil his will*, and to agree, and give their kingdom unto the beast, until the words of God shall be fulfilled.
>
> And the woman which thou sawest is that great city, which reigneth over the kings of the earth. (Rev 17:16–18)

Perhaps the most well known and terrifying enemy of Yahweh is the beast described in Revelation. The beast is a mighty kingdom and alternately a ruler which demands obedience and the worship of men, and which persecutes the saints. In this passage, we see that God controls the hearts of the kings who support the beast and do his will. God has "put in their hearts" (v. 17) to serve the beast, because in doing so they are fulfilling his purpose. God makes sure they are of one mind, and also hand over their kingdoms to the beast. One of the many things the Almighty accomplishes is that these kings persecute the harlot, who is truly deserving of punishment. As elsewhere in Scripture, Yahweh uses evil kingdoms to punish those who deserve punishment. In this case the harlot (likely Israel or Jerusalem) receives God's justice from the hands of evil men, who despite being sinners, are not acting apart from the will of God. Just as Scripture teaches elsewhere that God turns the hearts of kings, we similarly learn that God puts things into their hearts when he desires. Yahweh is also bringing about in the long run the victory of Christ and his people, as Christ will crush the beast revealing his power and bringing in his kingdom.

> Yet it pleased the LORD to bruise him; he hath put him to grief:
> (Isa 53:10a)

We will speak of pain and suffering shortly as we learn about it in the gospels, which provide the fullest understanding, and the fullest purpose of suffering in life. For now, I still wish to go over a few of the passages which show God's control over the crucifixion. This act, which some would call the evilest act to occur in history, the cruel murder of the God-man, was clearly willed and pre-decided to occur by God. Isaiah 52:13—53:12 describes much of what would occur in history, prophesying of Messiah's suffering in detail, and also provides a wealth of knowledge about the life-giving accomplishments of this act. Along the way, it gives us a plain statement of God's feelings about this evil event: It pleased God.

Not only does it tell us this act of cruel suffering and murder pleased him, but it places Yahweh as the active cause of this event. He is the one bruising the Suffering Servant. He is the one putting the Servant to grief. While that does not mean that the Jews or Pilate made no choices themselves, it clearly places Yahweh in the driver's seat, assuring that the act of injustice happens, and being pleased by its occurrence. Many men reject this notion philosophically, but it's right there in the Bible, whose truth is far greater than our mental objections. How can God be pleased by a sin? If God is perfect love, and is holy, how is this possible? This kind of question is very narrowly focused, and leaves out that Scripture itself shows the answer. God is pleased by a sin, and actually assures it comes to pass, because of what his Son accomplishes at the cross. This is what the ending of the chapter begins to reveal: The Servant justifies many and bears the sins of the people (v. 11). In short, he brings life. That is why sin pleases God. He brings about life through it.

> Him, *being delivered by the determinate counsel and foreknowledge of God*, ye have taken, and by wicked hands have crucified and slain: (Acts 2:23)
>
> For of a truth against thy holy child Jesus, whom thou hast anointed, both Herod, and Pontius Pilate, with the Gentiles, and the people of Israel, were gathered together,
>
> *For to do whatsoever thy hand and thy counsel determined before to be done.*
>
> And now, Lord, behold their threatenings: and grant unto thy servants, that with all boldness they may speak thy word,
>
> By stretching forth thine hand to heal; and that signs and wonders may be done by the name of thy holy child Jesus. (Acts 4:27–30)

Both Acts 2 and Acts 4 reveal something of how God's lordship and man's freedom interact. This is through discussing the saving act of the cross, which was an evil act done by men, but which was caused to occur for a pure purpose by God. Both passages make clear that Yahweh predetermined this evil act to occur. They also both make clear that the men who did the act are guilty. God's determined purpose put Christ on the cross. Men's lawless hands did the evil deed. Gentiles and Jews gathered together to do the evil, and when they did, they were merely accomplishing what God had already determined to come to pass. We see that God appoints evil to occur yet maintains his goodness in doing so. Men commit murder and will be rightly judged if they do not repent.

Jesus reveals basically the same point at the Passover, when he explains to the disciples, "And truly *the Son of man goeth, as it was determined*: but woe unto that man by whom he is betrayed!" (Luke 22:22). Thus the Lord reveals together God's determination of his capture and death, along with the guilt of the man who will betray him. Woe to that man who does this despicable act. Yahweh will judge him.

For some this presents too much conflict, and they reject it, or try to rewrite the passages to mean anything else. For others, we take it as given, and accept what we do not understand with a respect for the authority of God, and for the mystery there in his actions. Yahweh, being God and not a man, can accomplish this. You and I cannot. Where some Christians truly get angry, distressed, and confused at this thought, I believe we cannot object at all. It is simply not our place. If we think Yahweh is guilty of injustice, we must like Job, say, "[I have] uttered that I understood not; things too wonderful for me, which I knew not" (42:3b). Because, "I know that thou canst do every thing, and that no thought can be withholden from thee" (v. 2). We are simply not in the place of Yahweh to tell him how to rule, or to understand all his ways. We must know that his thoughts are not ours, and his ways are not ours. We must look to him with awe, and great love, and leave governing the creation up to him.

Remember, this is not a blind trust. This is a trust that comes with a knowledge of God's position, and of his character. It comes with knowledge of him which the Lord provided us through reason, conscience, and nature. It comes with further understanding given through Holy Scripture, which is perfect knowledge we can know is true. It comes with worshipping and obeying Yahweh in loving fellowship. Abraham brought his son Isaac to the altar, not thinking God cruel, but knowing that Yahweh was able to raise him up from the dead (Heb 11:17–19). We don't have to think we are blindly trusting in an unseen overlord who just might be apathetic to us or evil. Don't be ridiculous. Our trust is directed toward a God we know and love, and who has revealed himself to us. Moreover, we know it all ends in the cross. It ends in Christ being exalted, and in his people dwelling in eternal life without sin. We cannot remove any of the questions we have from that fuller perspective. All is finally for the good, and Yahweh is the good.

> And he said, Go, and tell this people, Hear ye indeed, but understand not; and see ye indeed, but perceive not.
>
> *Make the heart of this people fat*, and make their ears heavy, and shut their eyes; lest they see with their eyes, and hear with their ears, and understand with their heart, and convert, and be healed. (Isa 6:9–10)
>
> And in them is fulfilled the prophecy of Esaias, which saith, By hearing ye shall hear, and *shall not understand*; and seeing ye shall see, *and shall not perceive*:
>
> For this people's heart is waxed gross, and their ears are dull of hearing, and their eyes they have closed; lest at any time they should see with their eyes, and hear with their ears, and should understand with their heart, and should be converted, and I should heal them.
>
> But blessed are your eyes, for they see: and your ears, for they hear.

For verily I say unto you, That many prophets and righteous men have desired to see those things which ye see, and have not seen them; and to hear those things which ye hear, and have not heard them. (Matt 13:14–17)

Therefore they could not believe, because that Esaias said again,

He hath blinded their eyes, and hardened their heart; that they should not see with their eyes, nor understand with their heart, and be converted, and I should heal them.

These things said Esaias, when he saw his glory, and spake of him. (John 12:39–41)

Yahweh's words to Isaiah, and Jesus' application of these words to the people in his own day give us great insight into how God rules over men. Perhaps uniquely, they give us an example of how God hardens. Yahweh instructs Isaiah to preach to the people. Strangely, he instructs Isaiah not to soften their hearts, but to harden them, not to open their eyes, but to shut them. He does not allow that they see and hear at this time and become saved. It is his will to do the opposite. Make their hearts dull, lest they see, Yahweh commands the prophet. Yet we also see in the means of their hardening, which is the word of God itself, something of how God reigns over evil, and can appoint things to occur which are not good. The thing God sends is perfect and true—his word—but the reaction of the people is bad—they are hardened by it. So Yahweh need not lie, nor force anyone to make a wicked decision. He gives his word and they act exactly as he willed them to act—closed in eyes and ears to the message.

Jesus uses this passage to explain to his disciples why he speaks in parables. Parables, naturally, are not easy to understand, and some leave an audience scratching their heads. Jesus' explanation for the difficulty is to cite Isaiah,[6] whom God desired to shut the eyes of the people. Similarly, Jesus' parables are understood by only certain people Yahweh has chosen, but are not understood by the mass of the people, who in the long run remember, rejected Jesus. The teachings themselves had a part in hardening the people. It was not God's will at the time to heal all of them.

Those who understand and respond to Jesus in faith are simply showing that they are the ones God has chosen from the start to receive the message. Jesus expresses this at the very start of the passage:

---

6. A similar teaching to Isa 6 is repeated in Isa 44:18: "They have not known nor understood: for he hath shut their eyes, that they cannot see; and their hearts, that they cannot understand."

> He answered and said unto them, Because it is given unto you to know the mysteries of the kingdom of heaven, but *to them it is not given.*
>
> For whosoever hath, to him shall be given, and he shall have more abundance: but whosoever hath not, from him shall be taken away even that he hath. (Matt 13:11–12)

It is God who has decided who will have open ears, and who will have shut ears. We also see his choice of a people even in the grandly messianic Isa 53, "to whom is the arm of the LORD revealed?" (v. 1b). Yahweh has never purposed that all would understand his message. The parables of Jesus in themselves, like the words of Isaiah, play a role in hardening the people Yahweh has not chosen. The gospel message is perfect, but a carnal people respond by refusing to hear it. Only those whom he has chosen hear it, and respond, because he has given them that power. God is forcing no one to commit the evil of unbelief, but is simply communicating perfect truth, which assures the people are hardened. The Almighty is just. The people are responsible for their unbelief. He still saves his special people through the gospel, and lifts them out of the fire of sin and death.

Jesus makes a similar point following his teaching about being the good Shepherd of his sheep in John 10:

> Then came the Jews round about him, and said unto him, How long dost thou make us to doubt? If thou be the Christ, tell us plainly.
>
> Jesus answered them, I told you, and ye believed not: the works that I do in my Father's name, they bear witness of me.
>
> But *ye believe not, because ye are not of my sheep*, as I said unto you.
>
> My sheep hear my voice, and I know them, and they follow me: (vv. 24–27)

It is impossible to miss that being the sheep of Christ is not something that comes from our mere belief. Rather, our belief comes from being the sheep of Christ. In fact, the reason many of the crowd refused to believe was because they already did not belong to him. Those who are Jesus' sheep hear his voice and follow him. Our faith reflects that we are God's chosen to begin with. The truth, however well spoken, does not get through to them. At times God will use it for their hardening.

As in many other instances, offended readers may claim this is unfair. Yahweh has no right to choose some to receive the message, and to harden others through the same message. However, this is wrong. Beyond assuming that we have the right to decide what is fair or unfair, it also assumes that the Almighty owes us eternal peace and life in heaven. He owes us no such thing. He owes us only justice for our sins, and if we received the just reward for our sins, we would *none* of us receive the message of Jesus and none of us come to believe. We would all follow our dark hearts into hell. That means when Yahweh chooses a people to receive the words of Jesus, he is unjust to no one. He simply chooses whom he has mercy on, and lifts them out of condemnation to life. Just as it is the right of the governor to remove the penalty of death from a death row prisoner, that same governor does no injustice if he doesn't remove the penalty of death from every single death row prisoner. He chooses one or more prisoner to have mercy on, but the rest are already justly condemned. He has changed their state not the least. Similarly, Yahweh does no injustice to the sinners whom he does not choose to receive the gospel. They still are choosing to live as rebels, and they choose their own end in destruction. Yahweh simply pours out his love on those he has mercy on, and he is free to save whomever he desires.

Considering this bulk of passages from Scripture, and they are not even all that we find, evil is not out of control of a sovereign God. Rather evil is under his rule, and he can move the wicked this way and that as he chooses. God can bring good to come to pass by causing evil to occur. He creates the hearts of men, including evil men. He can predestine evil men to murder the Christ, and then judge those evil men for their deeds. These are challenging truths to nearly anyone. Granted there are many who would rewrite those words by complex philosophical means, or by injecting passages from elsewhere in Scripture, but taken as plainly written in context that's just what they say. They must be true regardless of the challenges.

Despite what I find to be overwhelming biblical evidence, there are still those that will cry out, "But you make God the author of evil!" It is clear though that I do no such thing, but the Bible does. The Bible teaches these things, and I am only citing and explaining them. We also have to look at the charge itself—of being the author of evil—and see if there is anything accurate in it. Like similar questions, it really depends on what we mean by the terms. If "author of evil" means that God commits evil, or is guilty of sin, then that is false. I have said no such thing, and the Bible does not. I have never heard anyone teach that God sins. God by nature cannot commit sin. However, if by "author of evil" you mean Yahweh causes evil to come to pass in some way, then obviously yes, God does so, but where is the problem?

Can you prove there is something wrong with that? Can you show from Scripture that God does not "author" evil? Can you show us where you gave a commandment that prohibits God from appointing evil to occur? Can you show where God gave a commandment to prohibit himself from causing evil to occur? If you can't show that, then it is a nonsensical charge to say God is the author of evil, because there is nothing wrong with that in the first place. Of course, he can do it. A simple review of Scripture will show that Yahweh predestines evil events to occur, and is sovereign over those events. He creates evil. He brings it to pass. The Bible teaches this is what Yahweh does, so there is nothing wrong with it.

What is actually wrong is this: that those making the charge seek to be in the place of God and to judge God. Those who make this charge seek to be the root of the moral law, rather than the Almighty. They make themselves the author of good. If they responded justly, they would be humble and recognize Yahweh has a right to govern his creation how he wishes. They would recognize he has a right to bring evil to a city for his own sovereign purposes. He has a right to wield evil kings as his whip. He has a right to send that earthquake in which children will die. Instead of seeking to charge Yahweh with violating their "author of evil" commandment, they should instead look within, see their own dark hearts, see that God justly brings down evil on mankind, and repent. They would repent of their sins. Repent of seeking to judge God. Trust instead in Jesus Christ to save them from their sins, and stop trying to prohibit Yahweh from being God. We alone are the guilty ones.

How Did the Fall Occur?

You might say to me: I get what you're saying about how God can cause sin to occur in this world, because it's already permeated with sin. I can even see how God is free to pull out of that fire whomever he desires, since everyone he leaves there is already guilty. But what about before Adam fell? There wasn't a guilty mankind then, so how did Adam fall? Doesn't it require either free will as we think of it, or God causing the fall or occur? While the Bible never explicitly talks about this subject, I believe the whole of Scripture does tell us God's purpose from the start, and this helps us know what the answer is. Yahweh has always desired to communicate his nature in the cross and resurrection. He even appointed the crucifixion to occur before the world even began:

> And all that dwell upon the earth shall worship him, whose names are not written in the book of life of the Lamb *slain from the foundation of the world*. (Rev 13:8)

Pass the time of your sojourning here in fear:

> Forasmuch as ye know that ye were not redeemed with corruptible things, as silver and gold, from your vain conversation received by tradition from your fathers;
>
> But with the precious blood of Christ, as of a lamb without blemish and without spot:
>
> Who verily was *foreordained before the foundation of the world*, but was manifest in these last times for you,
>
> Who by him do believe in God, that raised him up from the dead, and gave him glory; that your faith and hope might be in God. (1 Pet 1:17b–21)

> Blessed be the God and Father of our Lord Jesus Christ, who hath blessed us with all spiritual blessings in heavenly places in Christ:
>
> According as *he hath chosen us in him before the foundation of the world*, that we should be holy and without blame before him in love:
>
> Having predestinated us unto the adoption of children by Jesus Christ to himself, according to the good pleasure of his will (Eph 1:3–5)

God chose his special people before the creation, and God appointed the cross before the creation. That makes the fall of Adam in the garden a necessary measure to bring about this glorious future. The fall became the scaffolding for the glorious kingdom of God. While Adam was created good, and had neither a sin nature nor guilt, his choice of disobeying God was not an autonomous choice. God must have appointed this act to occur, as we see other acts predestined, yet without violently forcing Adam's will. Adam was freer than man became after the fall, not being bound to sin in his nature, but he was not autonomous of God's will fully either. Adam chose to disobey, for reasons Genesis does not give us, and God appointed that act to occur, to reveal whom he is in the cross.

The same Christians who find this answer too horrible to accept, will still admit that God permitted the fall to occur, set up events so that it would occur, placed the tree in the garden, allowed the serpent there, and did nothing to intervene. I find their objections weak, and while they might claim the moral high ground, they have none. Their God simply caused the fall in a less direct way, but he caused it nonetheless. If God caused it, we ought to be thankful for that, as we are thankful for Christ's blood and his mercy. We ought to be thankful for all that God does.

The cross manifests Yahweh's justice and righteousness, along with his mercy and love. It manifests his power and victory over all. It is a sign of his heart and his love. Yahweh made this world, and planned from the start for his Son to reign over it with his special people forever. Colossians 1:16 tells us: "For by him were all things created, that are in heaven, and that are in earth, visible and invisible, whether they be thrones, or dominions, or principalities, or powers: all things were created *by him, and for him.*"

This is one of many clear verses that show the Son to be the Creator, since all things were made "by" him. It's such a powerful statement of Christ's deity that Jehovah's Witnesses have to change the words of the text, making it "all [other] things" were created by him.[7] But it is important to notice that all things were made "for" the Son as well. This universe was purposed for the Son as a gift of the Father, and Christ was always to reign over creation with his chosen people, a much greater gift. God not only knew the end from the beginning, he declared the end from the beginning, and brought it to pass. A part of that was the fall, which despite Adam's choice to sin, is a part of God's plan. Adam is responsible for his choice, and Yahweh purposed it to occur for perfect and eternal ends according to his will.

If we recognize God's sovereignty, we can have no problem with how events have come to pass. However, if we import a high view of human freedom, and the presumption that God cannot judge man for events he caused to occur, only then does it become a problem. I would only tell you to drop the assumption that man has to be free in that sense, and stop telling God whom he can or cannot judge. Then you will see more clearly and understand. Then you will marvel at God's greatness,

---

7. Slick, "Col. 1:16–17." The Jehovah's Witnesses conceded at one point to put the word "other" in brackets, so readers would know it was not in the original Greek. However, in the most recent version of their Bible I looked at, they appear to have changed back, and "other" is no longer bracketed.

and goodness, and mystery. Then you will cease questioning, and simply understand. Yahweh is God. There is no other.

The Libertarian Assumption

I have endeavored to give you as biblical and as clear an answer as I possibly can. I believe I have remained true to Scripture, and shown that God rules over sin and suffering, and does so as our perfect Creator. However, this explanation is not what you will hear from most of Christendom. The more common Christian answer is to go on about human libertarian freedom, and how evil exists because God gave us this libertarian freedom. They will even go so far to suggest we couldn't possibly have "real" freedom if we didn't have the libertarian kind, in which we choose between moral opposites, or that we could not really love God fully without that same ability. They then bring the existence of evil down merely to man's choice, and God's permission. We have freedom. God permits us to use it for evil. They think this cleverly gets God off the accuser's hook. They may speak of predestination, because the Bible does, but it is a superficial predestination, based on God's foreknowledge of our actions. It may be an equally superficial one based on God's foreknowledge of our hypothetical actions in countless imaginary worlds, in which he will choose the best one, predetermining us only after responding to our hypothetical choices first. Let me deal with each form of this argument (which of course comes in differing varieties), and see if it holds water. It is, in a sense, their attempt to justify God, as if he needed justification, so it ought to be good.

What I find wrong with this common Christian argument, is that it ignores plain biblical teachings of God's sovereignty, as I've mentioned elsewhere, and also because it rests on bad assumptions. This thinking first assumes that God it totally reliant on a libertarian form of freedom in order to have a real relationship with us, when of course, God could have given us another kind of freedom, one that doesn't end up with people in hell. Some cannot imagine that option because they believe that you either have libertarian freedom or you're a robot, and who really wants to be a robot? How could a robot really make choices, including to love God? You should be grateful for not being a robot, and for your libertarian chance to end up in the fires of hell.

However, you cannot prove that those are the only two alternatives. It is a faulty assumption to begin with. If they *were* the only two alternatives, then the Father, the Son, and the Holy Spirit would all be robots, but they are not. They are all free. They are freer than we are, and they do not have a realistic choice to commit moral opposites They are never going to commit evil. Moreover, if one needed libertarian freedom to be free, then the saints in heaven are all robots too, and we've got to feel kind of sorry for them, and shouldn't be looking forward to heaven if we value our freedom highly. Yet the saints in heaven are free, and they are never going to sin. They have no realistic choice to sin anymore. Therefore, there are other ways of being free than libertarian freedom. If they have this freedom in the end, they could have had it in the beginning if it had been God's will. Therefore, the appeal to free choice is a poor attempt to sweep God's sovereignty over all things, including evil, under the rug. In this system, God would have had to create the libertarian kind of freedom, as opposed to another kind, with full knowledge countless souls would end up in eternal conscious torment. That means if one is the type to judge God, as one would judge a man, he would be found guilty as well. The libertarian God is clearly sovereign over evil also, just in a more indirect way, and a few steps back.

Now I can recall wandering up in the mountains, and enjoying the grandeur, and breathtaking beauty and power of the scenery. I marveled at it, and praised God as I walked. I praised God at the blue sky, the drippings of emerald greenery down the slopes, the palpable majesty of the jutting stone and cliffs. I was perfectly free to enjoy God's creation, and I would not have been freer if there had been an immediate option there to suffer and die instead, or if I had been getting shelled by paramilitary groups while on my hike. I would not have marveled any more at the beauty if the path had had hidden pits along the side, in which I could fall, and be bitten by snakes, or impaled by spikes. I would not have more of a choice to praise God if the path had become confusing, and I could have tangled myself up in the wilderness and died of the elements. I made a real choice to walk the path because I loved it, and I praised Yahweh because it was natural to do. I had the praise of God on my heart, and I made a choice to express it. The choice was real. A thousand venomous snakes off the side of the path would not have made my choice more real than it already had been. I was choosing to do what my heart desired.

Then there is the equally bad assumption that we would not be able to love sincerely if it were not for the glistening idol of libertarian freedom. Without that idol, we'd just be loving in a lackluster way, without sincerity of heart, or with only half a heart. We would not be loving by real choice. It is libertarian freedom that makes true love possible. This entire notion is grossly in error. We can know this immediately in the same way as mentioned before, since the Holy Trinity love in a truer and deeper way than we can even imagine, yet they will never choose not to love one another. The saints in heaven are capable of true and deep love, insofar as reborn souls in heaven can, and they are never going to love an idol instead of God. Therefore, one does not need libertarian freedom, the tug of sin on your heart, or anything like it, to love fully and completely. All you need is love on your heart and to act on that love. Then you have truly loved. Once again, God did not *have* to create this alleged form of freedom for us to be able to love, and we don't need to be grateful to this form of freedom for giving us the ability to fully love. In their system, God simply chose this form of freedom among other choices, and is sovereign over evil, just as the God I worship is.

I wonder if my wife would feel more fully loved, if I invited several exotic dancers to live in our basement. They would take up residence for a while, party nightly as you imagine that dancers do, and come upstairs and invite me to hang out, maybe take drugs with them, or have a back massage. Surely such a situation would make my wife feel more sincerely loved, because she would know that each night I came to bed with her, I made a real informed choice to do so, when there was a moral opposite imminent. Sure, she might miss me if I chose to spend nights partying with the exotic dancers, or debase myself with wild behavior and sexual sin, but she would know when I *did* love her, it was for real due to the existence in our basement of enticing moral opposites. Then our relationship would be "deepened," our love could be true, and our full love would reflect the full love of God, as it was always meant to be. It is the only way I could unite with my wife in love.

Or maybe not. Maybe I love my wife *just* as fully when I come to bed with her because it is on my heart to do so, as her husband, and because it is my role according to God. Maybe that is just as true and deep, despite not having any reasonable moral opposite present every night. I am following the will on my heart to love her, so I love her, and that is a love which is true enough. That choice reflects God's love to the ability a soul in Christ can reflect it on this earth. I do it because it's on my heart and it's on my heart because of the Lord. I am free, and I love her. I did not need present moral opposites to accomplish that. Nor do you when you choose to love.[8]

You see, thinking God can be judged to begin with is wrong. Justifying his sovereignty over evil with some necessity of human freedom is also wrong. It makes libertarian freedom the necessary basis of our relationship, when in actuality it is the other way around. God's freedom is the basis of our relationship. Any degree of freedom, and the kind of freedom we have, is totally dependent on God. Our steps are ordered by God. Our heart is turned by God. Yet in the libertarian system, Yahweh simply *has* to do something because we did something else. He is so useless in the situation he can't actually affect what we will do, but allows man's freedom to be primary, then uses his brilliance to make the most of it after the fact. Libertarian freedom then, is a false god, and shiny idol philosophers set up to worship before. Oh, how precious it is. We could not really be free without it. Treasure this idol. We could not have love without it. Oh, the preciousness and sacredness of free human will. Not only do we see them leaping and whirling around this golden cow, but we see their God leaping and whirling about its shininess as well, showing his devotion to its beauty, and his passion for its glorious nature. Oh, how would we ever have freedom or love without human autonomy? Oh, how would we ever justify Almighty God before his accusers without it? The defense team of God will rest its case on this.

Of course, the key is you cannot judge God to begin with. Never forget that. Yahweh needs no whitewashing from man. He needs no defense team. He is free to create man as he desires, and he is free to order man's relationship with him as he desires. Yahweh is free to appoint evil for his purposes, and never sins if he does so. What God does through evil is good, and he brings about a glorious paradise through it. Yet man may not sin, because we are commanded not to sin, and we are under God's authority. Attempts to explain God's rulership over evil through human freedom make man primary, and God secondary, and more so fail because they assume that God needs a justification in the first place. He does not. God is perfect by nature, and if he appoints the sin to be in the world, it is a good choice, and comes to perfect good in the end.

8. One might ask how what I say here—that a choice for evil is unnecessary for freedom—works in harmony with what I say elsewhere about how God uses pain to refine us, and how suffering is preferential to comfort in God accomplishing his goal in us. The passages harmonize because in the other instances I am speaking of how the Almighty uses pain in a sinful world, among fallen people. Here I am speaking in the abstract of the fact that a choice between moral opposites is not definitional to freedom or love.

Remember, much of what you hear about God and evil simply comes from the philosophical tradition, often from people who will admit they did not get it from interpreting biblical texts. It is man's ideas about how God should act, according to man's logic. Take note of the fact, over and over, when you hear people presenting God's lordship as merely responding to man's choices, that the Bible says nearly the exact opposite many times. Just as clearly as it teaches there is only one God, and there is no other, it also teaches that both good and evil come from God. It teaches that God turns the heart of the king wherever he desires. It teaches that God ends life, and predetermines acts of evil to occur. It says God does whatever he pleases, and no man or earthly power can tell him what to do. One has to sweep all that, and more, under the rug to imagine that God merely responds to our actions. Quite the opposite, He can appoint our actions to occur.

Basically the same points need to be made about a similar argument: the attempted escape that God knows all of man's choices in countless hypothetical worlds, and then responds to those choices by picking the best possible world, or set of events, in which things will come together for the good. Not only is this a far cry from anything that Scripture teaches, but it makes God the passive observer too. Yet he is not a passive observer anywhere. You see, if Almighty God were indeed imagining infinite hypothetical worlds, he wouldn't just be knowing our possible free choices in those worlds. He'd also be seeing how he made our hearts, how he moved our hearts, and what he decreed to occur, and see his own active power there determining what would come to pass in those worlds. Once you realize that, the idea of running to hypothetical worlds is meaningless, since God is just as sovereign there as he is here. Let's just jump back to the real world, and deal with reality as it is.

This hypothesis also ends up just as deterministic as the doctrines which men who hold it complain about. God may have surveyed infinite possible actions first, but once he determines an act based on that, there is only one outcome which occurs. The people will choose exactly as Yahweh appointed them to choose in those situations. Of course, this then makes their apparent list of choices, their apparent moral opposites at the time, totally illusory. There's only *one* thing they will choose anyway. So if this model makes moral opposites illusory for practical purposes, it makes little sense to complain that others do the same, and allege a violation of "freewill." You have done the same thing you complain about in others.

God on Trial

Were God a giant powerful man, and possible of being put on trial, the libertarian God would be found guilty. As much as they try to justify him, there's no avoiding this. True, the sovereign God would get a harsher sentence, being more actively involved in sin, but the libertarian God, at the minimum, would end up with a manslaughter or negligent homicide charge, for all his intentionally placing people in situations in which they'll sin, and knowingly permitting acts of evil to occur to them. Having the capacity to protect someone from evil, but not doing it, is also morally despicable for a man, and in some instances a crime. Releasing the tiger that tore up the child isn't that much morally superior to tearing up the child yourself. In fact, choosing to create libertarian freedom, versus another form of freedom that doesn't land souls in hell, would by itself make sure that the God of creation got convicted. Perhaps they should say of God's decision to give man that form of freedom, in the words of John Calvin, "The decree is dreadful indeed, I confess."[9] Likely, the sovereign God would get the electric chair, the libertarian God would get twenty years to life. Either way, they're both guilty by man's standards.

The route of claiming God merely permits sin does not successfully get God off the accuser's hook. Were God a man, either one would be unethical and could be tried and convicted. We know, however, that God is not a man. That is the key. God is not bound by our ethical laws or our preferences for how he behaves any more than he is bound by the law of gravity or the strong and weak nuclear forces. Yahweh is beyond those laws, and is completely free. There is nothing we can charge him with, but must only know he is God and love and worship him. That is what the righteous Job came to realize. He is so grand and we are so small. When it comes to sin, we must examine ourselves, not God, for sin, and repent of any that we find. We must ask God to search our hearts and make us pure. We must be washed clean of sin, which God promises he will do, if we repent and believe on his Son. That is the order of things, and at the judgment God will not be answering to us, but we will be answering to God.

---

9. Calvin, *The Institutes of the Christian Religion*, 3, 23, 7, 955.

PAIN | PART 1

Answering Children

Not long before I began this book, I had a short conversation with our four-year old daughter that reminded me much about theology. It was pertinent enough that I will give her a place here. My daughter was asking me "why" questions. As any parent knows, children like to ask why questions, and will often do them without end. My daughter had realized it was funny, and was finally just doing it as a joke. She started asking me about how our bodies took in food—why do we eat it, why is it good for us, why does it go down to our stomachs. I answered each question, and she immediately followed it with another single word: "Why?" Finally, I answered with, "Because God designed us that way." She asked once more, "Why?" I replied with God's name from Scripture, "Because he is who he is." "Why?" she asked again. I replied unchanging, "Because he is who he is." Every time she asked why, I gave the exact same reply. I offered no new insight. I offered no new angle on the topic. "He is who he is," I repeated over and over.

With this one reply I managed to be more stubborn than a four-year old, and I won the battle of the why's. She finally stopped asking. The game was over. It was an answer you just can't get past. This little situation of course reminds me of the reply we need to have sometimes when it comes to God's actions. Often that needs to be the final reply. God is who he is. It's a reply we need to give when people continually want to ask "why," and when the mind thinks the answers revealed in Scripture are not sufficient for their sophisticated minds. Yahweh is who he is. It's a fine answer for skeptics or for Christians who think God needs to act as they desire. We as men do not need the particular answer to everything God does, nor have we been promised it. We do not need to read the all-knowing mind of Yahweh. What we need to do is rest on God's character, and know he is Lord of the universe. It is a much better answer than falling into falsehood, or endless speculations looking for an answer. Yahweh is God and he does as he pleases.

> Who is like unto thee, O LORD, among the gods? who is like thee, glorious in holiness, fearful in praises, doing wonders? (Exod 15:11)
>
> For great is the LORD, and greatly to be praised: he also is to be feared above all gods.
>
> For all the gods of the people are idols: but the LORD made the heavens. (1 Chr 16:25–26)

> O the depth of the riches both of the wisdom and knowledge of God! how unsearchable are his judgments, and his ways past finding out!
>
> For who hath known the mind of the Lord? or who hath been his counsellor?
>
> Or who hath first given to him, and it shall be recompensed unto him again?
>
> For of him, and through him, and to him, are all things: to whom be glory for ever. Amen. (Rom 11:33-36)
>
> Surely every man is vanity. Selah. (Ps 39:11b)

DELIVERED INTO LIGHT

The purpose of suffering in Christ and the New Covenant

The book of Job is the solid answer to the suffering of the righteous in the Old Testament. It provides us the humbling answer that man cannot charge God with wrong. We need to recognize God's authority, and understand he can justly and righteously decide what comes to pass, including suffering in our own lives. It presents side by side a picture of suffering and death with God's final goal, which is presented in Job's restoration. His longing for a savior throughout the book will be realized finally in Christ, whose rewards are pictured in his restoration. Once Job has come to cease doubting and repent of his previous accusations, God's blessing pours out on him. He knows fully the goodness of Yahweh again for his life. If we are righteous, we will accept suffering. If we are righteous, we will not charge God.

The gospel provides us a deeper realization of the purpose of suffering, as well as of God's hand in it. It is what Job was anticipating. Through Christ's life death and resurrection, and his pouring forth of his life into the Church, we have a role that both accepts suffering, and is glorified by it. We have a redeemer who will cure us of our impurities. We also realize a goal that will surpass all suffering and death; that is a new creation, through the blood of Christ. That is a new heavens and earth where finally sin is no more. Do we not understand the suffering of righteous Job? In the gospel we have the only truly righteous Man who ever lived, and he is given the opportunity to suffer, and to suffer for the good of others. The Man volunteers.

Christ's suffering, and later that of his people, exists on more levels than one. Christ comes first out of love, and to deliver his people from sin and death. Christ suffers for love. Christ dies for love. His death is not fruitless, meaningless destruction, but is a willful sacrifice which bears with it great fruit; a restored creation, and the eternal salvation of his beloved people. His stripes are not meaningless brutal blows of a stick, but are healing wounds for all mankind. The blows come not from the out-of-control universe which hurts innocent men, but by God's meticulous plan. This Man willfully accepted the pain placed before him. This Man walked into it for our sakes, knowing what would happen. Jesus can tell us more about "why" suffering exists than those who run from pain, or those who are defeated by it, and is the most fitting Savior of humanity. What we must walk through, he walked through too.

The Lord of Glory

When God decided to become man, you could say this was the first step in accepting what you and I want to reject very often. He started by simply humbling himself, something not required at all for him to do. One who is spirit and dwells in heavenly light, took on our flesh, stepped out into space and time, placed himself under the law to live like us. The Ruler became a servant for our sakes. God did not need to do this, but he chose it; humility, suffering, and death. The Law Giver placed himself under the law and obeyed it, as his children must obey. In the flesh he would experience weakness, temptation, physical pain, tiredness, sadness, just as we do, all of this before the agony of the cross. He would accept the dirtiness and sicknesses of the earth to come and be with us. He welcomed that burden and lowliness.

This divine dwelling in the flesh, what we call the incarnation in history, is described at its inception in John 1: "And the Word was made flesh and dwelt among us" (v. 14a). The eternal Creator who made all things in the beginning, as in Genesis, entered into his creation. The passage also recalls the Lord's rejection by many, by the same people he came to: "That was the true Light, which lighteth every man that cometh into the world. He was in the world, and the world was made by him, and the world knew him not. He came unto his own, and his own received him not" (vv. 9–11). The King came to a wicked and rebellious people whom he had every right to judge immediately. Yet he walked as an average man of little repute. He used his flesh, his weakness, his tiredness, his grief, to walk with us and perfect the human nature which he'd taken on. Although he did not need to, God walked out all the statutes of the law, being obedient as we are to be obedient. He showed us what it means to be righteous, and loved the Father with all his heart through the weakness and pain of the flesh. He showed us what humanity was meant for.

In reminding us of how to practice Christian humility, the apostle Paul gives us this equally great description of God becoming man, and the kind of character it shows to do so:

> Let this mind be in you, which was also in Christ Jesus:
>
> Who, being in the form of God, thought it not robbery to be equal with God:
>
> But made himself of no reputation, and took upon him the form of a servant, and was made in the likeness of men:
>
> And being found in fashion as a man, he humbled himself, and became obedient unto death, even the death of the cross. (Phil 2:5-8)

The Lord Jesus intentionally lowered himself. He could have clung to his glory in heaven, but he chose to be lowly. Can you imagine doing that? Did you leave all that you own to live with the poor or the sick? Would you give up your freedom to become a slave to others? This is Creator of all, and it is amazing the humility he shows. At any time in his earthly life Jesus could have called upon his power as God, but chose to be lower than the Father. He did not call upon his power to end his hardship or destroy his enemies. God chose to be a servant, and practiced obedience, even though he is Almighty Creator. His obedience was so complete, he went to death on the cross rather than choosing to reject it. God had opportunity to sin. He experienced temptation in the flesh. Instead, he used human nature to save others, and did so to the point of the worst suffering. Some people like to imagine that God has it easy, and we've got to do all the work and the sweating on earth. There's a certain truth to that, because of God's perfect heavenly dwelling place, and his transcendent nature as spirit. However, God has joined us in all the work that we do, and in our sweat and our suffering. He did not reject having to work, or having to obey the law, but instead perfected it. How can we reject suffering if God himself embraced it.

In another major passage on God's incarnation, one of the richest in all Scripture, Paul writes of the unity of nature Christ has with us, saying:

> For it became him, for whom are all things, and by whom are all things, in bringing many sons unto glory, to make the captain of their salvation perfect through sufferings.
>
> For both he that sanctifieth and they who are sanctified are all of one: for which cause he is not ashamed to call them brethren,
>
> Saying, I will declare thy name unto my brethren, in the midst of the church will I sing praise unto thee.
>
> And again, I will put my trust in him. And again, Behold I and the children which God hath given me.
>
> Forasmuch then as the children are partakers of flesh and blood, he also himself likewise took part of the same; that through death he might destroy him that had the power of death, that is, the devil;
>
> And deliver them who through fear of death were all their lifetime subject to bondage. (Heb 2:10–15)

Yahweh chose a way to redeem us that involved becoming like us. Being God, I can't imagine he could not have chosen another way, or another thousand ways. However, Yahweh chose the best way, and it was to take on our nature. In doing so, the Perfect One needed to become perfected, to grow, to learn, to fulfill the expectations of the Father. It was suffering in part which acted to do this. It acted to perfect him. He let suffering do for him what we need to let it do for us. In accomplishing this, Jesus defeated death and the devil and set us free. By the very weak nature he took on, by following the order God laid out for mankind, his death was a victory. His resurrection won us life. Death could not hold him any more than the devil could lead him to sin. It was an act of suffering and death that brought us eternal life.

Jesus in becoming man accepted pain by accepting persecution. The scorn, threats, abuse, and eventual murder were welcomed by the Lord when he joined us here. As God he deserved full honor and worship. As man he not only accepted being under the law, and in a body which suffered and grew weak, but also the dishonor of men, their insults and hatred:

> And when Jesus came into the ruler's house, and saw the minstrels and the people making a noise,
>
> He said unto them, Give place: for the maid is not dead, but sleepeth. *And they laughed him to scorn.* (Matt 9:23–24)

For John came neither eating nor drinking, and they say, He hath a devil.

The Son of man came eating and drinking, and they say, *Behold a man gluttonous, and a winebibber*, a friend of publicans and sinners. But wisdom is justified of her children. (Matt 11:18–19)

Is not this the carpenter's son? is not his mother called Mary? and his brethren, James, and Joses, and Simon, and Judas?

And his sisters, are they not all with us? Whence then hath this man all these things?

And they were offended in him. But Jesus said unto them, A prophet is not without honour, save in his own country, and in his own house. (Matt 13:55–57)

His brethren therefore said unto him, Depart hence, and go into Judaea, that thy disciples also may see the works that thou doest.

For there is no man that doeth any thing in secret, and he himself seeketh to be known openly. If thou do these things, shew thyself to the world.

For *neither did his brethren believe in him*. (John 7:3–5)

There was a division therefore again among the Jews for these sayings.

And many of them said, *He hath a devil, and is mad*; why hear ye him? (John 10:19–20)

Then said the Jews unto him, *Now we know that thou hast a devil*. Abraham is dead, and the prophets; and thou sayest, If a man keep my saying, he shall never taste of death. (John 8:52)

From that time *many of His disciples went back*, and walked no more with him. (John 6:66)

And therefore did the Jews *persecute Jesus, and sought to slay him*, because he had done these things on the sabbath day. (John 5:16)

After these things Jesus walked in Galilee: for he would not walk in Jewry, because *the Jews sought to kill him*. (John 7:1)

When God joined us as man, he took on himself dishonor, insult, threats, and saw many men refuse to believe him, and many abandon him. Yet he never swerved from his aim in fulfilling the law and saving us. His aim was true. His love for his people was so great he gave up earthly honor and pleasure for us. God in flesh was abandoned by friends, accused wrongly, insulted, and not believed by his own family. It is some of the worst of the human experience. Anyone who comes to Christ can know they are delivered by one who knows them, their soul, and their experience deeply, having lived and suffered in the flesh with us. Our leader and father of our family is not far from us, unimaginable, and dwelling in a land past an unpassable ocean. He is right here beside us. Christ as a priest ministers to ones he understands through his suffering, relying not on transcendence or omniscience, but on a day to day walk in our world. The unspeakable glory of heaven is still within him in spirit. Eternal light in his soul. Yet he walks out each of our sorrows and overcomes them, loving and trusting in the Father. Those things we would not do, he does, and the love with which we would not love, he loves.

The Christ continues to receive public dishonor up to his end on the cross, which is exemplified in the description of piercing and persecution in Ps 22:

> I am poured out like water, and all my bones are out of joint: my heart is like wax; it is melted in the midst of my bowels.
>
> My strength is dried up like a potsherd; and my tongue cleaveth to my jaws; and thou hast brought me into the dust of death.
>
> For dogs have compassed me: the assembly of the wicked have inclosed me: they pierced my hands and my feet.
>
> I may tell all my bones: they look and stare upon me.
>
> They part my garments among them, and cast lots upon my vesture. (vv. 14–18)

The God who deserves public honor, public worship, and respect of the highest kind willingly receives public humiliation. He is robbed of anything he owns. His broken and gaunt body is displayed before all. The Lord of everything has made himself nothing for us. It's hard to imagine a lower experience in life than this public torture and humiliation. Yet his love led him to do this for us.

Christ's lowly, servant life ends in the passion and the cross. It is at once the fulfillment of his obedience to the Father, and a priestly offering up for our sins. But I speak here mostly of pain and death. The willingness with which he took on this death. No one took his life from him. He gave it up for us. Christ was not the weak being murdered by the strong. He was the strong being murdered by the weak, and he walked boldly into it because he knew what it would accomplish. More was accomplished in his death than in his miracles. More was accomplished in Christ taking on pain than in God's creation of the cosmos. It was a supernatural creative act. He birthed an entire people and delivered countless souls from eternal suffering, forming a new heavens and a new earth. A moment of infinite dishonor earned an eternity of bliss.

If one thinks there is no meaning in pain, or that death is the end of your life, one needs to consider the pain and death described in the Gospel:

> Then cometh Jesus with them unto a place called Gethsemane, and saith unto the disciples, Sit ye here, while I go and pray yonder.
>
> And he took with him Peter and the two sons of Zebedee, and began to be sorrowful and very heavy.
>
> Then saith he unto them, My soul is exceeding sorrowful, even unto death: tarry ye here, and watch with me.
>
> And he went a little further, and fell on his face, and prayed, saying, O my Father, if it be possible, let this cup pass from me: nevertheless not as I will, but as thou wilt. (Matt 26:36-39)
>
> Then cometh he to his disciples, and saith unto them, Sleep on now, and take your rest: behold, the hour is at hand, and the Son of man is betrayed into the hands of sinners.
>
> Rise, let us be going: behold, he is at hand that doth betray me. (Matt 26:45-46)
>
> What think ye? They answered and said, He is guilty of death.
>
> Then did they spit in his face, and buffeted him; and others smote him with the palms of their hands,
>
> Saying, Prophesy unto us, thou Christ, Who is he that smote thee? (Matt 26:66-68)
>
> Pilate saith unto them, What shall I do then with Jesus which is called Christ? They all say unto him, Let him be crucified.
>
> And the governor said, Why, what evil hath he done? But they cried out the more, saying, Let him be crucified. (Matt 27:22-23)
>
> Then released he Barabbas unto them: and when he had scourged Jesus, he delivered him to be crucified. (Matt 27:26)
>
> Then the soldiers of the governor took Jesus into the common hall, and gathered unto him the whole band of soldiers.
>
> And they stripped him, and put on him a scarlet robe.
>
> And when they had platted a crown of thorns, they put it upon his head, and a reed in his right hand: and they bowed the knee before him, and mocked him, saying, Hail, King of the Jews!

> And they spit upon him, and took the reed, and smote him on the head.
>
> And after that they had mocked him, they took the robe off from him, and put his own raiment on him, and led him away to crucify him. (Matt 27:27-31)
>
> And when they were come unto a place called Golgotha, that is to say, a place of a skull,
>
> They gave him vinegar to drink mingled with gall: and when he had tasted thereof, he would not drink.
>
> And they crucified him, and parted his garments, casting lots: that it might be fulfilled which was spoken by the prophet, They parted my garments among them, and upon my vesture did they cast lots. (Matt 27:33-35)
>
> And the sun was darkened, and the veil of the temple was rent in the midst.
>
> And when Jesus had cried with a loud voice, he said, Father, into thy hands I commend my spirit: and having said thus, he gave up the ghost.
>
> Now when the centurion saw what was done, he glorified God, saying, Certainly this was a righteous man. (Luke 23:45-47)

Christ, step by step, practiced obedience to the Father, as he, step by step, took on human experience, and went through weakness, tiredness, pain, and death. This obedience in human experience accomplished many things, including our deliverance from filth, earthly lusts, sin, and corruption. We are free of all that in him. Yet as Heb 2 points out, I want to remind that it accomplishes a union with his people, with his family. The incarnation and the experience of suffering brings us into his family, just as he came to join with ours. The human soul can know that his God is not a mere invisible force, or divine mind. His God is more than a cosmic spirit. His God is one with him, united with him in all things, including the suffering of this life. Christ also showed us all what obedience accomplishes. Christ, who did not need to obey, since he was the Creator from the start, obeyed the law and lived out righteousness for us. Going through this walk of righteousness, even when the body was weak and was broken, brought peace with God and paid the price for man's sin. Christ's suffering showed us the good in righteousness, that no matter the price, fulfilling the law of God is lifegiving, and a treasure to all. The good we frequently do not want to do, because it is not pleasurable, is the good which won salvation.

God entered into death for us. What many fear in itself, both the consequences and the dark mystery, was a destination God chose for himself—the door of death. We almost recoil at facing the frightening depth of entering death, leaving the light of this life, into something we cannot plainly see, and for many which gives off distant rumblings of judgment. God entered into this, and through his entrance, silenced its threat. He cured it of its promise of judgment. He cured it of its ending of our love and fellowship on this earth. The Savior went down and out again, as a diver in the black depth of the sea. There is nothing more to fear.

The experience of the cross also assures that God's nature is not a mere theory. This is true of Jesus' earthly life which preceded it. The Father did not appear to us as a vague pillar of light or a cloud of darkness. We don't need to envision God's nature or God's perfection in our mind through imagination, but we have him before us. He's called Jesus Christ. If you are sitting and waiting for God to reveal himself to you, he already has. Jesus taught, "If ye had known me, ye should have known my Father also: and from henceforth ye know him, and have seen him" (John 14:7). When Phillip asked Jesus to show them the Father, as if the disciples needed some vision or supernatural trip to heaven, the reply is different from what he expected: "Jesus saith unto him, Have I been so long time with you, and yet hast thou not known me, Philip? he that hath seen me hath seen the Father; and how sayest thou then, Shew us the Father? Believest thou not that I am in the Father, and the Father in me?" (vv. 9–10a).

The nature of God is revealed in Christ. This is true in his teachings, but even more deeply in his life, death, and resurrection. We are given a for-real glimpse into mysteries of heaven. This shows us not only God's capacity to suffer with us, but God's deep intention and deep love for us. His character, for any who ever doubted it, or for any who thought God does not love him, is revealed in Christ: He is love. He is love superabundant, and even offers grace and forgiveness to those who hate him. He is love unafraid, and purposeful, who will pour out his life to save us. If you're not sure who God is, look to Jesus Christ. That is nowhere else truer than in his suffering and love.

PAIN | PART 1

The Way to Life:

One feels like a child knowing that our heavenly Father brings us so much through his love and sacrifice. It's easy to think we just sit in the backseat, while he takes us out for ice cream with his hard-earned money. Or that we kick back in the recliner at his heavenly mansion that his blood bought us. But God's love is participatory, and so is his sacrifice. What we know as children, is who our parents are, and we learn to be like our parents, to take on their ways. So in Christ, suffering is not only in the several hours on the cross, or the several years of Immanuel's ministry. Rather, giving up life out of love is passed along to the children. Love in abundance is contagious.

Jesus instructed his disciples:

> This is my commandment, That ye love one another, as I have loved you.
>
> Greater love hath no man than this, that a man lay down his life for his friends. (John 15:12–13)

Just as the man-God was obedient to the Father to the point of suffering and death, so are we obedient, and will not be swayed from our faithfulness if it will end in death. As the Creator of this new creation went through work, tiredness, and pain to deliver others, so does the new creation work, tire itself, and suffer for the good of the world. As the Son's suffering perfected him and resulted in adoption by the Father, so our own suffering brings us closer to Christ. As Christ conformed the new humanity to the will of God, so do we conform our minds to the mind of Christ. As he went to death, we put to death the flesh. As he was persecuted for preaching, we too are persecuted for preaching, and do not stop, for the sake of bringing the world to Christ. A glorious new body Jesus Christ has created, and this new body practices goodness, and is not swayed from its goal by pain. You and I are in this body, if we are born anew in him.

Jesus promised:

> If the world hate you, ye know that it hated me before it hated you. (John 15:18)
>
> If ye were of the world, the world would love his own: but because ye are not of the world, but I have chosen you out of the world, therefore the world hateth you. (John 15:19)

> And ye shall be betrayed both by parents, and brethren, and kinsfolks, and friends; and some of you shall they cause to be put to death.
>
> And ye shall be hated of all men for my name's sake.
>
> But there shall not an hair of your head perish.
>
> In your patience possess ye your souls. (Luke 21:16–19)
>
> But take heed to yourselves: for they shall deliver you up to councils; and in the synagogues ye shall be beaten: and ye shall be brought before rulers and kings for my sake, for a testimony against them. (Mark 13:9)

The ministry of the apostles was also one of living through persecution, and hardships. This is for the glory of Jesus, and for the life of the whole church:

> Thrice was I beaten with rods, once was I stoned, thrice I suffered shipwreck, a night and a day I have been in the deep;
>
> In journeyings often, in perils of waters, in perils of robbers, in perils by mine own countrymen, in perils by the heathen, in perils in the city, in perils in the wilderness, in perils in the sea, in perils among false brethren;
>
> In weariness and painfulness, in watchings often, in hunger and thirst, in fastings often, in cold and nakedness.
>
> Beside those things that are without, that which cometh upon me daily, *the care of all the churches.* (2 Cor 11:25–28)
>
> For we which live are alway delivered unto death for Jesus' sake, that the life also of Jesus might be made manifest in our mortal flesh.
>
> So then death worketh in us, but life in you . . .
>
> *For all things are for your sakes,* that the abundant grace might through the thanksgiving of many redound to the glory of God. (2 Cor 4:11–12, 15)

It is no surprise that in being the disciples of Christ, the Christian is promised that he will be hated and persecuted. In the course of preaching the truth across the world, and in the course of doing righteousness, the men who first heard these words indeed suffered persecution. The apostles of Christ were nearly every one imprisoned and executed. John was imprisoned, tortured, and the exiled. Christ's followers in the generations following suffered similar attacks from local populations, Jews, and the Roman government. Yet the early Christians counted it an honor to suffer for Christ. Martyrs were remembered throughout the ages, and specially honored. To die was not some horror, but an opportunity to bring glory to Christ, and then to be with him in the next world. Apostle Paul said, "To live is Christ, and to die is gain" (Phil 1:21), so when we are in Christ either life or death is a benefit. We let God choose which one is for us; continued life here on earth to help our brothers, or worship in heaven in the presence of Christ. There is nothing for us to complain about either way. If the suffering of one Man on the cross brought salvation to many, we are the last people to wonder if our suffering on earth has purpose. Where others search endlessly for an answer to their pain, we have already been given one by God. It is not the immediate cessation of our struggle, but the binding of it to God's kingdom. Once we realize this, we know we can never reject our suffering.

Consider the explanation in this passage:

> Blessed be God, even the Father of our Lord Jesus Christ, the Father of mercies, and the God of all comfort;
>
> Who comforteth us in all our tribulation, *that we may be able to comfort them which are in any trouble*, by the comfort wherewith we ourselves are comforted of God.
>
> For as the sufferings of Christ abound in us, *so our consolation also aboundeth* by Christ.
>
> And whether we be afflicted, it is for your consolation and salvation, which is effectual in the enduring of the same sufferings which we also suffer: or whether we be comforted, it is for your consolation and salvation.
>
> And our hope of you is stedfast, knowing, that as ye are partakers of the sufferings, *so shall ye be also of the consolation*. (2 Cor 1:3–7)

Paul's teaching to the Corinthians in the opening of the book reflects much of what we can know elsewhere about suffering, though focusing on the work of the apostles, and perhaps other leaders. Paul makes crystal clear what the life in Christ is like, as he lays out his credentials as an apostle for those who seek to challenge him. Our suffering in Christ includes a great gift we give to other people, being able to comfort them in their trials also. Not only do we comfort them, but we do so in the same way Christ comforted us, through the same spirit. Just as we suffer in Christ due to persecution, we know we also are comforted by him. Our suffering gives us the resources to comfort others, and all of this flows from the Father, through Christ, to us. Just as a man warming himself by the fire will be able to warm others with his embrace or his touch, we provide warmth which comes from the source. We can never imagine our pain is without purpose for us or for others. We become healers through our pain.

Paul goes on to make a similar point as we see in Job:

> For we would not, brethren, have you ignorant of our trouble which came to us in Asia, that we were pressed out of measure, above strength, insomuch that we despaired even of life:
>
> But we had the sentence of death in ourselves, *that we should not trust in ourselves, but in God* which raiseth the dead:
>
> Who delivered us from so great a death, and doth deliver: in whom we trust that he will yet deliver us; (vv. 8–10)

Paul and his compatriots were persecuted to a degree greater than they thought they could endure. Yet it was at this point that it deepened their faith. They learned not to trust in their own strength, but to trust in God's, which is greater than all. Surely all these men were spiritually mature (Paul certainly was more mature than Job even before this incident), yet each one learned more greatly to rely on God and receive all their strength through Christ. The saints were refined in fire, as is often the case. Yahweh preserved them through the fire, as he did the young men in the furnace in Babylon (Dan 3), and showed his incredible power this way. We all can know, if the Almighty can deliver us from that hardship of persecution, he can deliver us through sin and death in Christ.

> And who is he that will harm you, if ye be followers of that which is good?
>
> But and if ye suffer for righteousness' sake, happy are ye: and *be not afraid of their terror, neither be troubled* (1 Pet 3:13–14)
>
> *Blessed are they* which are persecuted for righteousness' sake: for theirs is the kingdom of heaven.
>
> *Blessed are ye*, when men shall revile you, and persecute you, and shall say all manner of evil against you falsely, for my sake.
>
> Rejoice, and be exceeding glad: for great is your reward in heaven: for so persecuted they the prophets which were before you. (Matt 5:10–12)

One could do an entire study on Jesus' Beatitudes, on what they teach us about pain. In the Beatitudes it is blessed to mourn, because we will be comforted, and blessed to be poor in spirit, because we will enter the kingdom of heaven. Being "blessed," which can also be translated as "happy," reflects the life of the man who has been made new in Christ, and the man who is daily following Christ. Like in the passage above from 1 Pet 3, we are happy if we suffer for the good, and have nothing to fear, even in prisons and in abuse. Even in poverty and suffering the Christian is blessed, full of joy, because he rests on the Lord and has fellowship with his brothers. The Beatitudes turn common assumptions about what we should desire upside down.

The verses I've chose speak specifically of the blessing in being persecuted. Being persecuted surely includes being socially shunned by unbelievers, insulted, and hated, but it also includes the horrible sufferings of the day; of being imprisoned, tortured, and murdered for the faith. These sufferings, which are the most extreme any human being can face in this life, are not meaningless pain issued forth by a cruel, or capricious God. Rather, they are a blessing on us and on all of God's people. They unite the sufferer with God, and bring him into God's kingdom. They assure the sufferer he is in the line of God's prophets from the beginning of salvation history—men of great righteousness, who are highly honored in heaven. The martyr not only enters paradise, but does so as Isaiah, or Jeremiah, or John the Baptist. Like them, he also can know he brings forward God's work in salvation history, strengthening the people of God, and bringing into the family more children. "Precious in the sight of the LORD is the death of his saints" (Ps 116:15).

United with the Son of God in suffering

> Yea doubtless, and I count all things but loss for the excellency of the knowledge of Christ Jesus my Lord: for whom I have suffered the loss of all things, and do count them but dung, that I may win Christ,
>
> And be found in him, not having mine own righteousness, which is of the law, but that which is through the faith of Christ, the righteousness which is of God by faith:

> That I may know him, and the power of his resurrection, and *the fellowship of his sufferings, being made conformable unto his death*;
>
> If by any means I might attain unto the resurrection of the dead (Phil 3:8–11)
>
> The Spirit itself beareth witness with our spirit, that we are the children of God:
>
> And if children, then heirs; heirs of God, and joint-heirs with Christ; *if so be that we suffer with him*, that we may be also glorified together (Rom 8:16–17)

Other than faith, suffering is perhaps the greatest experience that brings us unity with God, through Jesus Christ. Suffering, in a sense, is sharing in Christ's own passion and his death. Scripture makes it sound obligatory, as if we're not entering heaven without suffering. For example, both of the above passages about suffering include an "if." We are his children *if* we suffer with him. Paul gives up everything in life, if by any means he may be raised in Christ. Suffering is part of the life of the believer, and is inseparable from the Christian walk. If we are not suffering, then can we be sure we are Christ's? Paul gave up his previous life, pushed aside his Pharisaic education, and willingly accepted social rejection, threats, abuse, persecution, and not long after the writing of his epistles, death. The audience of Romans, the church in Rome, also knew that to suffer with Christ included bloody and gruesome persecution. These things conform us to Christ's character, and bring us to be glorified with him.

For the Christian, of course, it is almost easy to say we would hypothetically accept martyrdom for faith, but then refuse to go through the average daily sufferings we must. But those are a matter of conforming us to Christ as well, and those unite us with his divine character too. They are obligatory. That is the suffering of giving up living for ourselves. The suffering of stepping down from pride and self-importance. The suffering of giving up our time and resources to serve others. The suffering of being a plain, simple, unfashionable person in a world that tells us we can be a diva instead, and looks down on who we are. It's the suffering of giving up the preferable and habitual sins we've grown accustomed to. It's the suffering of confessing our sins, and accepting rebuke. The average Christian rejects so many of these, while proclaiming he would die for the faith. Yet to be clean, to be at peace, to be conformed to Christ, all of these must become normal as well. They shape us, and chisel away at the hard flesh which has previously bound us. They set free our members to live as Christ will us to live, allowing us to follow his Spirit and his ways. These sacrifices get rid of the old, and bring to life the new.

> Grudge not one against another, brethren, lest ye be condemned: behold, the judge standeth before the door.
>
> Take, my brethren, the prophets, who have spoken in the name of the Lord, for an example of suffering affliction, and of patience.
>
> Behold, we count them happy which endure. *Ye have heard of the patience of Job*, and have seen the end of the Lord; that the Lord is very pitiful, and of tender mercy. (Jas 5:9–11)
>
> For consider him that endured such contradiction of sinners against himself, lest ye be wearied and faint in your minds.
>
> Ye have not yet resisted unto blood, striving against sin.
>
> And ye have forgotten the exhortation which speaketh unto you as unto children, My son, despise not thou the chastening of the Lord, nor faint when thou art rebuked of him:
>
> For whom the Lord loveth he chasteneth, and scourgeth every son whom he receiveth.
>
> *If ye endure chastening*, God dealeth with you as with sons; for what son is he whom the father chasteneth not?
>
> But if ye be without chastisement, whereof all are partakers, then are ye bastards, and not sons. (Heb 12:3–8)

James reminds us of Job, whom I've spoken about at length, while instructing Christians regarding hardship. Be patient, he is telling them, in waiting for the coming of the Lord. James knew how central the book of Job is to answering the difficulties of suffering. He reminds the Christian of Job's perseverance, how he endured to the end through suffering and remained faithful. He received reward, as the Christian will receive reward for his perseverance. Being faithful to the end is not one of many options, but is the only way for the Christian, who does not abandon Christ. We are faithful by doing good works and enduring hardship. Remembering the ending that God intends is key in this teaching. If we trust in God, we will know he purposes all for good, even when that intended blessing is not before our eyes. We suffer with a knowledge that God's kingdom will come about, as the prophets of old did, none of whom saw Messiah come to his people. The New Testament people of God are in the direct line of the prophets.

Paul in Heb 12 deals directly with suffering as a means the Lord uses to chastise believers. He does not merely speak of the suffering of persecution that Christians were familiar with in that day, but the suffering of God's scourge, which comes down rightly on a disobedient people. The churches he writes to have yet to successfully strive against sin (v. 4), so they are punished with suffering. Yet as we see in other passages about being conformed to Christ, suffering is the necessary and integral part of being one with Christ. Once Christ is our Lord, he punishes us for our wrongs, lovingly as a father does. In fact, that suffering only proves to us that we are his children, so necessary it is for the children of God to be disciplined. If we have not suffered, can we really be sure we are beloved by God? Can we know we are God's children? Paul says that we would be illegitimate in such a case. We'd not be children at all (vv. 5–9). We can know then, that the Lord is with us when we are chastised for our sins. It is right and good. Just as a father has the good of his son in mind when he punishes him, much more so the Lord Jesus has our good in mind when he scourges us. He is ridding us of the sin in our lives, relieving our guilt, and helping us to hate sin as he does. All of this punishment accomplishes. The fruit of our righteousness is long lasting, and the punishment by comparison is brief.

Paul ends, teaching:

> For they verily for a few days chastened us after their own pleasure; *but he for our profit*, that we might be partakers of his holiness.
>
> Now no chastening for the present seemeth to be joyous, but grievous: nevertheless afterward it yieldeth the peaceable fruit of righteousness unto them which are exercised thereby. (vv. 10–11)

I recall the Polish writer Aleksander Wat, who spent years in Polish and Russian prisons during World War 2. Wat had been a communist writer, being influential in bringing that terrible worldview into his country, and in creating the political conflicts that tore it apart. The evils of communist empires and political systems live with us to this day. Wat's story is amazing and everyone should read it. He would later come to believe in God while in prison, the same day that Germany invaded Russia, eventually leaving his previous worldview entirely to become a Catholic. He was through amazing circumstances freed from Russia, and returned to his own country, where he would produce writing more Christian in character, and speak out against the falsehoods of communism. He later moved and continued writing in France, and also recorded his autobiographical work while living in the United States.

When Wat suffered an agonizing illness in his old age, he came to see it as deeply connected to his earlier leftist work. "My illness is essentially demonic... The devil behind my illness is the devil of communism," he said to fellow writer Czeslaw Milosz, as they recorded his life story on tape.[10] Wat had played a part in the political movement that left many millions enslaved or dead. It seemed natural to him that his illness was sent to chasten him for that involvement, and so that he could learn from his suffering. His own illness was tiny compared to the pain he had caused to the world. For how many men had socialist empires starved, robbed, brutalized, and murdered? It is that kind of introspection that any Christian ought to have with his own suffering. He should ask God if it is there to correct him because of evil in his life. He can come to see it as God's chastening, and let it shape him and renew him through the pain itself. If every westerner viewed the horrors of violent crime and of terrorism as a scourge in the hand of God, imagine the repentance their nations would know. It is not a blind meaningless experience. That pain is a reminder and a lesson for Christians who sin. That scourge is far from the suffering of hell, but points our own sin and helps us to regret it. It further reminds us we belong to God, and will be united fully with Christ in heaven. We have a Father who loves us, and he will steer us rightly when he punishes us.

> When Christ, who is our life, shall appear, then shall ye also appear with him in glory.
>
> *Mortify therefore your members* which are upon the earth; fornication, uncleanness, inordinate affection, evil concupiscence, and covetousness, which is idolatry:
>
> For which things' sake the wrath of God cometh on the children of disobedience: (Col 3:4–6)
>
> For if ye live after the flesh, ye shall die: but if ye through the Spirit *do mortify the deeds of the body*, ye shall live. (Rom 8:13)
>
> I protest by your rejoicing which I have in Christ Jesus our Lord, *I die daily.* (1 Cor 15:31)
>
> *Him that overcometh* will I make a pillar in the temple of my God, and he shall go no more out: and I will write upon him the

---

10. Wat, *My Century*, 11–12. Wat's faith, like his conversion, was a largely personal and mystical thing. It should be noted that Wat, later in life, killed himself. However, that was likely as a result of his severe, ongoing, untreatable pain, and not an empty or miserable life.

name of my God, and the name of the city of my God, which is new Jerusalem, which cometh down out of heaven from my God: and I will write upon him my new name. (Rev 3:12)

He that overcometh shall inherit all things; and I will be his God, and he shall be my son. (Rev 21:7)

If at the core of uniting with Christ is suffering, and turning from sin, then the very life of that experience is in one thing: going to our death. If we are going to accept shedding our previous treasured sins, if we are going to accept being hated and beaten for our faith, if we're going to accept chastisement from Christ, we have to die first. That death we experience happens first through faith and baptism, when we are made a new creature. Passing through the waters of baptism take us, as Rom 6 explains, from death to life. Yet the dying of the old corrupt nature does not end there, but works itself out through our coming life in Christ. Paul spoke of dying as a daily matter, after having already believed and been baptized. The death the flesh experiences through the waters is applied to us in our suffering and our departure from sins. We put to death each of our lusts. We replace them with the will of Christ. Each of our false desires must die so that the heart of Christ within us lives and beats fully in a new man. This hurts. It sounds unattractive or even impossible to our flesh. The carnal man hates it. Yet if we are spiritual, and made anew, we will do this, empowered by the Spirit to act and be victorious.

Revelation promises that those who overcome will be in God's kingdom (21:7). It does not promise this for those who fall away and return to sin. It is the persevering who will be finally united with Christ, even having a new name by him. It is the persevering who will inherit everything, as a son inherits from his father. Revelation teaches many times to persevere over temptation and over struggles and suffering, presenting it as a necessity. To suffer for Christ ensures eternity with him. We will fully know our belonging, our sonship, at the end.

All Things for Good

The purpose of suffering is deepened and brought powerfully to reality in the life in Christ. Where for the man in the flesh, suffering is nothing but pain, and then an end in hell, for the man in the spirit, suffering will always work for the good. The suffering servant is an effective weapon in the armory of God. We are taught in Rom 8, "all things work together for good to them that love God, to them who are the called according to his purpose" (v. 28). That is an incredible statement about how God uses our whole lives. He is shaping all for the good if we are his children. There are even times that this good-working is visible to us, either at the moment or when we look at recent history. Yahweh is a God of mystery, but he is also a God of revelation, who manifests for us truth and shows us a glimpse of his glory. Though we are not promised particular answers, we sometimes get them, and we are shown them grandly.

One recent event which manifests how God uses suffering for the good came in the kidnapping of a group of Christian missionaries in Haiti. They were doing aid work and sharing the gospel when a criminal gang took them, and held them captive for a very large ransom.[11] Honestly, considering the size of the ransom, and the danger of criminals in Haiti, I didn't think they'd all make it. I thought at least we'd lose some of these brethren. However, regardless of whether these missionaries lived or died, I knew one thing confidently—this could be the greatest opportunity we could imagine. Who needs to hear the call to repent and believe in Christ more on earth than a gang of hardened criminals? These are likely men who see and hear all kinds of vulgarity, lewdness, and cruelty. They could be accustomed to darkness as the norm, to lies, crime, and violence as daily and acceptable activities. It was clear to me God had sent those missionaries there, not only to this dangerous country, but to the very presence of their captors. God had placed them there as his weapon. He was going to bring his laser light to those captors, and pierce their souls. Despite the danger of the captivity, and the fact I'd never want to be in the same situation myself, my heart could think about the hostages and rejoice. You see in man's fallen way of thinking these Christians are locked up with very dangerous men. In God's economy, very dangerous men are locked up with them. Rejoice, and know God is present in suffering, and not only this, but that it is his weapon against evil. He locked a bunch of dangerous hardened criminals up with his children. They will not come out the same.

The results of this long captivity ended up illustrating the truths of the Bible. I'd say it perfectly illustrated some of the points I've reviewed so far in this book. Firstly, God protected his children from death by a manner that sounds much like the book of Acts (5:17–23, 12:6–9), and the escape that Paul, Peter, and others had from immediate danger. The

---

11. McDonnell, Mozingo, and Kaleem, "Missionaries Kidnapped in Haiti."

captive missionaries discovered one day the door had been left unlocked. Not only that, but the way out was left unguarded. They had been preparing for a possible situation like this, and quickly organized themselves to depart. They made their way out of their holding cell at night, and crossed miles of land in pitch dark, until they finally came to safety. Their story, of captivity and of escape, became known to the entire world. I never thought it would happen myself, but it did.

What did the Christians testify to when they were released? They said that throughout their captivity, they had opportunity to speak directly to the criminals and to the leader of the gang. They had opportunity to tell them to repent of their sin, and that if they continued it would lead them to destruction. They proclaimed salvation in Christ, and called the captors to trust in Christ, for he is the only way to be saved. Not only this, but they witnessed the truth of Christ through their kind words, their chaste behavior, simplicity, modesty, and prayer.[12] It was a firebomb from God upon the enemy's territory and it came in the form of hardship and pain. The Christian need only trust in God, see his job before him, and he plays a role in the redemption of this world. His hardship is brought to glory.

Suffering is healing, both in our salvation, and in making us more Christlike—less selfish, less dependent on the flesh, more dependent on God, more prayerful, less lustful, more spiritual. Suffering can cleanse us within. Paul teaches that he keeps his body under subjection, "lest that by any means, when I have preached to others, I myself should be a castaway" (1 Cor 9:27). If we already understand that an athlete becomes a greater athlete through the pain of difficult training, we can understand that suffering expands the beautiful inner sanctuary of the human soul. If we already understand that the discipline applied to becoming educated, or a musician, or a soldier takes a man to meet his goal, we can understand that setting aside our desires, and putting to death our members, brings the child of God to run the race, and win the crown in heaven.

We see parallels to what God does in Christ all the time. Consider the painful, and sometimes deadly treatments that exist for cancer. No one wants to go through them, but that pain can be a healing experience and save us from death. It causes a level of destruction to the body, but may also kill the cancer. If we can recognize that mankind can heal the

---

12. Innerfire Ministries, "Haiti Missionaries Tell Their Story."

body through the cancer treatment, even though it comes with pain, we can recognize that God Almighty can heal the soul through the cancer itself. Again: if man can heal through the pains of chemotherapy, God can heal through the pains of cancer. He is not limited to using our medicine.

The Sorrow of Jabez

There's an interesting passage in First Chronicles, that has little introduction, and doesn't easily fit into biblical history. It's there nonetheless by the Holy Spirit, and it jumps right out at you, a sudden bright light compared to the surrounding chunky genealogies. That is the several verses describing Jabez:

> And Jabez was more honourable than his brethren: and his mother called his name Jabez, saying, Because I bare him with sorrow.
>
> And Jabez called on the God of Israel, saying, Oh that thou wouldest bless me indeed, and enlarge my coast, and that thine hand might be with me, and that thou wouldest keep me from evil, that it may not grieve me! And God granted him that which he requested. (1 Chr 4:9–10)

Of those who bring up these verses, many focus on the prayer for blessing and a grand territory. They use it to encourage prayers for prosperity, but I think they miss the greater point here, and misuse what is present regarding God's blessing.

Jabez was literally named after pain. His childbirth had caused his mother pain, and likely danger, especially in an age of greater death in childbearing. He became more honorable than his brothers, it tells us, so that we ought to seriously consider his words, as the words of the righteous. Jabez prayed for righteousness, and he prayed to not cause others pain. These should be regular prayers and meditations of the Christian heart. His being birthed in pain, perhaps seriously risking his mother's life, likely let him to more deeply respect the lives of others, and empathize with their pain. His prayer was an honorable prayer, and whatever Jabez may have asked for in material gain, he did for a specific purpose—that he might serve Yahweh with that gain.

Jabez did not simply want to be wealthy, but to bring about a world of righteousness, and protect human life and dignity. Through his mother's pain, he learned to hate causing others pain, and with it to love doing good. One woman's suffering forged in Jabez the light of goodness. So too, more than a millennium later, one woman's childbearing brought an end to all sin and death, through the righteous Child she bore. He kept us from evil and healed our affliction. Jabez tells us about righteousness, and about pain, and I believe finally about Christ. Being birthed in sorrow, he sought to heal the sorrow of others.

When I worked in ministry, I had a contact whose teenage daughter was being treated for cancer. That hardship would have been unimaginable to me growing up, and I would have thought of it as worse than death. She had her sixteenth birthday in the hospital, where other girls have them in far more pleasant and joyous circumstances. Yet I sensed nothing about this girl that was depressed, or bitter, or disillusioned toward her God. In all my conversations with her, as well as with her parents, I could see she had little fear, and trusted in God throughout her ordeal. She knows that if she doesn't survive she will be in the presence of the Son of God. She knows her experience in the hospital can be more of a blessing than the normal life of a teenage girl at home. There was no trauma to her mind or soul, or sense that her hardship was an injustice. Christ brought her peace.

I also have an old friend I know from ministry. He has been in a wheelchair since he was struck by a car in his youth. My friend cannot walk at all, and also has organ damage, that makes his gut not function properly. He was not a believer when he was struck, and thrown into this whole new world, but became a Christian during his ongoing trial and his pain. He understands that, despite the crippling effects of the crash, and despite God being loving and life-giving, that his suffering is not out of place for the wicked life he had been living. It could have come to him simply as a warning from God, before his time ran out to repent. It could have been a life-saving warning. I sent him an article recently on one of those amazing treatments, which as much as man's inventions can be called miraculous, looks miraculous. It was about some electronic machine that allowed paralyzed people to walk, by stimulating their nerves to talk to one another. My friend was not very moved by the article. He said he'd rather not have electronic devices in him. His wheelchair is the throne of God's glory. God has given it to him to manifest Christ for the world. This is not only because his suffering led him to call to the Lord, but because he goes out regularly in that chair and evangelizes the lost. He testifies to God's glory in Christ, and what God has done for him. What many would call a curse, he knows blesses the kingdom of

God beyond measure. On top of this, he can notice that people are more willing to talk with him when he shares the gospel, and less likely to be insulting and disrespectful, largely because he's in a wheelchair. Even in this vulgar and egoist culture, most people know it is tasteless to berate the severely disabled. So he has more people's ear when he tells them about Jesus. He has more people willing to take a tract from him. The brokenness in his body is there for God's glory.

The idea that suffering is a cursing is turned upside down in the life of a Christian, just as it is turned upside down at the cross of the dying Lamb. We know for a fact how our comforts and nourishment easily become a sinful snare, and how pain has come to bless us. We pray differently knowing this. We care for God's will to be done, even if the ax falls on us. During a recent spate of arrests in China of Christians and their leaders, a Chinese pastor said he was "grateful" for this chance to be arrested and go to prison. Another pastor said many Christians in his country view prison sentences as a blessing, adding, "Prison is a mission field . . . so many hungry and thirsty souls waiting to listen to the Gospel."[13] Prison sentences are common there when Christians are arrested, and these faithful disciples of Christ are able to put aside any fear, or outrage at injustice, and receive suffering in the same way as their Lord. Though outwardly they look weak, inwardly they are filled with supernatural power. Though outwardly they appear to lose, inwardly they conquer for Christ.

These are not random people I mention who just happened to be very strong or very wise in the face of adversity. They are common souls who continue in a long line of children of God, who have been given the answers they need by their faith, and finally from Christ. They know what the answer is. They are not confounded, but are informed and built up by their faith, and by the Holy Bible. Anyone can persevere with the same grace if he knows the Lord. A man must only give up his false notions about his life existing for his pleasure and for his own goals, to see why his life exists in the first place. For an unbeliever, a life of disability, or a young person with a fatal disease, seem like among the worst things that could happen on earth. They would do anything in the world to avoid it, and perhaps would seek to end their life through suicide if they ever had to live through that pain, having to drop all the dreams of their heart entirely. To end it all would sound better. The Christian knows it is

---

13. Lodge, "Chinese Pastor 'Grateful.'"

not our life that should end. It is our sin that should end, our vain glory, our living for self. If our life ends in the pursuit of that aim, we ought to embrace it. God and his ultimate good are glorified, whether by life or death.

A Summary

The answer of Christ and the solution of Christ to suffering surpasses Job's adequate answer. The revelation of God's Son teaches us that God binds suffering to the greatest good possible. In fact, the world is cured of sin and death through the balm of suffering. It reveals that God is not sitting impassively beyond our world of pain, but joins us fully in that pain, that we have a God who, despite being Ruler of all, practices humility, takes on the weaknesses of human nature, and endures suffering and death out of his love. That is the attitude we must take and our model for us. The gospel also shows us how all death and suffering will be conquered on earth and forever—through the cross and resurrection that God brought to pass. Suffering is a mere moment in our lives, in fact a mere moment in human history, which will end in eternity in a new heavens and a new earth. The terrible fall of mankind in the garden will be reversed, and is being reversed in Christ. Suffering is the result of the fall, and is also the cure for the fall; it was the cure for all at Jesus' death, and is the cure for us throughout our lives, as it unites us deeply with Jesus and assures us we are his children. We in turn take up healing others, as their comforters and teachers, being ambassadors for Christ's kingdom. We minister to others, help the oppressed, heal the sick, and preach the gospel by which men will know eternal life. In accepting the goodness of Christ's death, and of our own suffering, we become his hands on this earth in saving others. We do not reject suffering, or consider it injustice, but are honored to experience it for Christ's sake.

It simply is not possible to receive this truth from God, and then go on to pity ourselves when we feel pain. It is not possible to use pain, or the pain of our loved ones, as an excuse not to love God, or as a vain accusation against his eternal glory. In fact, once we know the answer, we marvel at God all the more, and we love him more richly and fully, as we know more richly and fully his goodness. Once we see what God has used pain for in our lives, we cannot just look back and reject it, but rather are grateful for it, that we were chosen to suffer to bring about his will. We can see its cleansing and purification in our lives. Pain is no more a nightmarish mystery, or a capricious demon that seems far worse than death. It has been unmasked. It has been revealed. Then we have been shown the hand of God in it.

I will end this section with the prayer of Polycarp at his death. In the words of this early Christian bishop and martyr, death for our Lord is an honor:

> "O Lord God Almighty, the Father of your beloved and blessed Son Jesus Christ, by whom we have received the knowledge of You, the God of angels and powers, and of every creature, and of the whole race of the righteous who live before you, I give You thanks that You have counted me, worthy of this day and this hour, that I should have a part in the number of Your martyrs, in the cup of your Christ, to the resurrection of eternal life, both of soul and body, through the incorruption [imparted] by the Holy Ghost. Among whom may I be accepted this day before You as a fat and acceptable sacrifice, according as You, the ever-truthful God, have foreordained, have revealed beforehand to me, and now have fulfilled. Wherefore also I praise You for all things, I bless You, I glorify You, along with the everlasting and heavenly Jesus Christ, Your beloved Son, with whom, to You, and the Holy Ghost, be glory both now and to all coming ages. Amen."

—From *The Martyrdom of Polycarp*, by the Church of Smyrna[14]

---

14. Church of Smyrna, *The Martyrdom of Polycarp*, X, 14:1–3, 207–208.

PART 2

5

Be cleansed of your filth

ONE MOMENT BROUGHT TO us all the corruption, falsehood, pain, and evil that we see. That is a moment of disobedience by man. One act can similarly cleanse us, which is the sacrifice of our Savior, which we receive through trust in him. When he touches upon our soul, we are free of guilt, united with the pure and eternal life of God, and will be brought into a land which is free of the suffering and death we see. Despite philosophical and theological questions on smaller matters, the diagnosis of our human state, and the cure for it, are essentially simple.

What is that faith which saves? According to the Holy Scriptures, it is the faith that Jesus is the Son of God, that he came down from heaven, died for our sins, and rose again on the third day (John 20:31, 1 John 4:15, 1 Cor 15:3-4, Rom 10:9). That is the simple faith. It is only by a gift of the Holy Spirit that a man can believe in this in a sincere and abiding way. At the same time, that faith is more than an intellectual assent. It is more than being convinced by an evidentiary argument. It comes with a love of Christ and a longing to be with him. It comes with a love for what Christ does and a desire to be like him, and to obey him. We believe real truths, but we also believe supernaturally, and with love. That is one reason why faith for many begins with simple love of Jesus, before right doctrine falls into place.

While many Christians cannot associate their faith with a simple moment in time, finding it became a reality gradually as they grew in personal knowledge of Jesus, I view one memorable and life-changing moment as the beginning of faith. It came after months of reading a pocket New Testament someone must have left in one of my dwellings. I don't know where I got it, but when I had time on my hands, I would be reading it, until I was writing tiny notes in the margins, and underlining my favorite passages. I was lying in bed one night, neither asleep nor awake, and I saw in my mind's eye a vision of darkness. It was utterly black. It was also a darkness that was sensory and personal, and that communicated a sense of evil. Next, I saw in my mind a light, and this was also sensory and personal, and the light battled the darkness, and the light defeated it. I knew that the light was good, and that the light came from God. God was that light. I could sense its goodness as by heat coming off a fire. It was in this moment that I desired to be on the side of that light, and I wanted to live with it forever. I wanted to embrace it. I looked and soon found myself together with that light, and with all of its forces. There had been in spirit a blood transfusion which transcended any intellectual complexities of unbelief. I was on a new side now.

That experience may not have been an infusion of doctrinal Christianity, but it brought to my soul the basic truth of God and Christ, and I believed in Jesus continually from that moment. It took me time to learn in the period after this, and surely my belief system was not orthodox in any manner for a few years. I read the Bible. I read much commentary, and looked to apologetics to answer many of the questions I had. I carelessly juggled biblical teachings with mysticism and personal ideas, until eventually I gave up the false notions for the doctrines of Scripture. One can look at becoming a child of God as a long process, but the life changed, the earth moved beneath my feet, in that one moment. It only took an instant. I was no longer on the other side. I was on God's side. Beneath any intellectual objections, or personal beliefs I held rightly or wrongly, I had gone from unbelief to belief. Everything else came afterward, and subordinate to it. I consider that act supernatural, and no wrong idea I ever held could have stopped it. It was simple and pure, and amounted to a man which was trapped in the flesh coming instead to dwell in the spirit, and coming to Christ.

To understand how the hand of God heals us in Christ, it's good to first take a clear look at what the disease is. It is multifold. One part of our experience stems from the fact our corruption came from disobedience: That is, we are in a state of guilt. We are outside of rightful citizenship, and are legally a criminal. When we stand before the judgment of God, we will be found guilty. Guilty people do not have peace with God, nor does a fugitive on the run from justice have peace with the law. We furthermore suffer a separation from the spiritual life of God, with whom we formerly had fellowship and connection. Just as your lamp will go out when you yank the plug out of the wall, the divine resources we had are now gone from us, and we know darkness; the corruption of the body which pains us, a blindness to the things of God. We are thirdly enslaved. Having committed ourselves to Adam, and in this to the devil, we rightfully belong to him, being held under his power, bound by his deceptions, and citizens of a kingdom of death. We are in bondage, as slaves, as Israel was in Egypt, a bondage we are both born into, and place ourselves under by choice. We cannot and we will not give God his due, and live as we should in righteousness. Our soul is bound to serve self and to serve Satan. It does not know the truth, and is enslaved to sin, even becoming hardened to sin, and making evil its norm until goodness seems harsh, blinding, and cold.

Impurity is in the depth of our nature, saturating the soul to the fiber of our being. What must happen to that blackened soul is a miracle. It must be made anew in a supernatural act akin to resurrection, and akin to the creation of the cosmos. That does not happen in outward acts, or in religious ritual. The nature of the Son of God must touch on our soul, and by his power he will bring newness, purity, knowledge, and love. His light and life must enter us. I can remember when I lived overseas, it occasionally happened that I'd get back home with meat I'd bought, and find when I tried to cook it, that it was bad. It smelled okay from the outset, but shortly into cooking it began to stink, and become oily. You could try all you like to season it and that stink would be there. You could put herbs and spices over it, but they would do little to mask the scent. You could try wine, and you'd just have bad meat saturated and encrusted with wine. The meat was bad to its core, and it would not change. Similarly, the human soul is corrupt to the depth of its being, and needs more than the garnishment of ritual and ethical deeds. It needs rebirth. It needs a power outside itself to bring newness and life, and destroy what was dead. That supernatural act, that finger of God, is Jesus Christ. Humbly repenting, and trusting in Christ, brings his power on you, and the dead filth will fall away, the new pure soul will be built. Every level of the problem of our guilt is done away with. Every layer of corruption cut away. Our identity as common criminal expunged, and our new life as a peaceful and submitting citizen created. Our ability to please God restored. Yahweh performs this in an instant, and then applies it to us over time through our new life. His supernatural power is the only one that can do this miracle.

The image of Christ on the cross is of a brutalized man. It is something that would bring anyone to weeping, and to deep grief, to see a loved one suffer. Even if it were not God himself; were it our brother, sister, or spouse, we would weep. We would long for it never to occur. We would instinctively cry out—No!—as if it were impossible to be happening, and cry out to God to stop the evil. We would cry to the heavens. More greatly should we weep over Christ our brother, to see him suffer; to see him go through injustice, indignity, and death. If we did not weep we would not be human. If we loved cruelty and injustice, we would be of the most depraved mind. It is right to be repulsed by seeing the only innocent man that ever lived treated like an animal, worse than garbage. Yet at the same time, were we to reject this act that occurred nearly 2,000 years before this writing, we would be condemning countless people to agony. If we said, "Let it never be so," Christ could right there answer us, like he did Peter, "Get thee behind me, Satan" (Matt 16:23). We know persecuting the innocent is evil. We also know it had to happen.

AN UPSIDE-DOWN WORLD

I can remember the first times I read the gospels as an adult, thinking there's no way that's going to happen. Jesus does nothing but good. The people need to receive this man as king. They can't really put him to death! Something needs to happen to stop this. Come on. The murder seems nothing more than a disappointment, and one we are dreading to read about. We want Jesus to keep teaching and doing miracles and become king, making the whole nation righteous, and striking down its enemies. However, today there is a very different way that I sometimes respond when I am reading about the passion of Christ, or when I am thinking about all that occurred before that bloody point. I respond to the scene with great joy. My eyes light up. Sometimes I come to laughter, and chuckle to myself over and over. I do not lie to you. It makes me laugh. Am I a sick monster to be lit up with life when thinking of a sadistic murder, or the death of one I love? I don't think so. Because when this joy strikes me, it is because I can see, behind the words and behind the acts, God's victory over Satan played out step by step. I see each part played in the passion as a public destruction of the devil and all of his powers, and a perfectly played hand by God. Dwelling on these acts, I am elated, as if walking on air.

Yahweh is in control the entire time his Son gave his life for us. There is an outward appearance of death and loss, when the hidden reality is of life and victory. We can see victory wherever we look. The persecutors of Jesus put a crown of thorns on his head, a cruel and intelligent way to mock him as king. Yet little did they know the meaning of their act. For since the fall, man has been cursed with such thorns coming up from the ground, a part of the curse that included our hard labor, and our death (Gen 3:17-19). When Christ bore those thorns on him, he bore our curse too, and put that curse into the ground, destroying it. Crowned with death, he put death to death.

Pilate, introducing Christ to the crowd of accusers, decked in his crown and purple robe, declared, "Behold, the man!" (John 19:5). He thought he was presenting a criminal, and one he desired much to get off of his hands. He was presenting instead the New Man, the head of the new humanity. Where the old man had rejected obedience, the New Man accepts obedience, and walks it out to his death. He is presenting the rightful head of humanity.

The prophet Zechariah had spoken of Messiah, saying:

> *Behold the man* whose name is The BRANCH; and he shall grow up out of his place, and he shall build the temple of the LORD:
>
> Even he shall build the temple of the LORD; and he shall bear the glory, and *shall sit and rule upon his throne*. (Zech 6:12b-13a)

Far from presenting a criminal, Pilate was presenting the Savior, according to the words of the prophet, who predicted his coming. He is publicly declaring the man for the messianic throne. Unwittingly he is declaring the beginning of his rule, and a kingdom which will branch out across the globe. This presentation even echoes Yahweh's own words, as he presents the fact that the original man has fallen into sin:

> And the LORD God said, *Behold, the man is become as one of us*, to know good and evil: and now, lest he put forth his hand, and take also of the tree of life, and eat, and live for ever:
>
> Therefore the LORD God sent him forth from the garden of Eden, to till the ground from whence he was taken. (Gen 3:22-23)

In the exact same words as God banishes the man from the garden, the prophet prophesies the Messiah, and the Roman governor unknowingly declares the new humanity to the public. Behold. Here it is. Look! This is what humanity really is. God presented the old man in his sin, while the Roman governor presented the New Man in His righteousness.

The death of Messiah on the tree also turns upside down the death brought from the tree in the garden. Where man had left behind the tree of life because of his sin, forbidden to return, Jesus walked to his tree willingly. By hanging on that tree, through death he gave us access to life—making an instrument of death become the tree of life instead. We live forever because of that tree. Coming into his kingdom we will also be forever united with the tree of life, which Revelation describes "in the midst of the street of it, and on either side of the river" (22:2a), being fully beyond the curse of sin and death (v. 3).

The very nature of this execution served God's purpose. Where the Romans sought out a form of execution that publicly humiliated the criminal, and caused ongoing pain, and where the Jews recognized it as too shameful to even speak about, the cross was more than an organ of torture. Yahweh would use the cross to fulfill prophecy, and even signify who the Man on it was. Where the Man was lifted up from the earth on this tree, he would also receive honor and worship, and men would come to him. It would be as a beacon seen from afar. Where his body was broken before all, being a public disgrace, the sight of his death would heal many. Like the serpent in the wilderness, men would look upon him and live:

> And the LORD said unto Moses, Make thee a fiery serpent, and set it upon a pole: and it shall come to pass, that every one that is bitten, when he looketh upon it, shall live.
>
> And Moses made a serpent of brass, and put it upon a pole, and it came to pass, *that if a serpent had bitten any man, when he beheld the serpent of brass, he lived.* (Num 21:8–9)
>
> Now is the judgment of this world: now shall the prince of this world be cast out.
>
> And I, *if I be lifted up from the earth*, will draw all men unto me. (John 12:31–32)

The very mode of execution it seems would bring worship to the King, and life to the nations. The prophesied lifting up on the cross only revealed more greatly the honor Christ is due everywhere. The centurion who saw him on the cross glorified God, and said, "Certainly, this was a righteous man" (Luke 23:47). It would not be long until kings of nations saw him lifted up and called him Lord. The purpose of humiliation would be reversed and bring honor. The importance of seeing is even present in one of the most well-known messianic prophesies: "and *they shall look upon me* whom they have pierced, and they shall mourn for him, as one mourneth for his only son, and shall be in bitterness for him, as one that is in bitterness for his firstborn." (Zech 12:10b). The One who was lifted up would be seen, would be grieved, and great righteousness and blessing would come to the children of Israel.

Christ's burial itself is pregnant with meaning as well. Laid in a tomb, the Lord of Glory seemed small, burdened by the whole world, dust like anyone else. He appeared to have returned to dust like all mankind under the curse: "till thou return unto the ground; for out of it wast thou taken: for dust thou art, and unto dust shalt thou return" (Gen 3:19). Jesus' own disciples were in despair, and didn't know what to do. They were confused that their Master had died. Yet the same man lying in the tomb had made the entire earth, as well as the cosmos, and the uncountable stars. What a small thing it is for him to dwell in a hole in the ground, for surely if Yahweh can dwell in human nature he can dwell in a small hole. As Yahweh is master of all things—the heavens, mankind, life itself—then surely he can rise out again. It is a miracle to us, but is it more unreachable than bringing on the dusk, or bringing on the dawn, to the God of creation?

Of Jesus, John says, "All things were made by him; and without him was not any thing made that was made" (John 1:3). Paul similarly writes, "For by him were all things created, that are in heaven, and that are in earth, visible and invisible, whether they be thrones, or dominions, or principalities, or powers: all things were created by him, and for him" (Col 1:16). The grave may be a place of corruption, but it is no more than an instrument in the hands of him who made it. His presence there further makes the grave a place of life for us, since he has entered and overcome it. The result of the curse now is our entrance to heaven.

The prophet Jonah would spend three days in the belly of a great fish. When he was spat out, he would preach repentance to a pagan people, and many would turn from their sins (Jonah 1:17—3:10). The Prophet who would come after Jonah would spend three days in the belly of the earth. When he rose out again, he would bring salvation to the ends of the earth, taking the light that was within Israel to all of the nations. As Jonah went to preach to a people beyond Israel, Jesus brought a gospel for Israel and the world. This worldwide victory was proclaimed many centuries before his time:

> And he said, It is a light thing that thou shouldest be my servant to raise up the tribes of Jacob, and to restore the preserved of Israel: I will also *give thee for a light to the Gentiles*, that thou mayest be my salvation unto the end of the earth. (Isa 49:6)

Again and again the appearance of death, loss, humiliation become manifestations of victory. Once you see what is going on, it is one long humiliation of the devil, at the hands of Christ. He made a public spectacle of him. The curse is put to death. The flesh and sin sent to the grave. The Savior of mankind drawing all men to him, out of the hands of Satan and into the hands of God. The Maker of all the earth, leaping up from the earth. There is much more to say about those details of the passion than I have mentioned, and I hope you study it to see for yourself. God is supreme at the cross, and is taking away the powers of hell.

I'M BLEEDING LIFE

People think Christianity is rather obsessed with blood. It's got blood to atone, blood to sanctify. People sing songs about blood, and speak of it like it is supernatural. There is a good explanation for this interest, and for why it frees mankind from the bonds of sin. Blood was necessary to free us. A part of why a man had to die was in keeping with Yahweh's plan and purpose he had before laid out. Yahweh desired to show his love and sacrifice in the cross, and had even desired this from before creation. The cross was consistent with the rites he had commanded in the temple, which required the life of an animal, usually the shedding of blood, to atone for sins. In a sense, God was being consistent with himself to do so. But that only demands one ask: Why was that pattern there from the beginning? Why did God desire blood? Why did he instruct in it? A part of the answer is in the simple truth given in Scripture. It tells us what the blood actually is, teaching:

> *For the life of the flesh is in the blood*: and I have given it to you upon the altar to make an atonement for your souls: for it is the blood that maketh an atonement for the soul. (Lev 17:11)

The blood is necessary because it contains the life. God had even commanded Noah long before, "But flesh with the life thereof, *which is the blood* thereof, shall ye not eat" (Gen 9:4). It is the blood, life containing, that makes atonement for our soul, covering our sins. The blood allows the life to pour out. The sacrifices in the temple bled as the normal way of dying, giving up their life for the guilty sinner, who should have given up his life. This practice, which lasted for over 1,400 years, slaughtering millions of animals over that time, was only pointing towards, and teaching about the eternal sacrifice: Christ pouring out his blood, and Christ pouring out his life. The animals were only able to cleanse man so deeply, and for so long. Yet Christ is able to cleanse man forever, through one single sacrifice of his life. The pouring out of blood is the pouring out of life, and God always intended to save through the death of his Son. The blood sanctifies us, as it did in the rituals of the temple, but now it sanctifies through the blood of the divine God-man, whose life is perfect, who forms us to his character, and fills our being with his life. Christianity is full of blood because it is full of life, and no one knows greater love, than to give his life for his friend (John 15:13). Who does not recognize the goodness and mercy of another who pours out his life for us? Who would not want to be bonded with the life of God forever? Who would not want to be sprinkled with the goodness which pours forth from the Father in heaven?

How another man's death can save the guilty sinner isn't intuitive to most of us. If anything, it might seem unfair, since it causes the innocent to suffer, and takes the just penalty away from the guilty. The Bible gives us further details of this truth which may help us understand, but doesn't seek to explain all the inner workings of redemption. Many Christians historically have allowed some flexibility in how we see the saving nature of the cross, at least within the basic bounds of the Scriptures. Let us look at what the giving of Christ's life does for corrupt man, in how it brings us peace with the Father. The accomplishments of the cross are multifold.

The Sin Bearer

Christ's act at the cross saves us first in removing our guilt. There are many Christians who wish to skip this layer of its power, but our fallen condition includes real guilt, and it must be removed. The Lord Jesus does this for us through the offering of his life on the cross. His priestly offering acts as a means of bearing our punishment for us, the pain that we were meant to endure. It also provides God the Father with a perfect offering, that of a life lived fully for God, and used fully to honor him. It gives God his due. For God does not merely plan to dismiss his judgment for our sin, as the evil we do deserves judgment. Rather, he displays his judgment at the cross, in the suffering and death of his Son. We can look at the cross anytime and see what our sin really deserves, and what we really deserve.

Isaiah 53 speaks of the suffering Messiah, and what his suffering would accomplish:

> But he was wounded for our transgressions, he was bruised for our iniquities: *the chastisement of our peace was upon him*; and with his stripes we are healed.
>
> All we like sheep have gone astray; we have turned every one to his own way; and the LORD *hath laid on him the iniquity of us all*. (Isa 53:5–6)

The wounds, and ultimately the death that Jesus would suffer, were because of our transgression. Just as the sacrifices of the temple bore our sins, the Servant too would carry our sins upon him as a part of the sacrifice. His chastisement, or punishment, is for "our peace," which is peace with God, and peace eternally. He had to suffer, as we should have suffered. He is being punished for the disobedient people. Hebrews 9:28 similarly mentions this function: "So Christ was once offered *to bear the sins of many*; and unto them that look for him shall he appear the second time without sin unto salvation."

This is consistent with the Mosaic animal sacrifices. The sacrifices atoned for individual sins, and at Yom Kippur, for Israel's national sins. The animal had to give up its life, and in most sacrifices, its blood would pour out and be used in purifying. It would purify people, as well as holy items. Before returning up Sinai to receive the law, Moses purified the people with sprinkling the blood of the covenant (Exod 24:8). Commonly the priest put his hand on the head of the sacrifice before killing it, and once it was dead it succeeded in making atonement for the sin, albeit of a shallower and more temporal kind than Christ offers. Perhaps the clearest description of how an animal bears sin is at the national Day of Atonement, and the scapegoat animal which would be led into the wilderness to die.

> And Aaron shall lay both his hands upon the head of the live goat, and confess over him all the iniquities of the children of Israel, and all their transgressions in all their sins, *putting them*

upon the head of the goat, and shall send him away by the hand of a fit man into the wilderness: (Lev 16:21)

The goat is bearing the sins of the people, which otherwise they would be bearing themselves. To bear sin is a common term for guilt, and we see it used frequently in the Old Testament. Leviticus 5:17, 22:9, Num 9:13, 18:32, and others each use this phrase to speak of carrying real guilt. This is a guilt bearing sacrifice. It is put in our place, so we do not need to bear the guilt, and then suffer as we should have suffered. Further sacrifices of Yom Kippur atone for the sins of the High Priest or of Israel:

> And Aaron shall bring the bullock of the sin offering, which is for himself, and shall make an atonement for himself, and for his house, and *shall kill the bullock of the sin offering which is for himself*:
>
> And he shall take a censer full of burning coals of fire from off the altar before the LORD, and his hands full of sweet incense beaten small, and bring it within the vail:
>
> And he shall put the incense upon the fire before the LORD, that the cloud of the incense may cover the mercy seat that is upon the testimony, that he die not:
>
> And he shall take of the blood of the bullock, and sprinkle it with his finger upon the mercy seat eastward; and before the mercy seat shall he sprinkle of the blood with his finger seven times.
>
> Then *shall he kill the goat of the sin offering, that is for the people,* and bring his blood within the vail, and do with that blood as he did with the blood of the bullock, and sprinkle it upon the mercy seat, and before the mercy seat:
>
> And he shall make an atonement for the holy place, *because of the uncleanness of the children of Israel, and because of their transgressions in all their sins*: and so shall he do for the tabernacle of the congregation, that remaineth among them in the midst of their uncleanness. (Lev 16:11–16)

Even modern Orthodox Jews, who have not had a temple for two millennia, recognize something of this transference of sin, from the people to the animal being sacrificed. Some sects of Orthodox still do a non-temple sacrifice on Yom Kippur, killing a chicken, instead of the prescribed animals. As they perform this modern sacrifice, they say a prayer such as this: "This is my exchange, *my substitute*, my atonement, this one shall go to its death, but I shall go to a good, long life, and to peace." That is the mandated liturgical prayer. After many centuries, traditional Jews have not forgotten the substitutionary nature of the sacrifice, nor the need for the animal to give its life. It is interesting that it appears as part of a longer, similar petition, revealing more layers to the meaning of the sacrifice:

> "Children of man who sit in darkness and the shadow
> of death, bound in misery and chains of iron—He will bring
> them out of darkness and the shadow of death, and will
> sunder their bonds. Foolish sinners, afflicted because of their
> sinful ways and their wrongdoings; their soul loathes all food
> and they reach the gates of death—they cry out to the Lord
> in their distress; He saves them from their afflictions. He
> sends forth His word and heals them; He delivers them from
> their graves. Let them thank the Lord for His kindness, and
> [proclaim] His wonders to the children of man.
> If there be for a man [even] one interceding angel out of a thousand
> [accusers], to speak of his uprightness in his behalf, then He
> will be gracious to him and say: Redeem him from going
> down to the grave; I have found expiation [for him]. "[1]

We see a fuller panorama of a modern Jewish idea of atonement here, which certainly parallels what Christ truly does for us. It includes the sinner's deadened and darkened state, the conquest over death, the breaking open of bonds, and healing of the soul. It speaks of our redemption coming from the atonement of this sacrifice. The sacrifice "expiates," or takes away our guilt. While we don't rely on the traditions of non-Christians for truth, this Jewish line of tradition is totally consistent with what we see in Scripture, and they will mention in their writings some of the same Torah passages that we do, including that the life of the flesh is in the blood, and the sacrificial instructions of Lev 16. This only shows I am not presenting you with some rare understanding of the text. Rather, the Mosaic sacrifices, the prophesies of Isaiah, and the New Testament sacrifice of Christ are consistent in their truths, because the sacrifice truly bears our sins, becoming our substitute.

1. Mangel, "Order of Kapparot," 2.

BE CLEANSED OF YOUR FILTH

The medieval rabbi Nachmanides perhaps spelled it out more clearly than any in his commentary on Lev 1, which is regarding the burnt sacrifices. While Judaism contains many mystical aspects, and more recently rationalistic ones, the prominent rabbi here just draws from the description of the sacrifices, and gives an obvious way it functions in atonement. After describing the parts of the animals which were burnt up, and how they each correspond to a part of our body and soul, he writes:

> All these acts are performed in order that when they are done, a person should realize that he has sinned against his G-d with his body and his soul, and that "his" blood should really be spilled and "his" body burned, were it not for the loving-kindness of the Creator, Who took from him a substitute and a ransom, namely this offering, *so that its blood should be in place of his blood, its life in place of his life,* and that the chief limbs of the offering should be in place of the chief parts of his body.[2]

Another interesting point about the Jewish understanding of atonement, not merely regarding the sacrifices instituted in Torah, is the fact that Jewish oral tradition has long taught a remarkably similar truth to the Christian faith—that a righteous man, through his suffering and death, can atone for the sins of others.[3] In Jewish commentary this may be the sins of a particular generation, or it may be the sins of the nation as a whole. They understand that beyond the animal sacrifices, there is a form of sacrifice a human being can make, despite their strong outrage against human sacrifice as a ritual. The suffering and death of a righteous man atones for the sins of many. This is very well documented in Jewish tradition, and is an ancient teaching.

Now many modern Jewish articles on the subject are quick to point out they are not teaching "the same thing" as Christian doctrine. They don't want to sound like they agree with Christians or justify their doctrine regarding Jesus' sacrificial death. They may argue that their doctrine does not relate to everyone, but only to one generation, or that it does not relate to the whole world, but only to Israel. Thus, they teach differently. However, it's very clear these are only surface differences. The key point is the same—a righteous man's death can atone for the sins of others.

---

2. Nachmanides, *Commentary*, Vayikra, 1:9.

3. Evan-Israel, "The Life of the Righteous Is Everlasting." In his article, Evan-Israel even cites Isa 53, the passage Christians take to be messianic, as an example of the principle that the death of the righteous man atones for others, though he doesn't present a substitutionary view.

If Jesus were only a man, or if he had committed sin in his life, Christians would be the first persons to agree with these Jewish claims, and place limits on what his death could accomplish. The difference in the Christian doctrine is there, not because the core point is different, but because Jesus is different—He is God and man, who lived a sinless life. It is the incarnation that shows the suffering and death of this righteous one atones for more than a mere generation, or more than a limited people group. It is infinite in its power, and covers all mankind through all time. You might say the Christian doctrine is the same principle as found in Jewish tradition, but empowered by the incarnation, and through Jesus' work, one more perfect than any man had ever done. Traditional Jews may make passing objections about Christianity endorsing human sacrifice, but at heart they understand what is really being said. One man can atone for the sins of another, for which he is not guilty.

The change that takes place through the substitutionary sacrifice is summarized powerfully in 2 Cor 5. When calling men to be ambassadors for the Savior of mankind, Paul teaches, "For he hath made him *to be sin for us*, who knew no sin; that we might be made the righteousness of God in him" (v. 21). This passage, outside of any idea of a legal transaction, and any idea of substitution, would be very opaque. You'd have to take educated guesses as to its meaning. Yet if we recognize that Christ truly bore our sins upon him, and then took our penalty, we can confidently make sense of it. Christ, though perfect, became sin for us by bearing our sin and taking our penalty for it. Our sin was punished. Then the perfect righteousness which Christ had, through his divine nature and his human life, was credited to us. Our debt was clear, and our penalty paid. This touches on a greater truth about Christ's righteousness in us, which I will speak more on later. Since the cross, we do not need to rely on the rags of our own goodness, but possess the perfect goodness of the Lord Jesus. That is the goodness of God. Paul writes:

> Yea doubtless, and I count all things but loss for the excellency of the knowledge of Christ Jesus my Lord: for whom I have suffered the loss of all things, and do count them but dung, that I may win Christ,
>
> And be found in him, *not having mine own righteousness*, which is of the law, but that which is through the faith of Christ, the righteousness which is of God by faith: (Phil 3:8–9)

This act of faith, of calling Jesus "Lord," and receiving his atonement for sin, brings us a new righteousness. This is one which is pleasing to God, because it was accomplished by his Son. We are pleasing to God only through his Son. It is nothing that is in us. Our accomplishments are worthless and do not make us good. It's all about his Son.

Christ's sacrifice, in taking our punishment for us, removes us from our guilt, and justifies us, making us in right legal standing before God. The status of criminal is no longer on us. The new status of citizen is ours. Our debt was paid by Christ, and justice was fulfilled. Not only does this reflect legal language of guilt throughout the Old Testament—which speaks of our sin, guilt, transgression, and judgment—but we see this also in the New Testament. In a chapter that may be the heart of the good news, Rom 8 opens with the central point, "There is therefore *now no condemnation* to them which are in Christ Jesus" (v. 1a). That word for condemnation is *katakrima*, meaning a "damning sentence" or "condemnation." It is used two other times in the New Testament, and this is when Paul speaks in Rom 5 about the condemnation we have in Adam (vv. 16, 18). We no longer have this on us when we are reborn. Later, in speaking of the assurance of our salvation in Christ, the finale of the chapter starts:

> Who shall *lay any thing to the charge* of God's elect? It is God that *justifieth*.
>
> Who is he *that condemneth*? It is Christ that died, yea rather, that is risen again, who is even at the right hand of God, who also maketh intercession for us. (vv. 33–34)

The opening literally means who shall "lay anything against" God's elect. To lay anything, *egkaleō*, means to come forward as an accuser or bring a charge against. This is a legal setting, and the legal matter has been taken care of. There is no means of accusation against God's people. This is because God justifies, so man cannot condemn whom God has justified. This word for justify, or bring to a right standing, is *dikaioō*. Its biblical usages include to render righteous, to show one to be righteous, or to declare righteous. This is a change of state that has occurred for those who receive Christ, because Christ has removed their condemnation. The question, "who is he that condemneth," uses a verb form of the word we saw at the start of the chapter, and means to judge against someone or to condemn. It is the same word Jesus uses when he says the chief priests and scribes will, "condemn him to death" (Matt 28:18b). A legal transaction clearly takes place at the cross, and includes the taking on of our sins by Christ, who suffers in our place. By His suffering and death we are brought to peace with God.

It is strange that those who are quick to deny that Christ took our penalty upon himself have to close their eyes to the situation in which he was nailed to a tree. The very situation fits with him being punished for our sins. That is the situation of a trial, before a judge. First, Christ is convicted at the local Jewish court, in a trial that breaks both Torah and traditional regulations of how a trial should function (Luke 22:66–71). Then the higher legal system, that of Rome, declares him innocent, saying, "I find no fault in this man" (Luke 23:4). Despite being found innocent of any transgression, the representative of Rome gives Jesus the punishment of a guilty man, due to pressure by the Jewish leaders and the mob (Luke 23:20–25). The Jewish leaders agree that the responsibility for his execution is on their hands, and Pilate washes his hands (Matt 27:24–25). According to the highest law in the nation, Jesus has been declared without fault. According to corrupt men he is guilty. He goes to the same death a guilty criminal goes, as according to prophecy, bearing the sins of the people. He takes our sin, our guilt, and our punishment. How a person can look at this trial situation and *not* see that Jesus bears our penalty, I do not know. It looks clear as day to me, despite not being explained as a teaching in one single passage. Catholics, Orthodox, and a few varieties of Protestants will basically mock the idea, but it is true nonetheless. A great and beautiful truth. What his people deserved for their sins, Christ took upon himself, in his stripes and in his death. He did not merely offer an offering to God, but took guilt and punishment for us. This is in part why the passion involves a trial, courts, and legal penalty. We will also be similarly judged on the last day before a perfect God, and we need redemption for our sins.

There are also those who flippantly brush off the idea that Christ took our penalty on himself with the notion that Christ's death is not a fair substitute. They reason that since we deserved eternal suffering in hell, and Christ only suffered temporally and died, that he couldn't really have saved us by taking on our punishment. It must be by another means. Yet this is too exact a demand, and ignores certain things about the sacrifice itself. There is nothing to say the substitute needs to be exact, but this is a presumption. Just as a lamb never could have been an exact substitute for Israel, Christ is not exact either, but is sufficient nonetheless. What Christ needs to pay is our eternal penalty. Christ paid that penalty not by suffering forever, as we should have, but by giving up his divine life, which is of infinite worth. Being God, and having God's infinite nature in him, Christ paid an infinite price. He is capable then of doing in several hours what we would have had to suffer forever due to his nature as God. There is no real problem here. It is a truly weak objection.

It's not wrong to recognize other facets of Christ's work on the cross, and how it accomplishes what it does. They can never be wholly separated from the sin-bearing role. Christ's work can be seen as a great offering given to God in the place of man's poor offering. It can be seen as the ultimate victory over sin and the devil. However, man has a real penalty to be paid, and no other explanation for Christ's passion deals directly with this. In fact, they would each still leave man guilty, and in sin. A criminal, deserving his sentence, does not merely offer to do something to make it right with the judge, or with society. He needs to serve his sentence as well. Likewise, we have no ability to join in with Christ in his passing through of death to life, if man is still alienated from God, and rightly sentenced. Guilty people aren't going to be doing that. Paying the penalty for sin is what clears us of our sentence, and really allows the other levels of the cross's power to function. The apostle teaches that Christ's atonement was "to declare, I say, at this time his righteousness: that he might *be just, and the justifier* of him which believeth in Jesus" (Rom 3:26). Christ's blood allows the Father to be both just and justifier; that is to both show his justice, in punishing sin, and his mercy, in making man righteous again, and restoring him to peace. God's deliverance is not a mere passing over our sins so he doesn't have to condemns us. Rather, it displays that he justly punishes sin, which itself is an outworking of God's love, and also shows mercy in restoring the lost criminal. The cross manifests all of God's character. When we look at it, we can think—this is where I belong. I belong on the cross. But Christ is there instead. That is why I live.

The Perfect Life

There is another level in which Christ took our place, and that is the level of righteousness. Jesus offered up to God the life of righteousness that we should have offered. His offering becomes ours. God did not merely incarnate just before the cross, and die for us there, but was working hard for us years beforehand to prepare. He led a full life of obedience to God, love of God, sacrifice, and worship, which is what man was meant to be doing in the first place. He resisted all temptations to sin. Having lived this way, when he reached the cross, he finally accepting death among all things, Jesus gave to Yahweh the offering that he deserved: one that fulfilled his expectations and brough him honor. His name which had been dishonored before the nations now was rightly honored. God was pleased not only in Christ's death, but in his life, a life which made Jesus the spotless sacrifice in the first place. Just as the animals offered on the altar were to be clean, and without blemish, our Lord was clean and righteous in all things. He became the righteous offering in our place, and gave what we would not give.

> If the priest that is anointed do sin according to the sin of the people; then let him bring for his sin, which he hath sinned, a young bullock *without blemish unto the LORD for a sin offering*. (Lev 4:3)

Being "without blemish" is the required norm for sacrifices, and this requirement is found in the same chapter in verses 23, 28, and 32 as well as other chapters of Leviticus and the rest of the Torah. A sacrifice was to be spotless. It showed the value of what was being offered up, and showed that Yahweh deserved what was perfect and clean.

> And walk in love, as Christ also hath loved us, and hath given himself for us an offering and a sacrifice to God *for a sweetsmelling savour*. (Eph 5:2)

Christ's offering was pleasing to Yahweh, being a sweet aroma to him. God accepted the sacrifice being pleased. This phrase "sweetsmelling savour" used by Paul is the same one used repeatedly throughout the Torah, in describing burnt offerings:

> And thou shalt burn the whole ram upon the altar: it is a burnt offering unto the LORD: it is *a sweet savour*, an offering made by fire unto the LORD. (Exod 29:18)

> And thou shalt receive them of their hands, and burn them upon the altar for a burnt offering, for *a sweet savour before the LORD*: it is an offering made by fire unto the LORD. (Exod 29:25)

> And he shall bring it to Aaron's sons the priests: and he shall take thereout his handful of the flour thereof, and of the oil thereof, with all the frankincense thereof; and the priest shall burn the memorial of it upon the altar, to be an offering made by fire, of *a sweet savour unto the LORD*: (Lev 2:2)

Just as we might find the scent of cooking meat a sweet aroma, Yahweh found the offering a sweet aroma, as it was a good offering, offered to him in the right way, with a clean heart. God has no taste for meat (Ps 50:13), but he is moved by a righteous and sincere offering. Christ's offering of himself was just so sweet.

In fact, Christ's offering of the righteous life is exactly what the sacrifices of the tabernacle and temple had been pointing to—God's true desire of righteousness in us. His desire that we live in truth. His desire we show mercy and love. The book of Hebrews, with its many comparisons to the Mosaic order, makes it clear Christ's offering fulfills the old order, and brings in the new:

> Above when he said, Sacrifice and offering and burnt offerings and offering for sin thou wouldest not, neither hadst pleasure therein; which are offered by the law;
>
> Then said he, Lo, *I come to do thy will*, O God. He taketh away the first, that he may establish the second.
>
> By the which will we are sanctified through the offering of the body of Jesus Christ once for all. (Heb 10:8–10)

It is very clear here it is not merely the physical pouring out of blood, but the righteous life and sacrificial nature of the life which pleases God. He has no more taste for human blood than for animal. We are made holy, then, by the holiness of Christ's offering, which is a life well led. The Scripture makes clear that Christ's offering was perfect, as Christ had led a life without sin. His obedience to the Father and sinlessness are seen in many New Testament passages:

> Who in the days of his flesh, when he had offered up prayers and supplications with strong crying and tears unto him that was able to save him from death, and was heard in that he feared;
>
> Though he were a Son, *yet learned he obedience* by the things which he suffered;
>
> And being made perfect, he became the author of eternal salvation unto all them that obey him; (Heb 5:7–9)

Jesus, though the Son of God, still went through the process mankind does in learning obedience, and he used that process to be perfected by the Father. He completed all righteousness which he needed to complete in the law. Once he had accomplished this, he won our salvation.

This perfection in his life is why his sacrifice was flawless and accepted by the Father. It had to be one of righteousness:

> And being found in fashion as a man, he humbled himself, and *became obedient* unto death, even the death of the cross. (Phil 2:8)
>
> For we have not an high priest which cannot be touched with the feeling of our infirmities; but was in all points tempted like as we are, *yet without sin.* (Heb 4:15)

We see in Philippians and in Hebrews that Christ's obedience was the fullest kind, even one willing to go to death. We see that Christ was without sin in his life, despite being tempted. This is the life and offering we are all meant to give, and the one which Christ accomplished, living in our nature. His perfect life was essential for the victory of the cross, even if we recognize the cross as bearing our rightful punishment. An imperfect Savior could not do that. Only the perfect One could accomplish it.

The need for a fully righteous life also explains why Yahweh saved us through becoming man. The sin offering was required by man, but man was unable to give it. So God himself became man, and did it for us. Only God himself could make this offering, as man universally commits sin, and is born in guilt. We are unable to please God. Christ, while being human, was without the stain of sin, being born of a virgin by the Holy Spirit, and never committed sin in his life. He fulfills the requirements required of man. His life was put in our place, not only as expiation, but as an unblemished offering, and a pleasing aroma. If Christ is pleasing to the Father, we are pleasing too.

We see the grand dishonor that had been given to Yahweh through the sins of Israel. Their wickedness publicly defames his name before the world. Yahweh speaks through Ezekiel, telling the people:

> And when they entered unto the heathen, whither they went, *they profaned my holy name,* when they said to them, These are the people of the LORD, and are gone forth out of his land.
>
> But I had pity for mine holy name, which the house of Israel *had profaned among the heathen,* whither they went. (36:20–21)

Amos likewise reviews the wrongs of Israel, which attacked the name of God:

> That pant after the dust of the earth on the head of the poor, and turn aside the way of the meek: and a man and his father will go in unto the same maid, to *profane my holy name*: (2:7)

Jeremiah writes similarly about the temple, "And they have turned unto me the back, and not the face: though I taught them, rising up early and teaching them, yet they have not hearkened to receive instruction. But they set their abominations in the house, which is called by my name, *to defile it*" (32:33-34). Apostle Paul uses the same language, and refers back to the same prophets, as he reminds the brethren of how universal sin is, teaching, "For *the name of God is blasphemed among the Gentiles* through you, as it is written" (Rom 2:24).

The sins of Israel more than any other nation, because it was a nation which represented Yahweh to the world, dishonored God in the grandest way. The character of God was made to look like a common thing, or a filthy one. The meaning of the word profane alone, in Hebrew *ḥālal*, is somewhat broad. Its usages include to make common, to pollute, or to dishonor. It's not hard to see how these may all go together as man sins, and brings disgrace upon the character of Yahweh, and what it means to have fellowship with him. His name no longer carries authority, goodness, and power in the eyes of men.

For the Lord's name to be rightly honored, it seems Israel would have needed to become perfectly righteous, but Yahweh had another plan for his people. He would restore them to the land simply for the sake of his name. His mercy on Israel would show the world who he is, not because Israel had suddenly become a perfect nation, honoring him, but because the Lord chose to use his power, goodness, and faithfulness to his promise to bring Israel back to the land. Yahweh did this apart from their good performance.

Yahweh explains through the prophet Ezekiel what he will do and why:

> Therefore say unto the house of Israel, Thus saith the Lord GOD; I do not this for your sakes, O house of Israel, but *for mine holy name's sake*, which ye have profaned among the heathen, whither ye went.
>
> And *I will sanctify my great name*, which was profaned among the heathen, which ye have profaned in the midst of them; and the heathen shall know that I am the LORD, saith the Lord GOD, when I shall be sanctified in you before their eyes.

For I will take you from among the heathen, and gather you out of all countries, and will bring you into your own land. (36:22–24)

Isaiah also speaks of Israel's redemption, and the unique mercy with which God would restore his name:

For my name's sake will I defer mine anger, and for my praise will I refrain for thee, that I cut thee not off.

Behold, I have refined thee, but not with silver; I have chosen thee in the furnace of affliction.

For mine own sake, even for mine own sake, will I do it: for *how should my name be polluted*? and I will not give my glory unto another. (48:9–11)

Despite Israel's need for righteousness, Yahweh was not dependent on their accomplishing this for his plan to succeed. Restoration would not rely on Israel's goodness but on his own. In his mercy Yahweh would restore Israel, and thus sanctify his holy name. This divine choice prevents Israel from being cut off forever, as they deserve, and shows that God fulfills his promises.

Once we recognize that the people of the church fulfill what God intended with national Israel, we can see how God's work through Christ parallels both Yahweh's warnings to Israel, and his promise to restore them. God brings the sinner back into his family only to show his goodness, not because the sinner has reached his holy standard. He does so for his name's sake, to restore its sanctity before the world. God has mercy and brings miraculous renewal despite our wicked performance. He provides the honor due to his name through becoming man and doing as you and I must. We have profaned it before the nations, and through the perfect offering of Christ, God has restored it.

Deceived is the Deceiver (Ransomed from Slavery)

The nature of Christ's life and death as the perfect offering, opens up another layer of Christ freeing us from sin and death. His life became a ransom, or redeeming price to set us free from slavery. He took our sins upon him, and he also paid the price for our freedom. While the New Testament does not explain the inner workings of this ransom, it does teach the ransom as a part of what Christ accomplishes. Jesus, while speaking of the servant nature of the ministry, taught:

> But so shall it not be among you: but whosoever will be great among you, shall be your minister:
>
> And whosoever of you will be the chiefest, shall be servant of all.
>
> For even the Son of man came not to be ministered unto, but to minister, and *to give his life a ransom for many*. (Mark 10:43–45)

Jesus refers to the giving of his life as a ransom. That giving of his life includes the righteousness of his living, as well as the sacrifice of his death. The same basic truth is repeated in the Epistles:

> For there is one God, and one mediator between God and men, the man Christ Jesus;
>
> Who *gave himself a ransom for all*, to be testified in due time. (1 Tim 2:5–6)
>
> For *ye are bought with a price*: therefore glorify God in your body, and in your spirit, which are God's. (1 Cor 6:20)

The ransom from slavery, or the ransom from ownership, is a principle throughout the Old Testament. It also plays a part in several commandments of the Torah. Men in the Old Testament are set free from captivity, and even set free from death by a ransom. The similar word "redemption" also often refers to a price paid for the freedom of a person, or the return of a property to its original owner. It should not be difficult to see the continuity of the redeemed slave in the Old Testament to the new life in Christ, for those who trust in him. Ownership is transferred by the payment of this price. Captivity is ended, and the slave comes to his new lord. Property leaves the hand of one holding it, and comes to the hand it now belongs to. The sinner in Christ has ended his belonging to the devil, sin, and death, and come to belong to God in Christ's kingdom.

> I *will ransom them from the power of the grave*; I will redeem them from death: O death, I will be thy plagues; O grave, I will be thy destruction: repentance shall be hid from mine eyes. (Hos 13:14)
>
> Then he is gracious unto him, and saith, *Deliver him from going down to the pit*: I have found a ransom. (Job 33:24)

Here the ransom in the Old Testament is from death. The passage from Hosea is the same one that Paul cites (although he uses the

Septuagint translation), when speaking of how death can no longer destroy us in Christ (1 Cor 15:55). He uses this to contrast the old corruptible body with the new incorruptible one. This is accomplished according to a ransom, or payment to set us free:

> For the LORD hath redeemed Jacob, and *ransomed him* from the hand of him that was stronger than he. (Jer 31:11)
>
> *And the ransomed of the LORD shall return*, and come to Zion with songs and everlasting joy upon their heads: they shall obtain joy and gladness, and sorrow and sighing shall flee away. (Isa 35:10)

Like countless passages in the Hebrew Scriptures, the prophets glorify God, speaking of how he set Israel free from captivity. Here the word "ransom" is used, where "redeem" is used elsewhere for basically the same liberating action. Ransom is the more general word for a payment (which interestingly can also mean a covering), while redeem is the more technical legal term for buying back. God's power has set the captives free and returned them. We may not see in the immediate verses a payment being made, but we can see this happen through the sacrifices of the righteous or of God. Sufficient payment was made for the people to leave bondage, and return to Yahweh, their Lord.

> And the LORD spake unto Moses, saying,
>
> Take the Levites instead of all the firstborn among the children of Israel, and the cattle of the Levites instead of their cattle; and the Levites shall be mine: I am the LORD.
>
> And for those that are to be redeemed of the two hundred and threescore and thirteen of the firstborn of the children of Israel, which are more than the Levites;
>
> *Thou shalt even take five shekels apiece by the poll*, after the shekel of the sanctuary shalt thou take them: (the shekel is twenty gerahs:)
>
> *And thou shalt give the money, wherewith the odd number of them is to be redeemed*, unto Aaron and to his sons. (Num 3:44–48)

The redemption of the firstborn was an actual payment made for some of the firstborn men of Israel so they did not have to serve in the temple for life, as the tribe of Levites did. Israel had the Levites to minister in the temple. They would take this role from the firstborn, whom God had chosen for himself by preserving the firstborn in the Exodus

(vv. 12–13). However, since the number of firstborn was greater than the number of Levites, there would be a group who were not replaced by them in service. A payment had to be made to set them free from their obligation in the temple. This redemption payment went to the temple and the high priest, and once made, those firstborn were free. They had been redeemed from their service. They could follow any number of callings besides priest.

> And if a sojourner or stranger wax rich by thee, and thy brother that dwelleth by him wax poor, and sell himself unto the stranger or sojourner by thee, or to the stock of the stranger's family:
>
> *After that he is sold he may be redeemed again*; one of his brethren may redeem him:
>
> Either his uncle, or his uncle's son, may redeem him, or any that is nigh of kin unto him of his family may redeem him; or if he be able, he may redeem himself.
>
> And he shall reckon with him that bought him from the year that he was sold to him unto the year of jubile: and the price of his sale shall be according unto the number of years, according to the time of an hired servant shall it be with him.
>
> If there be yet many years behind, according unto them he shall give again the price of his redemption out of the money that he was bought for.
>
> And if there remain but few years unto the year of jubile, then he shall count with him, and according unto his years shall he give him again the price of his redemption. (Lev 25:47–52)

A monetary payment accompanied the freeing of slaves. In certain situations, the slave could be set free with a payment, which would be higher or lower depending on how many years were left on his servitude. It also varied depending on how many years were left until the Jubilee, when slaves were set free, and debt cancelled. Once the payment was made, the slave left his master and returned to his life and his family. Here, a family member would have to make the payment. It had to be someone "nigh of kin" (v. 49).

This form of redemption uniquely is very similar to Christ's freeing of his people. This is not only because of man's slavery to sin, but also because of his identification of us as family. He takes on human nature, becoming like the ones he will free. Then he brings us into his family, and calls us his brethren (Heb 2:12–13). We become his children. His brothers (Rom 8:29). We depart from a servitude to one who loves us not, to a servitude and familial love to one who truly loves us. His payment is made not with silver, but with his more valuable precious life.

> And if a man sell a dwelling house in a walled city, then *he may redeem it within a whole year* after it is sold; within a full year may he redeem it.
>
> And if it be not redeemed within the space of a full year, then the house that is in the walled city shall be established for ever to him that bought it throughout his generations: it shall not go out in the jubile. (Lev 25:29–30)

The redeeming of property appears several times in the Torah as well. In this example, which contrasts with the normal practice of property returning to it owner, a house in a walled city can be sold permanently. However, if the owner wishes it back, he can redeem it within a year. If he doesn't do so in this time, it goes permanently over to the new owner. Just like with buying, redeeming makes ownership change hands.

> But because the LORD loved you, and because he would keep the oath which he had sworn unto your fathers, hath the LORD brought you out with a mighty hand, and *redeemed you out of the house of bondmen*, from the hand of Pharaoh king of Egypt. (Deut 7:8)
>
> Now these are thy servants and thy people, whom *thou hast redeemed by thy great power*, and by thy strong hand. (Neh 1:10)
>
> Go ye forth of Babylon, flee ye from the Chaldeans, with a voice of singing declare ye, tell this, utter it even to the end of the earth; say ye, *The LORD hath redeemed his servant Jacob*. (Isa 48:20)

As with the earlier passages about how God ransoms Israel from captivity, we see God redeems Israel from the same captivity, making the words practically equivalent. Israel's ransom in the Old Testament was most prominently from Egypt and from Babylon, where the nation was in captivity away from the land for years. However, there are many smaller captivities to pagan rulers and invaders, and the book of Judges includes many times Israel fell under the thumb of a foreign ruler. Then the nation was subsequently freed by a great judge or military hero. There may not be a monetary payment, but the principle of freeing is still there, and a payment made in human work and suffering.

God or Satan?

The goodness of Christ was a payment by our loving Father to free us from slavery. His divine life and obedience to God surpassed anything else in value. He paid our ransom. Still, many will ask to whom the payment was made. Historically, the early church mostly agreed the payment was made to the devil, since mankind became his slaves when they entered into sin. The church father Origen wrote, "But to whom did He give His soul as a ransom for many? Surely not to God. Could it, then, be to the Evil One? For he had us in his power, until the ransom for us should be given to him, even the life (or soul) of Jesus."[4] This understanding is written into ancient Eastern Orthodox liturgy, explaining how Christ tricked the devil into accepting his payment, and how the devil was defeated through being deceived. The West has mostly forgotten this explanation. Others argue that the payment was made to God, since God is the true authority, not the devil, and because we are still, in a certain sense, belonging to God while we are in sin. They may think that Christ paying a ransom to the devil gives Satan too much power, but if mankind being in captivity to sin did not give Satan too much power, then surely neither does a ransom payment.

It's true there is still a form of belonging to God as long as we live, but clearly mankind is under the dominion of sin, death, and the devil while we are fallen in Adam. That is our overall state. We are not enslaved to sin, death, and God. The devil is presented as the king of this earthly world until Christ's sacrifice. Our slavery to sin is also explicitly taught:

> And you hath *he quickened, who were dead* in trespasses and sins;
>
> Wherein in time past ye walked according to the course of this world, *according to the prince of the power of the air*, the spirit that now worketh in the *children of disobedience*:
>
> Among whom also we all had our conversation in times past in the lusts of our flesh, fulfilling the desires of the flesh and of the mind; and were *by nature the children of wrath*, even as others. (Eph 2:1–3)

The man before rebirth clearly does not belong to God, but belongs to the devil. He walks out his life following the ways of the devil, locked in the flesh, and is under God's wrath by his very nature. The devil is spoken of as the ruler of this world when Christ explains his coming victory

---

4. Origen, *Commentary on Matthew* xvi, 8, 65.

over him: "Now is the judgment of this world: now shall *the prince of this world* be cast out" (John 12:31). Christ also refers to the devil as the ruler of this world before the cross in John 14:30 and 16:11.

Sin is holding mankind in bondage, along with the rule of the devil. It is this bondage from which we are freed by Christ's ransom. Equally remarkable is the language used by the devil himself when he tempts Christ in the desert:

> And the devil, taking him up into an high mountain, shewed unto him all the kingdoms of the world in a moment of time.
>
> And the devil said unto him, *All this power will I give thee*, and the glory of them: for that is delivered unto me; and to whomsoever I will I give it.
>
> If thou therefore wilt worship me, all shall be thine. (Luke 4:5–7)

The devil promises Christ authority over the kingdoms of the world if only Christ will bow down to him. The devil, in harmony with Scripture's words, promises all those kingdoms because they belong to him, and he therefore can give them away if he desires. Those are the words of someone who owns something. Christ's immediate response does not reject the devil's ownership, but only cites Scripture's demand that we worship God alone (v. 8).

> Why do ye not understand my speech? even because ye cannot hear my word.
>
> *Ye are of your father the devil*, and the lusts of your father ye will do. (John 8:43–44a)

Here the Christ calls his accusers children of the devil. This may not be a reference to slavery per se, but refers to belonging to the devil, and sharing in nature with him. They are akin to descendants. Clearly for peace to be made, they would have to be freed from their familial attachment to Satan, and brought into the family of Christ.

> Jesus answered them, Verily, verily, I say unto you, *Whosoever committeth sin is the servant of sin.*
>
> And the servant abideth not in the house for ever: but the Son abideth ever.
>
> If the Son therefore shall make you free, ye shall be free indeed. (John 8:34–36)
>
> For the law of the Spirit of life in Christ Jesus hath made me *free from the law of sin and death*. (Rom 8:2)

These passages about our slavery to sin do not speak of a ransom payment, but they are clear that we are slaves who need to be set free. This shows us where our belonging lies, and it is not with God and with righteousness. It is with the devil, and with sin. We should have no problem then with the idea that Christ's payment for our redemption was made to the devil, for it is to the devil we are captive.

The nature of the payment was Christ's perfect life, which according to the early church understanding fooled the devil into plotting the capture, passion, and crucifixion of the God-man. The devil did his role in orchestrating those events. That's because he thought he'd have the perfect prize, and a better one than he currently had in holding mankind captive. However, what the devil did not see, because of the human nature of Christ and his willingness to suffer, was that he'd never be able to keep the payment he so desired. Christ's perfect life assured that the devil had no claim over him, as did the Lord's divinity. Christ appeared to him like the better end of the deal, but nothing in hell could hold this Servant of God. The devil had nothing to accuse him of. When Christ resurrected then, the devil had lost mankind, and also lost the prize he cherished. He had nothing. His reign was over. He can deceive the nations no more, and all the world can come to worship God, through Christ. One passage in the Orthodox hymn, Lamentations, which is for Great Friday, mentions this part of Christ's victory for us: "Deceived is the deceiver, deceived man is now ransomed, by thy great wisdom, O God."[5]

Saint Maximus the Confessor, a theologian and doctor of the church born shortly after the early church era, described this deception, writing:

> "The Lord mounted His flesh on the fish-hook of His divinity as bait for the devil's deceit, so that, as the insatiable serpent, the devil would take His flesh in to his mouth . . . [and] completely vomit the Lord's human nature once he swallowed it. As a result, just as the devil formerly baited man with the hope of divinity, and swallowed him, so too the devil himself would be baited precisely with humanity's fleshly garb; and afterward he would vomit man."[6]

---

5. Orthodox Church, "Lamentations" 3:21.

6. Maximus the Confessor, *Ad Thalassium* 64. Interestingly, in his remark, Maximus brings up the passage from the Psalms, "I am a worm, and no man" (22:6a). He uses this statement allegorically to point to the nature of Christ and the workings of the atonement.

The deception of the devil, you might say, is God's ultimate comeuppance on him for his own lying, which he had done from the beginning. The devil is hoisted by his own petard. The fall in the garden came through deception of Eve, which Adam allowed, with the lie, "Ye shall not surely die" (Gen 3:4b). The devil is associated with lies throughout Scripture, as are his demons. The gods that the nations worship are demons as well. Jesus teaches of the devil, "When he speaketh a lie, he speaketh of his own: for he is a liar, and the father of it" (John 8:44b). When Paul writes about the hidden nature of the message they preach, he notes that the devil is behind unbelief: "But if our gospel be hid, it is hid to them that are lost: In whom *the god of this world hath blinded* the minds of them which believe not" (2 Cor 4:3-4a).

We also see lies in Scripture, which come back upon the one who tells them. This is clear in the lie of Rebecca and Jacob when they plot to pretend that Jacob is Esau, so that Jacob can receive his father's blessing (Gen 27:6-17). They have him dress up in a hairy costume, so Isaac thinks the less manly Jacob is his other son. Jacob receives double in return from God, as he later is deceived by Laban and Leah, being tricked into marrying Leah, thinking she is her sister Rachel (Gen 29:23-26). He later is deceived by his sons into thinking Joseph has been killed by a beast, when they bring him his son's bloodied clothing (Gen 37:31-33). The liar here has to face his own methods, in a terrible way. Both are grievous to him, especially the imagined loss of his favorite son. The devil too, as deceiver, is justly being defeated by the very own method he uses. He thought he had a dead man on his hands to seize, but it was the God-man, and he could not claim him. He thought he had strength over God's Son. He had no strength at all. He either did not see or understand the incarnation.

I dove into the subject of deception earlier, and showed some legitimate ways that God deceives according to Scripture. This includes in the true faith itself. The gospel appears one way to men who are lost: as a waste, and as foolishness. But the gospel appears another way to those who are given by the Father: It is the power and the wisdom of God. Simple Christians also deceive the lost through the very nature of the faith; being sorrowful, yet having much to rejoice in, appearing weak, but providing strength, sounding guilty by slander, but being worthy of honor, being put in prison, yet having the only true freedom there is. This very same principle at work in deceiving the devil, and the blindness of the devil is what caused him to think he would be victorious. The

God-man looked weak, the God-man looked dead, the God-man looked defeated, but he was containing eternal life and strength which cannot die.

Further, God has power to deceive indirectly, and he does so through the mouths of false prophets, by his own angels. Though a challenging concept to some, the Bible makes this explicit in God's choice of action with wicked King Ahab. It is through deception that God assures that Ahab will go into battle and be destroyed. In the words of the true prophet Micaiah:

> And there came forth a spirit, and stood before the LORD, and said, I will persuade him.
>
> And the LORD said unto him, Wherewith? And he said, *I will go forth, and I will be a lying spirit in the mouth of all his prophets.* And he said, Thou shalt persuade him, and prevail also: *go forth, and do so.*
>
> Now therefore, behold, the LORD hath put a lying spirit in the mouth of all these thy prophets, and the LORD hath spoken evil concerning thee. (1 Kgs 22:21–23)

Ahab chose to listen to his false prophets, and subsequently died in battle, despite his best efforts to avoid being spotted by the enemy. By listening to the deception of his false prophets, he was slain as the Lord had desired. Despite his nature as truth, the Almighty can fool the wicked with deception. He simply does so by other means than lying—here it is through the impure mouthpiece of pagan prophets, and the words his angels give them. Those prophets are already full of falsehood, but God has chosen which specific falsehood and why. It should not be a surprise then that God tricked the devil, nor is it in conflict with his nature.

A deception brought death to mankind, a deception also brought eternal life and bliss, joy, peace, and love. The devil was locking the entire world into deception, so that they could not become children of God, so that only Israel knew Yahweh. His darkness over them made it impossible for them to receive the truth. Once the devil was defeated in the cross, his control over the nations, the spiritual blindness he had caused, was lifted. Israel is no more the ground of God's kingdom, but every people, nation, and language can become children of God. The nations of the world can now come to the light of God because of Christ, following demons no more:

> And he laid hold on the dragon, that old serpent, which is the Devil, and Satan, and bound him a thousand years,
>
> And cast him into the bottomless pit, and shut him up, and set a seal upon him, that he should *deceive the nations no more*, till the thousand years should be fulfilled (Rev 20:2–3a)

The gospel takes the treasure that was once contained within Israel, and brings it throughout the earth. It is by the command of Jesus:

> Go ye therefore, and *teach all nations*, baptizing them in the name of the Father, and of the Son, and of the Holy Ghost:
>
> Teaching them to observe all things whatsoever I have commanded you: and, lo, I am with you alway, even unto the end of the world. Amen. (Matt 28:19–20)

Christ's sacrifice ransomed his people from slavery. He purchased his special people for himself, with the cost of his toil, pain, blood, and death. That purchase price was more than worth the weak, mortal, sinful people he freed from slavery. His broken and bloodied limbs looked defeated, and the devil took the bait. We were won from the chains of sin, death, and the devil, by the perfect life of one man. All of us, once made gloriously free, I hope desire to be so valuable for our Lord. We desire our own lives to be precious and holy, because they were purchased with the precious, holy life of One who loves us. We should desire to give of our toil for the good of others, as we were won by hard labor. We should wish to return that love for the glory of our Father with work, sacrifice, and if necessary, our lives.

It is natural to point out that Scripture also teaches that Christ redeemed us from being under the law (Gal 4:4–5). We had been "in bondage under the elements" (v. 3) before Christ freed us, by becoming like us and living under the law. This seems to be another kind of redemption. But does that also mean he did not ransom us from the devil? Does it prove the previous point wrong? I cannot find any contradiction between the two. In fact, to continue in the law of Moses, or to continue in the law in our heart, after Christ has fulfilled the law, is satanic itself. It is bondage to seek to please God through the works of the law, be they the ethics of the Torah, or ethics you came up with on your own. Only the perfect life and blood of Jesus pleases God. His death and resurrection "[blotted] out the handwriting of ordinances that was against us" (Col 2:14a). The law is over and done with. That means Jesus' death indeed redeems us from bondage to the law, but that bondage is itself a bondage to Satan. The law was only meant to be temporal, until the Seed should come (Gal 3:19), and has never allowed man to save himself by hard work. Therefore, liberation from the law, and liberation from the devil, come together. This is further made clear in that liberation from the law is also liberation from the "curse of the law" (Gal 3:13). That does not suggest the law is itself a wicked thing, but the curse of the law is due to our sin, and our guilt. It is what we should have been punished with instead of Christ, but Christ took our penalty and hung on the tree. Being freed from that guilt, which is always associated with the law, is wrapped up in being freed from Satan. He inspired the fall in the first place and he tempts man to sin. In Christ he has nothing to accuse us of anymore. There is considerable and meaningful overlap between being freed from the law, from the curse of the law, and freed from the devil. Christ's accomplishment in giving his life buys us all of these together.

Put Death to Death

Christ is risen from the dead

Trampling down death by death

And upon those in the tombs

Bestowing life
—An Orthodox hymn[7]

While we can speak of how Christ accomplishes our peace on more than one level, there is only one level in which the New Testament speaks a good deal, and in detail: that is Christ's conquest of death. Jesus walked to his own death, because in going through death, he would conquer it for us, and set us free. He opens that passage for us from this corrupt world, and from bondage to death, so that when we join him through faith, we are assured eternal life with him, and a new incorruptible body. Death is nothing to be feared. It is an entranceway now into greater union with our Lord and King.

That purpose has been evident since Christ took on flesh:

> Forasmuch then as the children are partakers of flesh and blood, he also himself likewise took part of the same; *that through*

---

7. OCA, "Selected Liturgical Hymns."

> *death he might destroy him that had the power of death, that is, the devil;*
>
> And deliver them who through fear of death were all their lifetime subject to bondage.
>
> For verily he took not on him the nature of angels; but he took on him the seed of Abraham.
>
> Wherefore in all things it behoved him to be made like unto his brethren, that he might be a merciful and faithful high priest in things pertaining to God, to make reconciliation for the sins of the people.
>
> For in that he himself hath suffered being tempted, he is able to succour them that are tempted. (Heb 2:14–18)
>
> He that committeth sin is of the devil; for the devil sinneth from the beginning. For this purpose the Son of God was manifested, *that he might destroy the works of the devil.* (1 John 3:8)

Both of these passages speak about the incarnation of God in Christ side by side with the death of Christ, and explain their united purpose. Christ took on flesh so that as man, he would go through death. This would defeat death and the devil, and aid those who are in the flesh like him. John likewise points out that the incarnation destroys the "works of the devil," which in context is clearly sin. This is a victory over sin, death, and the devil.

> And you, being dead in your sins and the uncircumcision of your flesh, hath he quickened together with him, having forgiven you all trespasses;
>
> Blotting out the handwriting of ordinances that was against us, which was contrary to us, and took it out of the way, nailing it to his cross;
>
> And having spoiled principalities and powers, *he made a shew of them openly, triumphing over them in it.* (Col 2:13–15)

Here the cross is portrayed as publicly mocking the devil and his powers, and defeating them. While it appears Christ is the one being publicly shamed, hanging naked, and wounded from a tree, the devil is being openly put to shame, as nothing in those wounds or humiliation can hold the Lord of Glory. He both disarmed and triumphed over the powers of the devil publicly. The battle is over at the cross. Our sin cannot be held against us. Death cannot cause us fear. The devil has no hold over our soul in the next world, but will be in chains himself. Having taken on the flesh, having fulfilled the law completely, having gone through temptation, suffering, and death, Christ sets us free as he triumphs over death itself.

> Now is the judgment of this world: *now shall the prince of this world be cast out.*
>
> And I, if I be lifted up from the earth, will draw all men unto me. (John 12:31–32)

Christ has all authority now, and the devil has none. In predicting his passion and death, Christ also predicts the defeat of the devil through the same event.

> For whatsoever is born of God *overcometh the world*: and this is the victory that overcometh the world, even our faith.
>
> Who is he that overcometh the world, but he that believeth that Jesus is the Son of God? (1 John 5:4–5)

Coming into Christ through faith takes us through the same victory. We overcome the world through our faith, overcoming the world order, the lusts of the flesh, the bondage of the devil, held only by the authority of God and Christ. We follow his commandments. We learn love. We turn from sin. Christ overcame at the cross, so his children overcome.

> For this corruptible must put on incorruption, and this mortal must put on immortality.
>
> So when this corruptible shall have put on incorruption, and this mortal shall have put on immortality, then shall be brought to pass the saying that is written, *Death is swallowed up in victory.*
>
> O death, where is thy sting? O grave, where is thy victory?
>
> The sting of death is sin; and the strength of sin is the law.
>
> But thanks be to God, which giveth us the victory through our Lord Jesus Christ. (1 Cor 15:53–57)

That victory over sin also points to the victory over the mortal flesh. The bodies we have that grow weak, suffer pain, grow decrepit, and die will be replaced with new bodies, suitable to us in God's kingdom. In new bodies we will love and serve God forever, and suffering will be no more. That answer to pain which many seek through pleasure seeking, or drug use, or suicide is a real answer we can find. We cannot enter in through earthly means. We must enter in the right way. We can only enter through rebirth. We use that passage Christ opened up for us, and go from death to life unharmed.

Beyond destroying the enemy of mankind, it appears Christ's descent into the grave, and rising out of it, fulfilled his purpose in reigning over all things. By going into the pit for us, he forever brought his presence there, just as he is present forever in heaven having risen to the Father. He is present everywhere in between as well. The Son, being God by nature, has always shared in God's omnipresence, yet as the incarnation walking with us as man, he fulfilled that omnipresence just as he fulfilled all righteousness in his righteous life. In that sense, Christ's life, death, and resurrection brought his victory to all of known creation and to all of human life, including death.

In speaking about the spiritual gifts in the Church, Paul writes in Eph 4:

> But unto every one of us is given grace according to the measure of the gift of Christ.
>
> Wherefore he saith, When he ascended up on high, *he led captivity captive*, and gave gifts unto men.
>
> (Now that he ascended, what is it but that he also descended first into the lower parts of the earth?
>
> He that descended is the same also that ascended up far above all heavens, *that he might fill all things*.) (vv. 7-10)

This is a stunning short passage, just as it is stunning the truth it is used to explain. Christ made a captive of captivity itself, by invading and conquering the grave. He led it captive just as conquered kings were dragged off from their land, to serve their new rulers, and as the sinful nation of Israel had been taken off captive hundreds of miles away. One thinks of the wicked king Manasseh who was taken by Assyria and dragged away in chains by a hook through his nose (2 Chr 33:11, 2 Ki 19:28). Such mastery was shown by Christ over death, and it was taken into captivity as he rose far above all things.

In doing this, by descending into the earth, and then rising up to heaven, he would "fill all things" (Eph 4:10). Just as Christ brought his presence to baptism through being baptized, and brings his presence to the bread and cup of Communion, Christ brings himself to all of creation, covering it from bottom to top, from the pit to the highest heaven. In context, this shows how he brings heavenly things to the church, through the gifts brethren receive by the Holy Spirit. He can fill all the church just as he has filled all creation, and bring it in contact with the things of heaven. This seems a fulfillment of Ps 139, which teaches, "Whither shall I go from thy spirit? or whither shall I flee from thy presence? If I ascend up into heaven, thou art there: if I make my bed in hell, behold, thou art there" (v. 7–8). The Son also is revealed to be that ladder between heaven and earth (Gen 28:12, John 1:51), upon whom the angels ascend and descend, ministering to the sons of men. His conquest over death then cannot be limited to a mere moment. Rather it touches even on his final victory and the final kingdom in eternity. It touches on his ascension and his reign. It ensures our passage from death to life, but also ensures that Christ will rule everywhere we go. Nothing is withheld from his hand.

Unite with the Divine

Jesus Christ paid the price for our sin on the cross. His death and resurrection freed us from sin and death. Inseparable from that process is that we return to peace by coming back in intimate relationship with God. We get plugged back in to the source of power. We are restored to citizenship in the kingdom of our Lord. We are saved by departing from death in Adam, and coming into life in Christ. It is a change of status, you might say, and a reunion.

This reunion functions on various levels at once. It can be spoken of as coming back under the headship of God. It can be spoken of as being adopted into his family. It can also be spoken of as sharing in God's nature, even though we are men; we share in the glorious treasure of the divine, through our Savior who is God and, like us, a man.

Citizenship

If our previous existence was in the rebel kingdom of Adam, being servants of the devil, our new existence is in the kingdom of Christ, which he founded in becoming man. I brought up this parallel headship when speaking of our fall, and it must be mentioned again in speaking of our restoration. The first Adam brought us death, because he was our head. Christ, as the new Adam, brings us life, as he is our new head, and his saving work is accounted to us. Jesus' perfect righteousness represents his entire people:

> Therefore as by the offence of one judgment came upon all men to condemnation; even so by the righteousness of one *the free gift came upon all men* unto justification of life.
>
> For as by one man's disobedience many were made sinners, so by the obedience of one *shall many be made righteous*. (Rom 5:18-19)

Adam's people here may be the whole human race in the flesh, and Jesus' people are those who come to him through faith, but the principle is clear: When Christ is our head, his saving act counts for us. Just as Adam's sin brought judgment to us, Christ's death and resurrection brings peace to us. This is only possible since he is our head, and represents all of us. There is a new mankind now; a new human race, that with Christ as its head, can be pleasing to God the Father. His work accomplished a reunion.

> But now is Christ risen from the dead, and become the firstfruits of them that slept.
>
> For since by man came death, by man came also the resurrection of the dead.
>
> For as in Adam all die, even so *in Christ shall all be made alive*. (1 Cor 15:20-22)

This passage follows the same principle, but is highlighting the resurrection aspect of this saving work. Since Christ passed through to life, his entire people will pass through to life. Since Christ rose from the dead, we also will rise to life, dwelling with God in the next life as well, eternally one with God. We do so not as mere spirits, but in new bodies. As the head of the new creation rose in the flesh, we will also rise in the flesh, in new bodies that do not die. This is only possible through our union with the King, having accepted Christ as our Lord to be a member of his people. If he rose, then we rise too.

> But I would have you know, that *the head of every man is Christ*; and the head of the woman is the man; and the head of Christ is God. (1 Cor 11:3)
>
> For the husband is the head of the wife, *even as Christ is the head of the church*: and he is the saviour of the body. (Eph 5:23)
>
> And hath put all things under his feet, and *gave him to be the head over all things* to the church, (Eph 1:22)
>
> For in him dwelleth all the fulness of the Godhead bodily.

> And ye are complete in him, *which is the head of all principality and power* (Col 2:9-10)
>
> And Jesus came and spake unto them, saying, *All power is given unto me* in heaven and in earth. (Matt 28:18)

The Lord who died and rose is our new head, and we are his body. Scripture teaches he is the head of man, the head of the church, and the head of all things, bearing all authority in heaven and on earth. While I don't want to differentiate right now between each of these levels, the truth is clear: Christ is our authority. He is our representative. The head of a body leads a body, instructs it, corrects it, provides it with necessary resources. He uses his resources to care for and protect the body. All these things Jesus does with his church, which is called his body. In fact, our intimacy with Christ is so close as his people that when Jesus spoke to Saul, who was persecuting the early Christians, Jesus did not ask, "Why are you persecuting my people?" Rather, he asked, "Why persecutest thou me?" (Acts 9:4b). The Savior is able to call his people by his own name, the identification is so close. Being so close to him, Christ treats us as his own body, and just as a man who helped your body helped you, a man who harmed your body harmed you. In the new life, we are a part of Christ, so dear to him, he loves us as his own.

> Now therefore ye are no more strangers and foreigners, but *fellow-citizens with the saints*, and of the household of God; (Eph 2:19)
>
> For *our conversation is in heaven*; from whence also we look for the Saviour, the Lord Jesus Christ (Phil 3:20)
>
> But ye are a chosen generation, a royal priesthood, *an holy nation*, a peculiar people; that ye should shew forth the praises of him who hath called you out of darkness into his marvellous light (1 Pet 2:9)

With Christ as their head, believers gain citizenship in his land, and with it the fellowship, the priesthood, and the inheritance that comes with being among God's people. Gentiles now are grafted in, and are citizens of the New Covenant Israel. They are "the apple of his eye" (Deut 32:10). They were once strangers, but now are the nation of God. Their community is also one in heaven, sharing in a rightful place in God's kingdom, both in the now and in the next life, forever conformed to the righteousness of God.

PAIN | PART 2

Family

> And because ye are sons, God hath sent forth the Spirit of his Son into your hearts, crying, Abba, Father.
>
> Wherefore *thou art no more a servant, but a son*; and if a son, then an heir of God through Christ. (Gal 4:6–7)
>
> For ye have not received the spirit of bondage again to fear; but ye have received the Spirit of adoption, *whereby we cry, Abba, Father*.
>
> The Spirit itself beareth witness with our spirit, that we are the children of God:
>
> *And if children, then heirs*; heirs of God, and joint-heirs with Christ (Rom 8:15–17a)
>
> For whom he did foreknow, he also did predestinate to be conformed to the image of his Son, that he might be the firstborn *among many brethren*. (Rom 8:29)

Coming under Christ's headship, and becoming his body includes coming into his family. We are adopted, through Jesus, to be a member of God's family. The Bible speaks of God's people as children. It also speaks of us as his brethren, which is a word that can refer either to brothers, or more generally to family members. Where once we were alienated, and finding our family in Adam and the flesh, now we are close, finding our family in God, Christ, and spiritual men and women. This is one reason why we see so much of a changeover after we are born anew. Old habits, old people, old places fade out of our life, sometimes overnight, many slowly. Our life becomes full with new experiences, including a new church family, brothers and sisters who will love us the way the spirit wills, and help us to be members of Christ's family. They strengthen us, correct us, and build us in deeper unity with Jesus. We find new joys in the new family which we would not and could not know when we wanted to live in our flesh, and fulfill its desires. Our pleasures are godly, and our family is a source of peace, knowledge, and growth as it should be. Scripture is clear that our new state in Christ is not only a servanthood to the new master, but a loving family bond, comparable to a son or a brother. Christ becomes our kin along with our King. He is our loving Father, present with us.

This is a fulfillment of what Scripture previously reveals throughout, in growing truths. Yahweh is first compared to a father in Deuteronomy: "And in the wilderness, where thou hast seen how that the LORD thy

God bare thee, *as a man doth bear his son*, in all the way that ye went, until ye came into this place" (1:31). Scripture later more directly calls Yahweh a father, and often refers to his people as children. To Israel, who is the womb of Christ, Yahweh says, "*is not he thy father* that hath bought thee? hath he not made thee, and established thee?" (32:6b). This comes to its full measure in Jesus Christ, who is more literally the Son of God than anyone. Christ, as man, refers to God very often as the Father, over 150 times in the Gospels, showing us in human flesh the right way to approach God and to turn to him. It is as towards a loving father. When we come and receive Christ, he is like a father to us, interceding for us to the Father in heaven, having understanding of all our weaknesses through his human nature, and being one with God through his divine nature. If we are in Christ, his intercession for us is always successful, and he will lead us to peace and to holiness in life. We, as his children, share in all that he is. Because he is a Son, we become sons.

The family nature of the restored humanity pervades the New Testament thoroughly. Paul speaks as a matter of course to the churches as "brethren" and urges them to treat one another like brothers. The Messiah is called the Beloved of God (Eph 1:6), and the same term is used addressing the brethren by Paul, Peter, James, and John. They share aid and love as true family do. If we are family with Christ, who is firstborn among many brethren, then we are family with one another, of one mind and purpose. We follow his example, in humility, in helping others, in obedience to God. This is no mere idea of a great human family, it is a reality, powered by the Spirit of God, within the love and fellowship of the churches. No matter where we came from, we love one another as brother and sister in the same home, and we share in the inheritance we receive. We have the best Father imaginable.

It is impossible to speak about being brought into God's family through the man Jesus Christ, without speaking also of the source of Christ's human nature: his mother Mary. If we are restored into a new human family, through the cross and resurrection, we have a new human nature because God became man within Mary's womb. He drew from her flesh and blood. Though the term would have been meaningless then, from her DNA. God touched upon space and time in the incarnation, coming down within the womb of a holy virgin, Mary, the betrothed bride of Joseph. Just as the old humanity had a father and mother, in Adam and his wife Eve, the new humanity also has a father and mother, in Jesus and his mother Mary. It is wondrous if you think about it. Just as Eve was drawn from Adam's rib, Christ was drawn from the Virgin's womb. If all the saints can say that Jesus is my Lord, the mother Mary can also say, Jesus is my Son. We are in fellowship with God through Christ, with all of our brothers and sisters in the assembly, through the motherhood and humanity of Mary.

We see a picture of Christ presenting her to the church, when he presents her to the apostle John at the cross:

> When Jesus therefore saw his mother, and the disciple standing by, whom he loved, he saith unto his mother, Woman, behold thy son!
>
> Then saith he to the disciple, *Behold thy mother!* And from that hour that disciple took her unto his own home. (John 19:26–27)

After this moment, the apostle would have cared for and protected Mary in his home, along with other brethren in the church. She would have been revered by all who trusted in her Son. Mary is one we can all look to as a mother. In Mary is a picture of feminine purity. It is an example of how we can view women, in their purity, and holy use by God. It is an uplifting of motherhood, as if it weren't already a high calling, into sharing with God in salvation. The curse and pain of childbearing has become the most lifegiving power in Mary. Every Christian husband can look at his wife as a vessel of the future life of the faith, and every woman can know she is cared for as tender mother and vessel for God to use. When Paul writes that wives will be "saved in childbearing" (1 Tim 2:15), he is alluding to the newly sanctified womb, no longer reminding us of the curse, but conforming a woman to Christ.

Although there is nothing in the way of a physical description of the virgin Mary in Scripture, we know that she is holy, modest, and beautiful. She made herself the servant of the Lord, and said, "be it unto me according to thy word" (Luke 1:38). She believed God, trusted, and obeyed. But she is not just beautiful, she is also the mother of God. Mary bore in her womb both God and man, while God redeemed human nature, taking it on. Yahweh has existed for an eternity, and did not need a mother to come into being, but in becoming man, he used a mother to have life in the flesh. He went through each stage of development you see in your science books, from embryo, to fetus, to infant, and every moment of cellular reproduction was the restoration of human nature. I don't doubt the Creator could have generated human flesh to use out of nothing, but he instead chose to come to us as a baby from a human mother—Immanuel.

God with us. When we share in the nature of Jesus, then, we share in the nature of Mary, from whom he took on humanity. That is what it means to be mother of God, or as the early church called her: *Theotokos*, the God-bearer. The special people whom God has delivered to himself have a mother and father forever.

Divine Nature

Set your affection on things above, not on things on the earth.

For ye are dead, and *your life is hid with Christ in God.*

When Christ, who is our life, shall appear, then shall ye also appear with him in glory. (Col 3:2–4)

According as his divine power *hath given unto us all things* that pertain unto life and godliness, through the knowledge of him that hath called us to glory and virtue:

Whereby are given unto us exceeding great and precious promises: that by these *ye might be partakers of the divine nature*, having escaped the corruption that is in the world through lust. (2 Pet 1:3–4)

For I through the law am dead to the law, that I might live unto God.

I am crucified with Christ: *nevertheless I live; yet not I, but Christ liveth in me*: and the life which I now live in the flesh I live by the faith of the Son of God, who loved me, and gave himself for me. (Gal 2:19–20)

For if, when we were enemies, we were reconciled to God by the death of his Son, much more, being reconciled, *we shall be saved by his life*. (Rom 5:10)

At that day ye shall know that I am in my Father, and *ye in me, and I in you.* (John 14:20)

But the natural man receiveth not the things of the Spirit of God: for they are foolishness unto him: neither can he know them, because they are spiritually discerned.

But he that is spiritual judgeth all things, yet he himself is judged of no man.

For *who hath known the mind of the Lord, that he may instruct him? But we have the mind of Christ.* (1 Cor 2:14–16)

Being in God's kingdom, being in his family, comes with being united with his supernatural life. God dwells within us, and fills our life with his divine life. The New Testament portrays this union many times. In the passages here, we see that we have been given all thing, and are "partakers" of the divine nature (2 Pet 1:3–4). The word used for "partake" commonly means to be a partner, companion, or sharer in anything. While not by nature God, once we are restored, we are in connection to his supernatural being. We will see this reality in our life, as we grow to conform to Christ's character, as we are blessed with what we need to honor Jesus, and as our knowledge and love of God grows. Only Yahweh is God, but we are wrapped up in everything that Yahweh is. Our Lord Jesus, who gives all this to us, is just like us, and also just like God. It is this union of natures in Christ that powers much of this sharing of the supernatural and eternal life of God. To the degree that a man of normal body and blood can unite with Yahweh in essence, we do so. Christ has done so perfectly. We follow in his course.

Paul speaks of his inner life not as being his own (Gal 2:19–20). His inner life is Christ. All he needs to do is trust Jesus and put the flesh to death. Jesus' life will well up within him, like a fountain, and fill his being. His justification comes through Christ. His life comes through Christ. Nothing is of his own power. Paul is merely describing and explaining Jesus' own teachings of indwelling within his people (John 14:20, 17:22–23). Christ taught several times on his union with his people, paralleling it with his own union with the Father. Just as he lives eternally within the Father, he also lives in us, and we live in him. We have life, not only because a payment was made, and our punishment was taken for us. We have life because now we are united with his life, which is perfect and dwells in goodness forever. That is the life we have. It's not our own. That's why Paul can speak of the cross as atoning for our sins, and also speak of the resurrection, and the life of Christ saving us (Rom 5:10), because we truly are not finally saved without that union with Jesus' living body. When you hear a Christian speak of eternal life, remember he's not only speaking of the soul within us that will go on forever. He is speaking of the true eternal life that dwells in us, the life of God, which has now been welded to our own. Christ brings eternal life. Christ brings himself.

With Christ as our King, as our Father, as our life, we can depart from the flesh by becoming like he is. Many scholars, mystics, and pious of the Hebrew religion have put enormous effort and left no stone unturned to know the will of God, and done so failingly, yet the Christian has "the mind of Christ," simply because he has professed Christ humbly, and received the Holy Spirit (1 Cor 2:16b). That simple faith and repentance, more than any religious study in the world, made us family with God, and more intimate than imagined with the divine will. The son is like his father. Family resembles family. So too, when we come into the family of God, we become like our Father, and take on his ways. We learn obedience. We learn to be sacrificial. We learn to be humble. We are hammered into the shape of our Lord, chiseled be a representation of him here on earth. We break bread with him. We go through the waters with him. We belong to God now, and nothing can take away that union.

Truly as amazing as the indwelling of Christ within us, is our likeness to him. A likeness more intimate than we imagined awaits when our refining is complete. Apostle John writes, "Beloved, now are we the sons of God, and it doth not yet appear what we shall be: but we know that, *when he shall appear, we shall be like him*; for we shall see him as he is" (1 John 3:2). Even our father in the flesh Adam, made in God's image before sin was in the world, did not bear as much likeness as we will finally receive in Christ. As he shapes our soul, and chisels away at any hardness in us, we will find in meeting him in everlasting, we are like him. Everything fallen in us has been lifted up to glory. It is a soul more willing to go through sacrifice, and suffer pain, and one fully able to love.

I remember a moment, as a new believer in Jesus, when I had just read a striking passage in a book. It was an evangelical book a friend had lent me, and as a new believer much of it was unfamiliar territory. The passage spoke about how one can sometimes make a pact with the devil, and bring cursing into one's life. A curse struck me as realistic, and darkly possible. If anything, it described my life. I immediately thought back to the time when I was a little boy. I thought back to a time when I had renounced my life, and renounced anything good about me. In anger and despair, I had decided I wanted nothing of life, but only to destroy myself. Though much of childhood fades with time, this was a memorable moment and never will. This event sounded to me now remarkably like making a pact with the devil, a great pact of destruction which joined us together, and waged war against God's creation. In that moment, I closed my eyes and I asked God in prayer: "Did I make a pact with the devil? Did I give my soul to him?"

Now when I pray, I pray only to speak to the Almighty, and not to have a telephone conversation with him. I accept that God answers prayers in quiet ways, and often over time. He doesn't chat like a friend.

However, in this moment of prayer, I very soon heard an audible answer to my question. In the silence of my solitary apartment, a voice rang out and said, "Your soul belongs to me." I heard the Lord say this two times, and I listened intently for a few more minutes hoping to hear his voice again. It is often the new believer who needs much encouragement in his faith, and better grounding in the truth, and he receives it when needed. In this amazing moment, unexpectedly, God gave me the answer to my question. In a comforting voice He put to rest my fear. Through Christ and through my faith I was God's child. I was no possession of the devil. I belonged to him.

6

Walk Uprightly

WHEN I WAS LIVING in Austin, Texas, years ago, I still remember one brief moment, which stands out strongly among many others which remain. Driving along the road with my lady friend, I saw in passing a man by the side of the road who looked like Jesus. Why his looks stood out to me, I don't know. There are plentiful other bearded, long-haired types in the city, some of whom are questionable characters, and are far from embodying goodness. This man who stood there looking out appeared like Jesus to me, in his stature, and in his apparent spiritual power. I also remember the strange feeling that came with seeing him—fear.

Fear is something we associate with seeing a more dangerous looking character than Jesus, and certainly not when we're in a car and unable to be harmed anyway. I felt a sense of fear in my soul at that quick image of Jesus, who stood there, as if an icon. That fear came from an innate knowledge. I think anyone who has a Christian background, or even has heard the faith preached, can recognize it. That is the knowledge that Jesus is free, and we love that. Even non-believers love that about him. Societal traditions, unjust laws, daily routines, and personal desires do not stop Jesus from doing good. He is unrestrained by those externals. He walks in truth by himself. But if we were to become free as he is, become fully liberated to pursue righteousness, we would lose much of what we desire very quickly. Even the thought of being like Jesus makes us think of what we would lose. At that age, and as an atheist, I didn't have too much of a moral sense, at least not regarding most things. But I did know

I was holding on tightly to much that I loved, and that to be free, I'd have to lose it. I'd have to care far less for my life and my possessions.

I wasn't wealthy, nor did I have expensive possessions, but what I did have, I relied on. I trusted in a comfortable apartment, regular food, friends I was familiar with, and I sought to satisfy my desires, whether for pleasure or for sin. I prided myself on my books and my music, and got by on the melancholy-artist sense of self I'd patched together half convincingly over the years. That was all I knew, and lived by, and basically what made me, me. That means while to be free seems beautiful, a wonderful end to being slaves of desire, a glorious chance to seek out only what is good in this world, it also seems like a dreaded knife attack against us. It will tear at the flesh and destroy much of what we know and love. It snatches our desires out of our hand. It takes away our stability. That potent picture of righteousness found in the face of Jesus becomes an assault against the flesh. It makes everything we've build our life upon passing. That's frightening.

Yet when a man places his trust in Jesus, that miraculous act which makes peace with God immediately begins to bleed over into his life. There comes much greater willingness to let go, along with a true conviction to remove himself from any falsehood to which he is clinging. Light comes out of the darkness. The waters are separated from the waters. Continents begin to form. The one-time act of faith begins to work itself out over time, in moments, in years. Christ's righteousness which he received begins to act through him. It brings life to his members, pouring into every organ of the soul, invading each area of life and relationship. Laying down new laws and cancelling old. He surrendered to the King, and now the King will come down and govern this man, shaping him into the form of Christ.

The new heart and awareness that comes with faith is truly a new creation. You can call it a restoration of the old, but it indeed is new, since our Father calls it new. You are a new man. It is interesting that just as God, through his word, divided between the light and the darkness when he made the world, the new creation of the believer now can see between the two as well. Good and evil are clearly seen, and he knows to love the good and hate evil. He thirsts for the good, and he knows the eternal goodness of God which lies behind it. He no longer stays away from evil because of shame, or emotion, or fear, but because he has in his heart to love what is good, and loathe evil. He can feel real sorrow when he sins. He repents not because society demands it, or because he has upset someone, but because of his new knowledge of good and evil. It seems the dreaded knife assault of religion was a scalpel in the hand of a surgeon, removing the blade and the poison, and sewing the wound back together. It is not every knife that destroys.

There is a stillness to the soul when a man gives up his rebellion, and receives the love and mercy of God. There may also be an amount of ecstasy or elation, but these are purely passing. The ongoing result, after a life of sin and suffering, is stillness and peace. We know we are founded in God, and that he is an unbreakable foundation. We know we have love, which is eternal and perfect. We are not orphans alone in the world. We have a Father eternal we can speak to in heaven who cherishes us, and will correct us if we go wrong. We know that no matter our circumstances, eternal goodness and glory are our future with Jesus Christ. These things are healing to the soul, and the soul of the rebel, which only knew chaos, despair, anxiety, internal violence, now knows perfect relationship and what it means to be a son. It is healing to the disturbed mind, and to the mentally ill, feeding wholeness, sustenance, strength, and healing into their spiritual members. Just as a child who has been abandoned by his parents, bounced around from home to home, knows peace coming to a family which will love him forever, the human being, lost and vulnerable to the elements knows peace coming to the Father. Winds cannot shift this new man. The shaking of the earth does not make him fall. He may sway a little back and forth, but he is firmly bound together in his roots with the divine, defended by God's power and love.

TRUTH:

One of the first blessings that come with being washed clean is the knowledge that there really is truth. We have access to that truth now. We know that Holy Scripture is truth. We also know there is objective truth to be known in the world, through reason and conscience. The relativist needs to live with the belief that knowledge cannot be known in the deepest sense, and even morality is changing. He has a world in which you really cannot say that killing children is morally wrong, other than by personal opinion, or cultural consensus. We cannot really be certain the universe will function as it does day to day, as there is no basis to trust in randomly acquired laws of nature, which have themselves appeared by accident. Sure, the relativist may borrow the more satisfying beliefs of

Christians, as he does all the time, but he's got to deny his own system to do so, and at heart he knows he has no foundation. It is all restlessness and tossing about for him. There is no peace for the wicked. Yet in Christ we know truth, and know there is an eternal God of truth. There is a God from whom the moral law flows, along with all the foundational natural principles of this cosmos. This is a rock which dispels illusion, error, and deep confusion. We have solid ground to build on in our life.

The Bible teaches from Old Testament to New that Yahweh is truth—along with being love and light—and teaches that God's word, or his revealed will through the prophets of Scripture, is nothing but truth. This truth is deepened and applied to us most fully in God's revelation through his Son Jesus. While coming to save the world from its sins, Christ also provided a revelation. This is a revelation of who the Father is, in his character and in his will. The Son shows us who God is in a way never shown before:

> For the law was given by Moses, but grace and truth came by Jesus Christ.
>
> No man hath seen God at any time; the only begotten Son, which is in the bosom of the Father, *he hath declared him*. (John 1:17–18)
>
> God, who at sundry times and in divers manners spake in time past unto the fathers by the prophets,
>
> Hath in these last days spoken unto us by his Son, whom he hath appointed heir of all things, by whom also he made the worlds;
>
> Who *being the brightness of his glory, and the express image of his person*, and upholding all things by the word of his power (Heb 1:1–3a)

The New Testament teaches that God's Son makes the Father known. He declares or proclaims the Father. What we cannot see because Yahweh is invisible and is spirit, we see through Christ, not merely in his teachings but in his life, death, and resurrection. If you want to know most deeply who God is, look to Jesus' life, death, and resurrection. There is God. There is no tome on philosophy or metaphysics which can teach you more about God, nor can the Holy Scriptures before his coming reach this fullness of truth. Meditate on Christ to know God. The opening of Hebrews also makes it clear the superiority of God's appearing in the flesh to anything before it. The angels brought revelation to Moses, but the same angels bow down and worship the Christ (Heb 1:6). His revelation is the completion of what had come before in the prophets, who all merely pointed to Christ. This Son of God, who was the very hands of the Almighty as he created and shaped the universe, shows to us God's "brightness" and "express image." The exact image, or *charaktēr* in Greek, refers to an engraving or a stamp that produces a precise copy of the original. It is teaching the Son is an exact likeness of God, made visible for us here on earth. If Yahweh is a far-away star, the Son is the light streaming forth so we can see that star, coming forth from its very essence.

> Then said Jesus to those Jews which believed on him, If ye continue in my word, then are ye my disciples indeed;
>
> And *ye shall know the truth*, and the truth shall make you free. (John 8:31–32)

Jesus here was speaking to some among the Jews who showed, at least for the moment, belief in his teachings. He promised a way to know truth and to be free of sin, which is to "continue in my word." While the audience at the time did not like this answer, since it pointed to their own slavery to sin, all who seek to be free in Christ need to follow its truth. That demands not a momentary belief, but an ongoing abiding in the Son, a faith in his words, and obedience to him. This is similar language to John 15, in which Jesus likens his people to branches abiding in the vine, who have life as long as they are living in the vine, but who will be cast out and burn if they are not. Actively believing and living the Christian faith brings a knowledge of the truth. It is not the mere knowledge that Christ is Savior and his death and resurrection save us. It is an ongoing knowledge of truth, one that allows us to recognize sin, and turn away from it. It's one that allows us to do the works Jesus taught us to do, to love and serve one another, to live clean and pure. We know Christ's life within us as it works through us in our lives. We know God's goodness and trustworthiness as we depend upon him in all things, in sacrifice, and departing from the flesh, in overcoming evil. The knowledge of the truth is God's promise, which is always credible, and worthy of our trust. That Christian, if he is faithful, has knowledge of truth in the most intimate possible way.

> They are not of the world, even as I am not of the world.
>
> *Sanctify them through thy truth*: thy word is truth.
>
> As thou hast sent me into the world, even so have I also sent them into the world.

> And for their sakes I sanctify myself, that they also might be sanctified through the truth. (John 17:16–19)

Christ's revelation is a fulfillment of what had come before. The Scriptures from Genesis through the prophets declare God's truth in a similar sense; the truth of God's covenant promises, the truth of his judgment of sin and his mercy on the repentant, the truth of actively living God's law and seeing its results in history. His word is nothing but truth. This new vital connection to God will bring us holiness; Father pouring into the Son, Son pouring into his beloved people. It will lead us and clean us as God's vessel. It will show us the order of a new and different land from this earthly world, a heavenly land, which we possess together. We will carry that with us as we walk on this earth.

> *Thy word is true* from the beginning: and every one of thy righteous judgments endureth for ever. (Ps 119:160)
>
> For the word of the LORD is right; and all *his works are done in truth*. (Ps 33:4)
>
> He is the Rock, his work is perfect: for all his ways are judgment: *a God of truth* and without iniquity, just and right is he. (Deut 32:4)
>
> Into thine hand I commit my spirit: thou hast redeemed me, O LORD God of truth. (Ps 31:5)

In the Scriptures before Christ, we see that Yahweh, in his character and identity, is a God of truth. He contains truth and he is truth. He gives truth to us in the Scriptures. Yahweh's truth is not mere intellectual truth, but touches also on his righteousness and strength. There is no falsehood, no injustice, no weakness. We can trust in the Scriptures in their entirety, and we know all that God does is done in truth, so he will be nothing but faithful. From the creation of the world, to his guiding hand over our lives right now, his miracles, and his punishment of evildoers—it all comes from truth. It is rooted in truth. Its ultimate end is truth. Yahweh and his work are completely trustworthy and they are good.

This indeed gives rest to our soul. We can know the universe around us is not built for anarchy and chaos, but for order and truth. We can know that suffering isn't meaningless, but has a purpose. We can know Yahweh's truth is reflected in his creation, in nature and the natural laws all around us. We can know the promises of God's covenant are good and will come to pass. We can know his laws are good and good for us. The underlying fear and anxiety that comes with a denial of God are washed away then with coming to faith. Not one moment of our lives is outside of the direction of Yahweh, and the Creator we call on is good to answer.

One of the first things that the new believer in Christ desires to do is to fight evil, and to tell other souls the gospel of salvation. Often he does so before he has matured enough, or turned from sin fully, but it is a natural desire to have immediately. A man can now see the situation for what it is. The division between the light and darkness is coming clear. The division between things set apart for God and things which are not holy. The truth brings reality into focus. The warm bath we thought we were soaking in is actually a cesspool. What we believed to be love, is really selfishness and self-satisfaction. Our foods are actually poison. Our beloved friends and close family are lost, and are given over to the devil. The fact of warfare is plainly before our eyes and we want to go to battle and defeat evil, heal suffering, save souls made in the image of a loving God from ultimate darkness and fire. The truth did this to us. It has awakened the soul.

There is also peace to the soul, and greater harmony in daily existence when we know a consistent moral standard. The law of the Lord is consistently good for us, and based on his standard, rather than our personal preferences, and our feelings. We can no longer float without direction in a world that at heart we know makes up its morals to suit its inclinations. We can no longer stand on the tremulous ground of saying really bad people like murderers are evil, but the rest of us can behave with lewdness and vulgarity, blaspheme, fornicate, get drunk, and still basically be "good people." At heart, everyone who practices similar self-serving standards knows that they stand on quicksand. They know it's nonsense. Their worldview and ethics are unstable, and made up to suit the situation. Yet when we enter the life of God, and receive truth from him, we receive as a matter of truth a consistent law, one which is based upon the character and will of the Almighty, one which is given to benefit a people whom he loves, and whom he will guide perfectly. We have a set of ethics which fit the creation in which we live, which suits our natures, our sexes, and the way human society naturally works.

That law makes much more sense than a law of convenience or personal feelings. It is like an instruction manual; a set of instructions written by the same people who built the machine you are using. It's going to tell you how to rightly use that machine, and it comes from a source that knows how. God's law is so good for us, because it comes not only from a perfect mind and perfect love, but because it governs the creation which Yahweh made. Our souls and human relationships were built for it. Knowing this, and living our lives within the law of God, heals the soul. It takes what was confusion, self-will, anger, and brings the soul into right relationship with Yahweh, other human beings, and the whole creation itself. That pervasive alienation and fear each human soul can feel is washed away as we are washed in Christ. The simple knowledge of God's law by itself brings us back to right working order.

WALK UPRIGHTLY

The ongoing process of learning to live as a new creation is naturally associated with changes in the life. It is pictured to include better ethics, and cleaner living. The life ought to be full of prayer and worship, and a departure from a life built on fulfilling the flesh. These things are all true, but we need to remember they merely reflect what becoming holy truly is on the inside: that is a unity of the soul with Christ. It is the walking together of man's spirit with Christ's spirit, and the light of Christ working in a man. It would be an impossible burden to expect a man to live a life by his power and ethics which is pleasing to God. Yet there is nothing strange for the Son of God to do this within the life of a believer. To be sanctified is to be joined with Christ, and to continue living joined with Christ, to draw off of His truth, goodness, and knowledge. The changed life associated with departure from sin grows organically from this core. We give ourselves to our Lord, over and over, in each sphere of our life, and in various forms. We give even our contemplations, and longings to Him to use. Christ's work in the newborn soul is supernatural.

> I am the true vine, and my Father is the husbandman.
>
> Every branch in me that beareth not fruit he taketh away: and every branch that beareth fruit, he purgeth it, that it may bring forth more fruit.
>
> Now ye are clean through the word which I have spoken unto you.
>
> *Abide in me, and I in you.* As the branch cannot bear fruit of itself, except it abide in the vine; no more can ye, except ye abide in me.
>
> I am the vine, ye are the branches: *He that abideth in me, and I in him, the same bringeth forth much fruit*: for without me ye can do nothing.

> If a man abide not in me, he is cast forth as a branch, and is withered; and men gather them, and cast them into the fire, and they are burned.
>
> If ye abide in me, and my words abide in you, ye shall ask what ye will, and it shall be done unto you.
>
> Herein is my Father glorified, that ye bear much fruit; so shall ye be my disciples. (John 15:1–8)

The Christian is totally dependent on Christ and his life. Christ even teaches that "without me ye can do nothing" (v. 5b). The believer can only bear fruit in his life, the fruit of righteousness, because he draws from the life of the Son of God. The branches of a vine need to draw from the vine their life, nutrients, and water, so the Christian draws all life that he has from the true vine, which is the Savior. The life that he has in him is not his own. The good deeds he does are not his own. This passage also shows that there are those who dwell in the vine merely in a physical manner, but who are not truly dwelling in the vine in a spiritual fashion, nor truly drawing off the life of Christ. It is these latter, who are only attached physically to the vine, but not drawing from the vine's life, who get cut off and thrown into the fire. They did not bear fruit. They did not do righteousness in their lives. They did not draw from Christ's love. They are like dead wood, physically attached to the church, but with no life in them.

> Yet a little while, and the world seeth me no more; but ye see me: because I live, ye shall live also.
>
> At that day ye shall know *that I am in my Father, and ye in me, and I in you.*
>
> He that hath my commandments, and keepeth them, he it is that loveth me: and he that loveth me shall be loved of my Father, and I will love him, and will manifest myself to him. (John 14:19–21)

Jesus speaks similarly of this indwelling elsewhere in the same chapter, and in John 17. His followers will know at a later time about this indwelling, after Jesus has ascended to heaven to be with the Father. They learn this more deeply not merely because of his absence, but because the Spirit of God will come and live within them. This was fulfilled in power at the feast of Pentecost, also known as the Jewish feast of Shavuot. The young church, only ten days after Jesus departed, experienced the miracle of God's Spirit coming upon them. It filled them with joyous worship, and gave them the miraculous gift of languages (Acts 2:1–13), which helped spread the gospel across the globe. It furthermore guided them into truth, including the power of prophecy, as the apostles and their associates wrote the books of the New Testament. All believers receive God's Spirit, and know Christ in the most intimate way through him, although certain miraculous gifts such as prophecy, tongues, and healing, were only for certain saints in the early years of the church (1 Cor 13:8–10, Eph 2:20). Others, such as the gifts of teaching or evangelism, continue with us. God still gives gifts to men of faith and guides them though the Holy Spirit in them.

> I have yet many things to say unto you, but ye cannot bear them now.
>
> Howbeit when he, the Spirit of truth, is come, he will guide you into all truth: for *he shall not speak of himself; but whatsoever he shall hear, that shall he speak*: and he will shew you things to come.
>
> He shall glorify me: for *he shall receive of mine, and shall shew it unto you.*
>
> All things that the Father hath are mine: therefore said I, that he shall take of mine, and shall shew it unto you. (John 16:12–15)
>
> If ye love me, keep my commandments.
>
> And I will pray the Father, and he shall give you another Comforter, that he may abide with you for ever;
>
> Even the Spirit of truth; whom the world cannot receive, because it seeth him not, neither knoweth him: but ye know him; for *he dwelleth with you, and shall be in you.*
>
> I will not leave you comfortless: I will come to you. (John 14:15–18)

Just as we unite initially with Christ when we believe in him, we unite repeatedly over time through his Spirit working in us. It is as if on the moment of belief, the doctor entered our sick room. Throughout our treatment, he also comes and gives us medicine, counsel, and surgery. He watches over us and will restore us in an ongoing way. In this passage from John, it is clear that the Spirit speaks to the church just as Christ has spoken to it. The Spirit will speak nothing that is not of Christ. This flows from the order of the triune God, in which we see that the Son speaks words from the Father, and then when the Spirit comes to dwell in the church, he speaks words of Christ. This reveals our union with our Savior, and also reveals the full truth of the Holy Bible, as none can say only the words of Jesus are the true teachings. Truth in Scripture is one united whole. Just as we trust Jesus' words as the words of God, we trust the gospel writers as well, who were inspired by the Spirit, and we trust the Epistles and other New Testament books, which are likewise from the Father and Son, through the Holy Spirit.

The Christian hears from Yahweh whenever he reads the Bible. He also hears from Yahweh in a different form as the Spirit leads him to depart from sin, and helps him to understand the truths in the Bible. He hears from Yahweh as the Lord providentially leads his life and orders it for the kingdom of God. All things in the Christian's life are led by the Spirit, who brings life, truth, peace, and holiness. God speaks to him, not through new prophecy as given to the apostles, but through leading his life and guiding his heart. What once was a slavery to personal desire, ego, and sin, becomes full freedom to live out God's goodness in Christ. It is not only freedom from our condemnation, but freedom to live as human nature is meant to live, in a loving relationship with the Almighty, and filled with righteousness and truth. In uniting us with the divine nature, Yahweh hammers our human nature back into shape.

> So then they that are in the flesh cannot please God.
>
> *But ye are not in the flesh, but in the Spirit, if so be that the Spirit of God dwell in you.* Now if any man have not the Spirit of Christ, he is none of his.
>
> And if Christ be in you, the body is dead because of sin; but the Spirit is life because of righteousness.
>
> But if the Spirit of him that raised up Jesus from the dead dwell in you, he that raised up Christ from the dead shall also quicken your mortal bodies by his Spirit that dwelleth in you. (Rom 8:8–11).
>
> For ye have not received the spirit of bondage again to fear; but *ye have received the Spirit of adoption, whereby we cry, Abba, Father.*
>
> The Spirit itself beareth witness with our spirit, that we are the children of God:
>
> And if children, then heirs; heirs of God, and joint-heirs with Christ; if so be that we suffer with him, that we may be also glorified together. (Rom 8:15–17)

The new soul's unity with God will bring these amazing miracles as well. One miracle is that the same power that resurrected Jesus of Nazareth from the grave is inside the new believer. It gives life to our bodies, both the spiritual life on which we feed each day, as well as the new bodies we will receive at the resurrection of all flesh. God's family have a supernatural miracle living within them, which is power and life from beyond this world. It is sharing in the great miracle of Christ's resurrection. We also receive through the Spirit, and through unity with Christ, a spirit of adoption. We have been brought into our true and eternal family. The Spirit of God now leads us in calling out to Yahweh as "Father," something we can now say in the true sense. We have been born into his family through the working of the Holy Spirit, and through the waters of baptism. We have been united with One who truly is God's Son, Christ being a child of the Father eternally because he exists in God eternally, and Christ also becoming a child of God through his obedience to God's law and fulfilling of the law. We share in his sonship through his human nature. Amazingly, we share in his sonship through his divine nature, which we always have access to, despite our humanity. Just as Christ can go to the Father and speak to him as a beloved Son, we can do the same, being free of any condemnation, and being part of his family in the greatest possible sense.

> Know ye not that ye are the temple of God, and that *the Spirit of God dwelleth in you*?
>
> If any man defile the temple of God, him shall God destroy; for the temple of God is holy, which temple ye are. (1 Cor 3:16–17)
>
> Flee fornication. Every sin that a man doeth is without the body; but he that committeth fornication sinneth against his own body.
>
> What? know ye not that *your body is the temple of the Holy Ghost* which is in you, which ye have of God, and ye are not your own? (1 Cor 6:18–19)

The theological truth that our bodies are the temple of God is not a mere comparison, or a metaphor. There is some real literal truth in there. For our bodies, like the temple in Jerusalem, or the tabernacle in the wilderness, is a physical abode, and has God's Spirit dwelling within it. Just as Yahweh dwelt in the temple, in between the cherubim of the ark, in the holy of holies (Exod 25:22), Yahweh dwells in the soul and mind of the believer, who is not a ghost, but a real physical dwelling. Just as God came to dwell in flesh in Christ when he became man (John 1:14), he comes and dwells in us when we enter his family. Our bodies, then, are greatly holy, as the temple was greatly holy. Our bodies must be used for God's glory, as the temple was used during its day for his glory. We have within us the sacrifice of Christ, making peace, as the temple had sacrifices daily. We make intercession in prayer, as the priests did in the temple. We receive the bread and cup of Communion, as the temple offered the show bread in the holy place. All that we do with our bodies is now purposed for God, and washed clean of all that takes us away from that purpose. To sin with our bodies is especially terrible, since we make God's temple impure. This abode of our bodies now changes in its use, just as our minds, hearts, and all areas of our life change when we receive the Savior.

> And not only so, but we glory in tribulations also: knowing that tribulation worketh patience;
>
> And patience, experience; and experience, hope:
>
> And hope maketh not ashamed; because *the love of God is shed abroad in our hearts by the Holy Ghost which is given unto us.* (Rom 5:3–5)

Being united with Yahweh through the Spirit assures us of the attitude we can have. That is one of hope. We know even our sufferings are for the good of all, and God will use them for his kingdom. The entire universe is ordered to bring forth good from the people of God. We can rejoice in sufferings because we know that all is going to end in the glorious rule of Christ over all things, and we are forever with the Beloved. There is always something to hope for, where in our previous life there was no meaningful hope; only the final resting place of death, and at best, uncertainly over our fate. There was the distant thundering of judgment and wrath for the sin we kept in our heart. There was the suppressed guilt that kept growling, even beneath our whispers. Yet now our resting place in peace is assured, because God has made it known. That mindset and attitude comes from the love of Yahweh, which is known only in Christ. The life of God through the Spirit is a source of hope and healing for the soul.

> And be not drunk with wine, wherein is excess; but *be filled with the Spirit*;
>
> Speaking to yourselves in psalms and hymns and spiritual songs, singing and making melody in your heart to the Lord;
>
> Giving thanks always for all things unto God and the Father in the name of our Lord Jesus Christ;

> Submitting yourselves one to another in the fear of God. (Eph 5:18–21)
>
> This I say then, *Walk in the Spirit, and ye shall not fulfil the lust of the flesh.*
>
> For the flesh lusteth against the Spirit, and the Spirit against the flesh: and these are contrary the one to the other: so that ye cannot do the things that ye would.
>
> But if ye be led of the Spirit, ye are not under the law.
>
> Now the works of the flesh are manifest, which are these; Adultery, fornication, uncleanness, lasciviousness,
>
> Idolatry, witchcraft, hatred, variance, emulations, wrath, strife, seditions, heresies,
>
> Envyings, murders, drunkenness, revellings, and such like: of the which I tell you before, as I have also told you in time past, that they which do such things shall not inherit the kingdom of God.
>
> But the fruit of the Spirit is love, joy, peace, longsuffering, gentleness, goodness, faith,
>
> Meekness, temperance: against such there is no law.
>
> And *they that are Christ's have crucified the flesh with the affections and lusts.* (Gal 5:16–24)

Life in God's Spirit is an ongoing process of uniting with Yahweh's life. It is receiving his life, righteousness, and power. We do not just "have" the Spirit, but we "walk in" the Spirit as well. We are "filled by" the Spirit. That is Christ's presence in our thoughts and in our deeds. Our mind becomes filled with prayer and worship of the Lord, with thankfulness for all we receive, and we learn to be humble enough to serve one another. The Spirit first brings us the foundation of our home, then we build on that foundation with his resources step by step, with the wood, the nails, the brick, the mortar, the dry wall, the roofing, until the house is complete. It is the ongoing power to walk away from temptation, and to live in righteousness. It is our heart's desires being purified, departing from the slavery of our lusts, our pretentious goals, our self-importance, and arriving at a great peace, and love of mankind. It is the creation of a mind which dwells upon the treasures of God. A life ruled by passions is over, being put to death in Christ. Our life is one of prayer, worship, and spiritual joy. We have an attitude of thanks and dependency on our heavenly Father. The mind and character of God, in a sense, is being imprinted on our hearts.

> Know ye not, that so many of us as were baptized into Jesus Christ were *baptized into his death?*
>
> *Therefore we are buried with him by baptism into death*: that like as Christ was raised up from the dead by the glory of the Father, even so we also should walk in newness of life.
>
> For if we have been planted together in the likeness of his death, we shall be also in the likeness of his resurrection:
>
> Knowing this, that *our old man is crucified with him*, that the body of sin might be destroyed, that henceforth we should not serve sin. (Rom 6:3–6)
>
> Wherefore, my brethren, *ye also are become dead to the law by the body of Christ*; that ye should be married to another, even to him who is raised from the dead, that we should bring forth fruit unto God.
>
> For when we were in the flesh, the motions of sins, which were by the law, did work in our members to bring forth fruit unto death.
>
> But now we are delivered from the law, that being dead wherein we were held; that we should serve in newness of spirit, and not in the oldness of the letter. (Rom 7:4–6)
>
> But ye have not so learned Christ;
>
> If so be that ye have heard him, and have been taught by him, as the truth is in Jesus:
>
> That *ye put off concerning the former conversation the old man*, which is corrupt according to the deceitful lusts;
>
> And be renewed in the spirit of your mind;
>
> And that ye put on the new man, which after God is created in righteousness and true holiness. (Eph 4:20–24)
>
> Lie not one to another, seeing that *ye have put off the old man with his deeds*;
>
> And have put on the new man, which is renewed in knowledge after the image of him that created him; (Col 3:9–10)
>
> I protest by your rejoicing which I have in Christ Jesus our Lord, *I die daily.* (1 Cor 15:31)
>
> For we which live *are alway delivered unto death for Jesus' sake*, that the life also of Jesus might be made manifest in our mortal flesh. (2 Cor 4:11)

I spoke about the death we die when we believe and are baptized into Christ when I previously discussed how his death saves us from sin. The same also needs to be spoken in how Christ makes us holy. The action of the Spirit is not merely to direct us in leading more ethical lives. Rather, it is the creation of a new heart, the restoring of human nature in mankind. The believer is in his essence a disciple for that is what he has been made for and called to. The sinful man who lives for himself goes to death over and over, the new man comes to life and lives continually in us. Since sin has been put to death in us, because of the death of our Savior, we can no longer live for sin. We no longer live to fulfill the desires of our flesh. That part of us is dead. The New Testament speaks of taking off, and putting on our natures, as if they were clothing. We have taken off the old man, and put on the new man. The dirty garment is gone. This new man, molded to the presence of Christ within us, walks in righteousness. He loves what is good, and hates what is evil. He desires to honor God and lives in the law of God.

It is not wrong to envision this radical change as taking off or putting on clothing. In fact, some of the Greek words used have such physical meanings. The word for putting off in Eph 4 (*apotithēmi*) is also used in Acts when Stephen is "cast out" of the city to be stoned (7:58). The word for putting on, which appears in Ephesians, Colossians, and many other passages (*endyō*), is also frequently used for putting on clothing. In Mark 1:6, John the Baptist is "clothed with" camel's hair, using the exact same word. These two words rightly describe the casting away and putting on within our soul as we learn to walk in the spirit. This experience of acting on a new nature, alongside the indwelling of Christ, assures we do not simply receive the blood of Jesus, and then go on to live however our flesh dictates. It demands a change and activates a change. We are not controlled by a heart that thinks nothing of committing sin, but possess a restored human nature, that knows it is wrong, and will feel sorrow and repent of it. We live not in a mere obedience to the law, but in union with the very purposes of it.

When I was a new believer, within a year of being born again, I remember an instance when I experienced the response of the new nature to sin. I had committed sin perfectly aware that what I was doing was wrong. I had a bad feeling about my act, which I suppressed, and tried not to think about. The next night or the following, I had a certain dream. I was walking out by the ocean, on the sand. Strangely the ocean waters had shrunk back, as they would do if there was a great ongoing wind, or a tsunami. I walked out towards the receded sea, and saw on the ocean floor a rock, among other scattered items. The rock interested me, so I knelt down and lifted it, only to find that beneath the rock was a deep and black hole. I reached within the black hole to find a small note of paper. It had been rolled up into a scroll. Unraveling the scroll, I looked at the words, and saw the note read like this: "Your dark yew." Awakening shortly after this, and moved by what I'd seen, it did not take me long to see this dream was an unreal reminder of my sin. It was my spirit telling me my deeds were evil, and that I must not live like this. The dream had shown me the darkness of my act. True, in most cases, the believer will know this through thoughts or feelings, but at times, even if we wish to refuse to look at the truth, God's Spirit may lead us to see it in dreams. The believer in Christ then, in his new nature, has all the resources he needs to recognize, and turn from sin.

It bears telling that many Christians will doubt and have frustration if they commit sin after being born again. They may doubt their own faith. Unbelievers similarly often use sin in the life of a Christian to attack the faith, and claim it is not real, or that Christians generally are fake people. Such standards, however, need to be seen as irrational, because they truly are unreasonable and impossible standards for anyone. The Christian is a new and saved person, and their life will bear witness to that, even if they have sin to cast away from their lives. I can compare my life before being born again to my life after, and there is very little comparison. Before being Christian I sinned absolutely without shame, and lived for myself. If I ever felt sorry for my wrongs, it was only because they had brought serious negative consequences, or public shame. Otherwise, I was content to drink in the darkness like water. As a Christian, when I fell into sin, I had a new organ in my soul to recognize it, hate it, and repent of it. That was unheard of before. Repentance had been a meaningless term to my old self. I became in Christ's love an enemy of sin and made it a goal to turn away from it. The Spirit of God worked in me over several years until my life became far less wicked, and much more filled with goodness and truth. The difference is visible for anyone else to see as well. I have seen the same in the lives of other Christians, and can relate as a fact that any man of sincere faith will have a changed life, even if they sin on occasion. Do not be frustrated or torn with doubt over your own sin as a child of God. Jesus' promises are true. The work of the Spirit is real. Those visible changes you see ought to inspire you to continue to walk in the Spirit and work righteousness in your life. Everyone sins.

The new heart we have is also related to the new state of our relationship to the law. In suspecting some may think he is teaching lawlessness by teaching faith over works, Paul puts forth and answers that question: "Do we then make void the law through faith? God forbid: yea, we establish the law" (Rom 3:31). Rather than being done away with, the law is being establish in a new way. We are no longer under the law as a burden, or a ritual we can never really fulfill. We are no longer under its condemnation. Rather through faith we desire to do the law, as the law is within our hearts. That is why Paul writes elsewhere, "Wherefore the law is holy, and the commandment holy, just, and good" (Rom 7:12). Being turned to the goal of honoring God, and loving mankind, every principle of the law hangs on the new spirit God has placed within us. The law is now our friend, no longer condemning us, but directing us and empowering us to do good. It is a part of our inner programming.

After explaining how our life in Christ means we can no longer continue in sin, Paul again responds to the idea that being free from the law means we can freely sin:

> What then? *shall we sin*, because we are not under the law, but under grace? God forbid.
>
> Know ye not, that to whom ye yield yourselves servants to obey, his servants ye are to whom ye obey; whether of sin unto death, or of obedience unto righteousness?
>
> But God be thanked, that ye were the servants of sin, but ye have obeyed from the heart that form of doctrine which was delivered you.
>
> Being then made free from sin, *ye became the servants of righteousness*. (Rom 6:15–18)

Notice first that even though the Old Covenant has been done away with, there is still such a thing as obedience, and still such a thing as sin. The moral principles which the law taught are obviously present, even if the relationship to the commandments has changed radically, and even if some laws will not apply today. The Mosaic law has gone away, but it was not replaced with lawlessness. The apostle also speaks in detail here about whose control we are under. From what have we become free? Before we tried to be free of God, and were slaves of sin. Now we are free from sin, and are slaves of righteousness, with Christ as our Master. With a new Lord, we naturally will not continue serving our former master. We will serve our new Master, since now we belong to him, and righteousness is his character and his aim. We desire his goals and we are no longer held in bonds by slavery to sin. We should be further moved by the fact our former master did not love us, and was working in the end for our destruction. Our new Master loves us, and cares for our souls. He desires our good, provides all we need, protects us, and give us true freedom, which is the freedom to use our natures for the good. That was their purpose all along. His way leads us in the path of life, and it will never condemn us. In that path we fulfill all the goodness of the law, without being under its burden or judgment. We are truly free.

ACTS OF UNION

The Christian speaks of being made holy, or sanctified. This comes with many accurate details of what a holy life looks like, and what are clean and spiritual attitudes, but at its heart, it is ongoing union with the Lord of Glory. Just as being cleansed of sin involved coming over to the side of Christ, being made holy involves unifying with him over and over, in so many different ways, becoming part of that one organic whole—the true vine of John 15, the holy temple with all of its chambers, the body of our Lord. We live and breathe from the life of our Savior.

To do this, just as we died to our flesh when we believed, we continually put it to death, continually bring the divine life of God into our being. We unite through our worship, our good works, and everything that draws from his character into our thoughts, heart, and actions. Righteousness seems like an impossibility when one relies on the flesh, but when one fills up the soul with the goodness of Christ, who is good in his essence, temptation finds few places to take hold, and sin becomes much more of a far-off reality. Our soul is purified to live in him. The work of defeating the devil in our life becomes a reality because our strength is replaced with the Father's.

Let's look at some of the ways we unite with Christ once we are reborn. The Bible even connects some of them with salvation. They are all sacred, and awesome. They are nourishment for the new human soul.

Profess

We profess our faith with our lips, just as Christ will profess our names to His father (Matt 10:32). We speak forth our new reality as God spoke forth creation.

> But what saith it? *The word is nigh thee, even in thy mouth*, and in thy heart: that is, the word of faith, which we preach;
>
> That *if thou shalt confess with thy mouth* the Lord Jesus, and shalt believe in thine heart that God hath raised him from the dead, thou shalt be saved.
>
> For with the heart man believeth unto righteousness; and with the mouth confession is made unto salvation.
>
> For the scripture saith, *Whosoever believeth on him shall not be ashamed*.
>
> For there is no difference between the Jew and the Greek: for the same Lord over all is rich unto all that call upon him.
>
> For *whosoever shall call upon the name of the Lord shall be saved*. (Rom 10:8–13)

Announcing our faith with words comes side by side in this passage with believing. It even places profession with words together with belief in the activity of salvation, showing how closely wedded our words and faith are. As all Israel confirmed the covenant with words (Exod 24:3,7), the new son of God confirms his faith through his words. Profession is common immediately after we come to belief in Christ, and in the history of Christian liturgy it has been normal to do during each gathering of worship, as the people recite or chant a creed. In speaking it, we not only express our willful love and obedience to Christ, but we affirm that Christ does the same, who professes our names in heaven. Jesus taught, "Whosoever therefore shall confess me before men, him will I confess also before my Father which is in heaven" (Matt 10:32). There is no avoiding this spiritual connection between our words and Christ's words. We are both confessing a truth deeply wrapped up in salvation. Like Christ we also share in the willingness to suffer for our faith as we profess if publicly. We are now identified. The world will know who we are, and as it did with Christ, will often persecute us for it. It is powerful to profess belief, and also in the likeness of God.

Pass through Water

We go through the waters of baptism, as our Lord did (Matt 3:13–17), and die with him that way. It is the entryway into new life. It unites us with Christ and with his people, by going down into the water, and being lifted up.

> Know ye not, that so many of us as were baptized into Jesus Christ were *baptized into his death?*
>
> Therefore we are buried with him by baptism into death: that like as Christ was raised up from the dead by the glory of the Father, even so we also should walk in newness of life.
>
> For if we have been planted together in the likeness of his death, we shall be also *in the likeness of his resurrection*: (Rom 6:3–5)
>
> Jesus answered and said unto him, Verily, verily, I say unto thee, Except a man be born again, he cannot see the kingdom of God.
>
> Nicodemus saith unto him, How can a man be born when he is old? can he enter the second time into his mother's womb, and be born?
>
> Jesus answered, Verily, verily, I say unto thee, *Except a man be born of water and of the Spirit, he cannot enter into the kingdom of God.* (John 3:3–5)
>
> Then Peter said unto them, Repent, and *be baptized every one of you* in the name of Jesus Christ for the remission of sins, and ye shall receive the gift of the Holy Ghost. (Acts 2:38)
>
> The like figure whereunto *even baptism doth also now save us* (not the putting away of the filth of the flesh, but the answer of a good conscience toward God,) by the resurrection of Jesus Christ: (1 Pet 3:21)
>
> He *that believeth and is baptized* shall be saved; but he that believeth not shall be damned. (Mark 16:16)

Jesus was baptized by John, although he did not need to be cleansed or made new (Matt 3:15). In doing so he blessed baptism for all of us, and set a pattern for us to be like him. The Scriptures speak of baptism not only as a passing through from death to life, but also as an experience of our salvation, with both Jesus and Peter attaching it to salvation. The element of water brings us through the new birth. We were born once through our mother in entrance to the human family, and once through the waters in entrance into Christ. The act itself resembles death and rebirth in the grave, in likeness of Christ. It is interesting that just as Christ's baptism, the greatest accomplishment of John's ministry, included a public declaration by God that Jesus was God's Son, our baptism also visibly witnesses to our faith, and our state as a new child of the Most High. It is exhilarating to see another brother pass through the waters, as it is to see and hold your child for the fist time.

Eat Manna

We eat the manna from heaven which Christ gave us. This is what every Christian does in his gatherings, taking the bread and cup, breaking bread together as a people. Christ calls this food his flesh and his blood, and it becomes the new Passover meal, so his people may consume the Lamb of God in their departure from slavery. Jesus gave it the first time before his death to his apostles, and every meal after that has been presented by ministers of the church.

> *I am the living bread which came down from heaven*: if any man eat of this bread, he shall live for ever: and the bread that I will give is my flesh, which I will give for the life of the world.
>
> The Jews therefore strove among themselves, saying, How can this man give us his flesh to eat?
>
> Then Jesus said unto them, Verily, verily, I say unto you, Except ye eat the flesh of the Son of man, and drink his blood, ye have no life in you.
>
> *Whoso eateth my flesh, and drinketh my blood, hath eternal life*; and I will raise him up at the last day.
>
> For my flesh is meat indeed, and my blood is drink indeed.
>
> He that eateth my flesh, and drinketh my blood, dwelleth in me, and I in him.
>
> As the living Father hath sent me, and I live by the Father: so he that eateth me, even he shall live by me.
>
> This is that bread which came down from heaven: not as your fathers did eat manna, and are dead: he that eateth of this bread shall live for ever. (John 6:51–58)
>
> And as they were eating, Jesus took bread, and blessed it, and brake it, and gave it to the disciples, and said, *Take, eat; this is my body.*

And he took the cup, and gave thanks, and gave it to them, saying, Drink ye all of it;

For *this is my blood of the new testament*, which is shed for many for the remission of sins. (Matt 26:26–28)

Along with the singing of hymns and the preaching of the word, receiving the manna from heaven, or the Eucharist, has always been a central part of Christian worship. At times men have received it every day. During the Middle Ages the Catholic Church, afraid too many sinners were receiving Christ's body and blood, gave it to the congregation only rarely. The meal is a supernatural union with Christ through real food and drink, and is in imitation of Christ, who gave it at his Passover. While much of our union with Christ we think of in mystical terms, this kind of union could not be more physical, as Christ calls the food his flesh and blood, and we consume him into our physical being. In receiving him, we receive his righteousness and holiness, and are made holy. There is no church without Communion.

Wash Feet

We wash feet as Christ washed his apostles' feet, and commanded them to do. No servant is greater than his master, and he set for us the perfect example. It is an awkward task, that few people enjoy as a matter of preference. Yet in this challenge, and the possible aversion we feel, molds us to Christ the more.

> Jesus knowing that the Father had given all things into his hands, and that he was come from God, and went to God;
>
> He riseth from supper, and laid aside his garments; and took a towel, and girded himself.
>
> After that he poureth water into a bason, and began to wash the disciples' feet, and to wipe them with the towel wherewith he was girded.
>
> Then cometh he to Simon Peter: and Peter saith unto him, Lord, dost thou wash my feet?
>
> Jesus answered and said unto him, What I do thou knowest not now; but thou shalt know hereafter.
>
> Peter saith unto him, Thou shalt never wash my feet. Jesus answered him, If I wash thee not, thou hast no part with me.

> Simon Peter saith unto him, Lord, not my feet only, but also my hands and my head.
>
> Jesus saith to him, He that is washed needeth not save to wash his feet, but is clean every whit: and ye are clean, but not all.
>
> For he knew who should betray him; therefore said he, Ye are not all clean.
>
> So after he had washed their feet, and had taken his garments, and was set down again, he said unto them, Know ye what I have done to you?
>
> Ye call me Master and Lord: and ye say well; for so I am.
>
> If I then, your Lord and Master, have washed your feet; *ye also ought to wash one another's feet.*
>
> For I have given you an example, that *ye should do as I have done to you.*
>
> Verily, verily, I say unto you, The servant is not greater than his lord; neither he that is sent greater than he that sent him.
>
> If ye know these things, *happy are ye if ye do them.* (John 13:3–17)

Washing feet unites us with Christ. As an act, it teaches to serve others, and here it specifically teaches that even those in charge serve others. It teaches us about being clean as well, as the act of washing cleanses us bodily and spiritually. This is so much a part of our life in Christ, that Jesus tells Peter, "If I wash thee not, thou hast no part with me" (v. 8b). To reject this would be to reject our union with the Lord. To follow him in washing feet is to accept him, and doing this one humble act will shape us to his soul.

Suffer

We suffer with Christ in righteousness. I already dove into the importance and meaning of suffering in the life of the Christian. I will only briefly point out here that suffering, like other experiences in the life of a Christian, refines us and makes us holy. Scripture teaches we are heirs with Christ *if* we suffer with him. That suffering is a part of sharing in his sonship. It should be expected in the life of the believer.

> But the Lord said unto him, Go thy way: for he is a chosen vessel unto me, to bear my name before the Gentiles, and kings, and the children of Israel:

> For I will shew him how great things *he must suffer for my name's sake*. (Acts 9:15-16)
>
> Only let your conversation be as it becometh the gospel of Christ: that whether I come and see you, or else be absent, I may hear of your affairs, that ye stand fast in one spirit, with one mind striving together for the faith of the gospel;
>
> *And in nothing terrified by your adversaries*: which is to them an evident token of perdition, but to you of salvation, and that of God.
>
> For unto you it is given in the behalf of Christ, not only to believe on him, *but also to suffer for his sake*;
>
> Having the same conflict which ye saw in me, and now hear to be in me. (Phil 1:27-30)

Suffering was given to Apostle Paul as part of his mission after he was converted, and Paul writes to the Thessalonians that their own need to suffer has been "granted" for the sake of Christ. It seems persecution is a gift from the Almighty, one which comes along with following Christ. Here it is clear that suffering is for the sake of Christ. If glorifies his name, and brings His kingdom to be. The brethren need not be afraid of persecution, since it is only a witness that they are in Christ and are saved.

Persevere

We persevere through temptations and sufferings, as Christ persevered, never giving in to temptation, but fulfilling the goal. As Christ followed God's word over falsehood, we also rely on his word against any temptation.

> Then was Jesus led up of the Spirit into the wilderness *to be tempted of the devil.*
>
> And when he had fasted forty days and forty nights, he was afterward an hungred . . .
>
> Then the devil leaveth him, and, behold, angels came and ministered unto him. (Matt 4:1-2,11)
>
> There hath no temptation taken you but such as is common to man: but God is faithful, who will not suffer you to be tempted above that ye are able; but will with the temptation also make a way to escape, that ye may be able to bear it. (1 Cor 10:13)

> These things I have spoken unto you, that in me ye might have peace. In the world ye shall have tribulation: but be of good cheer; I have overcome the world. (John 16:33)
>
> For whatsoever is born of God overcometh the world: and this is the victory that overcometh the world, *even our faith*. (1 John 5:4)
>
> *To him that overcometh* will I grant to sit with me in my throne, even as I also overcame, and am set down with my Father in his throne. (Rev 3:21)

Since we are with Christ as he overcomes sin and death, we are also with him in overcoming temptation. His presence in us allows us to persevere through any suffering and temptation. As we turn to him for aid in overcoming this world, we draw closer to our Lord still. We become stronger in the spirit and defeat the devil with the Lord's strength. No child of God needs to overcome temptation by his own power of will, but does so through the Spirit of God, which will always defeat sin.

Teach

We teach as Christ taught. The three-year ministry and travels of Jesus of Nazareth are characterized by nearly constant teaching. From what we can see, and reasonably imagine, Jesus gave many of the same teachings in different locations. He gave longer forms and shorter forms of the same material. He was always opening his mouth, both in public and in private, to share the truth of God. He did not just teach by example. The Christian, and pastors above all, are charged with preaching God's word.

> And seeing the multitudes, he went up into a mountain: and when he was set, his disciples came unto him:
>
> And he opened his mouth, *and taught them, saying*, (Matt 5:1–2)
>
> What I tell you in darkness, that *speak ye in light*: and what ye hear in the ear, that preach ye upon the housetops. (Matt 10:27)
>
> Go ye therefore, and teach all nations, baptizing them in the name of the Father, and of the Son, and of the Holy Ghost:
>
> *Teaching them to observe all things* whatsoever I have commanded you: (Matt 28:19–20a)
>
> And he commanded us *to preach unto the people*, and to testify that it is he which was ordained of God to be the Judge of quick and dead. (Acts 10:42)

> *Preach the word*; be instant in season, out of season; reprove, rebuke, exhort with all longsuffering and doctrine. (2 Tim 4:2)

The preaching of the gospel, and the explanation of God's word is central to the mission of the church, and united the believer with the character of Christ. No one would believe without first hearing the word (Rom 10:14). Men also need to be instructed in the way of life, given encouragement and correction, and see the Scriptures explained and applied to practical life. The act of teaching, done persistently by the Shepherd, is also the act of the sheep. The elders of the church teach from the authoritative platform of the pulpit, which comes with their position, and the church member, with no ordination, teaches through conversation, and in giving a wise answer to those who come with questions. We are saved by faith, and that faith is explained by words.

Marry

We marry and picture the Lord and his bride through our union. While Jesus led a celibate life, and was not married on this earth, as Lord of all things, He marries with his people the church. Our marriages are a manifestation of this greater union. It is interesting that Jesus' first recorded miracle was at a wedding, in which he made the water into wine. The union of man with woman, like the union of God with his people, is found from start to finish in the Scriptures:

> Therefore shall a man leave his father and his mother, and *shall cleave unto his wife*: and they shall be one flesh. (Gen 2:24)
>
> I will greatly rejoice in the LORD, my soul shall be joyful in my God; for he hath clothed me with the garments of salvation, he hath covered me with the robe of righteousness, *as a bridegroom* decketh himself with ornaments, and *as a bride adorneth* herself with her jewels. (Isa 61:10)
>
> Then shall the kingdom of heaven be likened unto ten virgins, which took their lamps, and went forth *to meet the bridegroom*. (Matt 25:1)
>
> Husbands, love your wives, *even as Christ also loved the church*, and gave himself for it;
>
> That he might sanctify and cleanse it with the washing of water by the word,

> That *he might present it to himself* a glorious church, not having spot, or wrinkle, or any such thing; but that it should be holy and without blemish. (Eph 5:25–27)
>
> And I John saw the holy city, new Jerusalem, coming down from God out of heaven, prepared *as a bride adorned for her husband.* (Rev 21:2)

I would regard marriage as the deepest expression of union with Christ, and perhaps the greatest witness apart from sharing the gospel itself. The ways that marriage sanctifies us are many, including the sacrifice of the husband in providing for his household, and the difficulty and danger inherent in the wife's childbearing. Paul even teaches in 1 Tim 2 that the woman will be "saved in childbearing" (v. 15), if she continues in other virtues. Much like the cross itself, the childbirth in marriage appears almost as a reversal of the curse. It is bringing the woman to salvation. The final union of Christ with his people is nothing less than a great marriage.

Live Modest

We are modest and simple, expressing the humble heart of one saved by grace, and of the Servant of God who knew "no form nor comeliness." He had no beauty that we should desire him (Isa 53:2). Modesty in dress and lifestyle is sacramental, bringing the character of Christ to us, and expressing the humility and modesty of the invisible heart of our being.

> And Jesus said unto him, Foxes have holes, and birds of the air have nests; but the Son of man hath *not where to lay his head.* (Luke 9:58)
>
> *Lay not up for yourselves treasures* upon earth, where moth and rust doth corrupt, and where thieves break through and steal:
>
> But lay up for yourselves treasures in heaven, where neither moth nor rust doth corrupt, and where thieves do not break through nor steal:
>
> *For where your treasure is, there will your heart be also.* (Matt 6:19–21)
>
> Let your conversation be without covetousness; and *be content with such things as ye have*: for he hath said, I will never leave thee, nor forsake thee. (Hebrews 13:5)

> And having food and raiment *let us be therewith content.* (1 Tim 6:8)
>
> In like manner also, that women adorn themselves *in modest apparel*, with shamefacedness and sobriety; not with broided hair, or gold, or pearls, or costly array; But (which becometh women professing godliness) with good works. (1 Tim 2:9–10)
>
> Whose adorning let it not be that outward adorning of plaiting the hair, and of wearing of gold, or of putting on of apparel;
>
> But *let it be the hidden man of the heart*, in that which is not corruptible, even the ornament of a meek and quiet spirit, which is in the sight of God of great price. (1 Pet 3:3–4)

Modesty of heart is reflected in the attitude that we are servants. We are not trying to be someone more important than we are. If our Lord chose to come as the son of a carpenter and born among where animals lay, and if even those who heard of him asked, "Can there any good thing come out of Nazareth?" (John 1:46), we do not need to put on airs if we follow him. We are not looking to be wealthy either, but find fulfillment in heavenly treasures, content to have little. This modesty of heart is reflected by modesty of dress and the appearance of brethren. This is highlighted for women, who are not to find beauty in fancy hairstyle, jewelry, or fine garments. They are simply to have the beauty of the "meek and quiet spirit" (1 Pet 3:4), that of holiness and a quiet heart. Such light and love ought the characterize the Christian woman, not a slavery to fashion and cosmetics. The beauty of the woman pictures the beauty of the church, which is one which comes from the heart and is holy.

Pray

We pray as Christ prayed to the Father, knowing we have one who hears us and intercedes for us. Our life is a life of prayer. Words to our Father are always on our lips. We fast to remember Christ's suffering and to give the right spirit to our prayers, one of lowliness and dependency.

> At that time Jesus answered and said, *I thank thee, O Father*, Lord of heaven and earth, because thou hast hid these things from the wise and prudent, and hast revealed them unto babes. (Matt 11:25)

> And when Jesus had cried with a loud voice, *he said, Father*, into thy hands I commend my spirit: and having said thus, he gave up the ghost. (Luke 23:46)
>
> Then they took away the stone from the place where the dead was laid. And Jesus lifted up his eyes, and said, *Father, I thank thee* that thou hast heard me. (John 11:41)
>
> And Jesus said unto them, Can the children of the bridechamber mourn, as long as the bridegroom is with them? but the days will come, when the bridegroom shall be taken from them, and *then shall they fast*. (Matt 9:15)
>
> Rejoice evermore.
>
> *Pray without ceasing.* (1 Thess 5:16–17)
>
> Is any among you afflicted? *let him pray*. Is any merry? let him sing psalms. (Jas 5:13)

The life of prayer and fasting is in imitation of the source of life, who is Jesus Christ. As Jesus prayed throughout his ministry, it was God in human form calling out to God. Prayer is also a way we draw into the relationship which Jesus gave us—one of sons of God, and one in which we speak to God as our Father. It deepens our love and dependency on God the Father, and teaches humility. Prayer also provides for the needs of many, as our petitions are heard by God. Jesus even promises that which we ask the Father in prayer, the Father will give us (Luke 11:10–13). We can trust in his goodness and fatherly love.

Anoint the Sick

We anoint the sick, and lay on hands, as Christ healed in his ministry, making known his identity, manifesting his power. There is no promise of healing for all men, but God desires to utilize this ritual to draw us close to his Son, and to bless his children.

> And Jesus said unto the centurion, Go thy way; and as thou hast believed, so be it done unto thee. *And his servant was healed* in the selfsame hour. (Matt 8:13)
>
> And Jesus went forth, and saw a great multitude, and was moved with compassion toward them, and *he healed their sick*. (Matt 14:14)
>
> And one of them smote the servant of the high priest, and cut off his right ear.

> And Jesus answered and said, Suffer ye thus far. And *he touched his ear, and healed him.* (Luke 22:50–51)
>
> Is any sick among you? let him call for the elders of the church; and let them pray over him, *anointing him with oil* in the name of the Lord:
>
> And the prayer of faith shall save the sick, and the Lord shall raise him up; and if he have committed sins, they shall be forgiven him. (Jas 5:14–15)

While we do not have the miraculous gift of healing with us today, which we see described in the New Testament, we have the command to anoint the sick, which was done with oil, and came together with prayer, and the spiritual forgiveness of any sins. The New Testament does not give us great detail, but historically the church has seen anointing as both a spiritual and physical healing, with the anointed brother getting better if the prayers are within the Lord's will (1 John 5:14).

Forgive Sinners

As we speak of healing and forgiveness together in this rite, we should remember that the Christian heart to forgive exists also in union with Christ. A Christian's forgiving spirit and active forgiveness flows from the Savior and shares in him with all that he does:

> And when they could not come nigh unto him for the press, they uncovered the roof where he was: and when they had broken it up, they let down the bed wherein the sick of the palsy lay.
>
> When Jesus saw their faith, he said unto the sick of the palsy, *Son, thy sins be forgiven thee.* (Mark 2:4–5)
>
> If we confess our sins, *he is faithful and just to forgive us our sins*, and to cleanse us from all unrighteousness. (1 John 1:9)
>
> And when ye stand praying, *forgive, if ye have ought against any*: that your Father also which is in heaven may forgive you your trespasses.
>
> But if ye do not forgive, neither will your Father which is in heaven forgive your trespasses. (Mark 11:25–26)
>
> And forgive us our debts, as *we forgive our debtors.* (Matt 6:12)

Teaching about forgiveness is abundant in the New Testament. Even in these few passages it is clear that forgiveness is in imitation of Christ, who forgave men their sins during his ministry, and who also forgives us our sins when we come to salvation. He forgives us any time we confess and repent of sin. Learning to forgive others of their wrongs against us conforms us to our Lord to become like him. It also assures that God will forgive our sins in heaven, as if we act together with him in mercy. Just as some of Jesus' physical healings in the Gospels came with forgiving sins, the act of forgiveness, and of being forgiven, heals wounds and spiritual death on the soul. In unique cases today, forgiveness may indeed be linked to healing of physical disease, as a sign of what Christ accomplished.

The forms of unity with Christ I've briefly described here cover Christian teaching broadly, but I don't claim they are comprehensive. They don't say everything that Scripture says. I only want the reader to see a good and detailed picture of the Christian life, and highlight a few points: namely that each element of the holy life is a form of unity with the Son of God, and that they also accomplish good for the soul and for the community. They are not attempts to better ourselves, but are ways of loving God, and walking our steps beside our Lord. They bring us continually to his presence. The outwardly clean life of the believer is fed from the inward source of life, which is the eternal fountain of life, Christ our Lord.

One of the first urges I experienced after first knowing Christ was the hunger to love and serve others. We may come to that desire with our personal calling as well, often finding a unique desire to serve in one way, or in another way. I had to satisfy that hunger. I was given great opportunities very soon, being introduced to a woman who ran an orphanage overseas, and provided regular care, as well as surgeries, for babies who were often disabled. I experienced that the Lord answers our prayer if we come to him asking, and opens doors before us, as if supernaturally. This is just as the Bible teaches. The Lord had given me what I desired. I was able to work for this woman for several years, helping in infant care for part of it. I also worked online for several years to arrange for volunteers from overseas to come over, as well as for doctors to come on medical missions. It was, in the way that the new heart experiences, excitement and wonder for me. You see and experience God's hand working in the world, but you get to be a part of it. I can remember being at the home of one of the ladies who worked there, and seeing one of the infants who was soon to be adopted. She lay there with a wreath around her head. This was, in my new mind, a fulfillment of God's promise, who makes us kings who humble ourselves and come to him. He takes the meek, and lifts them up. He makes the blind see. This child, being unfortunate, would receive more rewards than most who started out with much more than she did. The truths of Scripture opened up, to reveal they are more than words. God's power is alive on this earth.

As a new believer after several years, I felt a calling to work in the pro-life ministry. I was appalled at the evil of abortion, and by its callous normalcy in society. I was inspired by those who fought against it, and could daydream of being on the streets in protest. Once I was back in my own country, I worked in pro-life witness for about seven years. It is grievous to be anywhere near the places where they kill babies in the womb. Much of the work there ranges between prayer, informing people of what is going on, and seeking to turn women away from the doors and save their babies. I've worked side by side with men and women who have been in that ministry for decades, and know it very well. They are dedicated, and willing to work continually, even though they see only occasional success. Even in the time I spent there, which was much more limited, I have seen women or couples decide to save their child. I have seen men and women responsive to the message we were preaching, and willing to hear it. Once a woman drove slowly past the street we were witnessing on. Then she lowered her window and reached into her bag. I wondered for a moment if she would pull out a weapon, as we receive regular insults, and are hated by much of the community. She pulled out a set of pictures and lifted them up to me. One was a photo of her child. "Some of you guys were out there one day when I was going to go get an abortion," she said. "I heard what you had to say and I decided to keep my child. Thank you for doing what you do." Then she drove off.

Like anywhere else in the world, I found that being in front of an abortion mill (we call them mills where the world calls them clinics) was a good place to share the gospel. Along with pro-life material, I would hand out gospel tracts. I would give short messages of the gospel, calling men to repent of sin, and believe in Jesus. Occasionally I was able to interact with passers by who asked me questions about the gospel. I always explained in simple terms, quoted a few passages I had memorized, and asked them if they would go home and read the Gospels. The abortion mill is further a place to prick the conscience. Preaching reminds men of their sin, and what better place to see sin, and recognize our culpability, than a place where children are murdered shamelessly every day. While some pro-life protesters avoid such talk, I remind people going into the building or walking by, that murder is evil, and against the law of a holy God. Men need to see the blackness of their sin, to repent and know the light of God.

That light Yahweh on the soul also urges the new believer to point others to Jesus. I was doing this, with plenty of flaws, from very soon after I believed. I am not naturally an outward person, and I don't say much. It causes me anxiety. However, when the opportunity arises, I do have much to say, and I could go on about the Bible, and Jesus, and answer objections at length. Some of the first people whom I told about Jesus were old friends, who of course objected, and wanted to argue against the faith. Others were family and acquaintances, and of course the long line of people waiting to argue about Christianity on the internet. The love of God acts on the soul to tell the good news to others, but it also acts on the soul in shaping us. As we study Scripture, teach and defend it, we become more wound up with God. We think less of our sins, and desire them less. I found before long it was much harder to sin when I was wrapped up in telling people about this wondrous life-saving discovery I had made, or when I was praying for them. When I was researching answers, either to their fair questions or hard-hearted objections, I became further changed. The life I had known went further into the past with each step I made in Christ.

THE GOODNESS OF THE LAW

In the Way of Jesus

God's way of life for us, in the walk that we have in Christ, is a part of the healing we speak of from pain, and from evil. It is healing to the soul of the believer, and healing to the world. The way of life which is a pleasing aroma to Yahweh, which fills him with satisfaction, is also goodness to us—relief, protection, aid, and the creation of life. To walk in the Spirit, in opposition to the flesh, overcomes death just as our faith overcomes it: "For if ye live after the flesh, ye shall die: but if ye through the Spirit do mortify the deeds of the body, ye shall live" (Rom 8:13). The newborn soul has all that he needs in life, not necessarily to meet physical desires, but to serve God in the kingdom, of which I will say much later. He has the way that leads to what the spiritual man desires, which is peace, love, joy, and the brotherhood of mankind.

The Christian lives with hope, and will not despair, for he knows that his Savior died for him, he loves him with divine love, and will be with him through any misfortune and death. This simple knowledge, along with the right way of life given by Yahweh, brings an end to much of the inner torment man knows in the flesh. It wipes out nearly any despair that leads to deep depression; to outbursts of anger; and to insecure, ego-building behavior. It provides a firm foundation for the mind, and is so fulfilling of the human soul, that sincere faith and life in Christ, by itself, would put nearly all psychiatrists out of business. They would shut their offices overnight. Sure, there would still be cause to study and deal with severe chemical imbalances, and brain damage, but in most ordinary cases, peace of mind would flow from the Spirit of God, and not from mental health professionals, and often ineffective medication. Most mentally ill people in fact have a spiritual problem, one which has morphed into mental, and even physical problems. That's why it is absurd to pay an advanced-degreed professional just to acquire contentment. Faith and love of God bring mental wholeness for those who truly believe, and live continually in their faith.

The Christian life is simple, humble, modest. It does not reflect the materialist mindset that wants high accomplishment, and all the worldly treasures and toys. It does not seek after a great level of security in life. The Christian is permitted to acquire wealth, which he can use to provide for the needs of his family, of ministry, and of the poor, but he does not seek after great gain. In contrast, he knows to be content with what he has, even if what he has is very little. The Lord may lift up some people to have businesses which are highly successful, and those men may be useful to the kingdom through their wealth, but this is not the norm. The norm is to accept what we have, and is not to be wealthy. The corruption that money brings, to everything from business, to churches, to governments, is explicitly detailed in the New Testament. It is very easy to turn from making decisions based on serving Christ to ones of personal power and wealth when large sums of money are involved. The mentality of the Christian is in using his life and resources for the kingdom of God, and not for himself. He does not need to meet societal expectations of what he ought to own, or how well he ought to live. He's not in a status competition. If anything, the Christian is in a competition of who can be the lowliest, and meekest, not the most wealthy and influential. This simple life breeds peace, a reliance on God, and a connection to other men and to the community.

In a similar manner, the Christian soul is not an image of fashion or sensuality. Rather, the Christian image reflects the Christian heart, being humble, modest, and plain. The Spirit of God teaches the practice of modesty specifically when addressing the lifestyle of women, but as a principle it applies in some ways to both men and women. We are not trying to decorate ourselves or look flashy. We are not concerned with what is popular, or will draw attention to ourselves. The beauty of the woman, and in a general sense of the bride of Christ, is in her gentle, meek, and humble heart. That modesty in the woman reflects her submission to her husband, and to leaders in the church. In the broader sense, it reflects the church's submission to Christ, as she follows him and gives up her puffed-up sense of self to become lowly, and obedient to God. This is reflected in a practical sense in dressing plainly, without ornamentation, sensuality, or showing much of the flesh. In the past ordinary modesty was not always strikingly different from the world of unbelievers, because at various times in history, unbelievers have had a sense of modesty, and at least avoided overtly sexual appearance. Today, the appearance of the Christian will be strikingly different from most of western culture, since that culture has become overtly lewd and vulgar in as many ways as it can find. The Christian's appearance, like his spirit, and together with his spirit, will create a sense of peace and goodness. It will show through its humility the goodness of the Savior. For to any soul who is open by the grace of God to Christ, even that appearance of the Christian will bring satisfaction and longing for the goodness which it reflects. It is a picture of Christ by itself.

The Christian is not an angry man. True, he may have legitimate anger based on love, against the evil in the world, but he has no anger against wrongs done to him, or because he needs to feel bigger than he is. He trusts God to take care of any wrongs done, and correct the evildoer if he will not listen to reason. If a man harms him, he still has all that he needs, both in the salvation he has been given, and in the fellowship of the church. There is no real loss. The only reason to be truly angry with someone would be due to the weight of ego and pride, and the Christian is losing these things by the Spirit of God. A wrong does not bring him low because he is not puffed up in the first place. He prays for the one who wrongs him. He is taught to love those even who persecute him.

On the most obvious practical level, this prevents ongoing inner turmoil due to anger and hatred, and prevents countless acts of violence or crime due to people who enact vengeance, almost as a duty. The one bomb that was set off by a wrongdoing isn't turned into a million bombs by a war. The Christian allows harm to come to him, and continues with grace and peace in his life. The more difficult and transformative teaching is to love your enemies. It is perhaps the hardest teaching in the New Testament, and something that no one accomplishes with perfection in this life. If sin and corruption was the master of the old human heart, love is the master of the heart in Christ. Learning to love men who have done you evil changes the heart. It can feel painful. The mind wants to reject it immediately. Yet it is the treatment which heals the cancer, and which moves the broken bone back into place. It shapes the soul to conformity with Christ, more than anything else. We must make it past the first brief sting of pain to be healed. If we are ever truly to love, we must love our enemies.

This lack of vengeance is repeatedly seen in other teachings. The Christian is not to sue other Christians, but to solve the problem through Christian intervention and discussion. If that fails, you allow yourself to be cheated (1 Cor 6:5–7). There is much more harm to be done by brothers fighting brothers in the legal system than by allowing a harm to come to yourself. It is out of step with the teaching not to seek vengeance, and with the fact we have all that we need in Christ. It would furthermore destroy the unity we ought to be showing the world as the people of God to turn on one another over a sum of money.

The Christian is taught a life of peace in which he turns the other cheek to those who wrong him, and does not answer an evil with an evil. He is not looking to return violence with violence, or make himself feel better by enacting vengeance. In a world in which entire societies have found vengeance acceptable, and at times mandatory, the spirit of the Christian defuses those situations, and disarms corrupt human nature. Among honor societies today, such as Yemen[1] and Albania,[2] taking vengeance can seem the only way to restore one's honor, and at times this includes bloodshed. Such practices were present at least in ancient Israel, as we see the Torah actively protects people who have accidentally killed someone, treating it as assumed that family members would seek revenge (Num 35:11–12). However, such vendettas, feuds, and simple revenge will not come about because the Christian is willing to accept

---

1. Al-Zaidi, "Revenge in Yemen."
2. Balkanista, "Blood feuds and honour."

some wrong, forgive it, and let the law handle any serious crime. This is at the center of the law of Christ.

When facing such broad teachings against violence, it is necessary to ask if there are times where it is morally mandated to fight against evil, due to the great harm it causes, especially when it causes death to men. There are some who follow an absolute understanding of the instructions not to resist evil, and would say you can never resist, even when human life is at stake. This is the Anabaptist view, and finds roots in several early church leaders who taught against any physical self-defense, and against serving in the armed forces.[3] This view rests largely on Jesus' teaching to turn the other cheek (Matt 5:38–39), and not return evil for evil, a teaching repeated in Paul's writing (Rom 12:17–19). However, there was no consensus in the early church on either serving in the military or self-defense. The other view is that there are moral mandates in the Bible to defend the afflicted, and to help the oppressed (Ps 82:3, Prov 24:11), and these moral mandates do allow self-defense, limiting the peaceful life of the Christian to nearly all ordinary circumstances. The New Testament also affirms the government's right to use violence (Rom 13:4). Exodus 22 allows citizens to use violence in protecting the home (v. 2–3). That means, for the sake of protecting human life, the Christian can resist, and even fight. This is not out of anger or vengeance, but out of the need to do good, if the circumstances truly demand it.

Christians over time understood that there were circumstances in which war could be justified, despite the mass killing involved. Certain conditions needed to be met, such as the need to protect life and a reasonable possibility of victory. In other instances, the war was not justified, and the Christian should reject fighting in it. While the complexity of the theory does not need to be discussed here, I will just provide this summary of it by Augustine of Hippo:

> "What is the evil in war? Is it the death of some who will soon die in any case, that others may live in peaceful subjection? This is mere cowardly dislike, not any religious feeling. The real evils in war are love of violence, revengeful cruelty, fierce and implacable enmity, wild resistance, and the lust of power, and such like; and it is generally to punish these things, when force is required to inflict the punishment, that, in obedience to God

---

3. Martin, "Early Church Fathers"; Morey, "The Early Church." The first source is an Anabaptist explanation of non-resistance using early church teachings, the second is a criticism of that view.

or some lawful authority, good men undertake wars, when they find themselves in such a position as regards the conduct of human affairs, that right conduct requires them to act, or to make others act in this way."[4]

One of the greatest ways in which the path of Christ leads to peace and healing is through marriage. The marriage of the Christian reflects the union of Christ and his bride, and is the most common visible witness the Christian can give the world of Christ's goodness and salvation. The lifelong nature of marriage, and the monogamous nature of marriage, contrast it with what God permitted previously, even of his people Israel. In the revealing of Jesus Christ to the world, the order of marriage was reestablished on God's will from the start of creation (Mark 10:5–9), with its lifelong nature reflecting the ongoing covenant between Jesus and the church, and the headship of the man reflecting the headship of Christ, who leads his people in all things. Marriage in Christ is what God has always intended.

Marriage itself is healing, not only to the people involved—man, wife, and children—but to all of society. It provides mental stability, virtue, and faith to each ongoing generation. It takes care of new souls, provides food and shelter for them, and puts guardrails on their lives so they are not doing evil. It trains them for a life of service and of doing good in the world. The closeness of the man and wife brings the other strength, joy, and peace. The man is able to grow fully in his role of ethical leader and spiritual priest. The woman is fulfilled in her role of becoming gentle and submissive to her husband, raising her children, and making the home a beautiful place to live. The simple fact that marriage takes our concerns off of our own desires and fulfillment, and onto that of other people, is healing to the soul. It is the most common and effective ministry that exists, channeling self-fulfillment into sacrifice for others, shaping us into the shape of Christ.

It is not hard to see what occurs when Yahweh's will for marriage is ignored. The results of broken homes, of fatherless boys, and of single-parent homes have been well documented for years, although anyone who respects the obvious truth and the teaching of the Bible does not need careful documentation to know that disaster results when you tear apart God's order. Yahweh calls tearing apart a marriage an act of violence, and commands men not to do it (Mal 2:16, Mark 10:9, 1 Cor

---

4. Augustine of Hippo, *Reply to Faustus the Manichaean* XXII, 74, 515.

7:10–11). The results of broken families, and of fornication, are a dirty bomb on all of human society. They include mental illness and physical harm to both man and woman. They include a greater likelihood of physical harm to the children, of crime by the children, of suicide of children, and a pattern of failed or nonexistent marriages of the children.[5] People who are unmarried are much more likely to kill their child in the womb than those who are married. Relationships outside marriage, such as same-sex relationships, which are essentially perverse, also come with documented harm.[6] The most obvious historically has been the overwhelming tide of disease and death which come from this unnatural practice, but there is ongoing harm done to human relationships which flows from the mindset that any two people can hook up, and that any relationship is valid. It makes the human mind believe its life is based on self-fulfillment and desire, rooting him again in the corrupt and unsatisfying mind of the flesh.

The Bible ensures the lifelong and monogamous nature of marriage in the New Covenant. This is a blessing of stability to all humanity. Despite a great deal of accommodation to divorce as well as polygamy in previous eras, Christ restored us to God's will and natural plan in creation, a plan that suits our inner being and our society—that is the exclusive and unbreakable nature of the marriage bond. The married cannot switch marriage partners through divorce, and if they do, they are practicing adultery, and must end it. Mankind can no longer seek to solve his problems, or find ego reward, by taking multiple spouses. Either one (divorce or polygamy) can be tempting, convenient, or be the pipe-dream of the selfish, but these alternatives to real marriage are half-baked and are not ultimately rewarding to humanity. Marriage is one man and one woman for life. It only ends when husband or wife dies (Rom 7:2–3, 1 Cor 7:39). The stability and peace brought by its unbreakable nature provide a visible picture of Christ saving his people, whom he has promised never to abandon, and provide blessing to husband wife and children.

Psalm 16 ends with the words:

---

5. Wilcox, *Why Marriage Matters*. This is a short book, and it is easy to find summaries and various portions of it online.

6. Collingwood, "Higher Risk"; Everett, "Sexual Orientation Disparities." These are both secular sources which show approval of same-sex behavior, but they still document the serious risk involved. If it is the responsibility of doctors to help the patient, they would warn against this behavior, and never think to approve it. There are Christian sources which are even more thorough in documenting the destructive results of immorality.

> Thou wilt shew me the path of life: in thy presence is fulness of joy; at thy right hand there are pleasures for evermore. (v. 11)

The path of life is fulfilled for the Christian because his Master is life, and lived the perfect life, pleasing to Yahweh. This psalm, which also prophesies of Jesus' resurrection (Acts 2:25-28), reminds us of the accomplishments of his resurrection, which are life and joy for eternity. If we join with Christ, whom death could not hold and who passed through Sheol and lived, we join with his righteousness, and we will see life and peace in the community of the saints. He is the path to life.

In the Commandments

The wonderful Christian song "The Love of God" extolls the greatness and depth of God's love on us. It is compared to the ocean, or the sky, and is greater than each. His mercy upon us saves us, despite our wicked deeds, and the punishment we deserve. Yet the love of God cannot be extolled without recognizing how Yahweh often applies that love to our life—that is through the law of God. Christians often treat God's law as the red-headed step child of the divine order, but the law is good, and the New Testament, despite removing the penalty of our sin, affirms it is good. God's law blesses us in countless ways. It provides order to society, and regulation that serves us. It encourages the good and punishes evil. God's law teaches principles of justice, care for the poor, care for family, honesty in business, and other forms of order given to all society. It is not always easy knowing precisely how much is a matter of the personal life, the church life, or the state, or which matters are serious enough to mandate or punish, but according to God's only divine perfect revelation of himself, the law of God is good. We should treasure and cherish it:

> I thought on my ways, and turned my feet unto thy testimonies.
>
> I made haste, and delayed not to keep thy commandments.
>
> The bands of the wicked have robbed me: but I have not forgotten thy law.
>
> At midnight I will rise to give thanks unto thee because of thy righteous judgments.
>
> I am a companion of all them that fear thee, and of them that keep thy precepts.

> The earth, O LORD, is full of thy mercy: teach me thy statutes. (Ps 119:59–64)
>
> The fear of the LORD is the beginning of wisdom: a good understanding have all they that do his commandments: his praise endureth for ever. (Ps 111:10)
>
> Praise ye the LORD. Blessed is the man that feareth the LORD, that delighteth greatly in his commandments.
>
> His seed shall be mighty upon earth: the generation of the upright shall be blessed.
>
> Wealth and riches shall be in his house: and his righteousness endureth for ever. (Ps 112:1–3)

It is common for unbelievers today to say the Christian God is horribly cruel, while in contrast they know the correct way to behave without the help of holy books. They are the ones to tell you what is right and wrong, not Yahweh. They believe, without Yahweh, that we ought to be fair, loving, help the poor, protect the innocent, help the oppressed, punish evildoers, but in doing so, all they say is that God's law, the same God they are denying, is a very good law. They want to call the child rapist evil. They want to condemn the mass murderer. They want God's law to rule over the earth, even if their understanding of it isn't perfect. They desire righteousness to abound forever. They want justice to be lifted up. They want the goodness of God's law, but without having to worship and obey God themselves. Perhaps more precisely, they want to pick and choose what they obey, which naturally precludes honoring God in any real and wholesome way. So they live in contradiction, claiming the God of the Bible is not true, but then demanding Yahweh's law reign over all. At least the parts they like.

These unbelievers ought to know at least that they are on the right track with wanting love and justice on the earth, but that if they truly want God's law, then they also need to want all of it, and to honor Yahweh who gave it to us in the first place. Anyone who is offended when a bystander is run over by an out-of-control vehicle desires God's law. Anyone who is appalled by robbery, crime, or corrupt politicians, desires God's law. If you're upset by a dishonest witness on the witness stand; a single mother who neglects her children and takes drugs, but will collect money every month; a building that collapses due to skimping on materials; people who become debt slaves for most of their lives, possibly facing prison for their debt; the incredible bodily harm, family harm, and crime that come from drugs; if you're upset by any of these things you long for God's law. However, to be consistent and reasonably you have to accept the whole package—that is Yahweh's authority over our lives, and our loving obedience to him.

The Torah is a word I will use to speak of the commandments in Scripture, even though it has a wider meaning much of the time. God's Torah, or his commandments and other related regulations, are spoken of as *a treasure* (Ps 19:10). They are called *a source of life* (Deut 8:1). They are *the way of life* (Prov 6:23). Some commandments even promise *a long life* (Deut 5:16). While the Torah certainly expresses something of God's character and will for us, these commandments are also given to us to provide a good path for humanity, and to protect and preserve life into the future. They are not mere entertainment for God. The Christian, in being washed clean and in walking in holiness, should learn them, understand their purpose, and apply them to life's walk, including larger-scale endeavors such as business, and the governing of society. They are good for the macro and micro scale of human society.

God's law both reveals his character, and it protects human life. In the context of salvation, it reveals our sinfulness, and fills us with the knowledge that we need God's mercy. In this section I speak primarily of just one purpose—caring for human life. The regulations of the Torah do just that, as do Jesus' higher ethical teachings, and teachings for the church. It is stereotypical of liberal Christians, and secularists, to portray God's commandments as mere rules, and overly restraining, but this is obviously false. God's law is the outworking of love, the outworking of love for God and love for mankind. They are love in action. In fact, you will find the same people who complain they shouldn't have to follow a bunch of stinking rules, believe that *you* have to follow their stinking rules, and they fully endorse many of the tens of thousands of rules society pushes upon its citizenry. Remember, many of the same people who complain a Christian is repressed to live in holiness and purity wanted everyone to wear a face mask during the COVID pandemic, stand about six feet apart from people, and even get forced to inject chemicals into their bodies. Those were their rules of purity they tried to force on an entire population. It was their holiness code. Moreover, they will try to conform your speech to their rules, demanding you use language that does not offend their special group, be it their favored race, homosexuals, or men pretending they are women. If you don't follow their prudish language rules, they will get very nasty, and even endorse that you lose your job or are punished. They will refuse to be your friend, and smear your name. You have broken their treasured commandments. Therefore, don't believe anyone who claims you shouldn't have to follow God's law, because those are the same people about to forcefully place their own law upon you.

While I don't have time in this book to cover all the laws in God's Torah, or explain their goodness, I want to cover many of them to show you how they order our lives in a good way. One of the first and most basic things that comes to mind is the commandment that *leaders must be righteous*, and honor God (Deut 17:19–20). In fact, the kings of Israel were required to write down all of God's law, which would have been a time-consuming task for them (v. 18). Nor were they allowed to live in decadence and pursue great wealth (vv. 15–17). The righteousness of the leader then, presumably would affect the righteousness of all society. Many kings of Israel practiced evil and idolatry, but they had to stray off of God's path to do that, and often the nation was punished as a result. In God's will, the leader is an example of righteousness and lives in righteousness. He should know God's law thoroughly and be obedient.

Justice should be fair, and we should be fair. Several commandments ensure this. For one, the multiple prohibitions on taking a bribe are there to ensure an objective judiciary (Exod 23:8, Deut 16:19). The law also prohibits discriminating in favor of either the rich or the poor (Exod 23:3, Deut 1:17), and there are always those judges, and in today's world those jurors, who would indeed discriminate in favor of either one. Dangerous murderers have been released because judges or jurors felt favoritism. This applies in today's world as well, to prevent us from discriminating in trials in favor of a certain race, either our own, or a race we believe just deserves a favor. We may not discriminate either way. The law prohibits giving false testimony, which includes not only ordinary lying, but more specifically false witness in a trial (Exod 20:16). Bearing false witness is spoken against multiple times, clearly and strongly in Scripture. In fact, in order to ensure a more accurate trial, there always needed to be more than one witness (Deut 19:15), and according to Jewish tradition the character of witnesses needed to be good.[7] A witness who was considered untrustworthy would not have been included in a trial. False witnesses could face being punished with the same punishment the accused would have faced (Deut 19:16–19). There must be no lies at a trial.

---

7. Jewish Virtual Library, "Witness."

The Torah *respects property*. This is clear in that it criminalizes robbery of all forms, as it does cheating and fraud (Exod 20:15, Lev 19:11). No one has a right to come and take what is yours, whether by stealth or by force. There are real distinctions between us as individuals, including our body, our personality, and our possessions. God's law respects this, as it respects the social order Yahweh has put in place. For a man to come and take what is ours is to violate that distinction between us, in a sense viewing the victim as nothing. Just like violence breaks down the barrier of the body, robbery breaks down the barrier of our home and possessions. It also causes practical harm, because what the criminal has stolen was meant to bring good; to the victim, his family, and society. Many people imagine robbery to be nonviolent, and sometimes it is, but just try and stop a robber from robbing what he is robbing and see how long it stays nonviolent. Robberies escalate to violence and murder all the time. Robbery is further typically motivated by greed or selfishness, and reflects a sinful materialism. In today's world the addict robs out of his bondage to drugs, and to feed his demonic addiction. It is rooted in the worst of spirits. A society which respects human beings also respects that what is mine is mine, and what is yours is yours, and if not, human dignity is attacked. To respect a man's property is a way to respect his person.

An interesting commandment regarding honesty, and fairness, is the commandment not to move *a boundary stone* (Deut 19:14). In its simple form, it prevents one neighbor or property owner from cheating another. The boundary stone, being for many the only immediate way we know where our property ends and another begins, could easily fool someone if it were moved slightly. Many would not notice unless a careful survey was done. Cheating is a form of robbery, and countless fights have resulted from disputes over a small slice of land. This law not only prevents cheating in land, but also applies to the boundaries we use in our thought and understanding. As we weight a concern and seek to find the truth of a matter, we cannot change our standards or our categories just to try and be right. That would be cheating and deceptive. We have to let the boundaries of our thought remain the same, so we can evaluate the world fairly. To change them in the midst of an evaluation would in essence be cheating. You will find in looking at men who try to change God's standards and avoid the teachings of the Christian faith, they slightly alter the language, alter the concepts, and once this is done, use the new language to permit what is wicked. An attack on clear language is nearly always necessary to pervert God's word. Respecting the boundaries helps us consistently draw truth from it, which is truth by which we live.

A similar commandment, which also applies to our mind, is the commandment to have *fair weights and measures* (Lev 19:36). It is not an uncommon practice for sales people who use weights to cheat customers by adding a little extra weight to the product to sell it at a higher price, or to use false weights. This still happens in some parts of the world today, where ordinary weights are used by the seller, and there is no advertised price. It's easy to do. This form of cheating is a kind of robbery, and is prohibited by the God of righteousness. The next time someone complains that the Torah is antiquated, let him see how he feels when he's ripped off by a seller. He will be suddenly proclaiming the law of God must apply. He does not wish to be cheated. As it applies to human understanding, this law similarly demands we use a consistent bar to find truth, or to discern value. We cannot change our standards to suit the occasion, in order to get what we want, or be right. We must weigh all things by the same honest set of weights. One of the clearest change of measures I have seen is with the standards humanists use to weigh the Bible. They will apply standards to Scripture that allow any doubt that comes in the deny the credibility of the Scriptures. However, in weighing their own authorities, they trust in the men they turn to for truth despite countless reasons for doubt, and even documented evidence that they have been wrong many times. They will trust an obviously fallible doctor with their life, an obviously fallible medical system which has killed many people, an obviously fallible media with its well-known lies. Yet they will not trust the Bible, because of an alleged flaw. Once you use consistent standards, it is easy to see that if human philosophies and men of learning deserve trust, then so does the Bible, if not more so.

Similarly, we do our best to use consistent methods to see truth when we read the word of God. The Scriptures are long, complex, and written in multiple forms. They speak on many subjects, and often provide truth that appears to point in two different directions. If we want to know and to teach doctrine, we should be interpreting Scripture according to the same rules throughout. We can't change our rules because we personally like one doctrine better. We use fair weights and measures. For example, if we accept through historical narrative that a man named Hezekiah built a tunnel, we also accept through historical narrative that a man named Solomon built a temple, and a man named Noah built an ark. Likewise, if we accept the moral commandment that you shall not murder, and that you must give to one in need, we similarly respect the moral commandment that a man may not lie with another man, and that what God has joined together in marriage, man may not sperate. We ought to be consistent with our understanding of words as well, and accept their normal definition, unless there is another definition within its range of meaning, which is truly demanded by context. There are indeed unique cases in seeking truth when special rules apply, but there's got to be a convincing argument for applying special rules, otherwise it's an obvious ruse to ignore what we don't like. That violates the divine order and hides the life-giving truth.

These laws of God help conform us to Yahweh's mind and will, for Yahweh is a God of truth. God is the same in his mind as in his actions. Yahweh doesn't have a false exterior. Yahweh is truth and all he speaks is truth. Since we are his creation and his children, we need to walk as closely to this as man can. We reflect God's image. That means our life and our walk must be rooted in truth and express inner truth. It should not waver, or be insincere. It does not lie. If we are holding onto falsehood, we must abandon it as being apart from God's kingdom. We know it, understand it, live it, walk it. The truth is a way we become one with Yahweh.

God's law mandates *caring for the poor* (Deut 15:11). It provides the poor with food, home, and clothing. Refusing to care for the poor is among the most condemned acts in the Bible, alongside idolatry. To give is a blessing and we should be thankful for the opportunity. A society working rightly should not have a single person who is without these basic needs. If it does, something is wrong. We do not give to receive something, or to make a name for ourselves, but only as a duty and an act of love. We should be grateful for the chance.

However, the Bible also commands that man work. It doesn't say work five days then relax all weekend, but work six days of labor (Deut 5:13). The New Testament clearly prohibits the church from feeding those who refuse to work (2 Thess 3:10), and also refuses church funds to people who are immoral, or who already have family to care for them (1 Tim 5:3–6). This ensures that there are consequences for being lazy or immoral. It also ensures that valuable resources are not wasted on people who do not truly need them. Such a teaching sounds harsh to some ears, but remember, we all practice a similar principle, for example, when we refuse a person funds because of fraud or fake injury. We can see there are people we should not be giving to. God's family is often portrayed as a hand reaching out to feed the hungry, with a plate of food. This is a fair picture. However, God's family can also be portrayed as a hand making the stop sign, and refusing those who wish to take advantage of others, and who cheat. God's people are fair to put up barriers against cheats, and to allow the lazy and immoral to suffer the consequences of their own actions. That kind of refusal helps steer people to realize they are responsible and cannot merely demand others give to them. It is the lazy man who demands free stuff who is being materialistic, not the one who rightly refuses him. In fact, if he were working instead, he'd be able to give to the poor himself, and be a blessing in that way. This would then free up many funds to help those who are truly in need. Nothing in Scripture demands endless indiscriminate giving. At times it commands the opposite.

The law of God includes other methods of protecting the poor apart from giving. The *prohibition of usury* is at least in large part aimed at protecting the poor, as several of the passages barring usury mention it is for their sake. The Hebrew was clearly barred from charging interest to a fellow Israelite, or to the poor (Exod 22:25, Lev 25:36). In one passage on usury, it is flat out prohibited towards a brother without mention of the poor (Deut 23:19). Christians in the West for many centuries barred all usury, based on these scriptures as well as natural law reasoning. The Catholic Church in the West upheld this prohibition, until they finally stopped enforcing it, without ever officially changing their doctrine.[8] If we respect at the minimum the clearest passages of the Bible, there would be large groups of people we would never charge interest to, including our brethren, and the poor. People would build homes and start businesses without the risk of losing it all and going broke due to interest in the future. They would not fear being put in debtor's prison. People would go to school without becoming debt slaves for decades, perhaps even paying off money until they were elderly.

The Torah further includes a *cancellation of debt* on the seventh year, which is the Sabbatical year of rest (Deut 15:1–2), being specifically for one's Hebrew brother, a practice which prevents ongoing debt among Israelites. One further protection, though not specifically to eradicate poverty, is that the law of God ensures that much of society would always have a home or property in their family. Outside of a walled city, you could not sell your home and property, but only could lease it, and it

---

8. Visser, "A Short Review," 175–189. This article covers usury in the teachings of various religions, but its three paragraphs on usury restrictions in Christendom provide an excellent overview.

would be returned to you on the Jubilee year, which was every fiftieth year (Lev 25:31). While this is in large part to keep properties in the right tribal territories, it also ensures homes for an enormous bulk of society, and frequently property on which productive work is done.

The Torah provided for Israel multiple *safety regulations*. Even though our technology has changed since then, the principles behind them are valid, and their purpose in protecting human life remains. The Torah demands that gates be built around the rooftop of a house, to ensure no one falls off (Deut 22:8). These would have been flat roofs, ones that people spent some time on, making this law a bit like having a gate on our balconies too. Pointy rooves need not apply. The Torah protects society from dangerous animals. A goring bull would be put to death if it killed a man (Exod 21:28). If the owner knew that the bull gored, and did not restrain it, the owner too could be put to death (v. 29). Filth had to be taken outside the camp and buried (Deut 23:12–13), and people who had leprosy were kept apart from the group (Lev 13:21). We may live in an overly regulated society today, with countless rules, and attempts to sanitize society to as high degree as possible, but at the minimum the basics of that system rest on the law of God. That law seeks to prevent accidents and protect from illness. Mankind is required to pass laws that protect human life in a similar fashion, and lessen at least the more serious risks. The trucker who must tightly chain his machine to his bed, and the builder who must build on stable ground, each follow the law of God.

The Torah regulates *gender distinction*. That is a concept that western society, long before the dawn of sanctioned sex changes, had been growing to ignore. The secular world despises sex differences and sex roles, but Yahweh loves them and gave them to us. This distinction is also revealed in nature, as we can see in the fact that, until a very modern era, nearly all cultures, nationalities, and religions in history respected that the sexes are different, and respected male headship. Yahweh created us male and female, and he gives us ways to keep the two sexes distinct, beyond the different bodily designs and mental makeup we already have. According to God's word, men must not wear the apparel of a woman, nor women wear the apparel of a man (Deut 22:5). They should be clearly distinct and not easily confused. In terms of roles in society, only men functioned as priests in the temple, and that was by the law of God (Exod 28:1–3). Nearly all civil leaders were men as well, although the Torah does not specifically prohibit women from holding that role. The New Testament not only reaffirms gender distinctions, but if anything makes them clearer. It is shameful for a man to have long hair like a woman, but if a woman has long hair, it is her glory (1 Cor 11:14–15). Women are to cover their head in worship to represent man's headship over them (vv. 3–7). Whenever modesty is specifically emphasized and taught, it is regarding women, and reflects their modest heart and their submission (1 Tim 2:9–12, 1 Pet 3:1–4). The woman's gentleness and meekness are emphasized in the New Testament. Man is taught to be leader and teacher in the church (1 Cor 11:3, 1 Tim 3:1–13). Man is also taught to be leader of the home, picturing Christ, and woman is his submissive helper, picturing the church (Eph 5:22–33). The differences in our body and souls are reflected in these instructions for us, which take advantage of how we are designed. God's law uses the man's strength by giving him the headship. It uses the woman's softness by placing her under his protection, and in the home. She is to be pure, and to bear and nurture children. Man and woman are two unique people each with a specific role, and with distinctions that aid in that role. There is harmony and fruitfulness when they each do their jobs.

The law of God *respects human life* and our bodies. It shows the highest respect for life by prohibiting murder and violence of all kinds (Exod 20:13, Lev 24:19–20). The prophets preach hard against violence, and condemn it many times over (Ps 7:14–16, Jer 22:17). A society ordered by God protects mankind against these evils, and punishes them when they do come about. Murder is punished by execution, which shows the highest respect for human life, both by giving the ultimate penalty, and by protecting the community from the killer. An attack on human life is an attack on the image of God (Gen 9:6). Many people view human violence, like other sins, as nearly inevitable, but if we are conformed to the Almighty this is not the case. People can live peacefully for ages with no violence. There are countless virtuous families, for example, who need not worry about a brawl breaking out, much less murder, when they spend time together. Entire communities can live in peace nearly endlessly. No written law would even be needed to prohibit murder because the heart of the people would be so far from it. This is the plan Yahweh has for mankind, as he makes us one in his Son.

We *worship only one God*, who is our rightful authority (Exod 20:2–3). We must not practice religious treason and worship other gods. Idolatry is forbidden (vv. 4–5). The first commandment—that Yahweh is God and we may not have any other gods before him—is more central than any other given at Sinai. There's a reason it comes first. It teaches that

Yahweh, being the Creator of all things, receives our singular allegiance. No other god does. Could there be any further commandments without this foundational one? The fact that there is one God, and no other true God besides him, is found throughout all Scripture (Isa 43:10, 45:21, 46:9). The gods of the nations are themselves called demons, even if the term god is casually used for them (Deut 32:17, 1 Cor 10:20). Somehow we recognize the importance of allegiance in the human heart, as we can recognize the great seriousness of treason to a nation, and we punish treason very severely. If we have one true authority, it is not a mere regulation being broken to follow after another authority, but the very nature of the relationship is being attacked. It is being struck at in the foundation. Threat by outside forces is opened up. Since Yahweh is the source of all life, goodness, and truth, it sends mankind into utter destruction to break that bond, and sends him off to be led by lies and evil instead.

Similar to the prohibition on worshipping false gods and worshipping idols is the *prohibition on sorcery* of all kinds (Deut 18:10, Exod 22:18). In the New Testament it is called one of the works of the flesh (Gal 5:20). This prohibition, and the threat of capital punishment for witches, is likewise central, since the use of sorcery seeks to circumvent doing things God's way. Instead of going to Yahweh through prayer, obedience, trust, and sacrifice, we try to manipulate the spiritual world ourselves, with our own special formulas. Sorcery isn't fake, even if some people fake it. Sorcery can indeed affect the physical world, whether for good aims or bad. However, all of it is sin, because like the treason of worshipping false gods, it disconnects us from God's way of working with us, and is a fundamental rejection of fellowship. Isaiah expresses this simply, asking, "And when they shall say unto you, Seek unto them that have familiar spirits, and unto wizards that peep, and that mutter: should not a people seek unto their God? for the living to the dead?" (8:19). Sorcery furthermore invites in demons, and seeks to manipulate spirits, making false gods out of these powers in place of the Almighty. The demons, coming in, then further separate us from Yahweh. Our faithfulness must always be to the one true God.

LIVING OUT THE NATURE OF THE TRINITY

Human life in Christ is a new creation. That is witnessed in the renewal of our inner being, reflected in our behavior. It is witnessed as well in a corporate sense, through relationships, marriage, people groups, and the church. This is because the rebirth in the Son of God brings us to human life as it was originally purposed—to reflect Yahweh's nature and character. Since Yahweh is Trinity, three Persons in One God, we see God-likeness not only in our individual virtues and character traits, but in the interrelations within our own communities. Mankind in the new creation shows endless images of the Holy Trinity.

On the most basic level, we can only have being through the being of our Creator. This truth is embedded in the Holy Name of God itself. When Moses first asks God to tell him what name to use, Yahweh tells him, "I AM THAT I AM." God makes it even clearer saying Moses should tell Israel that "I AM hath sent me" (Exod 3:14). When asked for a personal name, it seems, Yahweh immediately reveals that he is pure being, and true life itself. I am also not alone in seeing in this name, "I AM THAT I AM," a notion that God's being is also his doing. He is what he does.[9] This is further made clear in that the verb is in the future tense, more literally read "I Shall Be Whom I Shall Be." God's actions into the future are indicated here, as is the truth of prophecy and covenant promises.

The sacred name of God, used by Moses after this and used throughout the Bible, is revealed as YHVH, which some Christians historically have written as Jehovah, and which I write as Yahweh. God instructs, "Thus shalt thou say unto the children of Israel, The LORD [Yahweh] God of your fathers, the God of Abraham, the God of Isaac, and the God of Jacob, hath sent me unto you" (v. 15). While it would be difficult to give an exact meaning to this name, it is also rooted in the Hebrew verb *hāyâ*, which means "to be" and forms a number of other words related to being. This revelation of God as "being" continues into the New Covenant. Jesus referred to himself as this great I Am throughout his ministry and teachings, one of many ways he revealed that he is Yahweh. When speaking to the Pharisees about his eternal nature, he told them, "Before Abraham was, I am" (John 8:58). Perhaps most stunningly, when the Roman soldiers sought to arrest Jesus and asked him if he was the man they sought, the Lord answered with "I Am," and the soldiers immediately fell down as if in judgment (John 18:4–6). When we share not only physical life, but spiritual life with the Son of God, we also share in this true and

---

9. I do not mean this in the more literal sense that some philosophers mean it. I only suggest that God's action is fully consistent with his being, and will always express who God is.

eternal being from whom all other beings are created. We dwell with the eternal fountain of life.

This fountain of life is engaged in loving relationship eternally, dwelling beyond our world and communing in love between Father, Son, and Spirit. God is not merely love as an essence, but is love as a relationship and in action. The character of the Trinity is known through several elements, at least as it is known on earth: a vertical hierarchy, mutual love, and oneness. The world knows the Christian, and the world knows the church, through its manifestation of these heavenly realities. One of the clearest ways of showing the world the Trinity is through marriage. The husband pictures the Father, who sends out the Son from his essence, gives him words to speak, and tells him what he must do. The wife pictures the Son, who comes from the Father, and only does the Father's will, and speaks the words of the Father. Children picture the Holy Spirit, who springs forth from the Father and Son's will, after the Son ascends to heaven. Children are even brought forth physically from the loving act of husband and wife, as Spirit is generated spiritually through the communion of Father and Son. Each member shares love and resources with the other, often in a unique way. Through the husband's love and leadership, the wife receives all that she needs. She receives her physical needs through his hard work, and spiritual guidance through his priestlike role. Through the wife's love and submission, the husband's will is brought forth in the world. He receives peace, joy, and satisfaction through her gentle and loving obedience. Through their mutual love, children are born who receive life, teaching, and virtue from their parents. They are fed, clothed, and given a home through the sacrifices of their mother and father. The oneness, peace, and harmony that exist in marriage show the world the true life of God and that salvation in Christ is real. It shows men that Yahweh is one, that he is love, that he sustains, and that he brings eternal peace. Men will be brought to believe in Christ with the help of a godly and joyful Christian marriage.

All human relationships are guided and blessed in some way through the Trinitarian nature of Yahweh. It's not just the family. We have functioning, successful institutions because of this nature. Workers honor their bosses, work hard, and seek to make the company pleased with their behavior. Heads of businesses provide for their employees, help them to learn, and treat them as valued human beings. While not reflecting the deeper kind of love as in marriage, human love is also present in the work world through showing honor, and caring for the good of the other, whether one is above or below the other in station. Citizens and governments are also to reflect these traits. Those in power show love through their just use of power, and for providing even more than they need to, with a real concern for their people. Those who are citizens show love through their respect for the law, allegiance to their country, and working even beyond what they need for the good of society. As an inseparable whole, living in peace, it seems miraculous what an entire people group or nation can produce. It is equally startling what open conflict and fragmentation cause in a land, bringing civilization to a near standstill. We ought to be in awe and wonder, and praise God each moment for the wonders that come from ongoing, working relationships like these.

The church is tasked with sharing the gospel, caring for the poor, teaching right doctrine, and leading the assembly in worship. The church explicitly pictures the love between Father and Son in heaven. Not only do we see the same hierarchy existing in the church, with both headship and submission, but its unity with Christ also reflects Christ's unity with the Father. As the Church loves and lives in the spirit of Christ, it will be one; among its members, among churches, among individuals, and men will see God. Souls will come to believe by the preaching of the gospel, given alongside the living out of divine unity. Christ taught, "That they all may be one; as thou, Father, art in me, and I in thee, that they also may be one in us: *that the world may believe* that thou hast sent me" (John 17:21). Our Trinitarian union leads men to faith. The Father shares truth with the Son, the Son with the church, and the church with its members and the world. Its elders, servants, and ordinary members all have a role to play. Each have gifts. Each care for the good of the other. Elders lead with humility and love. The people follow with submission and diligent work. The lively action of the church is a witness that Christ loves and saves his people. It is rooted in the Trinity.

The Trinity act in harmony just as our mind must act with order and balance, and as the humans in any human family must practice right loving relationship. Each contributes thoughts, words, activities to the whole. We see a satanic breaking of this imprint of the Trinity when warring occurs. Each person views the other as an enemy. Men divide into factions. Ideas become acts of destruction rather than ideas proposed and reviewed. Suddenly brothers and sisters become the enemy, to be viewed from trenches with telescopes, or within the crosshairs of our weapons, not embraced or welcomed with love. What once were good ideas, become bad ones. This is obviously present in the churches as well, in a manner Paul warns against (1 Cor 1:10–13). The faction that proposes mercy in a matter is called the soft, feminized sissies, and the faction which speaks for justice is labeled the mean, heartless legalists. In reality they were both part of one familial whole, each with his rightful place. Men get deemed heretics over matters of philosophical guesswork, or over very minor teachings. The sharing of truth and of purpose between brothers is ended, and each faction holds onto his piece of the truth tightly. One religion becomes many. The name of God becomes many. The mind is divided and confused as in a state of madness. This is all in conflict with the mind of God. This is why Yahweh has given us his word and his Spirit, to live instead in trinitarian unity, conformed to the mind of Christ; each man distinct and honored, but in loving relationship with all men; each man serving the other, but serving from his rightful position, above or below. The divine law is being made real through our relationships, side by side with the gospel.

Human philosophers sometimes speak of history in terms of conflict. This is merely the human order; the order in the flesh. One idea comes along and gains great influence over human life. Then another idea comes and offers opposition. Through the push and pull of the old and the new idea, another idea is born and things start over. While this offers a loose description of human behavior over many centuries, it does not reflect God's will or the new creation. The new creation has different kinds of human relationships, rooted in our natural order and in harmony. It functions in peace, and not in war of ideas. Rather the head has an idea in obedience to Yahweh. His people seek to bring about this idea through hard work and prayer. That idea is then brought to fruition to the praise of God with joy. This is the life of the Trinity lived out, and it reflects the love, authority, and peace in the godhead. That is not to say there are no new ideas which need to be measured, but rather that the new ideas are measured and utilized in peace, not in conflict, and accepted only within the law of God. Nor does it mean that the servants may not share any ideas, only the heads, but that these ideas do not come in the form of disrespect for authority, or rejection of the law. Rather they are offered in peace, and discussed in terms of how they serve the good of all. Human life as it one day will be is one of expression of divine truth, through godly human relationships. It is one of an ocean of peace, through unique members who love and respect one another.

JOY OF CREATION

No one is ever a victim of the Almighty; we are a victim of our own sin. If anyone doubts the goodness of God's character one only need to look around and see the beauty and goodness even of a fallen world. We only need gaze up at the sky, on our drive home each day, and praise God for the heavenly vision of glory it is. If we did not see the sky daily we would consider it a miracle to see it once. It is mind blowing. Despite man's sin, despite his cruelty, treachery, and betrayal, we are still filled with goodness daily by a loving Father. We are given breath in the lungs, a mind the comprehend this world and solve its problems. We are given companionship and love of other human family members. We are given the overwhelming beauty and wonder of creation. We are given nourishment through food, which we may prepare to meet our own personal tastes of every variety. Fresh warm bread, by itself, is as good as anything a trained chef can produce, and as any expensive dish from a fancy restaurant. Its ingredients are simple, inexpensive, and it is not hard to produce. When I worked at a Mexican restaurant, I used to snack on warm corn tortillas, fresh out of the oven, with butter. I could hunger for those dreamily as much as any food I've ever tried. It's hard to imagine they eat anything greater than bread in heaven.

Those at war with Yahweh like to present him as overly cruel, but what overly cruel person, whether God or man, provides people with nourishment, satisfaction, and pleasure all the time? That doesn't make a lot of sense. Yahweh gives to man the incredible delight of intimacy in marriage, alongside the lasting peace marriage instills in the soul. God gives us jobs to do which fulfill our soul and use our unique skills. He gives us friends who bring us their encouragement, insights, new resources, and new horizons. He gives us wine that "maketh glad the heart of man" (Ps 104:15a), which we can freely enjoy without getting drunk. It simply cannot be argued, with any credibility, that a God who gives you sex and booze is out to get you. The suffering that continues throughout creation is man's doing. His personal misery flows from his ungratefulness. It is truly beyond words what we have been gifted with: the cosmos, the wonders of this earth, the human mind, the tools we have to work with. The exploration of this world is so grand and fascinating it could go on forever.

This fact is only multiplied when we realize that if we return to peace with God, we will have fellowship for an eternity, looking on his glorious face. We will learn forever. We will have loving companionship forever.

We will explore all things forever. We will uncover mysteries forever. We will eat and drink forever. We will pray forever. We are not limited to soaking up satisfaction in this pale world before it ends in darkness. Rather we touch on the nature of Yahweh himself by joining into eternity and living with him. God has given us a love that will not end with our life on this earth. His gift for us, as his children, is not going to run down like a mortal machine. It is his perfect gift. We are made in God's image and will be doing the work of God in joy forever. To share in all that Yahweh does is not the punishment of a cruel God, but the gift of a loving one.

If we were to fill the world and eternity only with our goals, it would be an empty endeavor, not even worth starting. The more financially conservative would fill up nation after nation, and planet after planet with his modern development, busy city centers, a tide of vehicles, factories, power plants, increasing wealth into a greater and greater mountain of cash and coins and electronic accounts. The western hedonist would bring his parties, his dating, his drugs, his orgies to every square inch of reality, in what he personally envisioned as heaven, so that the pleasure and ego were stimulated to his desired maximum. Man would set out with sinful goals and breakable buildings and make a mockery of the creation by doing so. Yet if we step back from our goals, and let God show us the goodness of creation, we find it is not found in the flesh. It is found in worship of God, and loving relation with one another. The materialist and the hedonist would give us a dystopic vision of eternity, one that would eventually throw anyone into blackened depression. It would be meaningless desire fulfillment. Yet the God of creation makes eternity with him a delight, through things which will not burn or die. We exist with him through love, which will not die. God will be praised and brotherly love experienced in every square inch of creation.

In Genesis we see the world before sin and God's intention with it. At each day of creation, the Bible teaches, God saw what he had created and "it was good" (Gen 1). This is also true of the light created at the beginning, but the phrase is strangely missing from the second day. At the end of the six days of creation, Genesis teaches: "And God saw every thing that he had made, and, behold, it was very good. And the evening and the morning were the sixth day" (1:31). We can see the whole creation and everything in it was good. The fall brought us pain, death, and sin, but it did not at all prevent Yahweh from using the creation to give us earthly life, protection, nourishment, and pleasure. Nor did it prevent Yahweh from continuing to use the creation to teach us, which it does through natural revelation each day. The Bible teaches the goodness of God's creation many times, and the creation itself proclaims the glory of God.

Psalm 33, which I have cited regarding God's control over all things, also speaks deeply of his creation of all things:

> Sing unto him a new song; play skilfully with a loud noise.
>
> For the word of the LORD is right; and all his works are done in truth.
>
> He loveth righteousness and judgment: *the earth is full of the goodness of the LORD.*
>
> By the word of the LORD were the heavens made; and all the host of them by the breath of his mouth.
>
> He gathereth the waters of the sea together as an heap: he layeth up the depth in storehouses.
>
> Let all the earth fear the LORD: let all the inhabitants of the world stand in awe of him.
>
> For he spake, and it was done; he commanded, and it stood fast. (vv. 3–9)

The passage teaches that God's goodness is here with us on earth. It also speaks of the method of creation, which is through the "word" and the "breath" of Yahweh (v. 6). This language suggests the Trinity, which becomes more fully revealed in later revelation. The perfect unity between a word and breath suggests the unity between the Son of God (who is called the Word), and the Holy Spirit (who is compared to wind). In fact, the word for breath in Hebrew (*rûaḥ*) is also the word for spirit, whether we speak of man's spirit or the Holy Spirit. God gave us the earth, heavens, and seas, and this act even says something about the deepest mystery of the godhead.

In one of several great passages in Proverbs about wisdom, it teaches:

> The LORD *by wisdom hath founded the earth*; by understanding hath he established the heavens.
>
> By his knowledge the depths are broken up, and the clouds drop down the dew.
>
> My son, let not them depart from thine eyes: keep sound wisdom and discretion:
>
> So shall they be life unto thy soul, and grace to thy neck. (3:19–22)

Yahweh used his perfect wisdom to make all things, and now we as men are given wisdom on this earth. In observing what God has made, we receive that wisdom, which will bring grace to our lives. That is the wisdom contained in the Scriptures and the commandments, as we see in the first verse of the same chapter, as well as natural wisdom found in solving problems and observing God's creation. We have received this second-hand wisdom ever since we learned to plant seeds, breed animals, or build huts. We can also think of the many creatures which have inspired new technologies in modernity, giving inspiration by God's design, such as the desert beetle which inspired new water harvesting material, or the iridescent butterfly wings, which revealed how to make new electronic readers. The wings of birds have brought about new airplane design. The stickiness of gecko feet has inspired man to make new adhesives. God's truth and goodness penetrate everywhere. Wisdom is compared to bread and wine in Prov 9, a food we are invited to eat to have life (vv. 5–6). It is not mere head knowledge, but serves our lives in powerful and practical ways, strengthening us. God's brilliance, majesty, complexity, mystery, and beauty are all around us all the times, and they benefit us in ways both seen and unseen. Who would reject this goodness that has been gifted us? Who would claim God erred, or was unjust? Even as guilty men we benefit every day.

Another section in Proverbs on wisdom seems to show a Torah of the world, side by side with the Torah of mankind. God placed this order in the world and man should follow it, not merely as a commandment, but because it is good, and is the foundation of the very world in which we live. Surely this Torah reflects the mind of God, his will for us, and his perfect character:

> When he prepared the heavens, I was there: when he set a compass upon the face of the depth:
>
> When he established the clouds above: when he strengthened the fountains of the deep:
>
> When he gave to the sea his decree, that the waters should not pass his commandment: when he appointed the foundations of the earth:
>
> *Then I was by him, as one brought up with him: and I was daily his delight*, rejoicing always before him;
>
> Rejoicing in the habitable part of his earth; and my delights were with the sons of men.

> Now therefore hearken unto me, O ye children: for blessed are they that keep my ways.
>
> Hear instruction, and be wise, and refuse it not.
>
> Blessed is the man that heareth me, watching daily at my gates, waiting at the posts of my doors.
>
> *For whoso findeth me findeth life*, and shall obtain favour of the LORD.
>
> But he that sinneth against me wrongeth his own soul: *all they that hate me love death*. (Prov 8:27–36)

This has been one of my favorite passages since I first picked up the Bible as an adult and started studying it. What more clear statement is there of the goodness of God's wisdom, and how it all is life sustaining? There is a wisdom present with Yahweh as he created the material world, the cosmos and all that is in it. There is also a wisdom for mankind, which to violate, would be to violate your own soul. Breaking the law is not only an offense to the Ruler, it is a harm to mankind. It brings death. What is clear also is the joy in God's created order, whether physical, or in human society. Yahweh finds delight in creating. He finds joy in using his wisdom in making all the things we see around us, and much that is unseen. Surely we touch on the mind of God when we search out the truths of the natural world, and when we seek to live with our brothers ethically, with love, justice, mercy, and right relationship. All of this follows the Torah of God, the living One, which flows from his mind in eternity.

As I pointed out when speaking uniquely on sovereignty, it is hard to miss that the Scriptures, while speaking of Yahweh's power in creation, often use it as an example of his power in human history, teaching us that Yahweh will accomplish his goals. The same God who made everything is going to accomplish his will in human history. We see this in Isa 45 and 42, and elsewhere. The very fact God created all these wonders we see and experience should teach us that he is wonderful enough to defeat his enemies, and to rescue his people. Yahweh created all things from nothing, and there is nothing that can stop God. A man contemplating the Scriptures should know that God is more powerful than whatever holds him in bondage. A man contemplating creation should know the same thing. His goodness and power are on display.

Romans 1:20 explicitly affirms this. We have a somewhat detailed knowledge of God through everything we see around us. Every single man can know God: "*For the invisible things of him* from the creation of the world *are clearly seen*, being understood by the things that are made, even his eternal power and Godhead; so that they are without excuse." Just as we know God's power and goodness through creation, we know all his attributes as well. We know his righteousness, justice, and holiness, enough to know our own guilt before him, enough that we have no excuse for our sin. What is made speaks about the Maker. In fact, it so closely expresses him, that the moment people cease worshipping the Eternal One, they begin worshipping nature, or spirits within it. They reject true worship, yet follow through with a close approximation, because they see something spiritual in nature. They are right to be in awe at God's handiwork, but they are wrong to worship it.

Perhaps the greatest review of the creation after the opening chapters of Genesis is the long description of Ps 104. The Holy Spirit does not slack in giving us the details and many wonders of Yahweh's creation:

> He sendeth the springs into the valleys, which run among the hills.
>
> They give drink to every beast of the field: the wild asses quench their thirst.
>
> By them shall the fowls of the heaven have their habitation, which sing among the branches.
>
> He watereth the hills from his chambers: the earth is satisfied with the fruit of thy works.
>
> He causeth the grass to grow for the cattle, and herb for the service of man: that he may bring forth food out of the earth;
>
> And wine that maketh glad the heart of man, and oil to make his face to shine, and bread which strengtheneth man's heart.
>
> The trees of the LORD are full of sap; the cedars of Lebanon, which he hath planted;
>
> Where the birds make their nests: as for the stork, the fir trees are her house.
>
> The high hills are a refuge for the wild goats; and the rocks for the conies.
>
> He appointed the moon for seasons: the sun knoweth his going down.
>
> Thou makest darkness, and it is night: wherein all the beasts of the forest do creep forth.
>
> The young lions roar after their prey, and seek their meat from God. (vv. 10–21)

This psalm goes on and on the same way, and ends with great praise of Yahweh who made all of this, and with condemnation of the wicked:

> Let the sinners be consumed out of the earth, and let the wicked be no more. Bless thou the LORD, O my soul. Praise ye the LORD. (v. 35)

It is as if in reviewing all the wonders of God's creation, we can see more clearly the destruction of God's creation found in sin. We can hate sin, and wish it more deeply never to be. We wish with greater depth to rebuke it. Since God and his creation are so wonderful, and he has made this our home, we immediately want it free from sin.

If we desired, we would see God's goodness everywhere we looked. We would likewise see his holiness, his righteousness, his eternity, his wisdom, his wrath against evil. We would be in awe at a living revelation at all times. Likewise, we would never stop praising Yahweh for all of this goodness. Praise would be on our lips at every moment and with every breath. We would shout praise, and cheer it with our hands raised. It is only hardness of heart the keeps us from seeing it and being grateful. Lack of trust. Hopelessness. Selfishness. They all blind our eyes to the goodness around us at all times. Wickedness itself is what attacks this beauty and goodness, and we should see how sin is often nothing more than what hides goodness from us, or blots wisdom from our mind. We would hate sin, and condemn sin, as the psalmist does here. Knowing God's goodness, knowing the goodness of his creation, we would say with conviction—let the wicked be no more.

Yahweh created a good creation. We still are nourished by it despite the scars and bruises from the fall. Most of mankind receives life, nourishment, and even pleasure daily even in a world full of man's evil and cruelty. Somewhere behind that creation we can see God's original creation, and his coming paradise hidden. We can see the grandeur of our mountains, and recognize there is one a thousandfold more awe inspiring in God's kingdom. We can be entranced by the ocean, and know the soothing of the waves, and the enchanting mystery will be revealed one day, through the supernatural, and in knowing Yahweh more fully. What we see here is only a picture, and a damaged one. Both in the mind of God, and in heaven, the revelation we see in nature will be fulfilled in a way so great, it is beyond words. Yet we complain about our blessings, and are ungrateful for this world. What stubborn childishness. We are decked out with gifts, and will receive much more.

My lips shall utter praise, when thou hast taught me thy statutes.

My tongue shall speak of thy word: for all thy commandments are righteousness.

Let thine hand help me; for I have chosen thy precepts.

I have longed for thy salvation, O LORD; and thy law is my delight.

Let my soul live, and it shall praise thee; and let thy judgments help me.

I have gone astray like a lost sheep; seek thy servant; for I do not forget thy commandments. (Ps 119:171–176)

7

The Future is a Miracle

When I worked as a musician in Spain, I used to play at a bar with a short goateed drummer named Keiko. He'd play the North African drums, along with the Spanish cajon, and a few rock and roll drums. He was very skilled, and could follow my lead, picking up on my musical signals, even though we had little time to practice together. One song I'd play all the time was the hypnotic number "Heroin," by the Velvet Underground.[1] I didn't want to promote the drug, just the music, and I knew people personally who were destroying themselves with it. I'd always warn an audience against being involved with narcotics, for their addictive power and the bodily destruction they bring. "Heroin" is a song about the utter self-destruction of the addiction, but a self-destruction that could only come about by one who desires much more. It is an addiction that fills a man with purpose, with meaning, with something to worship. It's like a dark version of love. It utterly consumes the soul.

Each verse of the song begins with a long slow exhale of the first few syllables. Then it builds up in stages to a quiet trot, that at times becomes frenzied, almost out of control, and excites the heart with its build up and its speed. Then it ends again with a final beat, quiet, back to droning hypnotism. It is the longing of a man who wants something much more than what he is, and what he has. He wants relief from all that oppresses him, crushing down on his soul. His drug is something glorious to him. When he takes it, for a moment, he enters the kingdom.

---

1. Velvet Underground, "Heroin," *The Velvet Underground & Nico*.

Like a number of irreligious pop songs, the lyrics throw in the word Jesus for what lies behind that name. As an unbeliever performing the song, it always felt good to me singing his name. Even the man who denies Jesus Christ knows that what Jesus Christ stands for, what he means, is *good*. He knows Jesus' very name is powerful. He has an underlying sense there is something spiritual, wholesome, eternal there. It is without difficulty or doubt that he compares his ecstasy to being a child of Jesus. While profaning him in his words, in his mind he is not profaning him, but rather soaking up one drop of the goodness that Christians live with in Christ. Milking from him what he believes the dead can receive. But it is only a feeling. It is temporary, this liberation which drugs offer from the world, this ecstasy, a ritual which needs to be repeated, stabbing into the vein over and over. It is a bloodier and more repeated sacrifice than men ever saw at the temple in Jerusalem. It is a man who knows he is lost, and has no answers. Only his drug.

It seems the only way to be free is to destroy yourself. The only escape the eye can see, the mind can imagine, is in self-nullification. It is exciting and terrifying at the same time. Somehow we affirm the goodness of life when we reject an empty or wicked one. When we hate our own slavery, we are pronouncing our love for freedom, even if we cannot see it. It is a suicide without suicide. When I was a boy I made a similar decision to give up on this life, and kill anything good about myself. It really was a clear statement, and commitment, or you might say an oath. I would not amount to anything in this world, and I was despised by it. I rejected this world and being a part of it, to walk instead like a ghost through it. We don't want to live anymore. But we still wish there was something good about this life, something pure beyond what we know. You can fill your consciousness up with all the entertainment or learning you want, you can keep a stable of lovers, but you know it is empty, and you wish to make them all go away. They cannot and will not help you.

The song gets quieter, continues with a long slow drone. The singer lets out the opening note, one single sound. It is still and comforting, like a little death, like worship of God, all the crowd looking up to that light which is on the stage. There is something wondrous about it. A light comes out of the darkness. The man pronounces the name of his master

In a chemical religion of drugs, the man finds death to self, and to the flesh, in the wondrous passageways that take his drug through his body and into his brain. It is better to experience this death than to be alive. The chemical is his master, his god, who brings him transcendent experience. The chance to finally be nothing. To be unaware is the dream of many men. It seems the world is so full of pain, confusion, meaninglessness, and cruelty, that escape from the flesh is the only way. To be dead, yet alive. Being locked in a body somehow is the source of evil. Being on the planet earth is the source of evil. Perhaps there is something beyond this material world that would be better. The flesh has to die. Our mind has to lapse. There is a man-made heaven on earth, at least until the drug kills you. It really doesn't take you anywhere better, but it destroys the flesh, which is enough to replicate it and satisfy the longings to be free of this earth. One cannot shout out the name of God, even in vain, without sensing its power. The name alone it makes you long for something more.

 I played rock and folk music for years, and made money on it. If I wasn't making music on the edge of my bed, I was performing in cafes and restaurants, or practicing with friends. I probably had hundreds of songs memorized, along with their chords, and even if I wasn't playing them, they played themselves in my head each day. They were the hymns to my religion. They uplifted me. They filled up the soul with what I perceived I needed, and gave me temporary meaning and hope. As a Christian today, that is over, and I listen to very little but religious music. My song lists are filled with family singers, choirs, and Eastern Orthodox chant. I sing hymns weekly with my family at home, on the same instrument I used for singing profane songs years ago. I can look at that old music now for the harm that it causes society, literally laying people low. It all points people in the wrong direction. Profane men, sexually immoral, vulgar, infatuated with self, and criminal minds fill the music world, and mass entertainment in general. Many lives and families have been ripped apart by these lost men and women who attacked all that is good, and presented themselves as gods for the masses. The music industry is full of such self-worshipping stars, who prance about seeking adoration. They are priests or even avatars of what they sense is a higher power. They are self-important, lewd, angry, ugly in spirit, and deadened to the truth. But there just one more thing you need to know about them: They're right.

 In a world apart from Yahweh, it is good sense to see there is no meaning in life. It is a normal desire to want to destroy what is ugly and painful, and escape it somehow. Watch it all burn. A world of the mere material, of overbearing desires, of oppression, is agonizing, and any normal person would seek paradise, if only by destroying that world. It's all got to burn. They sense the worthlessness of the flesh, and desire the beautiful kingdom of the spirit. They want something good, instead of something evil. But the only way they know is to destroy, if only themselves. Darkness never ending would be better than this world apart from God.

I used to know an older junkie couple from northern Europe who slept on the streets in Barcelona. They had marks up and down their bodies, fresh ones, old ones, endless scabs, and they were very kind and would stop me on the street sometimes. Once the old man told me: "Listen, I've got to tell you something, Tom. Listen to me. I've crossed over to the other side, and I'm not coming back." I liked the couple, and it was a refreshing chance sometimes to play them a few songs at their request. Since I usually played for money, it was a relief to play for free. One of my favorite numbers at the time was "Misguided Angel," and I poured out the song for them with my whole heart, at the end, finding the couple were weeping. It moved me to touch someone, and I was almost embarrassed that they thanked me so much for the music. One should be grateful to touch anyone's heart. To provide them something beautiful they can cherish. Does the musician want anything more?

One junkie I dated once told me that heroin addicts had strong hearts. They simply got disillusioned. The strong heart didn't know what to make of the world. It was constantly frustrated. I noticed the same thing when I got to be surrounded by them later in life. I always enjoyed their company more than the drunks, who were loud, simple, and sometimes violent. Junkies I knew had a gentle nature. They were feline. There was a young woman who used to make money playing the recorder in the main drag and the plazas. It's not an uncommon way for addicts to earn a little money in that country. She could have been in her late twenties, but her face and her teeth could have been of a woman much older, an unhealthy woman in her fifties or older, already weathered, and beginning to look wrinkled. She was a sweet girl who always came over and said hi to me, asked me about my music. I longed to help her. I wish I could have taken her home, locked her in a room, and gotten her free of her poison. I could have kept her there until she went through withdrawal, fed her, and let her go when she was free. It only seems right to liberate someone from their chains, and cruel master, and an act of love. But then if I did, it would be kidnapping, and I'd go to prison. So I knew the option was out the window. I couldn't set her free.

Apparently, a lot of people had crossed over, and they weren't coming back. A roommate I had for a while was being treated with methadone, which is a legal, and apparently safer alternative to heroin, and similar narcotics. He'd keep his cups of methadone in the refrigerator, covered in a cap, and he warned me if I had only a few drops of it, I'd die immediately. He could handle a large dose of it. Some people fill themselves with replacement drugs, at the minimum to function better than on the previous drug, or at best to gradually quit narcotics entirely. He and his other friend would sometimes return to heroin though, because of the inescapable attraction it had for them, and he eventually died, still in his thirties.

What's funny is that what anyone with a heart really wants, what they dream of, is actually real. It isn't a crazy dream. Or a Hollywood movie. It doesn't require our physical death. However, it's got a lot to do with dying. Blood really has to flow from a spike in the vein. Childish hearts that dream about a world of goodness, love, justice, beauty, and know the pale of death that hangs around us at all times, are not crazy or dreaming. There is a paradise for us. There is a kingdom in which goodness reigns, and men are at peace with each other. It is free from evil, and being free from evil, it is hardly boring. Opium is boring. Paradise is not. It is a kingdom full of joy, celebration, meaningful work, and worship of the most beloved Person we could imagine. Paradise just came about walking in a way we did not expect it to come.

THE SECRET

That human condition, ripe with suffering and emptiness, is destined to end. Purposelessness and void will dissipate into a new creation, consumed with glory. God has assured it. The New Testament begins with this revelation: That is the revelation of the kingdom of God, coming first in a man named John the Baptist, who prepares the way, and soon in the Man, Jesus of Nazareth, who is witnessed by the voice of God and many miracles. It came in the poor, in the dishonored, and in a long intentional death march, all proclaiming what was to come. I've already discussed how Christ's teaching purifies us, and to see the bigger picture, we should focus on the immanent nature of God's kingdom now, and see how exactly it comes to pass:

> The law and the prophets were until John: since that time *the kingdom of God is preached*, and every man presseth into it. (Luke 16:16)

The old order and the new order certainly overlapped in the work of John, who went living out in the wilderness, and baptizing in the Jordan

River. John was the last of the Old Testament prophets, and truly the greatest because he himself heralded the Messiah, and the new order. It was in the baptism of Jesus by John that Christ was publicly announced as God's Son. This baptism which John had been performing, while preparing men for the kingdom, and calling them to repentance, had another unique purpose: it would begin the saving work of Jesus Christ, and reveal him to the world, for those who would see. Then the new order, and the new creation began in a sense, even before the cross, as the kingdom was preached, as Christ worked miracles, as he gave his new law, and taught, even in mysteries, about what was soon to come:

> Now after that John was put in prison, Jesus came into Galilee, preaching the gospel of the kingdom of God,
>
> And saying, The time is fulfilled, and *the kingdom of God is at hand*: repent ye, and believe the gospel. (Mark 1:14–15)

The time given for Temple Judaism has finished. The prophesies of Messiah and the kingdom were being fulfilled now in Jesus as he began travelling, teaching, and working miracles. The time prophesied hundreds of years before had come. Jesus says that the kingdom is "at hand." This is language of immanence, showing an event is upon us right now, or in the immediate future. Repentance and faith are what the hearers must have to enter this kingdom. They must turn from their sins and believe in Christ.

> And it came to pass afterward, that he went throughout every city and village, preaching and *shewing the glad tidings of the kingdom of God*: (Luke 8:1a)
>
> And when he was demanded of the Pharisees, when the kingdom of God should come, he answered them and said, The kingdom of God cometh not with observation:
>
> Neither shall they say, Lo here! or, lo there! for, behold, *the kingdom of God is within you*. (Luke 17:20–21)

A single word is used for "shewing the glad tidings," and this is a Greek word *euangelizō*, referring to bearing good news. It is used throughout the New Testament for preaching the gospel, and in the Greek Septuagint (Old Testament) for sharing any good news, including the great works of God. I suppose one could imagine Christ and the disciples are bringing news of a kingdom that is far away in the future, but it appears their announcement is more like a knock at the door. It is immediate. It is within your reach. It stands before you. The immediate nature of the kingdom is made clearer in the second passage, as Jesus of Nazareth teaches the Jewish religious teachers that the kingdom is "within" you. This word "within" (*entos* in Greek) can also be translated "among," or "in the midst," and is the same word Jesus uses when he urges the Pharisees to clean the "inside" of the cup and dish (Matt 23:26), speaking of their interior being. The Greek Septuagint uses *entos* to say, "My heart was hot *within* me" (Ps 39:3a). This kingdom was already present in Jesus' time, and people could enter in through faith. It dwelt in the soul, and among the interactions, and human relationships of all who enter in. It may not have been in its final form yet, as he was laying down this kingdom step by step, but it was already beginning, and it would eventually put an end to all sin and death. The devil would be completely destroyed:

> And if Satan cast out Satan, he is divided against himself; how shall then his kingdom stand?
>
> And if I by Beelzebub cast out devils, by whom do your children cast them out? therefore they shall be your judges.
>
> But if I cast out devils by the Spirit of God, *then the kingdom of God is come unto you*. (Matt 12:26–28)

Jesus here is answering the challenge that he is casting out demons by the power of Satan. His answer, while silencing the accusers with their own logic, also demands we see that God's kingdom is present in the time he is speaking. Since Christ indeed casts demons out of people, and indeed acts by the Spirit, we know that the kingdom is already upon us.

> And he said, Whereunto shall we liken the kingdom of God? or with what comparison shall we compare it?
>
> It is like a grain of mustard seed, which, when it is sown in the earth, is less than all the seeds that be in the earth:
>
> But when it is sown, *it groweth up, and becometh greater than all herbs*, and shooteth out great branches; so that the fowls of the air may lodge under the shadow of it. (Mark 4:30–32)
>
> Another parable spake he unto them; The kingdom of heaven is like unto leaven, which a woman took, and hid in three measures of meal, *till the whole was leavened*. (Matt 13:33)

God's present kingdom includes its growth over time. It can be compared to a tiny seed, which needs to sprout, come up from the ground, and then develop into a bush large enough to shelter birds. Anyone familiar with gardening knows that some seeds are so small, you can hardly see them. They are tiny enough you'd have trouble just picking up one at a time. Yet with water, sunlight, soil, and perhaps some protection, that little thing you have to squint to see grows strong stems, flowers, and bears fruit. It seems miraculous, and its growth in size literally thousands of times over merely indicates the workings of the kingdom.

It can also be compared to a sprinkling of leaven, which over time raises a lump of dough until it is ready to be made into bread. This kingdom it seems acts on something else, on the dough which becomes our food. It enters into something, and transforms it to make it ready. What it enters into is the human soul, and human communities throughout the world, building them up, and making them righteous. The kingdom is not the same as the world, but it will over time permeate the world, bringing holiness throughout all of its lands, making it fruitful in faith and righteousness. The seed of leaven simply needs to be put in the dough, kneaded with work, and then it will take time to rise.

In Christ's ministry, the kingdom was not yet fully formed. It was a tiny seed. It went through stages of growth through his teachings, at his death and resurrection, and in the Spirit-filled church after his ministry, spreading throughout the known world. It continued to grow when Christ judged Jerusalem in AD 70, cutting the infant church from traditional Judaism when the temple was destroyed, and Temple Judaism destroyed with it. It has similarly gone through growth from the early church era up to the present. It went from being small scattered communities, whose leaders were arrested and murdered, to taking over the multi-national Roman Empire. It took hold in Europe, forming a new civilization out of the old, and even as belief fades in the western world today, new fruit is born in Asia, Africa, in people of many nations, languages, and belief systems. The kingdom of God is a present and future reality. It is not finished.

If we take the words of Jesus and of the Apostle John at face value, the kingdom has come. It may still carry a future reality to be completed in Christ, but the prophesies were fulfilled, and the kingdom brought in 2,000 years ago. Christ defeated the devil, taking away his power to deceive the nations. He promises us victory, the power to turn away from our sins, and to cast out demons wherever they dwell. The Holy Spirit in us, wherever he encounters Satan, will defeat him. Even our suffering and death will be for glory, and will bring us treasures in the world to come.

What Messiah brought in was prophesied many centuries before he accomplished it. Those prophesies give us a brilliant picture, at times in detail, of the kingdom. Let's look at a few of them:

Suffering Servant and Victory

> The meek shall eat and be satisfied: they shall praise the LORD that seek him: your heart shall live for ever.
>
> All the ends of the world shall remember and turn unto the LORD: and all the kindreds of the nations shall worship before thee.
>
> For the kingdom is the LORD'S: and *he is the governor among the nations.* (Ps 22:26–28)
>
> *So shall he sprinkle many nations*; the kings shall shut their mouths at him: for that which had not been told them shall they see; and that which they had not heard shall they consider. (Isa 52:15)
>
> *Therefore will I divide him a portion with the great,* and he shall divide the spoil with the strong; because he hath poured out his soul unto death: and he was numbered with the transgressors; and he bare the sin of many, and made intercession for the transgressors. (Isa 53:12)

Psalm 22, which describes in great detail the sufferings of Messiah, ends with a celebration of his accomplishments. Through his suffering he would rule over the nations. People all over the world would turn to Yahweh and worship him. The meek would eat and be satisfied because of him, a prophecy which we can understand either as the spiritually humble being fed, or the actual poor being fed, either of which is in harmony with the righteousness of God's kingdom.

Isaiah 52–53 is the most well known passage from the prophets about Christ. Being most known for its vivid description of Jesus' meekness, and his suffering on the cross, it also gives us a picture of his accomplishments. These include kings receiving the gospel, and entire nations being sprinkled, a sprinkling we can read in context of the whole of Scripture as referring either to the blood of Christ, or the waters of baptism. Just as Israel was sprinkled with the blood of the covenant at Sinai, the new peoples coming into the new covenant would also be sprinkled. Clearly Messiah's act on the world did more than reach many individual human souls, but also affects entire nations, and brings rulers to faith. It is earth shaking. Like a military victor, Messiah receives spoil for his victory, and divides that with those captains who fought with him.

> Behold my servant, whom I uphold; mine elect, in whom my soul delighteth; I have put my spirit upon him: he *shall bring forth judgment to the Gentiles*. (Isa 42:1)

Isaiah 42 opens with a long passage about Messiah. It includes some of the most well-known characteristics of the Lord and his work: He will not raise his voice. A bruised reed he will not break. He opens the eyes of the blind (vv. 2, 3a, 18b). Yet the passage opens by boldly proclaiming Messiah's goal, which is a global one: Messiah will bring justice to the nations. This is not merely a personal work on the soul of the believer, but a transforming work in entire people groups, one that touches upon law and upon governments. When the Lord says in Leviticus, "Ye shall therefore keep my statutes, *and my judgments*" (18:5a), he is using the same word, which is mišpāṭ in Hebrew. Here it means the commandments and ordinances. This word can also refer to a judge's decisions, such as in Deut 17:9, which teaches, "And thou shalt come unto the priests the Levites, and unto the judge . . . and they shall shew thee the sentence of judgment." Verse 4 of Isa 42 even tells us, "The isles shall wait for *his law*." The law here is the Torah, from the Hebrew *tôrâ*, used numerous times throughout the Old Testament to refer to the commandments of national Israel. While the passage otherwise emphasizes the Servant's gentleness and compassion, his mission is clearly beyond the conversion of individual souls. It is a governmental rule over nations of the earth.

Rule over nations

> Yet have I set my king upon my holy hill of Zion.
>
> I will declare the decree: the LORD hath said unto me, Thou art my Son; this day have I begotten thee.
>
> Ask of me, and I shall give thee *the heathen for thine inheritance*, and the uttermost parts of the earth for thy possession.
>
> Thou shalt break them with a rod of iron; thou shalt dash them in pieces like a potter's vessel.
>
> *Be wise now therefore, O ye kings*: be instructed, ye judges of the earth.

Serve the LORD with fear, and rejoice with trembling.

Kiss the Son, lest he be angry, and ye perish from the way, when his wrath is kindled but a little. Blessed are all they that put their trust in him. (Ps 2:6–12)

If anyone tries to present Jesus the Lord as a mere lovable hippie, leading a people of lovable hippies, read them Ps 2, among other similar passages. Here Christ rules over all the earth, which is a possession given to him by Yahweh. Those who rise up against him, he defeats, shattering them like a clay jar. Kings and other rulers must serve the Messiah, and fear his judgment if he is angry with them. Yet all who trust in him are blessed. This ownership of the nations extends to the "uttermost parts of the earth" (v. 8). The love of Christ clearly does not come apart from his just rule over all people, and the vanquishing of his enemies.

> And it shall come to pass, that *every one that is left of all the nations which came against Jerusalem shall even go up from year to year to worship the King*, the LORD of hosts, and to keep the feast of tabernacles.
>
> And it shall be, that whoso will not come up of all the families of the earth unto Jerusalem to worship the King, the LORD of hosts, even upon *them shall be no rain*.
>
> And if the family of Egypt go not up, and come not, that have no rain; *there shall be the plague*, wherewith the LORD will smite the heathen that come not up to keep the feast of tabernacles.
>
> This shall be the punishment of Egypt, and the punishment of all nations that come not up to keep the feast of tabernacles.
>
> In that day shall there be upon the bells of the horses, HOLINESS UNTO THE LORD; and the pots in the LORD'S house shall be like the bowls before the altar.
>
> Yea, every pot in Jerusalem and in Judah shall be holiness unto the LORD of hosts: and all they that sacrifice shall come and take of them, and seethe therein: and in that day there shall be no more the Canaanite in the house of the LORD of hosts. (Zech 14:16–21)

In this portrayal of the messianic times, all the nations worship Yahweh, coming to the house of God. Those who do not come to worship suffer judgment by not having rain in their lands. Some are even struck down with a plague. The temple is finally pure from the Canaanites, meaning either the pagan Canaanites who had been forced to serve in

THE FUTURE IS A MIRACLE

the land (Josh 17:13), or similarly impure people who were defiling the house of God. The many commands of Yahweh in the Toah to be separate from wickedness are being fulfilled. Holiness is so widespread it comes to every pot in Judah, the family's dishware pure enough to use in the temple. Holiness shall spread throughout all the land, as the nations of the earth come to worship the King.

> Arise, shine; for thy light is come, and the glory of the LORD is risen upon thee.
>
> For, behold, the darkness shall cover the earth, and gross darkness the people: but the LORD shall arise upon thee, and his glory shall be seen upon thee.
>
> And the Gentiles shall come to thy light, and *kings to the brightness of thy rising*.
>
> Lift up thine eyes round about, and see: *all they gather themselves together*, they come to thee: thy sons shall come from far, and thy daughters shall be nursed at thy side.
>
> Then thou shalt see, and flow together, and thine heart shall fear, and be enlarged; because the abundance of the sea shall be converted unto thee, *the forces of the Gentiles shall come unto thee*.
>
> The multitude of camels shall cover thee, the dromedaries of Midian and Ephah; all they from Sheba shall come: they shall bring gold and incense; and they shall shew forth the praises of the LORD.
>
> All the flocks of Kedar shall be gathered together unto thee, the rams of Nebaioth shall minister unto thee: they shall come up with acceptance on mine altar, and I will glorify the house of my glory.
>
> Who are these that fly as a cloud, and as the doves to their windows?
>
> Surely the isles shall wait for me, and the ships of Tarshish first, to bring thy sons from far, their silver and their gold with them, unto the name of the LORD thy God, and to the Holy One of Israel, because he hath glorified thee.
>
> And the sons of strangers shall build up thy walls, and *their kings shall minister unto thee*: for in my wrath I smote thee, but in my favour have I had mercy on thee.
>
> Therefore thy gates shall be open continually; they shall not be shut day nor night; that men may bring unto thee the forces of the Gentiles, and that their kings may be brought.

> *For the nation and kingdom that will not serve thee shall perish;*
> yea, those nations shall be utterly wasted. (Isa 60:1–12)

In Isa 60, as in other passages, the nations of the world all serve Yahweh, and will be destroyed if they do not. We see in some detail how nations come from afar to bring gifts, bringing great wealth into the kingdom, the economic wealth of entire lands, surely including gifts from kings, ordinary men, and the wealthy. Kings come to worship and to serve Yahweh. What was once a singular and quite small nation of God now extends to a multi-national domain under one God. The bright glory of God pours down upon Israel, which shines for the entire world, as a center of divine worship. This great era is a result of Yahweh's mercy on Israel and the people's repentance from sin.

New Testament Reign

Although the New Testament focuses on salvation in Christ through his sacrifice and resurrection, we clearly see his reign portrayed as well. That includes his defeat of the devil, and rule over the earth. There is no doubt that the Savior is in charge, not just over individual souls, or a religious institution, but over the world.

The Devil Cast Out

> Now is the judgment of this world: *now shall the prince of this world be cast out.* (John 12:31)
>
> And having spoiled principalities and powers, he made a shew of them openly, *triumphing over them* in it. (Col 2:15)

Like other passages in the Gospels and Epistles, these are not ambiguous about Christ's defeat of the devil. Through his death and resurrection Christ cast out the devil, and triumphed over him and all of his powers. No demon on earth can stand up to the Spirit-filled church, nor do any more than temporarily hold back the kingdom. Christ has the authority, and not them. That is why we see the casting out demons in Jesus' name a multitude of times. His name carries real authority, and nothing can stand against it. The demons must leave.

> And I saw an angel come down from heaven, having the key of the bottomless pit and a great chain in his hand.

> And he laid hold on the dragon, that old serpent, which is the Devil, and Satan, and *bound him a thousand years*,
>
> And cast him into the bottomless pit, and shut him up, and set a seal upon him, that he should *deceive the nations no more*, till the thousand years should be fulfilled: (Rev 20:1–3a)

Many Christians try to present Rev 20 as the ultimate evidence that Christ's kingdom is somewhere in the future. However, that is a big assumption, as nothing in the passage demands it is in the future. Read in harmony with New Testament passages teaching that God's kingdom is upon us, and with the historical evidence of the spread of the kingdom, this passage is describing past events, as is the book as a whole. Nothing in the text itself demands it is not already occurring. Revelation 20, along with the reign of the saints with Christ, shows the devil being bound for a thousand years. This binding has a specific purpose—that he can no longer deceive the nations. This kind of binding makes good sense in light of what we see in the church era: Israel is no longer a unique people of God, but men from all nations, tribes, and tongues come into full fellowship with Yahweh, God of Israel. The hold the devil had over those nations is gone, and they are free to be a part of the covenant people. We now have one new people, made up of the believing Jewish disciples of Jesus, and the Gentiles, who came from afar to the light of Messiah. The devil then, is bound already. All are free to come into the kingdom.

All Authority Given to Me

> And Jesus came and spake unto them, saying, *All power is given unto me in heaven and in earth.*
>
> Go ye therefore, and *teach all nations*, baptizing them in the name of the Father, and of the Son, and of the Holy Ghost:
>
> Teaching them to observe all things whatsoever I have commanded you: and, lo, I am with you alway, even unto the end of the world. Amen. (Matt 28:18–20)

There is no real question about who has authority, Jesus or the devil, when Jesus himself teaches that all authority has been given to him. That includes authority on earth, placing him above any ruler or magistrate on the earth. All of those men must serve the Lord. He is King. The church, while not ruling in a political sense as an organization, makes disciples of entire nations, and those nations will serve the Lord. The kingdom expands from the saints to other souls, who will also rule nations. The sons of their faith, whether serving as president or shopkeeper, will be baptized, and will obey the authority of Jesus. He is with us always, as this great expanse occurs.

> Sing, O barren, thou that didst not bear; break forth into singing, and cry aloud, thou that didst not travail with child: for more are the children of the desolate than the children of the married wife, saith the LORD.
>
> Enlarge the place of thy tent, and let them stretch forth the curtains of thine habitations: spare not, lengthen thy cords, and strengthen thy stakes;
>
> For thou shalt break forth on the right hand and on the left; and *thy seed shall inherit the Gentiles*, and make the desolate cities to be inhabited. (Isa 54:1–3)

Following the more famous Suffering Servant passage, Isa 54 jubilantly teaches us more about the results of Messiah's work. I include it in this New Testament section because of how it appears after Isa 53. The nation will expand both to the right and the left, a description that conforms to the Abrahamic promise to bless all the nations, and to have descendants as numerous as the sand of the sea. The barren woman, a spiritually dead people, will be made fruitful with life because of her faith, fulfilling and echoing the many barren Old Testament saints who were miraculously given children. It even suggests an expansion through childbirth itself, including of the miraculous kind. This passage of celebration, and of God's mercy on Israel, like others promises that the children will "inherit the Gentiles" (v. 3), showing rule over all the earth. It cannot be read apart from Ps 2, which promises the same to the Son of God (v. 8a). It points to the renewal and restoration which will pour out through Christ, as uninhabited or destroyed cities are rebuilt, as are other things made new.

> Thou madest him a little lower than the angels; thou crownedst him with glory and honour, and didst set him over the works of thy hands:
>
> *Thou hast put all things in subjection under his feet.* For in that he put all in subjection under him, he left nothing that is not put under him. But now we see not yet all things put under him. (Heb 2:7–8)

Psalm 8 is quoted a number of times in the New Testament. Here Paul uses it to indicate the rulership of Christ, while he is also describing his becoming man, and suffering for our sake. He is fulfilling that dominion which mankind was originally meant to have, since he came as man. Just as the Old Testament teaches, Christ is ruler, but we do not yet witness it fully, seeing only his victory over death at the cross. It is with time that we will more fully see all things being under his feet, like a conquering king, which has been started at his victory over the devil at the cross. This is language of power. Yahweh will put him over all creation, just as he put King David's enemies "under the soles of his feet" (1 Kgs 5:3). This complete submission of all creation to Christ fits in doctrinally with the book's emphatic point that Christ is greater than all that came before. He truly is the promised ruler. Don't let the bloody sacrifice at the cross make you think he doesn't rule.

> And what is the exceeding greatness of his power to us-ward who believe, according to the working of his mighty power,
>
> Which he wrought in Christ, when he raised him from the dead, and set him at his own right hand in the heavenly places,
>
> Far above all principality, and power, and might, and dominion, and every name that is named, not only in this world, but also in that which is to come:
>
> *And hath put all things under his feet, and gave him to be the head over all things to the church,*
>
> Which is his body, the fulness of him that filleth all in all. (Eph 1:19–23)

Ephesians 1 uses similar language, and speaks more specifically of Christ as head over all things "to the church" (v. 22). The church is like his body, through whom he acts and in whom he dwells. It may be only the church which worships him as Savior, but as more people and nations place their trust in Christ, his body will grow, as will the extent of his indwelling. Christ is the one who "filleth all in all" (v. 23). The phrase itself is an interesting one. It could be one of varying ways to just say: everything. It could also more specifically mean he fills everything in everyone, or everyone in all places. It reflects the totality of his indwelling. We see the same phrase used in 1 Cor 12, speaking of the diversity of gifts throughout the church, and in 1 Cor 15, speaking of the Almighty.

This passage also refers to Christ's authority by saying he is seated at God's right hand (v. 20). This is a position of authority next to the Father.

It is an image that would have been immediately recognized in the culture at this time as signifying someone who had power alongside the king. We see this image appear also in Stephen's vision at his death, "Behold, I see the heavens opened, and the Son of man standing on the right hand of God" (Acts 7:56). The position of authority is present, and is not far off. His saints also share in his position in heaven, as Eph 2 teaches, "Even when we were dead in sins, hath quickened us together with Christ, (by grace ye are saved;) And hath raised us up together, and made us sit together in heavenly places in Christ Jesus" (vv. 5–6). His people share secondarily in his rule. His people join with Jesus as a part of him, and even before we die on this earth, we are lifted up. We have a place at his side.

> Then cometh the end, when he shall have delivered up the kingdom to God, even the Father; when he shall have put down all rule and all authority and power.
>
> For *he must reign, till he hath put all enemies under his feet.*
>
> The last enemy that shall be destroyed is death.
>
> For he hath put all things under his feet. But when he saith all things are put under him, it is manifest that he is excepted, which did put all things under him.
>
> And when all things shall be subdued unto him, then shall the Son also himself be subject unto him that put all things under him, that God may be all in all. (1 Cor 15:24–28)

First Corinthians 15, which also presents the simple gospel in its opening, describes the finality of Christ's reign which he brought to us. He will deliver that kingdom to the Father, showing the Father what he has accomplished, bringing the earth to a knowledge of Yahweh and to righteousness. The passage teaches that Christ will rule until he has put all enemies under his feet (v. 25), this phrase which keeps coming up indicating the totality of Christ's rule, and defeat of his enemies. That certainly must involve many battles over time. Enemies must be crushed one after another. The passage even indicates that death in some form will be ended *before* the kingdom is presented to the Father (v. 26). Since Jesus took authority 2,000 years ago, the defeat of his enemies is going on before us now.

THE FUTURE IS A MIRACLE

Revelation

Perhaps no other passage of the New Testament speaks more plainly of Messiah's reign and kingly status than the book of Revelation. Christ is without a doubt conqueror and victor over all. His victory comes before the resurrection and the final judgment. It includes his return as King, and rule over the earth, which Revelation is unique through all the Bible in calling a thousand-year reign.

> And the armies which were in heaven followed him upon white horses, clothed in fine linen, white and clean.
>
> And out of his mouth goeth a sharp sword, that with it he should smite the nations: and he shall rule them with a rod of iron: and he treadeth the winepress of the fierceness and wrath of Almighty God.
>
> And he hath on his vesture and on his thigh a name written, KING OF KINGS, AND LORD OF LORDS. (Rev 19:14–16)

Here Christ returns from heaven. The sword of his mouth is the word of God, and he has real authority, able to punish those disobedient among the nations. He brings with him the wrath of God on all who oppose him, echoing the description in Ps 2. This does not sound at all like a leader who is tolerant of evil, but rather who will destroy it, nor like one who leads by gently pointing to the better way, but rather who commands all to obey. He is a King over all other kings. The King's reign is described in the following chapter:

> And I saw an angel come down from heaven, having the key of the bottomless pit and a great chain in his hand.
>
> And he laid hold on the dragon, that old serpent, which is the Devil, and Satan, and bound him a thousand years,
>
> And cast him into the bottomless pit, and shut him up, and set a seal upon him, that he should deceive the nations no more, till the thousand years should be fulfilled: and after that he must be loosed a little season.
>
> And I saw thrones, and they sat upon them, and judgment was given unto them: and I saw the souls of them that were beheaded for the witness of Jesus, and for the word of God, and which had not worshipped the beast, neither his image, neither had received his mark upon their foreheads, or in their hands; and *they lived and reigned with Christ a thousand years*. (Rev 20:1–4)

The devil is defeated and shut up, for a period of a thousand years. The kingdom of Christ is a thousand years. That number, if we look at how it is used elsewhere in Scripture, likely is not meant to mean the exact length of time. Rather it means the kingdom goes on for a very long time, and its extent is immeasurably great, similar to passages such as Ps 50, "For every beast of the forest is mine, and the cattle upon a thousand hills" (v. 10), or Ps 84, "For a day in thy courts is better than a thousand" (v. 10a). The main characteristic of binding the devil is that he may not deceive the nations anymore. This does not signify that he may not tempt any to sin, but rather that he cannot blind the nations to the one true God and the Messiah anymore. We now have a family of God that extends throughout the world, and not one centered on the Hebrew people.

We also see not only Christ reigning over the earth for a thousand years, but we see the saints reigning with Christ. They sit upon thrones from which they can do judgment. Later in the same passage, there are also those martyrs whose souls are raised to life, called the "first resurrection" (Rev 20:5), who reign with Christ for the thousand years. The mention of a first resurrection, separate from a second resurrection, does not appear anywhere else in Scripture, and there is fair debate as to its meaning. The reference to the martyred saints may be speaking of a spiritual reign, since their souls are in heaven having been raised, or it may be speaking symbolically of those who have suffered for Christ being restored to rule civilly. Either way, this passage puts the emphasis on the saints holding power, and not as much on Christ, though they reign with him.

Jesus Christ brought about, through his work for us on earth, the defeat of the devil, and the kingdom of God. While the book speaks a great deal in allegorical language, as does other prophecy, Revelation details real events in history, mostly what has already occurred: the coming of the promised Child, the persecution of the church, the evil leaders who dominated the world at the time and sought to destroy the saints, the destruction of those false rulers, and the establishment of the rule of Christ and his holy ones. It leaves only the final chapters for the future, the resurrection of the dead, the final judgment, and a world taken wholly beyond sin and death. Yet we are living in what Christ told us plainly he was bringing about, and we are spreading that throughout the world—that is that germ, or seed, of the kingdom, which grows to such great extent, it is thousands of times grander than when begun, and the mighty birds of the air find rest in its branches. Kings will bow down before him, and nations become his followers. We have seen this come to pass, and we will see much more to come.

Now Means Now

As I mentioned before, Jesus speaks of his kingdom as coming soon to pass. This is unavoidable. He and John both use imminent language, such as "at hand," when introducing the kingdom. Similar and same language is used to speak of the coming judgment on Israel, Christ's return, and the whole series of events that will lead to an eternity without evil or death. Let's quickly look more broadly at the imminent language, and see how normal it is to understand it to mean an event which is very near in the future.

At hand:

> And as ye go, preach, saying, *The kingdom of heaven is at hand.* (Matt 10:7)
>
> Now after that John was put in prison, Jesus came into Galilee, preaching the gospel of the kingdom of God,
>
> And saying, The time is fulfilled, and *the kingdom of God is at hand*: repent ye, and believe the gospel. (Mark 1:14-15)
>
> But *the end of all things is at hand*: be ye therefore sober, and watch unto prayer. (1 Pet 4:7)
>
> Blessed is he that readeth, and they that hear the words of this prophecy, and keep those things which are written therein: for *the time is at hand.* (Rev 1:3)
>
> And he saith unto me, Seal not the sayings of the prophecy of this book: for *the time is at hand.* (Rev 22:10)

Shortly:

> The Revelation of Jesus Christ, which God gave unto him, to shew unto his servants things which must *shortly come to pass* (Rev 1:1a)

And he said unto me, These sayings are faithful and true: and the Lord God of the holy prophets sent his angel to shew unto his servants the things which must *shortly be done*. (Rev 22:6)

And the God of peace *shall bruise Satan under your feet shortly*. The grace of our Lord Jesus Christ be with you. Amen. (Rom 16:20)

This Generation:

Verily I say unto you, All these things shall come upon *this generation*. (Matt 23:36)

Verily I say unto you, *This generation* shall not pass, till all these things be fulfilled. (Matt 24:34)

Verily I say unto you, that *this generation* shall not pass, till all these things be done. (Mark 13:30)

Not Taste Death:

But I tell you of a truth, there be some standing here, which *shall not taste of death*, till they see the kingdom of God. (Luke 9:27)

And he said unto them, Verily I say unto you, That there be some of them that stand here, which *shall not taste of death*, till they have seen the kingdom of God come with power. (Mark 9:1)

While doubters will try and find ways around these passages of immanence, if taken according to the normal meaning of the Greek words, there's really no doubt that Jesus and the apostles here were speaking of events occurring in their own time, or within a biblical generation. Words like "at hand" and "shortly," really mean the same thing they mean in our language: a soon-to-come event, even one which is already beginning to occur. "Shortly" means in haste, with quickness, or near. Someone could speak to us today with the same terminology, and we'd know exactly what they meant.

Likewise, "this generation" doesn't mean anything different in Greek. "This" is a near demonstrative, just like our word, and "generation" typically refers to people living at the same time period, with lifespans according to Scripture being seventy to eighty years (Ps 90:10). A man of twenty hearing Jesus speak could easily expect to be around in AD 70–80. A man of thirty had a very good chance as well. In fact, every usage of the phrase "this generation" in the New Testament is without dispute speaking of the generation of people present at the time of its writing. There is no reason we should take this usage as meaning anything different from the others. It would be purely arbitrary to claim its meaning has suddenly changed. When an author wants to speak of a far-off generation, such as in Hebrews 3:10, he says, "*that* generation." I recommend anyone who doubts that "this generation" means anything different from what it means in English to go to the concordance and read every New Testament usage. You will see how strong the biblical evidence is for the ordinary reading of the phrase.

We further see that the kingdom would come in soon when Jesus goes so far as to say there are those standing and hearing him preach who will "not taste death" until they see the kingdom of God come in power (Luke 9:27, Mark 9:1, Matt 16:28). The same passage from Matthew includes that they will see "the Son of Man coming in his kingdom." These were Israelites and others who heard Jesus preach in the first century. They were standing in the land of Israel. They were not of your and my generation. They were not wearing blue jeans, and t-shirts, and sunglasses. It is *they* who would not taste death until these events occurred. That is phenomenal, and does not allow us to imagine we've got to wait for Jesus centuries later to keep his word. The fact he says these words to those standing and hearing him speak further assures us that we make no mistake when we take "this generation" to mean the people at that time.

Those who try to avoid this teaching will often claim that his words about the kingdom only refer to his transfiguration, which comes immediately afterward in the gospel narratives (Luke 9:28–36, Mark 9:2–9, Matt 17:1–9), and was approximately one week later. I don't think many people would choose to understand "the kingdom of God come with power" that way unless they were trying to get out of a passage they found difficult. There is nothing in the text which would say that, and logic does not demand it, despite the general sequence of events. It is quite a leap of logic. Moreover, the transfiguration, in which Jesus revealed a level of his divinity, does not resemble other teachings in all of Scripture about the kingdom. Whether we speak of the Old Testament prophesies, Jesus' parables, or Revelation, a glowing light from heaven does not really resemble the kingdom. For that reason, I find this to be reading into Scripture quite a bit. Nor does it qualify as the Son of Man coming, since Jesus had already come in his incarnation, and was only revealing more of his nature briefly. He describes his coming in judgment in Matt 24, and it does not resemble a light from heaven a week later.

Now there *is* a grain of truth there, in that heaven is the source of the kingdom, and Christ is the source. From this flows everything. However, it is clear in numerous teachings that this is not a mere spiritual kingdom, nor a distant one. It is here with us. It is among us. It is practical. It is found in human righteousness. It is found in justice. It will grow over all the real physical earth. It will tread down the enemies. A vision of heaven is not the kingdom coming in power, nor is it Christ coming in power. Christ was speaking of what was still further off, but within that generation. That's why he speaks in general language about the time frame, limiting it to some of those hearing him preach, but perhaps not all, since some will have died. It's not a week later, as the transfiguration was. It is nearly certain that none of his audience had tasted death in that week, making the comment superfluous if he only spoke of the transfiguration. The entire scenario alongside Jesus' words fit with a coming that came when only a portion of the hearers were alive.

What that means to some Christians is absolutely shocking: Jesus and the apostles really meant it when they said the kingdom was coming in at their time. They weren't speaking to a people in a future millennium. They were speaking to the people of their day about the situation of their day. The beast spoken of was a well-known pagan ruler, and the anti-Christs false spiritual teachers of that day. Jesus really returned as he promised, poured out judgment on Jerusalem, and is reigning with his saints. Earthly powers, no matter how formidable or deadly, really have no power against the powers of heaven, and their rebellion will be struck down. The earth, as a whole, really will be subdued to the rule of Christ and the worship of him. All enemies of God and of righteousness will be crushed under the feet of Christ, and finally death will be put away in at least some of its forms. We are living within a growing kingdom of peace, joy, righteousness, and the worship of God. Right now.

An Everlasting Light

> And hath put all things under his feet, and gave him to be the head over all things to the church, (Eph 1:22)

THE FUTURE IS A MIRACLE

> But to which of the angels said he at any time, Sit on my right hand, until I make thine enemies thy footstool? (Heb 1:13)
>
> And the LORD shall be king over all the earth: in that day shall there be one LORD, and his name one. (Zech 14:9)

The Bible speaks forcefully about a great darkness being lifted. It speaks of a light dawning, and peoples all over the earth coming to that light. It says that God's people will be righteous. It says God's kingdom will come, and it will never end. Yet many Christians, while believing other doctrines of the Bible, cannot believe these words too, except as a far-off reality, or a mere spiritual truth. One of the main objections they have, one shared by atheist critics of the Bible, is that these things just did not come to pass. In the minds of Christians, that means that the words have to mean something else, and these events must not have been at hand after all.

I believe that a short review of the language, as well as a review of human history, both shoot down this dark doubt about the Bible. We have already looked at much of the language. Let's look at history, and see if these things really are coming to pass. If they are, there's no reason to expect they all occurred in one moment. We can see them occur over time, often in grand triumphant ways, often in slow, incremental ways. Peace, worship of God, righteousness, and long life are appearing from heaven on this earth, and they are growing.

I want to say first, that as a new believer, with only a pocket New Testament in my hand, one of the first things that struck me is that the civilization which embraced the gospel, and received Christ, is also the one that had been blessed with the ability to have advanced technology, heal previously unstoppable illnesses, and greatly lengthen lifespan. That civilization is western Christian civilization in Europe, and it has spread its blessings throughout the globe now, not only in sharing technology and medicine, but in spreading the learning tools so that everyone can use, develop, and increase their knowledge to help human life. It has been an incredible outpouring of life, and that fact struck me immediately. The Son of Man spoke of having life in abundance, and the nations which received him also received an earthly sign of that abundant life in being able to increase their life and their health here on earth. Just as Jesus' physical healings were a sign of who he is and what he does, it seems our life-sustaining technologies that started in the Christian world do much the same. That picture of heaven was appearing on earth, even if much still lies in the future, even though all fully relies on Christ. We live today, largely because of the Christian West, in so much comfort, health, and free of deadly dangers that previous people would regard it as supernatural. They would regard us as wealthy, even if we don't see ourselves that way. Even in looking back on history it seems a miracle occurred. Many technologies we use daily we could call without hesitation a miracle. We have been cleaned of much of the filth of the earth, and of its pains. We have made it more beautiful, peaceful, and long lasting for our King.

Before we look at the incredible increase in righteousness and life, let's look at the fulfillment of the judgment and persecutions predicted in the New Testament. I don't believe anyone contests that the judgment on Jerusalem was fulfilled. Within forty years of Christ's ascension, Roman armies sieged Jerusalem, and then destroyed the temple, leaving not one stone standing, as Jesus predicted. Early Christians took his teaching as referring to their own time, not a distant one, as they followed his instructions, hiding out in the hills to survive the slaughter (Matt 24:16). They knew Messiah spoke to them and the events of their day, as he bid them pray not to have to flee on the Sabbath or in winter (v. 20). Several ancient historians attest to this flight. Adam Clarke summarizes both Eusebius and Epiphanius saying:

> "It is very remarkable that not a single
> Christian perished in the destruction of Jerusalem,
> though there were many there when Cestius Gallus
> invested the city; and, had he persevered in the siege,
> he would soon have rendered himself master of it; but,
> when he unexpectedly and unaccountably raised the
> siege, the Christians took that opportunity to escape . . .
> [As] Vespasian was approaching with his
> army, all who believed in Christ left Jerusalem and fled
> to Pella, and other places beyond the river Jordan; and
> so they all marvellously escaped the general shipwreck
> of their country: not one of them perished."[2]

In contrast, well over a million Jewish unbelievers were slaughtered, and sold into slavery during the Roman destruction of their nation.

---

2. Clarke, *Adam Clarke's Commentary*, 818. Clarke also makes note of this in his section on Rev 7 in the same book. One short quote from church historian Eusebius can be found in his *Ecclesiastical History*, book 3, chapter 5.

During Passover, the same time that they had crucified the Messiah, over half a million visitors were trapped in Jerusalem, awaiting their own destruction.[3] Temple Judaism ended in bloody smoking ruins. A second revolt in the next century, led by the false messiah Bar Kochba, resulted further in millions of Jews either being killed or enslaved, and the banning of all Jews from the land promised to Abraham.[4] Until the very modern era, in the twentieth century, the Jew apart from Messiah has been in exile, living under the boot of other rulers.

The time preceding the temple's destruction, was filled with signs and the supernatural, just as we would expect. According to Jewish oral tradition, much of which was to be written down as the Talmud, the forty years preceding the destruction of the temple were strange indeed: The signs that the scapegoat sacrifice on Yom Kippur had pleased God were no longer functioning. The massive doors of the temple would swing open on their own (an event like this is also mentioned by Josephus). One of the lamps in the temple, considered the most important, went out every night for forty years. The lot used to choose the goat for the sacrifice on Yom Kippur always came up in the left hand.[5] It seemed as if God revealed to Israel that the sacrifices now meant nothing since Christ had shed his blood, and that the end of the old system was upon them. As if these signs were not enough, it is recorded that a face like an angel appeared above the holy of holies.

According to other histories, in the period leading up to the siege of Jerusalem, a great light shaped like a sword hung over the city. A sword shape, in its basic form, with the handle on top and the blade pointing down, is only the shape of a cross. According to the Hebrew book of Yosippon, the first thorough history of Israel since Josephus, "For one year before Vespasian came, a single *great star shining like unsheathed swords* was seen over the Temple. And in those days when the sign was seen it was the holiday of Passover and during that entire night the Temple was lit up and illuminated like the light of day, and thus it was all seven days of the Passover." The book also records a miracle over the most holy place in the temple, saying, "Now it happened after this that there was seen from above over the Holy of Holies for the whole night *the outline of a man's face, the like of whose beauty had never been seen* in all the land, and his appearance was quite awesome." Great armies were witnessed in

3. Bible History, "The Destruction of Jerusalem."
4. Kerstein, "The Bar-Kochba Revolt."
5. Federoff and Peterson, "Talmudic Evidence."

the skies, replete with armed soldiers and chariots, like a heavenly army showing who is really in charge of the coming destruction. Christian historian Eusebius, citing Josephus says, "For before the setting of the sun *chariots and armed troops were seen . . . in mid-air*, wheeling through the clouds and encircling the cities." Tacitus likewise records, "There had been seen *hosts joining battle in the skies*, the fiery gleam of arms, the temple illuminated by a sudden radiance from the clouds."[6] These wondrous signs, some of which are recorded in multiple sources, come from Jewish, Roman, and Christian records, often written with amazement by the author.

One interesting section in Josephus describes the Roman catapults throwing rocks into the walled city. Even these stones carry a sign of the meaning of the city's destruction. He writes, "As for the Jews, they at first watched the coming of the stone, for it was of a white color and could therefore not only be perceived by the great noise it made, but could be seen also before it came by its brightness. Accordingly when the watchmen that sat upon the towers gave them notice when the engine was let go and the stone came from it, they *cried out aloud in their own country language (Aramaic), 'The son cometh.'*"[7] Every time the great stones came down from high up in the air, the watchmen would cry in warning, "the son is coming!" This was indeed the coming of the Son of Man just as he promised. The watchmen in Jerusalem, unwittingly I believe, were indeed acting as the watchmen of God, proclaiming the coming of Christ from heaven. It was the Son of God who wielded the pagan ruler Vespatian and the pagan general Titus, and destroyed the faithless city.

Apostle John's description of the beast also fits into the pagan rulers of that time. The term itself, as well as the number of the beast (Rev 13:1–2, 18), point convincingly to Emperor Nero. He had earned himself the name "beast" because of his compulsion towards senseless violence, and he lived up to that name, not only slaughtering Christians in large number, but also torturing and murdering men and women for his own personal enjoyment. He even had his own mother killed. Roman historian Suetonius writes, "He showed neither discrimination nor moderation

---

6. David, "Historical Records."

7. Josephus, *Wars of the Jews*, 5.6.3. There are several translations which refuse to write the word as "son," but write it instead as "stone," assuming a mistake was made between the two Hebrew words. However, "son" is how it reads in the ancient Greek text. The source I cite here is an interlinear of the text, so you can see the Greek itself.

in putting to death whomsoever he pleased on any pretext whatever."[8] Nero led one of the largest ancient persecutions of Christians in the Roman Empire. Apostles Paul and Peter were likely martyred late in his reign. Appolonius of Tyanna, a first century philosopher and ascetic, wrote of Nero, "In my travels, which have been wider than ever man yet accomplished, I have seen many, many wild beasts of Arabia and India; *but this beast, that is commonly called a Tyrant, I know not how many heads it has*, nor if it be crooked of claw, and armed with horrible fangs . . . And of wild beasts you cannot say that they were ever known to eat their own mothers, but Nero has gorged himself on this diet."[9]

The number of the beast found in Revelation, which is 666, also matches the numerical value of his name according to Hebrew numerology of *Caesar Neron*. The variant number found in a handful of texts, 616, matches the numerology according to an alternate spelling without the n, or Hebrew *nun* at the end of Nero.[10] The period of forty-two months in which the beast spoke blasphemies and waged war with the saints (Rev 13:5), matches the main period of Nero's persecution of the saints, which started after the great fire of Rome in AD 64, and ended with his death in AD 68. The seven kings spoken of in Rev 17, match the seven Caesars very well. The sixth king reigning as Apostle John writes is Nero (v. 10). The seventh, who would rule only a short time, is his successor Galba,[11] who was assassinated less than a year after becoming Caesar.

You would be hard pressed to find any pagan king of that era and location who matches the number given in Revelation, and the fact he would lead a great persecution of the saints. The fact that Nero matches on other points, including being called "a beast," the length of his persecution, and the succession of seven Caesars, leaves little doubt this is specifically the beast of whom the apostle speaks. That is why John begins and ends the book noting that these are things which must shortly take place (Rev 1:1, 22:6).

---

8. Suetonius, *Nero*, 58, 37.
9. Philostratus, *Life of Apollonius*, 4:38.
10. Gentry, *The Beast of Revelation*, 33–35.
11. Gill, "A Look at the Lives." This is counting with Julius as the first Caesar, as some ancient sources do, while others list Augustus as the first. Julius Caesar did not hold the formal title of Caesar or Emperor, but he had made himself dictator at the time he was assassinated.

RIGHTEOUSNESS OF THE KINGDOM

> And I will betroth thee unto me for ever; yea, *I will betroth thee unto me in righteousness, and in judgment*, and in lovingkindness, and in mercies.
>
> I will even betroth thee unto me in faithfulness: and thou shalt know the LORD.
>
> And it shall come to pass in that day, I will hear, saith the LORD, I will hear the heavens, and they shall hear the earth;
>
> And the earth shall hear the corn, and the wine, and the oil; and they shall hear Jezreel.
>
> And I will sow her unto me in the earth; and I will have mercy upon her that had not obtained mercy; and I will say to them which were not my people, *Thou art my people*; and they shall say, Thou art my God. (Hos 2:19–23)
>
> For I the LORD love judgment, I hate robbery for burnt offering; and *I will direct their work in truth*, and I will make an everlasting covenant with them.
>
> And their seed shall be known among the Gentiles, and their offspring among the people: all that see them shall acknowledge them, that they are the seed which the LORD hath blessed.
>
> I will greatly rejoice in the LORD, my soul shall be joyful in my God; for he hath clothed me with the garments of salvation, *he hath covered me with the robe of righteousness*, as a bridegroom decketh himself with ornaments, and as a bride adorneth herself with her jewels.
>
> For as the earth bringeth forth her bud, and as the garden causeth the things that are sown in it to spring forth; so *the Lord GOD will cause righteousness and praise to spring forth before all the nations*. (Isa 61:8–11)

What the suicide hopes to eliminate by slaughtering a human being, God more successfully eliminates by changing human life through his Son. God's act on the individual, and God's act on history, bring peace to the soul even before the believer goes to heaven when he dies. That peace is a great sign of his eternal salvation, and a sign he is reigning right now, just as he said he was, over all things in heaven and on earth. What the agonized man seeks to do by blowing his head off, throwing himself off a tall building, with drinking poison, with gassing himself in his car, with a razor blade, a knife, a rope, through drug overdoses, through the long slow dying of drug use, Christ does when he takes us to the grave, and raises us up again. He obliterates that world of sin and suffering. He squeezes the poison out of our veins. He purifies our heart from its guilt. He fills our head with knowledge. He cuts out the old, and places within us the new. He more successfully allows us to die than our own physical death would do, and brings us where there is grace, hope, and love.

There are many effects that being born new has on the individual, but since we are speaking of Christ's kingdom, which is over all the earth, let's look at its historical and global power. This is something one can begin to witness early in the Christian era, when we are looking only at the small seed of believers, and continue to see all the way to the present, as its blessings are instilled in entire nations, people groups, and empires. Even the modern atheist and the pagan has inherited some of the blessings of the kingdom, and live according to some of its ways. Much more conquest is to follow. It cannot be stopped.

At the time prophesied by Daniel over four centuries earlier (Dan 9:24–27), Christ was the power of God coming down on earth. Yahweh came in power in Christ's incarnation, death, and resurrection. He came before the temple was destroyed, and he came to put away sin, to seal up prophecy, just as Daniel wrote. Christ was a light both to Israel, and then the nations of the earth, as prophesied by Isaiah (Isa 49:6). If all this is true, we should expect to see the power of God's kingdom at work in human history from that point onward, and in no mild and minor way, but drastically and earth changing in its scope. The effects of this fulfillment should be clearly visible. We should see that new reality at work.

The kingdom of God indeed began with his coming, as Christ's words indicated. One of the first visible building stones beyond the individual was the great respect for human dignity which spread beyond any borders. This is first witnessed in the preaching and life of the church, and then as it spreads throughout the globe, instilled in laws, and in the hearts of national leaders. It is the image of God in man revealed in divine revelation, and brought to its fullness in God becoming man and living as a servant. The kingdom is at once a healed humanity, a religious community, and a presence in human governments. I have never heard anyone refute this fact: the Christian faith has healed more sick, clothed more naked, fed more hungry, taught more uneducated, and helped more oppressed human souls than any religion or belief system on earth. That's only speaking of churches and ministries themselves. This awesome life-healing blessing also includes governments and other institutions which have been shaped by Christ, and being so accomplish the same loving goals.

The early church, from the earliest documented era, prohibited both abortion and infanticide.[12] Neither Roman law nor religion prevented the murder of infants and very young children, and it was normal to leave them out to die. Roman orator and politician Cicero even wrote, "deformed infants shall be killed," while the philosopher Seneca wrote, "unnatural progeny we destroy; we drown even children at birth who are weakly and abnormal."[13] What would have been common for the pagan of the multi-cultural Roman Empire, was wrong for the Christian. His leaders taught him this in authoritative, dogmatic fashion. I know there are many that will claim it's wonderful they stopped killing newborn children, and not so wonderful they prohibited abortion; but those who would say this need to recognize how very small the difference is. The difference between throwing a child over a cliff upon the rocks and having an abortion are a brief moment in time, and a thin layer of flesh of a mother's belly. Perhaps that similarity is why many pagan cultures accepted both abortion and infanticide, and why today, in a less-than Christian West, secular intellectuals are endorsing infanticide[14] and states are proposing laws that would decriminalize it.[15] The unborn child and the newborn child are factually not far apart at all, but it is the Christian faith that recognizes, as a dogma, that human life has value from its point of genesis. It does not lose its value just because it's small. That high respect for human dignity, and also for science, protects the unborn baby just as it protects the newborn one. It reflects the grander human dignity that the faith recognizes in us all. If you like the fact that Christians saved small children from murder, you ought to like the entire respect for human dignity dwelling within the faith. Countless children were saved, and are currently saved, because of that one act of God's power in human history, through Christ, and through men who follow him.

Christians did not merely live their lives without abandoning children to die, but they actively went out and picked up the children that

---

12. Brown, "What the Early Church."
13. Early Church History, "Infanticide."
14. Cimmino, "University of Chicago Professor."
15. Unruh, "Lawmakers in 3d state." The secular left would deny such laws allow infanticide, but I find those objections disingenuous. They prevent investigation of infant deaths after birth, and similar laws allow newly born infants to die of their injuries. As of 2022, nearly half of U.S. states allow babies who survive abortions to be left to die.

pagans left to die, adopting them as their own. Some who had the means would educate them. According to Augustine in his *Epistle to Boniface*, "Again, sometimes foundlings which heartless parents have exposed in order to their being cared for by any passer-by, are picked up by holy virgins, and are presented for baptism by these persons, who neither have nor desire to have children of their own."[16] The *Abt-Garrison History of Pediatrics* describes the decisions by the early Christian Council of Nicaea, and other later councils, to aid abandoned children, along with other poor and vagrants, reporting:

> "The Council of Nicaea (325 A.D.) decreed that, in each Christian village, a *xenodochion*, or hostelry for the sick, poor and vagrant, should be established. Some of these *xenodochia* became *brephotrophia* or asylums for children. The Council of Vaison (442) provided that an abandoned child should find sanctuary in a church . . . This was confirmed by the Councils of Arles (452) and Agde (505), and mothers, who were driven to abandon their new-born offspring through shame or poverty, now left them in the marble receptacle at the church door. This privilege was freely granted at the Council of Rouen. The Council of Constantinople (588) compared the crime of infanticide to that of homicide."[17]

Christian protection of abandoned children continued beyond the Roman era, as the practice of abandonment was also found among invading barbarians whose children would come to have a safe haven in Christian communities. Beyond being protected from death, and having basic needs provided, such children regularly received education from monasteries and convents, as well as from some of the wealthy.

This proactive manner of saving life has always been characteristic of the Christian faith, and the western civilization it made its home in. The Christian does not merely avoid doing evil, but actively works for the good of humanity, and seeks to protect and preserve human life. When Christians became emperors of the formerly pagan empire, they passed laws protecting abandoned children, and some subsidized adoption, helping their fellow brothers in Christ along in their pursuit of exalting Christ, and respecting humanity.[18] I suppose saving children from death

---

16. Augustine, *Letter 98*, 6, 902.

17. Abt, *History of Pediatrics*, 57.

18. Tate, "Christianity and the Legal Status," 124–141; Di Berardino et al., *Encyclopedia of Ancient Christianity*, 499.

might frustrate those who believe we've too many of them on the planet, but to God's heart, saving their lives is good, and to the hearts of countless children saved, it is good as well. We take this respect for human dignity for granted often in the West, since it was Christian for so long, but it didn't appear at random, and most of it did not come from the pagan world. It came uniquely from the Christian world, as God's promised kingdom worked its way through the many peoples of the earth. It's not just something we're all born with.

Another immediate, and large-scale act of conquest by God's kingdom was the ending of the gladiator games. The games held for entertainment in the colosseums featured to-the-death battles of warriors, of prisoners, and the brutal killing of prisoners by various wild animals. It was a regular, normal form of entertainment, just like fictional killing is for people today. Some of its warriors became famous, and had abundant fans. Others were no-name people who were simply suffering an execution by another name. Christians at times were killed in the colosseums, as well as criminals and political prisoners. What was entertaining to the pagan world, was darkness to the Christian kingdom. The final ending of the murderous games came through an eastern monk named Telemachus in AD 404, in a rather amazing story. According to church historian Theodoret, "After gazing upon the combat from the amphitheater, he descended into the arena, and tried to separate the gladiators. The sanguinary spectators, possessed by the demon who delights in the effusion of blood, were irritated at the interruption of their cruel sports, and stoned him who had occasioned the cessation." The Christian emperor Honorius soon heard about the killing of this monk, and according to Theodoret, "After being apprised of this circumstance, the admirable emperor numbered him with the victorious martyrs, and abolished these iniquitous spectacles."[19] It was not the first time Christians had attempted to end the colosseum's deadly entertainment, but it was the event which ended them for good. It left the games merely as a remembrance of pre-Christian darkness.

The Christian knew the gladiator games were wrong, without needing to look up the commandment which teaches you shall not murder. Both the killing of innocents, and the use of cruel deaths as entertainment, were an affront to God. The Christian had an entirely different view of God's will, and of human dignity than had come before, or

---

19. Theodoret, *Ecclesiastical History*, 5, 26.

elsewhere among civilizations of the world. The Christian influence on the empire, once Christianity was accepted by its leaders, and by much of its population, put a final end to the gladiator games. They wiped them out of history, showing God's power and presence came in with Christ, and it is not something we are waiting around for, you and me. Christ acted here through his body, the church. He is reigning and defeating his enemies. God is putting them under his feet.

Giving to the poor and aiding the suffering entered the world of the Roman Empire in abundance through God's people. These things are obligations for the Christian. To the pagan, they were more likely to be obligations only to those close to you; not to anyone in the world, and not to your enemies. Some pagan thought viewed giving to the needy to be a sign of weakness, and to be avoided. Through God's kingdom, these became hallmarks of western civilization, ones which continue to the present year. The pagan emperor Julian, who sought to restore worship of the Greek gods after the empire had gone Christian, complained that Christians were drawing people away from their gods, saying:

> "Why do we not observe that it is their [the Christians'] benevolence to strangers, their care for the graves of the dead, and the pretended holiness of their lives that have done most to increase atheism [unbelief of the pagan gods]? . . . For it is disgraceful that, when no Jew ever has to beg, and *the impious Galileans [Christians] support not only their own poor but ours as well, all men see that our people lack aid from us.* Teach those of the Hellenic faith to contribute to public service of this sort."[20]

Notice Julian, after complaining about the Christians, encourages men of his faith to do the same thing. This appears to be not because he recognizes it is good, but because he doesn't want to lose more members to the Christians.

When pagans gave to the poor in that culture, it was often to increase their stature, or to gather people under themselves. Julian, had he reigned longer, would have simply had a government system of giving under him, and likely used it to increase his power, as socialistic governments today do. According to Amundsen and Ferngren in *Beneficience and Health Care*:

> "Such benefactions were not made out of disinterested 'love of mankind' but rather *out of a desire for personal recognition,*

---

20. Julian, "Fragment of a Letter," 69, 71.

which the Greeks and Romans regarded as the natural motive for giving. The impulse for giving was not pity: "broadly speaking, *pity for the poor had little place in the normal Greek character*, and consequently for the poor, as such, no provision usually existed ... there was nothing corresponding to our mass or privately organised charities and hospitals."[21]

In contrast, Christian belief places the primary emphasis on private giving. It is not to increase anyone's stature, except that of Christ the Savior. It does not win servants for the wealthy, or dependents for the government. There may be the occasionally wealthy public giver, but giving from a biblical and a Christian perspective has generally been to help humanity, because humanity has worth, and to witness to the goodness of the Savior.

James Kennedy and Jerry Newcombe record in *What if Jesus Had Never Been Born?*:

> The world before Christianity was like the Russian tundra—quite cold and inhospitable. One scholar, Dr. Martineau, exhaustively searched through historical documents and concluded that antiquity has left no trace of any organized charitable effort. Disinterested benevolence was unknown. When Christ and the Bible became known, charity and benevolence flourished.
>
> Will Durant writes about ancient Rome, which was the zenith of civilizations in antiquity: "Charity found little scope in this frugal life. Hospitality survived as a mutual convenience at a time when inns were poor and far between; but the sympathetic Polybius reports that 'in Rome no one ever gives away anything to anyone if he can help it'—doubtless an exaggeration."[22]

Souls grow up in our culture today assuming everyone just knows to behave with charity, but apparently souls do not just know to behave this way, as it was not present in the pagan culture beforehand, and was also much more limited in other non-Christian civilizations. Even leaders of eastern religions will acknowledge Christianity has a much more active approach to helping the suffering than they do,[23] and of course Hinduism, practiced by over a billion people, teaches that a low station in life and poverty are a part of your journey through reincarnations. You should not try to lift people up, for fear of robbing them of their spiritual growth.[24]

---

21. Amundsen and Ferngren, *Beneficence and Health Care*, 6.
22. Kennedy and Newcombe, *What If*, 29.
23. Vecsey, "Dalai Lama."
24. Staff Reports, "Poverty."

Many monks of eastern religions are beggars themselves, unable to give to the poor nearly the aid, protection, and education that Christians do because of their belief. Both the Muslim, and the modern humanist have borrowed straight from the Christian faith their mandate to help the poor, or relieve those suffering from a disaster. The vast injection into culture and into history of supporting the poor, one which is now imitated by even non-Christian cultures, came through Christ and his people, because Jesus really did what he said he would do. He really is ruling right now, over all things.

It was through Christianity that the Bible, the divine revelation of God, was brought to the entire world. It began through the time-consuming work of scribes, who copied thousands of New Testament books which went across the Mediterranean world, to the era of the printing press and mass production, bringing over the millennia between five and seven billion copies of God's word across the globe.[25] While it is the supernatural life of Christ that saves men from death, it has been the supernatural revealing of the Bible's pages which pointed countless men to Christ. When people do not have the opportunity to have the book in their hands, its truths are available through radio, television, recording devices, and now the internet. Early Judaism was more proselytizing than it is today, but even in that early era rarely reached souls in large numbers, or entire people groups. Modern Judaism does not expand rapidly either, despite its access to the same tools Christians have. It was through the church that virtually every nation, tribe, language-speaker on earth received God's word, came to worship the one true God, learned the commandments of God, and entered into a unity with God's people; the same people who dwelled in tents in Canaan, who left Egypt, who crossed the Jordan to enter Israel, who remained faithful through centuries of idol-worshipping kings and countrymen, who joined with Christ before the destruction of the Second Temple, and who are with us today dwelling in every nation. What was impossible through the old people of God, became possible with the new, and clearly fulfills the prophecy of the knowledge of God going out through all of the nations (Isa 11:9). This is why Abraham was to be a blessing to all the nations. This is why his seed would be so many, as many as the sand of the sea in multitude (Gen 22:17–18). God's real acts in history, God's supernatural power in history, and God's present kingdom are what brought it about.

25. Klein, "The Shocking Truth."

In bringing the worship of the one God, and the commandments of God, the church also put an end to idolatry and witchcraft. Entire nations who formerly worshipped many gods, or who worshipped spirits, or the forces of nature, now bowed down to the King of the universe. Certain portions of Christendom allowed some of it to hang on, but it did so in much smaller numbers, and it was never allowed to have the power again. The early Christian emperors ruled over Christians and pagans alike, with most pagans converting to the Christian faith through missionary efforts, or eventually being pressured by laws to abandon their idolatry.[26] Witchcraft, which God prohibits and punishes with capital punishment, was in part replaced by prayer and divine miracles, as well as by science. At times it became a shameful practice, and kept under the cover of darkness, at times prosecuted as a crime, and at others not. Temple prostitution disappeared, as did human sacrifice, where it had existed. As Thomas Cahill writes of the European Celts:

> "They sacrificed prisoners of war to the war gods and newborns to the harvest gods. Believing that the human head was the seat of the soul, they displayed proudly the heads of their enemies in their temples and on their palisades; they even hung them from their belts as ornaments, used them as footballs in victory celebrations, and were fond of employing skull tops as ceremonial drinking bowls."[27]

It was into this culture that Christian saint Patrick brought the light which had arisen in Galilee, and such demonic practices were no more because of Christ. The minds which were blinded by the devil were allowed to see the glorious light of the gospel of Christ (2 Cor 4:4). Into similar cultures in Europe, Africa, and the Americas, Christian men, not all of them missionaries, confronted such evil and vanquished it. The worship of the one true God is fundamentally different than the worship of the gods of the world. Now, instead of turning to the powers of demons, as the Bible calls the gods of the nations, men turned to the power of God, who is light, and who brings all the blessings of life to us. Men left the religion which enslaves man, to the religion which frees him.

In one of the greatest events in human history, Christian settlers, conquerors, and missionaries who opened up the Americas for Christ ended some of the most large-scale violent, and sadistic human societies

---

26. Little, "5 Ways Christianity Spread."
27. Cahill, *How the Irish Saved Civilization*, 136.

on the earth. Pagan societies which sacrificed men and children to their gods were eradicated, nearly overnight. Priests who sliced the skins off of their victims, then wore the disembodied skins for religious purposes[28] were replaced with priests who offered up the body and blood of Christ. North American tribes for whom the massacre of enemies was the norm, and by whom the cruelest torture was inflicted on nearly every prisoner they took, were provided a new and more humane existence, in which brutal death and cruelty were very far from the norm. People who lived brutally came with time to live peacefully. It's not the least a bad thing those societies were subjugated by Christians from Europe, in part by using violence. It is a truly great thing which ought to make us praise God.

When Pizarro came to the Inca empire, he stood before the Inca king and his forces of tens of thousands of soldiers, with under two hundred men himself, a few dozen on horseback. In his own letters, he wrote, "Fear lies on the men like a black blanket, everyone can now see the madness of this enterprise, all know only a miracle can save us, and we doubted Heaven thought us worthy of a miracle." The Incan king and several thousand of his men came to the Spanish camp the following day, hoping to capture them. When the king was presented with the Holy Bible by a friar, he looked at it for a few moments, said "There is no magic in this," and then threw it on the ground. At this moment, Pizarro and his forces called upon God, and led a charge against these men, outnumbered many times over. As in the miraculous victories recorded in Scripture, the Spanish soldiers threw the Incas immediately into disarray, and chaos. The king's stand was toppled. Many of his warriors fled. The Spanish soldiers rode about killing the Inca forces until the sun went down, sealing the end of its pagan bloody rule. They didn't lose a single man. Later they took the Inca capital itself without a struggle, soon subduing an empire of millions.[29] It required the sword to do that. All of the men who did so were sinners themselves. Yet events like this turned the flood of history for the good, and brought the knowledge of Christ to many millions of human souls. It ended a demonic, primitive, and much more violent existence in an entire continent. It was merely a part of what Scripture prophesied about the knowledge of God flooding the earth.

---

28. Associated Press, "Mexico Finds Flayed God."

29. Prisoners of Eternity, "Francisco Pizarro and the Conquest." Pizarro's meeting with the Incas and victory in that battle is recounted in much detail in Jared Diamond's *Guns, Germs, and Steel*. Different recountings I've read vary on a few details.

Remember, I'm not reviewing all of this for the sake of everyone agreeing it is all a great thing, although it is a great thing. I'm reviewing all of this to show that God's kingdom came with Jesus Christ. It has begun. It's not going to reveal itself in some future political or religious event. We're not waiting for an incarnate Jesus, ruling from Jerusalem, to send out forces against some modern-day Assyrians. The prophecies were true, the words of Jesus and the apostles mean what they plainly mean, and God's kingdom came in and spread across the globe. It led men personally, and it led nations. Kings bowed down to Christ. It's important to recognize that the fruit of the kingdom are life, goodness, and peace, which are not always found in soldiers who conquer, but that's not my primary point here; it's just to show that history is brilliant evidence for the kingdom being with us in the present. God is trampling down his enemies through Christ. Its overall effects have been towards goodness and peace. Those who have trouble accepting the goodness of bringing down pagan empires through the sword, usually have no problem with the goodness of Allied planes flying over Europe, bombing it to a crisp to bring down the Nazis. They have no problem with millions of soldiers pumping lead into millions of other soldiers to take down Hitler's empire, in a slaughter that sounds reminiscent of E.E. Cummings's passage of poetry, "how do you like your blue-eyed boy, Mister Death."[30] If man can recognize the value in shedding rivers of blood to take down a mass-murderous empire such as the Nazis, he should have no trouble seeing the goodness of taking down primitive, murderous, child-sacrificing pagan empires as well. It rids the world of great evil, and the enemies of God:

> Thou shalt break them with a rod of iron; thou shalt dash them in pieces like a potter's vessel. (Ps 2:9)
>
> And the carcases of this people shall be meat for the fowls of the heaven, and for the beasts of the earth; and none shall fray them away. (Jer 7:33)

God's power in his people also brought to us one of the great stabilizing and civilizing elements of human society: lifelong monogamous marriage. The early church, much more than today, took seriously the New Testament teachings against divorce, and against remarriage. It also took seriously the stated nature of marriage itself: a one-flesh union between man and woman for life. This ruled out evils like fornication, like remarriage, like religious prostitution (which was prevalent in the pagan

---

30. Cummings, "Buffalo Bill's," 94.

world), like homosexual behavior, like regular prostitution, like polygamy. It made it much more difficult to break up marriages, and bring about the social instability which comes with it. Although Christians have been attracted to some of these sins through the ages, the church always taught this stable and ethical form of marriage, and later prohibited much of the rest in civil society. Many Christian nations had laws against sodomy. Polygamy became illegal, where it previously had been tolerated in parts of the world. Despite Christian failure to live up to this doctrine, it changed the world. It provided many more homes in which children would be raised by both parents, and in which they would be much safer and better trained than in other living environments. It protected the woman from being used simply for prostitution or for rape. It gave less motivation to commit abortion or infanticide, because of the loving union that children would be born into. It avoided the clear problems in polygamy, which tends to allow men to monopolize the women, leaves some wives without the resources and attention of their husbands, and puts family members in the same household who are not closely related, and are much more likely to have conflict.

Christian marriage is safe, and rooted in the same biblical teaching, and the same basic respect for human life, that the rest of God's teachings are. Both spouses are highly valued. Each spouse has a role. The organism has a head, who leads lovingly, and a submissive wife, who gently follows his lead. The children are raised to have virtue and faith, and have the attention of their parents, rather than an entire crowd of people, who may not love them, or who are more likely to desire their harm. If any one thing in God's kingdom is a fountain of life, it is marriage. It reveals the salvation present in the faith, and gives us a future. Even today, long after the civilizational change Christian marriage provided, it stands as superior to a life of using the opposite sex for temporary selfish pleasure, and provides stability and sanity for any who leave behind lifestyles of fornication or perversion for real love instead. Man's heart desires to sin, but even in this state he can sense the goodness and warmth of the family. The child from a broken home needs no lessons to desire both his father and his mother to care for him. He doesn't need to learn a religious doctrine to know angst and sorrow at being abandoned by a parent. Marriage given by God is a fount of mental and spiritual health, while the instability of lifestyle fornication leaves men with more anxiety and depression. It pours forth unwanted and uncared-for children. In a world of youth crime, violence, suicide, and fatherless households, Christian marriage has not ceased being incredibly relevant. It is a grand signpost to God's love in this very day. It contains real power.

Similarly, and deeply related, is the fact that the kingdom of God quickly brought better treatment of the woman. Not only was she highly valued as a virgin or a godly wife, protected and provided for throughout her life, but she is recognized as a fellow sister in Christ. She went from being much like a piece of property in the pagan world, to a valued member of the new human family. She is recognized as sharing in salvation. She is a full member of the church. The simple use of women witnesses testifying to the resurrection shows a higher honor regarded to women than ancient Jews[31] or neighboring societies. Just as it was shocking to many Jews that the Gentiles came into the covenants of God, it would have been shocking to some that women came in as well, having full fellowship with the covenant people. While God does not give woman the same role as a man, and she is still to be submissive to his leadership, she is given much more value than women of the pagan empire that preceded the church, or than first century Jewish tradition allowed. Most early converts were apparently women.[32] She was a sister in Christ to any man, who was a brother in Christ to her. She was to be honored for her purity, virtue, and motherhood. Man's leadership role over her became tempered with benevolence and protection, rather than simply a desire to use her, and further recognizes her God-given dignity. Men likewise became held to higher standards in other ways, including that he be faithful in marriage, not take concubines, or use women for sex while single.

Accusers of the Christian faith like to blame Christians for slavery, as if Christians were unique in having slaves at various times and places throughout history. However, not only were Christians not unique in this—it has existed for thousands of years in societies of all kinds across the globe—but it was Christians who ended slavery in their nations, and later influenced non-Christian nations to do so as well. Britain ended slavery step by step in the early 1800s, the United States in the middle of the same century.[33] By the middle of the twentieth century, it was abolished in international law.[34] If a man really dislikes the practice of slavery, he ought to respect that its end was largely a Christian

---

31. *Babylonian Talmud*, Sanhedrin 3, 79. The wording of this passage sounds as if women were prohibited from various kinds of trials, but not from all.
32. Aquilina, "A Radical Equality."
33. Carpenter, "A Secular Jew"; Coffey, "The abolition of the slave trade," 1–6.
34. Reuters, "Chronology—Who Banned Slavery?."

accomplishment, and then thank God for it. Christians ended it directly, and they influenced other cultures to do the same. You need to give credit where that credit is due. Christians were able to see the slave like a brother, a view we see clearly taught in the book of Philemon, and we have records of Christians setting free their slaves from the earliest centuries after Christ. Paul writes to the disgruntled slave owner, "For perhaps he therefore departed for a season, that thou shouldest receive him for ever; *Not now as a servant, but above a servant, a brother beloved*, specially to me, but how much more unto thee, both in the flesh, and in the Lord? If thou count me therefore a partner, *receive him as myself*" (vv. 15–17). Paul asks the slave owner to receive the slave in the same way he'd receive Paul, who is a freeman, a fellow Christian, and an apostle. Once one sees the slave as a brother in Christ, his need for protection and his humanity come into the picture, and it becomes less imperative to hold him. At the minimum, he is more of a member of the family. You receive him with joy and friendship, even if the working relationship of servitude remains present. It will never be the same.

As I've pointed out before, the main problem with slavery from the word of God is its misuses, and its existence in overly cruel forms. Slavery is a broad term that covers a variety of forms of servitude, and it's hard to find the more humane kinds to be evil. However, much slavery that has existed in history is certainly in conflict both with what the Bible explicitly teaches about slavery, and against Christian principles in how we treat humanity. Slavery which involves kidnapping men is clearly prohibited in the Torah, as is cruel injurious treatment of a slave. A man who kidnapped another man to sell him into slavery would be executed (Exod 21:16), and a Hebrew slave was to be freed on the seventh year of captivity (Exod 21:2). A more humane form of indentured servitude would not necessarily go against Scripture, and servitude has been used to lift people out of poverty many times over, or at least help them survive in very difficult circumstances.[35] Where is the evil in that? They get a better life through a willingness to work a number of years, and millions of people today still seek out such servitude arrangements. The mission of the Christian church naturally includes ending the evils of slavery, although in its zeal it has ended more humane forms of servitude, which are not in themselves wrong. The New Testament respects the roles of

---

35. Tardi, "Indentured Servitude." This article mostly reviews indentured servitude in early U.S. history, but similar institutions have existed in other places and times in history. It is still practiced today illegally.

master and slave, and never prohibits them. It calls on masters to behave with goodwill, without threatening, reminding the master that both he and the slave are looked on without partiality by God (Eph 6:5–9). Either way, the cruelties of slavery, literally across the globe, were not ended by traditional Jews, by Hindus, by Muslims, by Buddhists, by Taoists, by Shamanists, by Wiccans, or by any other religion on the globe. It was ended by the new creation started by Jesus of Nazareth twenty centuries ago. Freedom in Christ, which every born-again soul has, is reflected in freedom on this earth. When the child of God prays—Thy kingdom come, thy will be done—he can know his prayer is being answered.

Similarly, the eternal life brought by uniting with the Son of God is reflected in the blessing of life on this earth. The Christian faith is rooted in truth, both in God's word and the natural laws of creation, and through both of these God has blessed Christendom with extraordinary advancements in the sciences, and in the long run with a longer lifespan. Trust that a God of goodness and wisdom runs the cosmos has led to goodness and wisdom to come to mankind. Knowing that Yahweh is a God of truth has led to seeking out that truth in the laws of nature, expecting its orderly functioning.[36] Christian centers of learning developed the methods of science over time, getting out and testing the prevalent theories, rather than relying on them as philosophical claims, as the Greco-Roman world had primarily done. Its centers of learning and universities trained minds that would develop technologies far exceeding civilizations which came before it. The earliest places of higher learning were monasteries. Monks preserved and copied books, produced and protected works of art, and in doing so continued civilization and protected learning during long periods of invasion and political instability. Universities began in the twelfth century in Bologna and Paris, and soon spread across western Europe. The universities founded in the early United States, including Harvard and Yale, were Christian in their character and purpose.[37] In Europe, the arts and sciences were often sponsored by Catholic popes and kings. The growth of learning was comparatively slow at first, and its advancement more comparable to other advanced civilizations for hundreds of years, but learning took off at a higher rate around the time of the Renaissance, providing Christian civilization with advances which no society in history ever had, ones which it subsequentially took across the globe. This

---

36. Pearcey and Thaxton, *The Soul of Science*, 21–29.
37. Ways to Faith, "The Christian Origin."

race forward saw the final development of the scientific method, and developments such as the steam engine, the telescope, the microscope, and the flush toilet.[38]

As far as its effect on human life alone, between having more peaceful societies, better nutrition, good hygiene, and modern medicine, the average lifespan has increased immensely, and infant and childhood mortality decreased until child deaths are extremely rare. In the past any large family could expect to lose more than once child. Today most families never lose a single one.[39] Through modern medicine and hygiene, along with social stability, where the average lifespan at the start off the eighteenth century was under forty years old, it is now eighty to ninety in the more advanced countries, and much higher than forty even in war-torn and undeveloped nations.[40] The Christian nations of the world went to primitive, pagan societies, and through their advancements they have eradicated illnesses, provided successful treatment for others, brought safe drinking water, access to medicine and modern comforts, useful training and education, and significantly increased lifespan in these societies as well. Much of this they did for free. The rest came through political influence or colonization.

Pain and suffering in general have been suppressed by the advancements of Christian society, whether by painkillers, treatments of diseases, or eradication of famine and hunger. Where it would have been normal for struggling humanity to go extended periods of time with very little, or no food, we now live in a society in which even the poor people get fat, and even in poorer nations certainly do not starve. Famine and death by starvation have become extremely rare, reaching historical lows by the last part of the twentieth century.[41] Where we once suffered in the steaming heat, or the deadly cold, we now choose the exact temperature we want for our home, and feel inconvenienced if it's not where we want it. We have so many mountains of food, our wasted food alone could feed the undernourished two times over.[42] We can go to a snack closet and choose whatever morsel or treat fits our taste, and choose from any variety of countless fruit juices, coffees, teas, or alcoholic beverages. It is impossible not to see the words of the messianic Ps 72 coming to pass,

38. Seaver, "What Were the Most Important."
39. Roser, "Mortality in the Past."
40. Roser et. al., "Life Expectancy."
41. Hasell, "Famine Mortality."
42. World Food Program USA, "Is There a Global?"

which extols the reign of the king and his son, preaching, "There shall be an handful of corn in the earth upon the top of the mountains; the fruit thereof shall shake like Lebanon: and they of the city shall flourish like grass of the earth" (v. 16). This super abundance can indeed tempt man into arrogance and into living for the flesh, but it is nothing less than a sign of the goodness of the new creation in the risen Savior. Many of the burdens of sin, along with physical pain, have been relieved of us, through the blessings given through Christendom. Even unbelievers, whether the Muslim, the Hindu, or the Shamanist, have been blessed through this outpouring of life. The supernatural life has taught us how to rightly treat the natural life. We see a fulfillment of the word of truth, which teaches, "The law of the wise is a fountain of life, to depart from the snares of death" (Prov 13:14). We should all see where that law originates in the first place, and bow down before him, and his Son.

The Holy Spirit infused himself into the human soul as God's family came into Christ. Through that family, God's presence pervaded human society; through human love, the work of the churches, and the men who filled up human institutions, working them to bring glory to God. The earth was brought into subjection to Christ the King, and this is still going on. The cathedral is still being built, even as slowdowns occur, and even as bombers attack it. Do not let failure here, or disaster there, make you ever doubt that. Do not let hatred or persecution against men cloud your vision. This change in the world is what God promised in Scripture, and it has been visibly seen over 2,000 years so far, in a drastic and undoubtable reality. The evidence is all around us through the kingdom, as it is from the Creator, through the creation. Failure is a temporary setback, there to chastise us as God's children, and in the long run, draw us deeper into him. It is there to work his plan to greater glory. The church, and the presence of God's kingdom on earth, are clearly visible to all mankind.

> In his days shall the righteous flourish; and abundance of peace so long as the moon endureth.
>
> *He shall have dominion also from sea to sea*, and from the river unto the ends of the earth.
>
> They that dwell in the wilderness shall bow before him; and his enemies shall lick the dust. (Ps 72:7–9)
>
> And the sucking child shall play on the hole of the asp, and the weaned child shall put his hand on the cockatrice' den.

THE FUTURE IS A MIRACLE

> They shall not hurt nor destroy in all my holy mountain: for *the earth shall be full of the knowledge of the LORD*, as the waters cover the sea. (Isa 11:8–9)
>
> All the ends of the world shall remember and turn unto the LORD: and all the kindreds of the nations shall worship before thee.
>
> For the kingdom is the LORD'S: and *he is the governor among the nations*. (Ps 22:27–28)
>
> Our Father which art in heaven, Hallowed be thy name. Thy kingdom come. Thy will be done, as in heaven, so in earth. (Luke 11:2b)
>
> Go ye therefore, and teach all nations, baptizing them in the name of the Father, and of the Son, and of the Holy Ghost:
>
> Teaching them to observe all things whatsoever I have commanded you: and, lo, I am with you alway, even unto the end of the world. Amen. (Matt 28:19–20)

There is much left to come. Clearly, we still have terrible suffering on earth, and we still have death. Our future though is not to wait around until Christ's final coming when all will be completed. It is to continue to subdue Christ's enemies, and to love and protect human life. It is to make disciples of all people on the earth. As this continues, his enemies are put under his feet. The end of all things, promised in Scripture, is to dwell in perfect righteousness and bliss with the Lord. We will see that one day. The evil and unbelieving will be cast into hell, to suffer eternally. The righteous and believing will be in eternal intimate communion with the Lord. He who is righteous will now remain righteous. He who is wicked will now remain wicked, apart from God and his people (Rev 22:11). The children of God will see the face of Christ eternally, and know pure love, apart from the sins, doubts, pains of this world. They will know the true love of God forever (vv. 3–5).

ANSWERS

The Christian faith has both the answer to pain and the solution to pain. There may be some of that solution which we do not see immediately before us, just as there was some of it we could not see when Christ was hanging on the cross. However, much has been revealed already, and the goodness that comes from Christ's love on this earth is a sign of the eternity we will have with him later. It is an experience of it. All pain will be put away. The cross and the blood of Jesus assure that. In this world, despite the pain that still exists, the saints of Christ bring the experience of heaven to earth. Its doings. Its love. Its worship. Its communion. Its beauty. They are manifested through the church which Christ created and rules, just as he rules over all things.

Despite the wealth of passages from Old Testament and New which show Messiah and God's people ruling over this earth, it is common to hear people deny this earthiness, and claim that the kingdom spoken of by Christ is purely spiritual. Our inheritance is simply after death. We get eternal life, and basically, that's it. People who make such claims rely heavily on John 18:36, in which Jesus says to Pilate, *"My kingdom is not of this world*: if my kingdom were of this world, then would my servants fight, that I should not be delivered to the Jews: but now is my kingdom not from hence." They may similarly point to a "heavenly" kind of kingdom, relying on teachings such as 1 Pet 1:4, which says that Jesus has begotten us, "To an inheritance incorruptible, and undefiled, and that fadeth not away, *reserved in heaven for you.*"

It would be strange if these statements, and others like them, denied any of the truth of the passages we've already gone over. The Bible is one revelation of God, who is a God of truth and does not deny himself. We should know from the start it is more likely that statements about a spiritual kingdom simply harmonize with the whole, without denying Christ's rule here. We also need to remember that most people who make such arguments do not wholly deny that the spiritual kingdom will make itself present physically on the earth. They simply disagree about *how* it will appear on the earth, or *when* it will appear. They fully recognize that no matter how otherworldly the source of the kingdom is, it is present in the physical. For that reason, I find arguments based on these scriptures to be dead on arrival. The people making them don't really believe in them to begin with.

In John 18:36 Jesus is indeed locating his kingdom beyond this world. However, he is speaking in terms of its source, which is simply where it is coming from. It is rooted in heaven. It is rooted in the soul of the believer. If Jesus really meant it is simply an invisible and intangible kingdom we would have some problems, since he taught people that his kingdom was coming in during their lifetimes, and he rooted that kingdom in actions, in righteousness, in good human behavior right here. Those things are not purely spiritual, but break forth into this earth. In fact, if you stretched "not of this world" to its fullest extent in the abstract, you would end up gnostic, and deny the godly purpose of the material world. I think anyone can see that would not be biblical at all. Could Jesus have been saying the kingdom is only rooted in individual ethics, and not in government? Well, that's not precisely what he said. However, some may guess it because he remarks that this is why his servants do not fight for him to take the throne. Thus, they conclude he was denying any political actions in the future. However, this comment just refers to Jesus' purpose in his earthly ministry, which was to proclaim the glad tidings, and call people to obedience, meekness, and service to others. It does not specifically rule out anything to do with government in the life of the believer. If it did, we would then have to say the Christian could not vote today, could not lobby, be an activist, or seek to change wicked, unjust laws. Yet very few Christians make that interpretation, so they are misusing this passage even according to their own standards. Christ was only speaking of the source of his kingdom, which of course hints at his divine nature, and the purpose of his earthly ministry, which did not include becoming king by warfare. He could have had he chosen, but his mission was to change the human heart, and then use that new heart for his kingdom. Jesus was not ruling out anything involving government to come.

Next we can look at Peter, who speaks in his first epistle of awaiting an inheritance which is reserved for us in heaven (1:4). It is not the only passage like this in the New Testament. This may lead some to wholly spiritualize other teachings about the kingdom, and even assume that's all they really were referring to anyway, being just allegories of the next world above. This is clearly wrong, since we have much else which speaks on God's kingdom which makes clear it refers to the earth we live in, and human behavior here. Now the kingdom of heaven, and the kingdom of God can often be used interchangeably, but much of the time when we think of heaven, it is the after-death experience we consider. In this passage from Peter, I believe it is speaking of the after-death portion of existence. That's because he speaks of being incorruptible, and because in the following verse he speaks of being kept by the Spirit until the last time (v. 5). However, the fact this reference is likely about the heaven which is future, that does not mean the kingdom which is present does not exist. It only means the culmination and perfection is in the future. Nothing here then demands that we rewrite or entirely spiritualize everything else we see in both testaments. Jesus says his kingdom is with us now. He also teaches it is in the next world. We should find no problem.

We see further confirmation that the heavenly nature of the kingdom does not deny the earthly reality in the opening of the book of Acts. This is in that short period between the resurrection and the ascension. While Jesus speaks of kingdom matters with the apostles, we see a relevant question asked and answered:

> When they therefore were come together, they asked of him, saying, Lord, wilt thou at this time restore again the kingdom to Israel?
>
> And he said unto them, *It is not for you to know the times or the seasons*, which the Father hath put in his own power.
>
> But ye shall receive power, after that the Holy Ghost is come upon you: and ye shall be witnesses unto me both in Jerusalem, and in all Judaea, and in Samaria, and unto the uttermost part of the earth. (Acts 1:6–8)

The apostles seem to be asking a question related to prophecy; that is the restoration of the kingdom to Israel from its oppressors, as was promised, which would involve great earthly prosperity and power. It would come with a great defeat of its earthly enemies. In his response, Jesus does not deny that he will restore the kingdom. He only tells them it is not for them to know the times, and that they will act as witnesses to Christ across the world. That indicates a future reality of the earthly kingdom. Now some may interpret the kingdom in the New Covenant to mean all the church, or all Christian lands. Others may see it in this passage to refer only to national Israel, God doubling back to deliver the nation, since they have not been abandoned for good. However, either way you have it, the apostles are only told to wait. They are not told it will not happen.

In fact, it is part of the prayer of every Christian that God's heavenly kingdom make its appearance on earth. Every time the Christian prays, "Thy kingdom come. Thy will be done in earth, as it is in heaven" (Matt 6:10), he is praying for the spiritual perfection of heaven to break forth here. This is how God's kingdom operates. It does not remain purely invisible, but pushes forth into this world by God's grace and the faith of his people. That is why Jesus can speak of his kingdom as not of this world, and also speak of God's will being done here, just like in that transcendent world of perfection. There is no contradiction. Nor is there a hard barrier between the righteousness of Christian communities, and the actions of government. God's will can be done in both. It penetrates everything on this earth, as Christ has become all in all.

THE FUTURE IS A MIRACLE

It is natural to ask, if what I am saying is true, then what role does pain still have for us? The New Testament teaches our role in being hated, in suffering persecution, in being sanctified through pain. How does this fit in with the present reality of God's kingdom, and a growing victory over Christ's enemies? It fits in with our present reality, since we are not yet at the completion of God's kingdom. Pain still is a mechanism, as I have written about extensively in this book, for bringing about the good. It still is the tool Yahweh uses to make us greater men of God, and increase our dependency upon him. It is still a chastisement for our sins. It will be conquered completely in the long run. For the present it has become God's tool of victory. Our sacrifice, like Christ's, defeats his enemies in this world. Our death is a victory. Our spirit, which is not longing for wealth, power, greed, sensuality, or lust fulfillment, is still the freest to serve God and be molded to Christ's character. Being brought down lifts us up. Therefore, suffering fits into all I have said, because it is God's chosen vehicle. It is his means.

What about other historical views of God's kingdom and the end times? Are they blatantly false? Is what I have described the only way to view God's action through his people and in history? It's important to see, that even though other views differ either a little, or a lot from what I've said, all of them agree to certain same truths in the future. They all agree the faithful will end in a state of bliss and union with the Lord forever. They all agree the wicked will end in hell. They all agree in the long run that sin, corruption, and death will be destroyed completely. Until that future point, they have some differences.

One view holds that Jesus brought in the kingdom during his work on earth, but this kingdom was always meant to be a spiritual one. It only exists through believers and the church. Scriptures which refer to vast earthly rule and kingdoms were exaggeration or symbolism. It's only a spiritual reality here on earth. This view, which has represented the majority of Christian belief in history, while different in how it draws the border of the kingdom, has considerable overlap with what I have said. An optimistic spiritual view will still recognize that God's kingdom, through his people, transforms this world towards life and love. It has great influence until Christ's return. It may not go so far as to portray a political rule over the entire globe, or a Christianizing of the entire globe, but the world will see extensive change, and vast numbers in every nation brought to Christ. This is because there is no avoiding the fact that the same person who obeys Christ in his private life obeys him in his public life, if he is consistent. The man who practices righteousness among his friends and neighbors, will practice righteousness through his job, or his business. The man who deals justly in his personal relations, will deal justly when he works for the government, becomes a judge, a police man, or the head of state. Once we see how Christ's character pervades all society, there is much less separating a spiritual view of God's kingdom from a view that it reigns over nations and empires, and is truly global.

The other major understanding of the kingdom sees a true earthly reign over all nations as I have described, but places this reign in the future, upon a bodily return of Christ. He will rule personally over the nations, and there will be a glorious reign of righteousness, while sin still exists and people still die. Once that reign is complete, then we go on to the final judgment and eternity. A view like this was common in the first few generations after Christ, but later died out, as the spiritual view became the more or less official one. It has reappeared in the modern era, in usually a different form. The future view requires taking the immanent language of Jesus and the apostles as meaning something besides immanence, but it still sees the same basic things occurring through Christ, and the same long-term solution. Christ will rule over nations. Christ will be victorious over all enemies. It has simply been put off for ages, and we are just waiting. On questioning, some who hold to this view will basically fall back onto a modified view. They may acknowledge that Christ *did* bring in a spiritual fulfillment of the prophecies in the first century, but will claim that what is future is simply a more complete and greater fulfillment. Insufficiencies in the interpretation that the kingdom is purely future really demand this kind of modification; a lesser fulfillment in the past, and a greater one in the future. While it is possible that some prophecies are indeed fulfilled twice—there are examples of messianic ones which were twice fulfilled a second time in Jesus' ministry (Hos 11:1)—nothing in the Bible ever says that the arrival of the kingdom includes such a double fulfillment. It would be speculation to say that it is. Considering the clear words in the New Testament of a soon fulfillment, the events they explicitly describe are ones which already occurred. That is all we can know for a certainty.

Until then, the children of the Lord spread the knowledge of God across the globe, and bring righteousness to the world. They worship Yahweh with their brethren, receive Jesus into their being in Communion, and share the glad tidings to unbelievers. They live according to righteousness, as neighbors, citizens, business owners, and government officials. They bring the earth into subjection to Christ, being God's tools in putting all things under the feet of Messiah. The supernatural power of the Holy Spirit works through them. It may not come all at one time historically, but it comes in a large scale and visible way. We will see the worship of God, peace, abundance, and goodness cover the whole earth like a tide. Evildoers will be punished by the law of God.

HELL

In the end God's people will not experience pain anymore, but there will always be a place for suffering. That is in the domain of hell. This reality itself plays a role in the beautiful redemption that God's people will receive. Hell is one of the last things which men want to accept. We have a hard time imagining that anyone deserves eternal suffering for their sin. We like to think that even the worst of sinners will repent eventually, and imagine hell might not be necessary. However, it is not up to our preferences to decide what is real. There is no objection which man has to the suffering of hell which make it a teaching we can dismiss or otherwise minimize. Hell justly punishes sinners, and glorifies Yahweh as a righteous God.

The Bible teaches that Yahweh will not justify the wicked, but will punish them forever in hell. It teaches explicitly many of the things which lead men to hell, including unbelief and many sins. Paul warns the churches in his letters several times of various sins which will lead to hell. In 1 Cor 6, he writes, "Know ye not that *the unrighteous shall not inherit the kingdom of God?* Be not deceived: neither fornicators, nor idolaters, nor adulterers, nor effeminate, nor abusers of themselves with mankind, Nor thieves, nor covetous, nor drunkards, nor revilers, nor extortioners, shall inherit the kingdom of God" (vv. 9–10).

In Gal 5, he similarly teaches:

> Now the works of the flesh are manifest, which are these; Adultery, fornication, uncleanness, lasciviousness,
>
> Idolatry, witchcraft, hatred, variance, emulations, wrath, strife, seditions, heresies,
>
> Envyings, murders, drunkenness, revellings, and such like: of the which I tell you before, as I have also told you in time past, that they which do such things *shall not inherit the kingdom of God*. (vv. 19–21)

Revelation 21 gives us another sin list:

> But the fearful, and unbelieving, and the abominable, and murderers, and whoremongers, and sorcerers, and idolaters, and all liars, *shall have their part in the lake which burneth with fire* and brimstone: which is the second death. (v. 8)

Hell is the domain which was prepared for the devil and his angels, as well as for sinners who do not repent (Rev 20:10, 15; 21:8). It is better, according to Jesus' teachings, to cut off your hand or put out your eye, than to end up in hell (Mark 9:43, 47). It is called a place of fire, and of torment (Jude 7, Mark 9:44, Luke 16:24). Despite the fact that men understand the concept of justice, and even desire the wicked to be punished, they step back at this kind of teaching as overly harsh. Despite the fact that many men, when faced with the fact of a child-killer on trial, will cry out that he deserves to "burn in hell," they will still think of excuses to deny this theological truth in the Bible. Yet this is the clear teaching of Scripture.

Perhaps the greatest objection to the reality of hell is that the punishment is eternal, the suffering is never ending. Matthew 25 refers to hell as "everlasting fire" and "everlasting punishment" (vv. 41, 46). In the final verse, it is even set parallel to the "eternal life" of heaven, so that to deny its eternal nature would be to deny the eternal nature of heaven as well. Revelation 20 teaches that the beast and the false prophet shall be tormented in hell "day and night for ever and ever" (v. 10b). How can a single sin, no matter how grand, warrant a punishment which seems much worse, and out of proportion to that sin? Isn't sin just temporal? This is what most people ask. Yet this reaction stems from not seeing what sin really is, or not seeing fully God's goodness and justice. Every sin is not merely a sin against man, who is finite, on an earth which is finite, but is a sin against Yahweh, who is infinite, and whose kingdom is eternal. Sin ends in eternal torment because it is sin against an eternal God. Sin also logically leads to such eternal consequences because it severs us from the life of God. Once severed, our life will go on apart from fellowship with God, and without his saving grace unless we repent. Brought to eternity, that severing means we suffer all things apart from grace, which will include pain, corruption, hopelessness, and a rotten fellowship with evil men and with demons. This goes on and on, and it is natural that even apart from judicial punishment from God, the separation from his grace and the connection to evil brings the consequences of sin down upon us forever. Those temporal decisions we made in life become eternal in the next world.

Hell is also a factor which assures that heaven bears the qualities of heaven. It assures the redeemed will be received into eternal bliss, and into beautiful fellowship with the Savior and with the saints. Were sinners to enter in, there would be no such thing as heaven. That is why the Scriptures teach that no impure thing will enter in (Rev 21:27). Those who practice lawlessness will never enter (Matt 7:21–23). We should find this easy to understand, since even in our own homes, there is much evil we would never allow to enter. We keep out filth, things which cause disease, and dangerous people, just as the Almighty does in far greater ways. A father would not allow a rapist to climb in through his daughter's window, but would strike him down if he even tried. Similarly, God does not allow wickedness into his kingdom, and all who enter must enter through the narrow way, which is through Christ. We must be restored to righteousness. We must be cleansed of sin. Then we will enter his kingdom, where there is no corruption or death.

The reality of hell points to God's justice. God's justice by itself points to his goodness, since justice is a righteous reaction against evil. The fact we see the wicked suffer, even on this earth, reveals that Yahweh is good in his character. Just as we would not want a child killer to go free, without any punishment, Yahweh allows no sinner to go free without punishment. He reacts against evil because he is by nature good. Just as Yahweh is revealed through the mercy he shows to those who repent and believe, he is shown just through the punishment he gives to those who go on in sin and deny him. This is clear in Rom 9, when Paul writes,

> What if God, *willing to shew his wrath*, and to make his power known, endured with much longsuffering the vessels of wrath fitted to destruction:
>
> And *that he might make known the riches of his glory* on the vessels of mercy, which he had afore prepared unto glory (vv. 22–23)

God's entire plan to save his children is a manifestation of who he is in his character, in mercy, love, righteousness, and justice. His punishment of the evil displays his justice. Bringing his saints to glory displays his mercy. We should not allow the difficulty of the reality of hell to hinder us from seeing this, as we should always be looking to God for the truth. We cannot complain that he punishes evil, but must only seek his mercy, and turn from sin, which leads to his wrath. The redemption he offers us is eternal, and it is far from any sin and evil, in perfect peace.

We may live on an earth now in which pain and death come upon the good, as well as the evil. There may be unique suffering for some due to breaking God's law, but every human living will experience pain through being conceived corrupt, and through the evils in this world. The best of men may suffer the most horrible pain. Yet this will not always be so. Suffering will end for the righteous. On the last day, pain will only have one purpose—that is to bring justice to those who do evil. It will only be a response to cutting oneself off from the source of all goodness. Pain will remain in hell forever, upon those who have rejected Yahweh. We may wish that no one ever goes to hell, but if no one went to hell, then God would not be righteous, the wicked would get what they want in the end, and heaven would be a place of suffering and death just as earth is. If you feel pity for those people in hell, do not complain about your Maker. Pray for them. Teach them the gospel, and plead with them to come trust in Christ. God sends you to rescue people from such a horrible end.

It is interesting that unbelievers who reject their Creator, yet desire a future of peace, do not see the source of the problem itself. They want to place God as the source of the world's suffering, but close their eyes to the fact that over and over again it is mankind, breaking God's laws, which is the source of suffering. The justice they say they want, is brought by Christ. The care for the needy and suffering they claim to desire is brought by Christ. The love for children they claim to have, is brought by Christ. Cruelty, violence, rape, murder, and lack of love all stem from going against God's will. Yet this reality is hidden beneath the shadows of unbelief. It is lurking beneath the surface. The guilt for sin. The need for self-sacrifice. Our desire for forgiveness. These truths and more come bubbling up in the unbeliever's life, because he was designed by Yahweh and he lives in Yahweh's world, even if he denies it. The emptiness and desire to die he may sometimes feel are only an expression of man in need of God. They show man's insufficiency. It is only pride that prevents him from kneeling down, and humbly confessing his sins, and asking for God's love forever. If he would repent God would hear him. Yet he holds onto himself, as he fears losing the only god he knows, and his life of corruption he's learned to adore. He doesn't want to give up the god of self, so he assents to all evil and pain. He casts his vote for Adam.

The New Mount

SEVERAL MILES SOUTH OF Council Bluffs Iowa, in the southwest corner of the state near the border with Nebraska, the body of young Gloria Slump was found on a railroad bridge in 1967. She had been beaten and stabbed many times with an unknown object. Gloria worked in Omaha, just across the border, and had recently told her parents she had met a "nice guy" and would be bringing him home to meet them. The main suspect in her killing, the presumed nice guy she had met, was questioned by police, failed a lie detector test, and soon after committed suicide with a shotgun. No one was ever arrested for Gloria's murder. As part of their investigation, police had entered her apartment to search it. They found the young woman's Bible sitting out, and in the Bible was a note she had written, with these words:

> "I am a stranger here. Heaven is my home. Danger and sorrow stand around me on every hand. Heaven is my fatherland. Heaven is my Home."[1]

It was as if the young Gloria had left a message for everyone, so that they would know where to find her. Hauntingly, it even suggested her own demise. She knew the state of this darkened world and her danger in it. I don't think that the officers who entered her home will forget finding her note, or the meaning it took on in light of the murder.

The words of the poem are similar to the opening verse of a song by the same name. The following verse continues:

> "And if I suffer hard, Heaven is my home
> I will not question God, Heaven is my home
> Christ suffered even more, And promised to adorn
> Me with a crown of gold. . . Heaven is my home"[2]

---

1. Bowers, "Heaven is My Home."

2. Khorolskiy & Friends, "Heaven is My Home." According to Mr. Khorolskiy, the words of this song are similar to various Russian hymns from the nineteenth century.

There has been a pathway opened to that better land, our homeland, since soon after the fall. Yahweh showed his mercy and his righteous way to us; the animal skins he gave to Adam and Eve to cover them; the words of warning he gave to Cain, and the undeserved protection he provided to him even after Cain had committed murder; the warnings of the impending great flood, and the ark which he commanded righteous Noah to build; the ladder he revealed to Jacob with angels ascending and descending. God has always provided lost man an opportunity and a path to depart from this stained and impure world into a better one.

Yahweh revealed his perfect law through Moses, on top of a mountain, with great supernatural occurrences. He provided his law in smoke and fire and tremblings of the earth. It was a great law that would bring life and peace to all who follow it. The Son of God from heaven likewise ascended a mount, and gave his preaching on the law, revealing its true meaning in the spirit, and revealing God's original purpose for us at the creation. Far from being a national law which Moses had brought, and full of criminal punishment, it was the way of the spirit made for a place called heaven:

> Blessed are the poor in spirit: for theirs is the kingdom of heaven.
>
> Blessed are they that mourn: for they shall be comforted.
>
> Blessed are the meek: for they shall inherit the earth. (Matt 5:3–5)

It called for a spiritual change within us, not a mere obedience. It called for a meekness, and childlike nature which any saint must have. It called for dependency on the Father and not on ourselves. Then the Son of God provided a means to attain that law—not just a path to walk and hard work to accomplish. He provided a means to that better world by giving us his own righteousness, his very own perfect and eternal being to share. Our hard work would not lift us up. He singular work would take us there.

Christ has a home for us with God, far above this world. It is neither Moses' mountain nor Jesus' mount. It is a home with Christ in his love. The homeless on earth has a home in heaven. We are established there even before we arrive:

> But God, who is rich in mercy, for his great love wherewith he loved us,
>
> Even when we were dead in sins, hath quickened us together with Christ, (by grace ye are saved;)

THE NEW MOUNT

> And hath raised us up together, and made us sit together in heavenly places in Christ Jesus: (Eph 2:4-6)
>
> If ye then be risen with Christ, seek those things which are above, where Christ sitteth on the right hand of God.
>
> Set your affection on things above, not on things on the earth.
>
> For ye are dead, and your life is hid with Christ in God. (Col 3:1-3)
>
> In my Father's house are many mansions: if it were not so, I would have told you. I go to prepare a place for you.
>
> And if I go and prepare a place for you, I will come again, and receive you unto myself; that where I am, there ye may be also. (John 14:2-3)

The perfect world of our Father is so far beyond this world we cannot imagine it. His home is beyond space, time, and the material elements. It is beyond the invisible forces, and tiniest particles modern science can recognize. It exists beyond human logic and desire. It is a world of communion in pure love, without darkness, or evil. It is so far from us it almost seems impossible to reach it.

Yet we can know that world of the spirit here, even if it is a distant place that we desire to go. God's very words, which he reveals to us, come from this unseen world, and from his mind. His angels come to us from this world. The Word took on flesh and walked on earth, in *our* world, healed men and raised them from death to life, right here. The distant land we long for can be present in some form as we walk out these tired, and sometimes painful steps on earth. The material world will be completely filled with the spiritual. The angles are ascending and descending on the Son of God, who touches both earth and sky. Heaven is coming down to be with us.

Everyone has their complaints about pain on this earth. Some turn those complaints into an indictment against the Creator, and a chance to accuse him of sin. How could God have made this world if it was going to include such suffering? How could he have allowed me to continually suffer as I do? Why would any God have allowed the serpent into the garden in the first place? The list of complaints against the God of heaven could go on endlessly, from the mouths of men convinced that God had done something wrong. We could hear their cries throughout human history:

> "Our child was kidnapped by witchdoctors and killed for his organs."

"I was just going for a nice walk in the autumn woods when I was chased down by wild hogs, and they ate me alive, taking my flesh bite by bite."

"I was working on my roof and a strong wind blew me off. Here I am paralyzed, I cannot work, and now my wife has to go into town and work in the brothels."

"I was supposed to get married this year, but the man who promised marriage lied to me, stole from me, and left with another woman. I have nothing left, but only shame."

"When the soldiers came into town, they rounded us all up, whipped us, and then took the women for themselves and abused them as much as they liked."

"I was arrested for betraying the king. They impaled my body on a spike and as I hung there in agony, the sharp wooden beam ripping apart my flesh, they brought my family before my eyes, and slew my wife and children one by one."

"I was taken as a little girl and used by men. Now they keep me in this room to entertain men until the day I die. I can feel the rash on my back sticking to the moist bed, and itching blisters on my body that ooze puss. I wish I could strip off this body, like I'd strip off clothes, and be free of it forever."

The response to such horrors is often overwhelming sadness, fear, hopelessness, and a sense of an absent God. In fact, some men have such a dark response to far lesser difficulties in life. Some men experience simple failure as that millstone upon the neck. Yet Yahweh has not left us here, wishing in vain to fly away, hating being stuffed into this suffering body, like a spirit in a box. If we look up to our Maker, and call out to him, he gives us a far greater picture. He shows us the Christ, taking on that mass of suffering, in his own tortured flesh, and lifting it up to God. He shows us Christ walking in our flesh, revealing the love, kindness, sacrifice, and honor that our very nature was meant to reveal. He shows us his perfection of that mass of pointless meat we call humanity, shaping us into his perfect love, often through the very own acts of suffering that we hate. He will cleanse us of the poison within us. He will squeeze that corruption out of our flesh even to make a new body for us. Just as a doctor heals with medicine, he will heal us through our afflictions. Whether in our own short lives, or in the panorama of human history, God is redeeming the world to himself. No sin will be left unpunished. No righteous man kept from his kingdom.

THE NEW MOUNT

I spent much of the opening of this book relating my own experience with severe depression. I distinguished depression from ordinary human grief, sadness, and other human pain. It is something which I believe stemmed from an extraordinary distance from humanity I felt, and experienced since my earliest memories. I remember being separate in my mind since I was two years old. I can, if I wish, examine that pain, and the root of that pain, and today see God's purpose, just as I see my own hand in that pain. The brilliance of Yahweh's working reveals itself.

The unique kind of detachment I was given, if I had responded simply by using it for virtue, could have led me to devote myself to great study, or to making much art. I may not have had the same life as others, or been able to befriend others so easily, but the Lord would have given me people who loved me, and whom I could love. My state would not have seemed a curse or a disease, as it did. It would not have given me endless pain without apparent hope of ending. It would simply have been one piece of human variety among many others, which can be used to honor God and to serve man. There is no sin in being separate inside.

However, in desiring to be the same as others, and desiring the enjoy lives which they had, this unique gift of God acted much like a curse. It did not let me do as I desired. It kept me from having the same life as others. It stuck around despite my desire to reject it. This in turn almost mechanistically led to unhappiness, and eventually the inescapable pit of depression. My reaction, which was ungodly, led my life down the path of suffering. If I had received God's gift like a humble child, and not desired to be something other than I'd been created, I can easily see a path of peace, happiness, and love, rather than the never-ending, nauseating darkness that came with depression, and which lacked all hope. I would not have spent half a lifetime wondering what was wrong with me.

In my view today, God did not curse me, or punish me with my condition. Yahweh placed a great blessing upon me by creating me separate in my mind. It was my own rejection of my identity that turned it into a curse. God did not curse me with depression as I grew up, but my own attitudes, hardness to God, and ongoing sin placed me in that prison. My envy of the world did that. If I had been thrown into the depth of the sea, to sink endlessly away from the light, it was no accident, but was fully just. I cannot claim to be a victim.

The hell and destruction which was on *my own heart* was before the Lord, and being judged. I was able to taste, for a small moment, the chains of darkness in hell, reserved for the angels who sinned.

One of the blessings in knowing isolation as I did is to prepare me for being God's child. For the Christian, if he truly lives like one and speaks like one, will be rejected by his peers. He will be rejected by his friends. The same people I wanted to be accepted by in my life would nearly all of them have rejected me for the beliefs I now hold. The fact the Christian will suffer rejection is especially true in this secular society, which has deemed Christian belief, beliefs also common to other faiths for thousands of years, to be evil and have no place in society. I have faced that rejection today, and tell you the truth, it does not throw me into any depression. I don't fear or hate it. I can feel a godly sorrow on my heart when I see the world hate Christ. I can feel a sorrow because I won't be able to have fellowship with those people. However, the rejection I have experienced by this world does nothing to bring me the emptiness and self-hatred I knew through depression. It is an honor to be rejected for Christ, and I can see it as a natural consequence of God bringing about his will on this earth.

I can tell you the exact moment I was first shunned by an acquaintance because I do not accept the behaviors the secular world accepts. I can tell you the exact moment I was first shunned by an old friend, and a supposedly good friend, for the same thing. I could relate other close friends who have excommunicated me from their society either because I openly preach Christ or because I do not celebrate the sins this world celebrates. I have been threatened by employers as well, both Christian and secular, for my beliefs. I have lost jobs for my beliefs. I have no difficulty seeing myself as a second-class citizen at best, in a society in which all are presumably equal. In my previous life and belief system, all of that rejection could have greatly upset me or deepened my unhappiness. Who wants to be cut off from everyone they know to have no place in the world? Who wants to lose all their friends? Yet none of this has felt threatening to me, or caused me depression. None of it makes me doubt God. I praise Yahweh for all of it. I am free from the black waters of the abyss to rest upon them in the ark of my Lord, passing through them into safety. Knowing my eternal home in Christ, and the goodness of God, leaves me with a peace that remains through all things. It simply does not end.

The same is true of other hardships in our pilgrimage. My wife and I were unexpectedly faced with losing our second child years ago. He was discovered to have a serious genetic disorder which included severe heart problems, and other more minor debilities. We knew his chances were slim, and he was born early through c-section because the doctors thought it best to begin working on him early. It turned out they could not keep the boy alive more than slightly over two weeks, and he died as the result of the many attempted treatments. It was all the life our child had on earth with us beyond the womb. We visited him in the natal intensive care unit. We watched him die before our eyes. We experienced ordinary human grief, which comes out of love. We shed tears for a lost loved one. We remember him with love and with tears. Yet none of this began to approach the depression I had known earlier in my life. None of it left me with a sense of emptiness, deadness of soul, or a lack of love for life. I continued to know goodness and peace in Jesus Christ. Ordinary things in life still brought me joy. I thank God for the short time we were blessed with our child. Every moment of that was a gift. I only ask the Father show me a way to use our boy's short life here for the glory of Jesus. That's what we all are here for, whether we live long or short lives. It's all just a gift.

It is remarkable how the Almighty turns everything we thought to be true on its head. In my former life of self, and of deadness, I wanted aggressively to be different. I sought to be special, and not conform to the world. It was a point of pride. Many of my peers thought that way as well, taking pride in being different from the system, or in artfully crafting a rebellious spirit. Yet strangely, nearly everyone I knew went along with the prevailing liberal views of the time, the expected lifestyle of the group we belonged to, listened to the popular media of the times, and went passively with the cultural flow, which pretended as best it could to be counter-cultural. I did not fail to notice this as a young man, wondering if I was so different, what was I doing watching their televisions shows, and holding more or less the same beliefs. That doesn't sound too different. It really strains the mind to try and pretend uniqueness when you're like everyone else. It is only since becoming a Christian and learning to live like one that I find I go against the flow of the culture. Without even trying to be different, I find I am one standing against many. I am in revolt against the prevailing powers, beliefs, and institutions set up around me. I do battle anytime I interact with the godless world, and take any amount of hatred and ridicule without ceasing to walk the path before me. One does not need to be a biker in a leather jacket to stand against the powers, but only be a simple Christian convinced of the words of truth. The simple step of getting on our knees to come to Christ, it seems, fulfills the wrongheaded goals we once had of being different. It fulfills them not by wiping them out, but by reordering them, and bringing them into the kingdom of God. Then we go and turn the world upside down.

There was a time I crossed over into death and hopelessness in my life, and also a time I crossed over into something I had never seen before: light and life to be changed forever. I walked into a strange new land far off of the path I had been walking for many years. I would never return to the disease and affliction I had known in bondage. In being a Christian, I know I am a new person. I will never go back. Rebirth did not bring me into a new life of little but laughter and pleasure, to be in comfort with the rest of the world. Rather it showed me the beauty and healing, and creative power of tears; the peace and strength that can exist in pain. It revealed that any wounds of the enemy or hatred of the world will not harm my soul, because my being is forever wedded with God. I do not fear losing the approval of the entire world, but only cling to the love of God. I cannot desire to be like the happier man, or the more popular man, the wealthy, the talented, the ruler. I can only desire to be what God makes me. I can only speak to my Father and ask: make me into whatever you desire. I am in bondage to no man on this earth. I am free to serve the Lord.

Long ago I would have thought that nothing could take me out of the darkness of my life. There was nothing but a great chasm before me. There was an endless pit beneath me. Any light from the world above had disappeared long ago as I was dragged down in the waters endlessly. I see in my mind a young man, leaning against the wall of a flat, hurling knives across the room into the opposite wall. I see another curled up into a ball on the floor for hours, crying out as if in physical pain. The emptiness was an unspeakable horror I would have given anything to leave. I dreamed of death literally thousands of times. Yet I think about that unspeakable horror today, and I know no matter how terrible it was, if God used even a single moment of that suffering to bring me to Jesus Christ, I don't regret a thing. I would never wish away even one of its terrible hardships. None of that was a mistake. If that is what it took to draw me from the life of a guilty sinner, enslaved to the flesh, to be cleaned in Jesus Christ and know his love forever, I do not reject a moment of my agony. I could never say it was unjust to have that long season in my life, because I know that God has done it.

Bibliography

Abt, Isaac A., ed. *Abt—Garrison History of Pediatrics*. Reprinted from *Pediatrics*, by various authors Vol. 1, Philadelphia and London: W.B. Saunders, 1965.
Al-Zaidi, Hassan. "Revenge in Yemen: Between the Tribal Culture and Absence of Justice and Law." *The Yemen Times*, June 30, 2005. https://yementimes.com/revenge-in-yemen-between-the-tribal-culture-and-absence-of-justice-and-law-archives2005-855-culture/.
Amundsen, Darrell and Gary Ferngren. *Beneficence and Health Care*, ed. Shelp, Earl. Dortrecht, Holland: D. Reidel, 1982.
Aquilina, Mike. "A Radical Equality: Women in the Early Church." Catholic Answers, September 10, 2019. https://www.catholic.com/magazine/print-edition/women-in-the-early-church-a-radical-equality.
Aquinas, Thomas. *Summa Theologica*. 1a2ae, Q6, Art. 4. In *Introduction to St. Thomas Aquinas*. edited by Anton C. Pegis, 486–487. New York: The Modern Library, 1948.
Associated Press. "Mexico Finds Flayed God Temple; Priests Wore Skins of Dead." Associated Press, January 2, 2019. https://apnews.com/article/e4e92bc35ead46309f632ec12df8ddf8.
Augustine of Hippo. *Letter 98, 6*. In *Nicene and Post-Nicene Fathers, Series 1*, edited by Philip Schaff, 1: 902. Grand Rapids: Eerdmans, 1887.
———. *Reply to Faustus the Manichaean XXII, 74*. In *Nicene and Post-Nicene Fathers, Series 1*, edited by Philip Schaff, 5: 515. Grand Rapids: Eerdmans, 1887.
Babylonian Talmud. 2nd ed, edited and translated by Michael L. Rodkinson. Boston, MA: New Talmud Publishing Company, 1918.
Balkanista. "Blood Feuds and Honour, a Tragic Tale of Albanian Tradition." The Balkanista. November 7, 2020. https://thebalkanista.com/2020/11/07/blood-feuds-and-honour-a-tragic-tale-of-albanian-tradition/.
Bible History. "The Destruction of Jerusalem in 70 AD." Bible History. https://bible-history.com/jerusalem/destruction-of-jerusalem-in-70-a-d.
Blech, Jörg. "Melancholy Without Shame." *Der Spiegel*, February 5, 2012. https://www.spiegel.de/politik/schwermut-ohne-scham-a-37ed126a-0002-0001-0000-000083865282.
Bonn, Scott, A. "The Twisted Tale of the 'Co-Ed Killer.'" *Psychology Today*. March 17, 2014. https://www.psychologytoday.com/us/blog/wicked-deeds/201403/the-twisted-tale-the-co-ed-killer.
Bowers, Nancy. "'Heaven is My Home': Murder of Gloria Slump 1967." Iowa Unsolved Murders: Historic Cases. February, 2010. https://iowaunsolvedmurders.com/

beyond-1965-selected-unsolved-iowa-murders/heaven-is-my-home-murder-of-gloria-slump-1967/.

Brown, Michael. "What the Early Church Said about Abortion." Christian Post. June 2, 2022. https://www.christianpost.com/voices/what-the-early-church-said-about-abortion.html.

Cahill, Thomas. *How the Irish Saved Civilization*. Anchor Books, New York, 1996.

Calvin, John. *The Institutes of the Christian Religion*. Volume 2. Edited by John T. McNeill, translated by Ford Lewis Battles. Louisville: Westminster, 1960.

Carpenter, John B. "A Secular Jew Makes a Surprising Discovery about Christians and American Slavery." Action Institute. April 17, 2019:1–6. https://www.acton.org/pub/commentary/2019/04/17/secular-jew-makes-surprising-discovery-about-christians-and-american.

Church of Smyrna. *The Martyrdom of Polycarp*. In *The Apostolic Fathers*, edited by J.R. Harmer, translated by J.B. Lightfoot, 207–208. London: MacMillan, 1891.

Cimmino, Jeff. "University of Chicago Professor: Infanticide is Morally Acceptable." *National Review*, July 19, 2017. https://www.nationalreview.com/2017/07/infanticide-morally-acceptable-professor-argues/.

Clarke, Adam. *Adam Clarke's Commentary One-Volume Edition*, abridged by Ralphe Earle. Grand Rapids: Baker Book House, 1967.

Clench, Sam. "Pope Francis Has 'No Explanation' Why God Lets Children Suffer." news.com.au. February 8, 2022. https:// www.news.com.au/world/pope-francis-has-no-explanation-for-why-god-lets-children-suffer/news-story/3b4e215fbd74d77a6a9a0bd74de9819f.

Coffey, John, "The Abolition of the Slave Trade: Christian Conscience and Political Action." *Cambridge Papers*. Cambridge Papers Limited. Vol. 15, n. 2. June, 2006.

Collingwood, Jane. "Higher Risk of Mental Health Problems for Homosexuals." *PsychCentral*, May 17, 2016. https://psychcentral.com/lib/higher-risk-of-mental-health-problems-for-homosexuals#1.

Cook, Bev. "Holy Fools." *Orthodox Christianity*. September 16, 2015. https://orthochristian.com/82170.html.

Cummings, E.E. *Tulips and Chimneys*. New York: Thomas Seltzer, 1923.

David. "Historical Records with Some Signs (AD 66–70)." Fulfilled Theology (blog). March 5, 2010. fulfilledtheology.ning.com/forum/topics/historical-records-with-some.

Diamond, Jared, *Guns, Germs, and Steel*. New York: W.W. Norton, 1999.

Di Berardino, Angelo, Thomas C. Oden, Joel C. Elowsky, and James Hoover, eds. *Encyclopedia of Ancient Christianity*. translated by Joseph T. Papa, Erik A. Koenke, and Eric E. Hewett. Downers Grove, Illinois: IVP Academic, 2014.

Early Church History. "Infanticide in the Ancient World." Early Church History. September 5, 2018. https://earlychurchhistory.org/medicine/infanticide-in-the-ancient-world.

Ehrman, Bart. "Leaving the Faith." The Bart Ehrman Blog, July 19, 2017. https://ehrmanblog.org/leaving-the-faith.

Eusebius, *Ecclesiastical History*, b. 3, c. 5. In *The History of the Church*. Translated by G.A. Williamson, 111. New York: Barnes & Noble, 1995.

Evan-Israel, Adin. "The Life of the Righteous Is Everlasting." Chabad.org. https://www.chabad.org/library/article_cdo/aid/5271031/jewish/The-Life-of-the-Righteous-Is-Everlasting.htm.

BIBLIOGRAPHY

Everett, Bethany G. "Sexual Orientation Disparities in Sexually Transmitted Infections: Examining the Intersection Between Sexual Identity and Sexual Behavior." *National Library of Medicine*, February 16, 2012. https://www.ncbi.nlm.nih.gov/pmc/articles/PMC3575167/.

EWTN, "The Glory Be (Gloria Patri)." EWTN. https://www.ewtn.com/catholicism/teachings/glory-be-gloria-patri-12744.

Federoff, N., and T. Peterson, ed. "Talmudic Evidence for the Messiah at 30 C.E." My Hebrew Bible. February 13, 2016. https://myhebrewbible.azurewebsites.net/Article/523.

Forcén, Fernando and Carlos Forcén. "Symeon the Holy Fool." *The British Journal of Psychiatry* 205, no. 2 (August 2014): 94. https://www.cambridge.org/core/journals/the-british-journal-of-psychiatry/article/symeon-the-holy-fool-patron-of-the-mentally-ill.

Gentry, Kenneth. *The Beast of Revelation*. Tyler: Institute for Christian Economics, 1989.

Gill, N.S. "A Look at the Lives of the First 12 Roman Emperors." ThoughtCo. updated June 30, 2019. https://www.thoughtco.com/coins-of-the-12-caesars-4126834.

Hasell, Joe. "Famine Mortality over the Long Run." Our World in Data. March 22, 2018. https://ourworldindata.org/famine-mortality-over-the-long-run.

Innerfire Ministries. "Haiti Missionaries Tell Their Story." YouTube. February 1, 2022, 1:33:55, https://www.youtube.com/watch?v=3c4Yopjz8Pk.html.

Jewish Virtual Library. "Witness." Jewish Virtual Library. 2008. https://www.jewishvirtuallibrary.org/witness.

Josephus, *Wars of the Jews*. In *The Bible and Related Texts*, translated by Patrick Rogers. https://www.biblical.ie/page.php?fl=josephus/War/JWG5#06.

Julian III. "Fragment of a Letter." In *The Works of the Emperor Julian III*, edited by E. Capps, T.E. Page, and W.H.D. Rouse, translated by Wilmer C. Wright, 69, 71. London: William Heinemann, 1923.

Kaonga, Gerrard. "Child Shoots at Cops over McDonald's Order Dispute — Police." *Newsweek*. February 22, 2022. https://www.newsweek.com/shooting-4-year-old-father-mcdonalds-police-salt-lake-city-utah-1681251.

Kelley, John. "Antidepressants: Do They 'Work' or Don't They? A New Study Finds Little Difference between Pill and Placebo." *Scientific American*, March 2, 2010. https://www.scientificamerican.com/article/antidepressants-do-they-work-or-dont-they/.

Kennedy, James D., and Jerry Newcombe. *What if Jesus Had Never Been Born?*. Nashville: Thomas Nelson, 1994.

Kerstein, Benjamin. "The Bar-Kochba Revolt." World History Encyclopedia. August 30, 2018. https://www.worldhistory.org/The_Bar-Kochba_Revolt/.

Khorolskiy, Simon & Friends. "Heaven is My Home." YouTube (June 19, 2018). https://www.youtube.com/watch?v=on7VPe_SG7s.

Klein, Camilla. "The Shocking Truth: How Many Christian Bibles Have Been Sold?" Christian Educators Academy. March 4, 2023. https://christianeducatorsacademy.com/the-shocking-truth-how-many-christian-bibles-have-been-sold.

Little, Becky. "5 Ways Christianity Spread Through Ancient Rome." History. June 8, 2023. https:www.history.com/news/5-ways-christianity-spread-through-ancient-rome.

BIBLIOGRAPHY

Lodge, Carey. "Chinese Pastor 'Grateful' For Prison Sentence." *Christianity Today*. October 14, 2014. https://www.christiantoday.com/article/chinese.pastor.grateful.for.prison.sentence/41643.htm.

Mangel, Nissen, trans. "Order of Kapparot," 2. Excerpt from *Machzor for Yom Kippur*. Merkos L'Inyonei Chinuch, Brooklyn, NY: 2004.

Martin, Lynn. "Early Church Fathers on War, Violence, and Pacifism." Anabaptist Faith. https://anabaptistfaith.org/early-church-fathers-on-war-violence-and-pacifism/.

Maximus the Confessor. *Ad Thalassium 64: On the Prophet Jonah and the Economy of Salvation*. In "The Divine Bait." *Classical Christianity*. October 19, 2011. https://classicalchristianity.com/2011/10/19/the-divine-bait/.

McDonnell, Patrick, Joe Mozingo, and Jaweed Kaleem. "Missionaries Kidnapped in Haiti." *Los Angeles Times*. October 16, 2021.

Morey, Robert. "The Early Church, War and Pacifism." The Church in History Information Center, January 19, 2009. churchinhistory.org/pages/misc/ch-war-pac.htm.

Nachmanides, *Commentary on the Torah*. Vayikara, 1:9. In *Commentary on the Torah by Ramban (Nachmanides)*, translated and annotated by Charles B. Chavel. New York: Shilo, 1976.

OCA (Orthodox Church in America). "Blessed John of Moscow the Fool-For-Christ." Orthodox Church in America. https://www.oca.org/saints/lives/2023/07/03/101881-blessed-john-of-moscow-the-fool-for-christ.html.

———. "Selected Liturgical Hymns," Orthodox Church in America. https://www.oca.org/orthodoxy/prayers/selected-liturgical-hymns.

Origen. *Commentary on Matthew*, xvi, 8. In *Christus Victor, An Historical Study of the Three Main Types of the Idea of the Atonement*, Gustaf Aulén, translated by A.G. Hebert, 65. London: SPCK, 1953.

Orthodox Church. "Lamentations," 3:21. "The Lamentations of Holy Friday." *St. Mary of Egypt Orthodox Christian Church*. https://stmaryofegypt.net/homeprayers/lamentations/.

Pearcey, Nancy R., and Charles B. Thaxton. *The Soul of Science: Christian Faith and Natural Philosophy*. Wheaton: Crossway, 1994.

Philostratus, *The Life of Apollonius of Tyana*, 4:38. In *Philostratus I*, edited by T.E Page and W.H.D. Rouse, translated by F.C. Conybeare, 437, 439. London: William Heinmann, 1912.

Prisoners of Eternity. "Francisco Pizarro and the Conquest of the Incas." Prisoners of Eternity. March 3, 2021. https://www.prisonersofeternity.com/blog/francisco-pizarro-and-the-conquest-of-the-incas/.

Reuters. "CHRONOLOGY—Who Banned Slavery When?" Reuters. August 9, 2007. https://www.reuters.com/article/uk-slavery-idUSL1561464920070322/.

Roser, Max. "Mortality in the Past: Every Second Child Died." Our World in Data. April 11, 2023. https://ourworldindata.org/child-mortality-in-the-past.

———, Esteban Ortiz-Ospina, and Hannah Ritchie. "Life Expectancy." Our World in Data. 2013. https://ourworldindata.org/life-expectancy.

Seaver, Carl. "What Were the Most Important Inventions of the Renaissance?" History Defined. https://www.historydefined.net/what-were-the-most-important-inventions-of-the-renaissance/.

BIBLIOGRAPHY

Sederstrom, Jill. "'Wasn't What I Would Call a Bad Person,'" Oxygen. July 31, 2020. https://www.oxygen.com/true-crime-buzz/friend-describes-charles-manson-childhood-in-west-virginia.

Slick, Matt. "Col. 1:16–17, '. . . All [Other] Things Were Created by Him . . . ' and the Jehovah's Witnesses." CARM. Dec. 5, 2008. https://carm.org/jehovahs-witnesses/col-116-17-all-other-things-were-created-by-him-and-the-jehovahs-witnesses/.

Staff Reports. "Poverty for Hinduism's Dalit Class." BORGEN Magazine, August 12, 2014. https://borgenmagazine.com/poverty-hinduisms-dalit-caste/.

Staff Writer. "Christian Apologist Tyler Vela 'Deconverts' from Christianity." Protestia. November 2022. https://protestia.com/2022/11/20/christian-apologist-podcast-announces-his-deconversion-from-christianity-because-god-did-not-comfort-him-after-divorce.html.

Suetonius, *Nero*, 58. In "The Life of Nero." In *Suetonius; Complete Works*, translated by Alexander Thomson, 37. Delphi Classics, 2016.

Tardi, Carla. "Indentured Servitude: Definition, History, and Controversy." Investopedia, September 19, 2022. https://www.investopedia.com/terms/i/indentured-servitude.asp.

Tate, Joshua C. "Christianity and the Legal Status of Abandoned Children in the Later Roman Empire." *SMU Scholar, Journal of Law and Religion*. Vol. XXIV 2008: 124–141.

Team Seven. "The Butcher Baker." True Crime Seven. February 17, 2021. https://truecrimeseven.com/the-butcher-baker-the-true-story-of-robert-hansen-the-human-hunter.

Theodoret of Cyrus. *Ecclesiastical History*. In *The Greek Ecclesiastical Historians of the First Six Centuries of the Christian Era*, edited and translated by Edward Walferd, 5:327. London, UK: Samuel Bagster and Sons, 1843.

Unruh, Bob. "Lawmakers in 3d State Promoting Plan to Allow Infanticide." WND News Center, March 27, 2022. https://www.wndnewscenter.org/lawmakers-in-3rd-state-promoting-plan-to-allow-infanticide/.

Vecsey, George. "Dalai Lama Says Buddhists Could Learn From Christians' Activism." *New York Times*, September 8, 1979. https://www.nytimes.com/1979/09/08/archives/dalai-lama-says-buddhists-could-learn-from-christians-activism.html.

Velvet Underground. "Heroin," Track 7. *The Velvet Underground & Nico* Verve, 1967, Vinyl.

Visser, Wayne A.M. and Alastair McIntosh. "A Short Review of the Historical Critique of Usury," *Accounting, Business & Financial History* 8, no 2 (July 1998): 175–189. https://doi.org/10.1080/095852098330503.

Wat, Aleksander. *My Century*. ed. Richard Lourie. New York: New York Review, 1988.

Ways to Faith. "The Christian Origin of Universities." Ways to Faith. May 31, 2021. https://waystofaith.net/christian-origin-of-universities/.

Wilcox, William B. *Why Marriage Matters: Thirty Conclusions from the Social Sciences*. New York: Institute for American Values, 2011.

World Food Program USA. "Is There a Global Food Shortage? What's Causing Hunger, Famine and Rising Food Costs Around the World." World Food Program USA. November 16, 2023. https://wfpusa.org/articles/is-there-global-food-shortage-whats-causing-hunger-famine-rising-food-costs-around-world/.

www.ingramcontent.com/pod-product-compliance
Lightning Source LLC
Chambersburg PA
CBHW050331230426
43663CB00010B/1818